CULTURAL PLURALISM

CULTURAL PLURALISM
The Indian Scenario

Editors
S.A. Azeez Saheb
B. Francis Kulirani
K.K. Misra

Indira Gandhi Rashtriya Manav Sangrahalaya
(National Museum of Mankind)
Bhopal

GYAN PUBLISHING HOUSE

ISBN : 978-81-212-1147-5

Published by
Indira Gandhi Rashtriya Manav Sangrahalaya
Shamla Hills, Bhopal-462013 (Madhya Pradesh)
E-mail: directorigrms@gmail.com

Gyan Publishing House
23, Main Ansari Road, Daryaganj,
New Delhi - 110002
Phones : 23282060, 23261060
Fax : (011) 23285914
E-mail: books@gyanbooks.com
website: gyanbooks.com

Laser Type Setting : Rajender Vashist, Delhi
Printed at : Salasar Imaging System, Delhi

Contents

PART–III
RELIGIOUS PLURALISM

PART–IV
LINGUISTIC PLURALISM

PART–V
CULTURAL PLURALISM AND ETHNIC GROUPS

Foreword

Ajit K. Danda

Contemporary India comprises several physiographic regions, each of which in socio-cultural terms divides itself into several States, and/ or Union Territories. People of various ethno-cultural and economic backgrounds at different points of time migrated to and occupied variegated terrains, which in turn helped to a considerable extent in preserving their respective special attributes. Thus, the initial differences between them in terms of ethnicity, culture, and economy were not only maintained, but over the period, due to support from the then system of socio-cultural management, got further reinforced. Given the level of development of the system of communication those days, there was neither much awareness about the nature of disparities existing in the Indian soil as a whole, nor did they come into sharp attention as possible irritants. Obviously, therefore, not many serious endeavours were visible to overcome the differences.

Variation in the degree of peoples' exposure to modernisation as such, without adequate support from any effective media of communication, under the influence of differential eco-cultural niches, preserved the tendency of maintaining distinctive identities. The people of India by and large have lived under such circumstances rather too long; a fact that, instead of evening out the differences, further strengthened their respective independent identities.

The characteristic socio-cultural background of the people of India, under the influence of the framework of *varna-jati,* invested this arrangement with a sort of legitimacy. Even the stark economic disparities were thus provided with an apparent rational basis for their continuation. As a result, until recently, there was no major attempt from among the people themselves, to wipe out the differences. Therefore, nationality defined in terms of ethno-cultural purity or likeness, never grew or was seriously aspired for in India. Instead, the heritage of India's ethnic and cultural heterogeneity not only persisted over time but during the recent decades, has become exposed to almost two opposite sets of forces: homogenisation and differentiation. The peoples' exposure to forces of modernisation—administrative, political, market, industrial, urban, and such others—are all directed towards their consequent state of homogenisation. The process of evolution, on the other hand, by and large manifests itself through the resultant mechanism of differentiation. Until the processes culminate into the development of a sort of steady equilibrium on the basis of the establishment of some symmetrical relationships, expression of occasional stresses may not be construed as the natural outcome. Contemporary developments in various parts in India, therefore, appear as the expression of ethnic processes which have set in historically and have been sustained largely by physiographic, cultural, economic, and socio-political factors. A close understanding of the same is considered essential for an appropriate comprehension of the processes of national integration.

Some of the essential prerequisites necessary for the purpose of maintenance of any system of dynamic equilibrium are extraordinary alertness and constant vigilance. Having India's ethno-cultural diversities and socio-economic disparities in view, even an ever-alert eye may not prove sufficiently adequate unless some balance can be struck between their opposed tendencies. Cultivation of an atmosphere of mutual tolerance between cultures as well as between ethnic groups seems imperative in this respect. An assurance of equality in sharing of authority as well as resourcesalso appearsimportant in this regard.

However, no assurance or spirit of mutual tolerance is likely to have the desirable lasting impact until the people themselves can be directly involved in the programme of achieving the goal and made responsible for retaining the promised benefits. A massive endeavour for liberal education and dissemination of imaginative non-formal teachings emphasizing extra-parochial identities, particularly through mass media, may provide some basic support.

Achievement of the ultimate objective of the society has to be programmed in phases and deliberate distinctions are required to be maintained between the methaphysical goal and the ideographic objective. Until some mechanism is evolved to transform India's vertical segments initially into a system of horizontal divisions, the strata within which through mutual interaction could in the long run even out their mutual differences, and an in-built system is ensured to maintain the same; achievement of the goal may remain elusive. Appropriate synchronisation of the programme of socio-economic planning with the declared objectives of the cultural policy and adequate support of political will as well as wisdom with particular emphasis on the pan-Indian and universal ethos seems urgent and indispensable.

The volume : ***Cultural Pluralism : The Indian Scenario*** edited by Shaik Abdul Azeez Saheb, Baby Francis Kulirani and K.K. Misra is likely to supply sufficient required data for such planning.

Preface

It is almost a universally accepted view that there are as many expressions of truth, beauty and goodness as there are cultures. Individuals undergo a process of enculturation. The current emphasis is on the worthiness of many ways of life. In the aftermath of colonialism the emerging nation states like India had to come to grip with the new social reality of multi-dimensional diversity. Inspired by Ramkrishna it was Vivekanda who constructed a doctrine of pluralism and tolerance. This construct was fine tuned by Gandihiji whose humanistic approach transcended the Hindu spirituality-more universal, spiritual and humanistic. Gandhiji believed in participatory pluralism of every Indian citizen, because each one has imbibed a little bit from our multi-religious, multi-lingual, multi-ethnic heritages. In order to strengthen our pluralistic heritages, the domain has to be periodically revisited and emerging issues need to be analyzed form various academic stand points. It is in the above context that the Anthropological Association, Mysore decided to organize a two day national seminar on the topic 'Cultural Pluralism: The Indian Scenario' during 5-6 December 2009.

The selected papers for publication are broadly on the themes of 'cultural pluralism and tribes', 'religious pluralism' and 'linguistic pluralism'. The inaugural address by Prof N S Reddy deals with 'What is the right kind of Secularism for a Multi-Religio-Cultural Nation like India?' and the key note address by Prof Imtiaz Ahmad examines 'Pluralism and Cultural Diversity in India'. The two articles that are part of this publication set the rest of the papers in context.

The organizers are grateful to the Director, Anthropological Survey of India, Kolkata and the Director, Central Institute of Indian Languages, Mysore who sponsored the two day national seminar that was held in the auditorium of the Central Institute of Indian Languages, Mysore. The Department of Studies in Anthropology, University of Mysore, Mysore collaborated in organisational aspects of the seminar.

The organizers wish to put on record our gratefulness to the Director, Indira Gandhi Rashtriya Manav Snghrahalaya, Bhopal for arranging to publish the proceedings of the seminar.

Editors

Introduction

B.F. Kulirani, S.A. Azeez Saheb* and *K.K. Misra

Geographically the Indian Union of today is one of the largest countries in the world. In fact the present political geography of India is but a small part of a culture and civilisation that extended right from present-day Afghanistan to Cambodia, Burma and Sri Lanka. The spread of this civilisation spanned millennia. What comprises the Indian Union today is an area that extends from islands in tropical seas to snow-clad mountains with a population over a thousand million. The rain forests of Assam, Arunachal and Meghalaya form the eastern border, while on the western border lay the Thar Desert of Rajasthan. Obviously not all inhabitants of such a vast area enjoy a similar life-style. Millions of Indians live in the metros, and many of them have life-styles that can easily compete with that of people living in any advanced urban center of the world. On the other hand, many still live in forests and practise hunting, gathering for subsistence economy as their forefathers have done for millennia. In between these extremes live the rest of the Indians. In fact, it is because of these extreme differences that the first Prime Minister of India referred to India as a country which exhibits "unity in diversity".

Needless to say, the residents of India not only differ in their way of life regionally, but also in the population composition adaptations. Thus in India we find 15 official languages apart from the national languages, Hindi and English. The followers of all the major religions of the world are present in India and have their separate places of worship. Even the sub-sects of the major religions are very much active in India and rivalries between these sub-sects are quite common. This clearly indicates that though we all are Indians, we have many grades of Indianness; hence all these differences thrive.

Adding to the complexity of Indian pluralism is the tribal population of India, spread over this huge territory. At one time it was they who had complete control over the area. Over time, however, they were marginalised. The spread of road and rail networks in the nineteenth and twentieth centuries, and the gradual opening up of these areas to modernity, paved the way for many variants of culture. Even today, however, pockets of primitive tribes exist in areas isolated from the influence of modern civilisation. The Cholanaicken tribe of Kerala and the Jarwas and Sentinelese tribes of Andaman are examples of pristine culture shielded by isolation. Similarly, difficult terrain and isolation has protected the tribal population of Jaunsar Bawar in the Himalayas, Chotanagpur and Bastar. But forces of modernity and the profit motive of civilisation are so strong that such barriers are easily penetrated.

Yet another dimension of plurality is the Village India. Just because we find that the villages of India are agricultural, it does not necessarily mean that every individual residing in the village owns cultivable land or actually tills the land. For the proper functioning of the agricultural system it is essential that a number of other services are available to the tiller so that he must have access to proper agricultural implements and arrangement for the maintenance and repair of the same, drought animals to pull the plough, and the carts for transportation of the produce to the market, system for the disposal of dead animals, arrangement for supply of water to the fields as well as potable water for the kitchen, and so on. Moreover, after the mundane requirements have been met and taken care of, there are other needs which also include spiritual needs. Such varied requirements necessarily mean division of labour and specialisation. Over the millennia such specialisations have resulted in a unique system that is referred to as the caste system. The caste system is, as already explained, basically a system for the division of labour. In time, however it proliferated into a system which, at least in parts, possibly created more problems than it solved.

India is no exception to the influence of the world's religions. Judaism was followed by Christianity in early centuries. During the last millennium there were a number of Islamic invasions from the West, although Islam reached the Malabar shores in the 9th century as one of the religions of the traders. The followers of Islam, a religion that took birth in the deserts of the Middle East, brought a different culture and way of life all together. During the invasion, obviously the first wave consisted of soldiers and their camp followers, along with the Sufi saints. But other families soon followed. Over generations Muslims have settled in India and through a process of syncretisation, have assimilated practises that were being followed in India. Thus today we find caste-like practises being followed even in the Dargahs of Muslim saints. Although theoretically denied, we find that in India both Islam and Christianity have imbibed the Indian hierarchical system of castes. In fact, it is not uncommon to find Indian Christians continuing to use the original surnames of their forefathers especially if they belong to the higher castes. The tendency is also visible among converts to Sikhism another religion, whose founder had egalitarian goals; but its followers also followed the syncretisation process.

Indian culture can be compared to water which is neutral in nature. Though it consists of explosive components of Hydrogen molecules (Hindu culture) and Oxygen molecules (other cultures like Muslim/ Christian/Sikh), they have combined to form the un-flammable water substance. Similarly, elements of Indianness unite the Hindu, Muslim, Christian and Sikh communities. The seminar on "Cultural Pluralism: The Indian Scenario" provides a platform for examining the common threads of Indianness that bind us together and also an opportunity for a dialogue between religions. The Anthropological Association proposes to hold a two-day national seminar on the above topic. The following broad sub-themes are identified.

The multitude of eco-cultural and biological adaptations made by the people of India has been the subject of study for the Physical Anthropologists, Human Geneticists and Human Ecologists. Environmental degradation and fast changes in life-styles are posing great challenges and serious concerns about the well-being of the Indian population. We need to address these social realities and suggest corrective steps.

Indian plurality has many shades. At the same time, Indian religious philosophies, thoughts and knowledge have worldwide influence and there is no corner of the world that is untouched by the Indian Diaspora. India is also in turn influenced by the homogenising forces of globalisation. The multiplicity of these cross currents has brought in a state of flex. We need to look closely at the social reality that is being played in contemporary India.

Majority of the Indians favour inclusive development, national unity and an emergent, developed India. The ethnic and regional identities have become very critical in the present day socio-political scenario. Continued neglect of the marginalised groups has snowballed into major crisis due to the armed appraisals in many parts of the country.

The seminar on "Cultural Pluralism: The Indian Scenario" was held in the auditorium of the Central Institute of Indian Languages, in Mysore on 5th and 6th December 2009. Prof. P.K. Misra the President of the

Anthropological Association welcomed and introduced Dr. L.K. A. Iyer awardee, Prof. N.S. Reddy from Hyderabad. He was presented with the medal and citation by the President of the Association. Prof. Reddy delivered his talk on "What is the right kind of Secularism for a Multi-Religio-Cultural Nation like India?" He said that the word secularism was coined in England by Holyoake in 1851 from the Latin word, "speculum", meaning a specific span of time, with its derived meaning of a concern for here and now: It meant giving importance to what is empirical as against what is transcendent. In modern age there has been an obvious shift in the balance of power between the church and the state. In this changed context, secularism has come to mean non-interference in each other's affairs, by the state and the church an attitude of live and let live. This, to Prof. N.S. Reddy, is the apt meaning of secularism as it is relevant today. However, he felt that there are some social scientists and thinkers for whom secular and sacred are mutually antagonistic. He closed with a quotation from that quintessential secularist, Jawaharlal Nehru who wrote (in 1930s): "Personally I am convinced that nationalism can arise out of the ideological fusion of Hindu, Muslim, Sikh and other groups in India. That does not mean extinction of the culture of any one group, but it does mean a common national outlook" (1937:60). So any label should reflect the plurality of our society and the inclusiveness of our national culture. He thinks that Bharatiyata fits the bill, not Hindutva. He further feels that integrating different sections into a national unity is Indian ethos often smudged by time-serving politicians and community leaders. One should realise that any campaign based on hatred of others cannot thrive in India in the long run. As for the majority community, it should stand by what Vivekananda said: Hinduism sees all religions to be true. That should continue to be the world-view of our national culture. Prof. H.K. Bhat, Vice-President of the Association, proposed vote of thanks. This session was followed by a tea break.

After the tea break, the academic sessions of the seminar "Cultural Pluralism: The Indian Scenario" started. Dr. B. Francis Kulirani welcomed the delegates and introduced the seminar and requested Prof. V.G. Talwar, Vice-Chancellor of Mysore University to inaugurate the Seminar. In his inaugural address, Prof. Talwar referred to the fact that India is a land of varieties. He said that geographically the Indian Union is one of the largest countries in the world. Since the middle of the second millennium BC, Indian civilisation has played host to several streams of migrant groups and communities. Present-day political India is but a small part of a culture and civilisation that extended right from present day Afghanistan to Cambodia, Burma and Sri Lanka. Even today Indian Union is spread from islands in tropical seas to snow-clad mountains with a population over a thousand million. While many have their life-styles comparable those of people living in advanced urban centers of the world, others still live in forests and are practising hunting, gathering for subsistence economy like their forefathers. Most of the Indian population lives between these extremes. In fact, it is because of these extreme differences that the first Prime Minister of India referred to India as a country which exhibits "unity in diversity". The process of adaptation and interaction among various groups brought about India's characteristic diversity.

Dr. Talwar also referred to the fact that India is multi-ethnic in nature, inhabited by maximum number of linguistic speakers following all the religions being practised in the world today. It has been the seat of various dynasties from time to time. Obviously, with so many civilisations, religions, and long history, India has harboured a variety of cultures. India has seen the rise and fall of various empires. These dynasties may have vanished as political powers, but have left the relics of their culture making India a rich mosaic of cultures. The diversity of cultures in India comprises several strata from the most rudimentary tribal cultures to the most advanced cultures of the 21st century. It is hoped that the present seminar will be able to throw light on this variety.

Even though the process of globalisation and liberalisation is operational, the diversity of Indian cultural tradition still continues to survive. He expected the scholars deliberating in the next two days to present a number of papers covering the whole spectrum of Indian population.

Prof. Talwar also said that India has also been influenced by world religions. Apart from Hindus we also find Buddhists, Jains, Parsis, Jews, Christians as well as Muslims in India. Over generations, the followers of these religions have settled in India and through a process of syncretisation have assimilated practises that were being followed in India. Thus, today we find caste-like practises being followed even in the Dargahs of Muslim saints. Both Islam and Christianity have imbibed the hierarchical system of Indian castes. Besides these major religions, about five hundred ethnic groups in the country practise their own religions. Though we generally categorise them as "animists", each group is distinct from each other in matters of worship and world-view. Prof. Talwar hoped that by making people aware of the inherent similarities of the culture of India, despite the apparent differences, such seminars may strengthen the unity of India.

The key-note address of the seminar, "Pluralism and Cultural Diversity in India", was delivered by Prof. Imtiaz Ahmad, from the Jawaharlal Nehru University, New Delhi. He referred to the fact that contemporary academic discourse on multiculturalism in India has been centered on a single salient point viz. a fundamental difference between pluralism (and one might as its variant include diversity) and multicultural pluralism. Most self-proclaimed theorists on the subject have characterised societies throughout history, but remain silent on the question of the nature of the relationship between the different pluralities. On the other hand, multiculturalism is concerned with the issue of mutual interrelations among the various types of pluralities that might be found to exist in society. This is concerned with the issue of equality. It asks whether the different pluralities co-exist as equals in the public and political arenas. Thus having nailed itself down to a fundamental difference between pluralism and multiculturalism, the academic discourse on multiculturalism in India bemoans very deeply that multiculturalism as a theory of democracy and citizenship has received little attention. As one theorist notes, "It appears quite paradoxical that in a country, which was among the first few democracies to endorse the principle quality between groups, there has been no serious attempt to theorise the idea of multicultural democracy." He stated that his point of departure on this question is that this mode of formulating the difference between pluralism and multiculturalism is seriously flawed and ignores the differences between the societies where multiculturalism as an ideology of the state and a theory of ensuring democracy evolved. He further stated the he does not quite deny the relevance of the substantive point that pluralism can be characterised by the presence of diverse groups, communities and cultural orientations or world-views without being concerned with the nature of the relationship between different cultural pluralities. He feels that it is possible that groups or communities may exist in a framework of back-to-back pluralism, that is, within a framework where they exist in relative isolation and independence from one another without coming into interaction except for limited purposes. Or, they may be involved in daily mutual interaction, but their interrelations may be regulated within a framework of dominance and subordination or hierarchical ordering. However, placing undue emphasis upon the difference between pluralism and multiculturalism ignores the historical difference over how societies have looked at pluralism and in what ways they have legitimised it. This has serious implications for the programmes by which they seek to deal with the question of preservation and sustenance of pluralism within national polities. There is, therefore, no escape from focusing on how these differences have shaped the attitudes of the polities towards both looking at and handing cultural pluralism, religious as well as other, and providing for the preservation of pluralism and diversity in the public-political domain.

Prof. Rajesh Sachdev, Director, Central Institute of Indian Languages, Mysore, delivered the presidential address. Dr. Shaik Abdul Azeez Saheb, proposed a vote of thanks to the Honourable Vice-Chancellor, Prof. V.G. Talwar, who despite his extremely busy schedule graciously agreed to inaugurate the national seminar on Cultural Pluralism: The Indian Scenario: "We are fully aware, Sir, how difficult it must have been to keep yourself away from your duties to inaugurate this seminar and deliver the inaugural address. On behalf of the gathering and the Anthropological Association of Mysore, and on my personal behalf I extend to you, Sir, my heartfelt thanks for your gracious presence."

He next thanked Prof. Imtiaz Ahmad thus, "Professor Imtiaz Ahmad, whose books we have all read, since many of us were undergraduate students, needs no introduction to anthropologists not only of India but of the whole world. If Professor Ahmad does not mind my divulging a secret I would like to share with you all that Prof. Ahmad had a slight fever till yesterday and was indisposed. But his love for Anthropology made him ignore that in this position and come all the way for delivering the key-note address. I am sure the whole gathering here, will join me in thanking Prof. Ahmad Sir, for extricating himself from his busy schedule at JNU and coming all the way to Mysore to deliver the key-note address which we all enjoyed."

He went on to thank Prof. Rajesh Sachdeva: "We are also thankful to Prof. Rajesh Sachdeva, Director, CIIL, Mysore who not only most graciously agreed to allow us to utilise the facilities of the institute for conducting the seminar but also extended the necessary financial support. He also agreed to preside over the inaugural function of the seminar. The financial support extended by Prof. Sachdeva Sir, will take care of the lunch, tea and snacks as well as free accommodation for the outstation delegates. On behalf of all of us present here, and on my own behalf, I thank you sir, for all your assistance."

He continued to thank all those who contributed to making the seminar possible saying, "I am thankful to the representatives of the media who have kindly, agreed to cover this national seminar, without whose presence the main purpose of organising the seminar would not have been met.

"I will be a miss in my duties if I do not thank all those who have performed their duties unhesitatingly behind the curtains. Moreover, on my own behalf, I thank all the participants and the authors who will be presenting the papers in the following sessions.

"I am aware that I have not been able to thank each individual with whose help the seminar could be organised. Please believe me that the omission is not because of intension but due to shortage of time. Thank you one and all."

Prof. H.K. Bhat in his paper "Plural Societies and Cultures in Modern Nation-States with Reference to India : Anthropological Perspectives", stated that society and culture are the two most important basic concepts of Anthropology. Historically speaking, the British Anthropologists gave more prominence to the concept of society while the American Anthropologists considered that culture is the key-concept for Anthropology. However, in contemporary Anthropology, although the distinction is maintained between society and culture, they are not considered in dichotomous terms, but as an integrated term that is referred as socio-cultural, while addressing the various issues related to humans. In some contexts, it may be even necessary to view them as separate entities.

In her paper entitled "Development and Diversity: A Deliberation of Nationalism" the author Dr. Elizabeth Zhakerya presented a gist of her extensive field work, which she carried out for decades, in various capacities. From her long experience she feels that many among the marginalised groups oppose typical development programmes for various reasons and are aware of the shortcomings of such programmes to bring them into the mainstream advancement. Some of the opposition is due to fear about losing their inherent culture, values and life-style. A number of persons have expressed the view that it is humiliating to give up a proud tradition for some alien culture and existence. Many insist that it is arrogance on the part of the "developers" to assume that their culture, tradition and life-style are superior to some others. Yet others are opposed to the losses incurred in the process of introducing modern development; they perceive that the losses are being forced upon them. Outlined in this paper are direct observations of some such changes that have occurred, or are occurring, during the course of several field visits covering a number of years in predominantly tribal areas of Kerala. She also attempted to verify and analyse most of these assessments to whatever extent possible. Learning from these experiences, she has taken heed to pay as much attention to details in planning and implementations, during her different work assignments in various projects in rural and tribal areas, keeping in mind many local variations and aspirations of populations where the projects were executed.

Smt. Rajalaxmi Misra presented the Young Anthropologist Award for the best paper of the Seminar titled "Cultural Pluralism: The Indian Scenario" to Dr. D.V. Prasad, Mysore, for his paper, "Religious Pluralism and Tribal Identity: An Anthropological Study on the Nicobarese of Katchal, Central Nicobar Islands". In his paper, he discussed the unique features of the Nicobarese institutional framework and its role in maintaining their cultural identity even after conversion to Christianity or Islam, and peaceful coexistence with multiple religious faiths in a syncretic manner. Despite their extended association with new religious faiths, the Nicobarese still maintain their tribal identity by sharing basic or compulsory institutions like *Tuhet* (maximal lineage) system, *Manula* (council), *Misang* (contribution of resources), *Hayaken* (cooperation during plantation), *Manuvula Hinengo* (collective effort), *Minakren Tavahava* (cooperation during illness), *Inlom* (bi-local residence), etc. Furthermore, living together in lineage clusters and sharing customary ways of economic, political, and ritual life of their own, eventually projects their original identity as Nicobarese rather than as Christians or Muslims.

In their paper, "The Jarawas, Stone-Age People in the 21st Century", Dr. B.R. Ghosh, and S.S. Ghosh, from Mysore expressed the opinion that cultural pluralism in India is perhaps not as apparent anywhere else as in Port Blair, the capital of the Union Territory of Andaman and Nicobar. On first appearance, the town appears similar to any other small town in India. But even a small drive for about half an hour takes the tourist beyond the borders of the town, either to the jungle or the beach. Both appear to be far from "civilisation", not only in space but also in time. Entering the moisture-laden dense tropical forests, where the sunlight never reaches the forest floor, the tourist feels himself removed from urban life not just by miles only but by centuries. In these jungles the tourists may confront a group of Jarawas, one of the most "marginalised" communities in India. Immediately, innumerable questions crop up in their minds. Unfortunately, more often than not, these questions are not correctly or even satisfactorily answered by the people around. Some of these questions are, aren't these people Negroes?

Why are they almost naked? And so on. The questions increase substantially if they see the settlements of the Jarawas in their drive on the ATR (Andaman Trunk Road) across the Great Andaman or to the coastal belt. But the fact is that the Jarawas represent one end of the spectrum of the cultural pluralism that exists in present day India. An attempt has been made to describe and discuss how the Jarawas have maintained a way of life that has continued practically unchanged for millennia and is presently under severe threat by the forces of modernity.

In the next paper, "Cultural Diaspora: Tribal Migration as a Survival Strategy", Dr. Amitabha Sarkar from Kolkata suggested that survival strategy is the key factor because different locales offer different occupational opportunities. These are often altogether different from the opportunities available in the natal village. Tribals are thus forced to adapt to local situations. At the same time they are also being incorporated into local cultural milieu in the new place as elements of survival strategy. These are the kind of diasporic situations in various corners of the country where the tribals are pushed in view of their bread and loaf. It can also be said that being unable to maintain their bare subsistence, the tribals are pushed to some areas where occupational opportunities are available. This is a very alarming signal for planners and administrators because it clearly shows that the area from where the tribals were/and have migrated, are not fully covered under the schemes of the government developmental programmes. Here lies the root of social disharmony and unrest that is very much common in some parts of the country.

The paper "Religious Pluralism among the Khasis" by Dr. M. Sasi Kumar and C. Raghu from Mysore, tries to analyse how the Khasis have been able to follow the matrilineal system of descent and inheritance pattern despite embracing Christianity. The Khasis are a tradition-bound society, which often persuades its members to cling to their age-old customs and traditions by enforcing various kinds of sanctions on deviants. In a close-knit society no one can live as a social isolate and hence they observe the traditional norms and values as strictly as possible. The deep-rooted attachment of the Khasis to their tradition and culture together with the Christian missionaries' rigid attitude that the converts should give up everything native resulted in an initial rift between the converts and the Khasis. The Christian missionaries soon realised that they should give up their rigid attitude as the age-old cultural practises distanced a major section of the Khasis from embracing Christianity. This made them rethink and tolerate certain degrees of aberrations.

While earlier a convert had to abandon traditional customs, now-a-days Christians more pragmatically seek to blend into local cultures. The economic freedom and facilities for modern health care and higher education created by the missionaries attracted the Khasis. Gradually both the sides restrained themselves from direct confrontation and compromised on certain respects. It can be seen that though a considerable section of the Khasis embraced Christianity, which brought considerable changes in their socio-religious and economic life, they still follow the matrilineal system of descent and inheritance. The close link of matrilineal system with their traditional social life and culture helped them co-exist.

Dr. B.R. Vijayendra in his paper on "The Idea of Health: Medical Pluralism and Management of Treatment among the Jenu-Kurubas of Karnataka" mentioned that during the last few decades, medical researchers and public health specialists have shown an increasing interest in Anthropology. The main reason for this interest has been the realisation that there is more to health and disease than physical and biological processes. It has become clear that in order to overcome barriers to the uptake of health interventions and develop culturally appropriate, sustainable interventions, it is first necessary to understand the social and cultural context of health and disease. Much of the enthusiasm for including Anthropology is because it holds the key to the target populations' culture, that is, their beliefs, attitudes and practises; the anthropologists can advice on how to improve adherence in clinical trials or influence and change problematic beliefs, attitudes and behaviours through culturally appropriate interventions (Robert Pool and Wenzel Geissler, 6-7, 2005). Jenu-Kuruba is a primitive scheduled tribe community in Karnataka. They are distributed in the three southern districts viz. Mysore, Kodagu and Chamaraja Nagara. According to 1981 Census, their population was 34,747. Traditionally, they were forest dwellers and their subsistence economy was based on honey collection, food gathering and hunting of wild animals. The study was conducted in a modern settlement inhabited by 66 Jenu-Kuruba families. The total population of the settlement is 331. The Jenu-Kuruba concept of health is in tune with their traditional living habitat. They prefer to be lean and short statured which enables swift movement in the forest. They consider honey, yams and leafy vegetables as energy giving food. Illnesses are classified into four major categories on the basis of etiological categories. These include both naturalistic and supernaturalistic dimensions. Ideas such as hot-cold, three humors of the body, spirit intrusion, wrath of the deities, and sorcery are quite strong among the Jenu-Kuruba. The people have very good knowledge of the plant medicines available in the forest. Their pattern of health care is mainly based on etiological factors. They also consult allopathic doctors in nearby towns. The Jenu-Kuruba society is patterned on the theme of suspicion and distrust for each other. This is reflected in their ideas of health and treatment. In the study, an attempt was made to describe the medical pluralism and management of treatment among the Jenu-Kuruba.

Nilanjan Khatua, in his article on "Disease and Health Care among the Kamar Tribe: Ecological and Demographic Perspectives", states that medical anthropologists distinguish between illness and disease and these two concepts are again distinguished from sickness. Illness is viewed as the subjective experience of the patient and the immediate members of his family, friends and neighbours. This is an emic perspective of the reality. Disease, on the other hand, is an etic perspective which refers to the clinical manifestation of abnormality of physical function or infection by a pathogen in an individual or host. Arthur Kleinman uses a generic term "sickness" to include both illness and disease. Disease is considered a biological phenomenon, while illness includes psychological and social dimensions as well. The distinction between disease and illness begs the question what is "health", and a concept that is notoriously difficult to define. Health is the most precious possession of human beings. It is the solid foundation on which man's happiness rests. According to Carter of the WHO (1948), "Health is a state of complete physical, mental and social well-being and not merely an absence of disease or infirmity". The ecological approach in medical anthropology focuses on how human cultural and behavioural patterns shape the complex interactions of the pathogen, the environment, and the human host, and produce both infectious and non-infectious diseases.

Dr. S.A. Azeez Saheb in his paper "Syncretism in India: Shared Traditions among the Lingayats in Karnataka" tried to show that Lingayatism attempted to carve out a new path for itself, but failed, and fell in line with traditional Hinduism. Over a period of time it equated ritual status with social status, and conformed to the traditional ranking of castes based on birth and occupational differences. New converts were looked down upon by those who were born into the faith. Sub-caste endogamy and inter-dining between the sub-castes were the main points of the founder Basavanna's pristine revolutionary zeal for equality and the absorption of the sub-castes of the Lingayats into the mainstream of Hinduism. These issues were discussed in detail in the paper.

Dr. B. Krishna Reddy in his article "Cultural Harmony in India: The Role of Mystics and Saints" (with special reference to Sai Baba of Shirdi) states that communal harmony is *sine qua non* for national integration, peace and prosperity in a vast country like India inhabited by people following a variety of religions, speaking numerous languages and dialects and observing cultural pluralism. In addition, the issue of communal harmony is quite relevant and significant under the present circumstances in which communal frenzy, religious intolerance and social turmoil have been posing a serious threat and danger to our national unity. The problem of communal harmony needs to be tackled at various levels. It is often understood that communal harmony is basically a religious problem though it is not so. This fact can be demonstrated by depicting the socio-religious conduct of mystics, saints and Sufis.

Dr. Francis Kulirani in his paper on "Indian Christians: Regional Ethnic Formations and Denominational Pluralities" discussed in detail about the Indian Christians and stated that the Indian Christians in general have been described as "Hindu in culture and Christian in Religion." The acceptance of this religion has not distanced them from their socio-cultural milieu. At the same time they have also been subjected to the ramifications of Christianity and when it occurred in the western countries, was transported to India by the missionaries who carried the cross after the sword, especially during the 18th and 19th centuries.

Dr. V. Jayarajan in his paper on "Multiculturalism in the Ritual Performance of Kerala : A Study on Teyyam" states that Teyyam, a ritual dance tradition in Kerala is vogue in the northern districts such as Kannur and Kasargod. Teyyamis performed in the shrines, *Kavus*, houses, ancestral houses, and public spaces in fixed intervals. The ritual is performed by the lower communities who are not allowed to enter the shrine or house during the non-performing days. Although Teyyamis performed in the Hindu shrines, it has multicultural dimensions as there are several Muslim characters in the Teyyam cult. It is also to be noted that the shrines where Teyyam is performed belong to the Jain tradition. Furthermore, Buddhist tradition can also be traced from the vegetarianism followed by some shrines.

In their joint paper "Persistence and Change among the Sacred Specialists of the Nagore Andavar's Dargah in Tamil Nadu", the authors Prof. K.G. Gurumurthy from Dharwad and Dr. S.A. Azeez Saheb from Mysore agree with the statement of Prof. Vidyarthi that the combined functioning of the three components of a sacred centre reflect classical as well as Folk-Islam (Sufi) tradition. The sacred specialists of a place of pilgrimage maintain a distinct style of life and transmit certain texts, organising pilgrimages and officiating as the *Dargah muzawars*. Further, the sacred complex in general and the sacred specialists in particular undergo modification and transformation as a result of general development in the larger universe of Islamic Civilisation, of which they are a part. The position and the status of *faqirjamas* that are peculiar, and which enable them to persist in their occupation of saint worship, though the people derive faith from their concrete relation to the *Dargah* and its *muzawars*, rather than a direct relation to the distant and metaphysical God, have not received the attention of the scholars so far. The role of sacred specialists and the spiritual descendants of the saints of Nagore Andavar's Dargah, which encompasses folk-Islamic traditional aspects with the Classical Islamic Civilisational content, not only integrates the two cultural traditions but also opens up new vista in understanding the basic resilience of the two different civilisations juxtaposed, proving that there exists unity in diversity in Indian culture, which is unique with multi-ethnic, multi-linguistic and multi-religious traditions.

Dr. V. Pragati from Pudhucherry, and C. Raghu from Mysore, argue in their paper "Religious and Ritual Practises among *Arundhathiyar*: A Socio-Religious Perspective" that practically no significant change is perceptible in the religious and ritualistic behaviour of the *Arundhathiyars*. The impact of technological and modern materialistic culture has not been as powerful as that of religious culture on the *Arundhathiyar*. Worship and other religious acts form part of their daily life. However, the present day modern and sophisticated youngsters do not generally conform to these practises, though the old and the aged still live up to them. They further conclude that the *Arundhathiyar*, like most other castes of Puducherry attach prime importance to religious practises in every walk of life. Human life as perceived by them is full of hazards; hence, they need the help of the supernatural powers. Thus, in the day-to-day life of *Arundhathiyar*, religion is incorporated.

R. Rajendra Prasad, in his study on "The Sacred Complex of Vailankanni: A Study in Cultural Pluralism", stated that the study of sacred complexes in India would reveal the underlying cultural and religious syncretic processes by the congregation of people belonging to various faiths and beliefs. The established cultural influences reveal the origin and traditions of a particular pilgrim center. Vailankanni is one such sacred complex in south India where the cultural traditions of different religions can be observed among a congregation of devotees who visit the shrine in large numbers throughout the year.

In his paper "The North-East Scenario : A Linguistic View", Dr. Senkuttuvan from Mysore describes India as a museum of languages. According to him the vast heritage and rich tradition of the country can be understood completely and comprehensively by more and more extensive and synchronic studies of languages and dialects which are the manifestation of the cultures found in the length and breadth of the country. The pluralistic cultural diversity ensures more or less harmonious co-existence of several sub-cultures and value systems in a diverse society.

The fact that the Sino-Tibetan family of languages with a number of dialects plays a dominant role in the context of cultural pluralism in North-East India has been brought out in historical detail by Dr. Harka Bahadur Chhetri Atreya. His paper "Cultural Pluralism: The Indian Scenario: In the Context of North-East Region" deals with the cultural diversity of the North-East Region from a historical perspective. The Sino-Tibetan Language family as mentioned in the Linguistic Survey of India has been divided into three groups, i.e., Chinese, Thai and Tibeto-Burman groups. The Tibeto-Burman group is of our concern in the present paper. It is again sub-divided into Bodo (Boro), Burman and Tibetan groups. The Bodo group, as the dominant mongoloid family group in the North-East India, covers nine sub-groups. These are Chutia in the far North-East, Garo in Western Meghalaya, Hasong in West Assam, Rabha in South Assam, Kok Borok in Tripura, Koches in the Middle and West Assam, Mech in West Assam and Nepal, and Moran, Motok, Tiwa or Lalung in the North-East and middle-South Assam. The author is of the opinion that all these groups have variously contributed into the cultural pluralism in North-East India.

In their paper "Emerging Patterns of Cultural Pluralism among the Burmese Settlers in Great Andaman: An Anthropological Perspective", Dr. D.V. Prasad and Dr. S.A. Azeez Saheb from Mysore expressed the opinion that the continued existence of diverse ethnic groups in India in general and Andaman Islands in particular demonstrates the mutual coexistence of different categories of people. Of the existing diversity, the Karen and Burmese settlers in Andaman Islands are particularly contributing to this fact. Though they form a sizeable population in these remote islands, they have attracted no attention for wider scientific study. They hailed from mainland Burma during colonial annexation.

The Karen is an agricultural community inhabiting nearby villages in Mayabunder District in Andaman. However, the main Burmese population are scattered in different parts of the island including South, Middle and North Andaman, and are professing diverse occupations for subsistence. The organisational flexibility of the Burmese enables them to adjust in the multicultural set-up of Andaman Islands. The process of acculturation through alliances with their neighboring non-Burmese settlers facilitated them to learn the techniques of adaptation by emulation of other customs and traditions. Despite this plurality, observance of their own traditional life cycle rituals, annual festivals and religious practises are found even today among them. With this backdrop, the present study attempts to highlight the existence of cultural pluralism in their social living ranging from rites de passage, annual ceremonies, and other customary practises in view of the predicament of minority ethnic identities in Andaman Islands.

Prof. P.R.G. Mathur in his paper on "Society and Culture among the Kallu Pandarams of Kerala" states that the Jangam Pandarams speak Telugu, subsist on ritual begging and farm labour. The Poo Pandarams speak Tamil, were traditionally garland makers for the Pattar (Tamil Brahmin) temples, ritual mendicants, and have been recently engaging themselves as farm labour. The third community known as "Pandaram" is the Kallu Pandaram or Kall-Andi. They are distinguished from the other two communities by their occupation; they are highly skilled and engage in polishing navaratnam gem stones. They speak Telugu in the family and among themselves; however, they cannot write the script. They use Malayalam for all other purposes and most of them are also fluent in Tamil. They say that originally they were Jangams, but because of their occupational pattern, they differentiated from that community.

Dr. Samira Dasgupta from Kolkata, in her paper, "Bishnupur: A Site of Cultural Pluralism", states that Bishnupur is a treasure land of arts and crafts. It has an excellent tradition which includes weaving of Baluchari saris, terracotta works, dush avatar tash, sankha industry, etc. The excellent music of Bishnupur Gharana brings a heavenly atmosphere, which gives joy, peace and satisfaction to the people. It has a very important position in the cultural life of Bishnupur. All these along with the temples and other important places have given Bishnupur a very important position in the itinerary of the tourists. Lastly, the researcher observed that tourism as an exogenous component and a stimulating agent has caused occupational opportunities. Due to promotion of tourism, this heritage site is getting protection and proper conservation.

Dr. Bhamini Raghavaiah, K., Dr. Subramanya, C.E., and Prof. Rajasekhara Reddy, K. are of the view in their paper "Indian Pluralism: Changes and Concerns" that Indian civilisation has played host to several streams of migrant groups and communities from different parts of the world. Since ancient times, India has represented a melting-pot of races and cultures. The process of acculturation and integration has been extensively at work at the regional level. Though each group or community has a distinctive identity and ethos of its own, it does not exist in a social vacuum.

PART–I
Cultural Pluralism: General Perspectives

1

What is the Right Kind of Secularism for a Multi-Religio-Cultural Nation Like India?

N. Subba Reddy

We often use the word secularism; hence, there is a need to spell out in which sense we use it. For, it has acquired different connotations at different points of time in its long evolution. To go back to the beginning of history, the spirit of secularism is implicit in the biblical saying, "render unto Caesar what is Caesar's." It conveys the message that men of religion should not get involved in worldly matters, which are best left to the men of the world. Towards the end of the medieval period the cry for secularity took the form of a clamour of both kings and commoners to escape from the oppression of Papacy which reached the pinnacle of its mundane power and the nadir of its moral decay. Coinciding with the beginning of enlightenment, secularism stood for an attempt to free the pursuit of physical knowledge from religious interference. This thrust had its roots in Reformation and the Lutheran assertion of an individual's right to decide on his own ways of work and worship. This process eventually culminated in the separation of the church and the state.

The word secularism is said to have been coined in England by one Holyoake in the year 1851 from the Latin word, *speculum*, meaning a specific span of time, with its derived meaning of a concern for the here and now. It meant giving importance to what is empirical as against what is transcendent. In the modern age, there has been an obvious shift in the balance of power between the church and the state. In this changed context, secularism has come to mean non-interference, in each other's affairs, by the state and the church—an attitude of live and let live. This, to me, is the apt meaning of the word "secularism" relevant for our times.

However, there are some prominent social scientists and thinkers for whom the secular and the sacred are mutually antagonistic. According to Bryan Wilson (1987:159), the process of secularisation is marked by "a decline in religious activities, beliefs and ways of thinking." He also spoke of the secular humanism which places trust in human intelligence rather than in divine guidance. He later altered his stance, saying that secularism is not against religion *per se*, but against superstitious religion. This kind of antithetical perception of secularism and religion seems to persist among some social scientists even now. T.N. Madan who edited the book, "Religion in India", assumes that religion will fade away in a secular society, and that the strong presence of religion means weak secularity. He writes in the concluding chapter as follows: "secularism as the widely shared worldview has failed to make headway.........Signs of weakening secularism are in evidence particularly among the Hindus. Religious books, a newspaper report said, continue to outsell all other books in India.........Religious pilgrimages attract larger and ever larger congregations counted in millions. Buildings of religious worship dot the urban landscape . . . . The Godmen and Gurus sit in seminars and roam the streets" (1991 : 396-97). But a secular society, in the sense I take it, can also be one with a vibrant religion or religions. Secularism should only imply delineation of the respective spheres of religion on the one hand and of the state on the other, such that one does not transgress into the domain of the other.

An analysis of the situation observed in America may help clarify things. W.M. Mc-Clay, in an article entitled "Two Concepts of Secularism" says: "The sociologists from Max Weber to Peter Berger were convinced that secularism was one facet of the powerful monolith called modernisation.......If by secularism we mean the perspective that dismisses the possibility of a transcendent realm of being...then we should have expected the religious beliefs and practises to wither away by now.........yet at the dawn of the 21st century, America remains, energetically and even maniacally religious" (2001:7). Referring to the attempts to confine religion to the margins, he states that religion shows no signs of going away quietly. He then cites the growing numbers of churches, church associations and church attendance.

Still there remains the problem of overlap. In spite of careful demarcation, the religious and the secular do not remain in their respective compartments, but overflow. In the American Constitution, the first

Amendment provided for free religion (or no religion) for the citizens and prohibited the establishment of religious institutions by the state. On the basis of the wall built between the state and religion, the Federal Court ruled against any prayer conducted in state-funded schools and even the running of state buses to schools which conduct prayers. But still there are chaplains employed by the congress session. There are instances of Presidents invoking the help of god when they launch important programmes. These overflows between the two domains are there in all the countries including India. After all, the functionaries of the state are not required to be atheists. But what kind of limits should be set on the overflows is an important question which has a bearing on the working of secularism.

Proceeding further, Mc-Clay divides secularism into two kinds. Based on the concepts of positive liberty of the philosopher, Berlin, he divides secularism into positive secularism and negative secularism. Negative secularism is based on independence from religious injunctions, and it has the virtue of openness to diverse perspectives. On the other hand, positive secularism, as he says, implies established unbelief and the obligation to liberate people from misconceived religious beliefs. The positive secularists, according to him, take a radical stand for "excluding all religious thought from any serious part of public life" (*Ibid.*:25). He prefers negative secularism to positive secularism. After the above classification of secularists, Mc-Clay refers to an interesting demonstration held in Delhi in 1999 by an organisation called Citizens for Secularism to protest against the demolition of Babri Masjid which coincided with two other demonstrations, one demanding the building of the temple and the other demanding the rebuilding of the mosque. He is all appreciation for the first group which did not demand any building or rebuilding a place of worship, and wanted the state to act in a non-theocratic way

Regarding the question whether secularism should be opposed to religion *per se, Saral Jhingran (1995:54)* writes: "Once the facts are faced, the entire argument being repeated even now in our own country regarding the negation of religion being integral to secularism comes crashing down."

Secular State

A secular state is one which places all the religions of its citizens on an equal footing as opposed to a theocratic state, which favours one religion as state religion and confers on it special privileges. We have a secular state in India, which does not favour any particular religion and does not discriminate against any. It is expected to maintain equidistance from all religions as is expressed in the concept "*Sarva Dharma Sama Bhava.*" The Constitution offers to citizens freedom to profess, practise and propagate any religion (or no religion), to build and run their own shrines, mosques, temples, etc., subject to certain conditions like the maintenance of public order. The Constitution also grants an affirmative privilege to the minorities which is denied to the majority. They can establish their own educational institutions and administer them without any interference from the state even if they are aided by the latter. The Constitution forbids the state to utilise its funds to promote religion or religious institutions of any kind.

The above provisions go to show that the Indian Constitution was founded on a firm secular base. Yet, when one comes to the level of practise, many lapses become apparent. A highly pessimistic view of the possible success of our secularist creed is expressed by T.N. Madan (1991:392) in the following words: "I submit that in the prevailing circumstances, secularism in South East Asia as a generally shared credo is impossible, as a basis of state action impracticable, and as a blue-print for the foreseeable future impotent. It is impossible as a credo because the great majority of the people are active adherents to some religious faith. It is impracticable for state action either because, Buddhism and Islam are state or state-protected religions or because the stance of neutrality is difficult to maintain since the religious minorities do not share the majority's views as to what it entails for the state. And it is impotent as a blue-print for the future because by its very nature, it is incapable of countering fundamentalism and fanaticism." While he reiterates the view that the large-scale adherence of people to religious faith rules out any secularism, a few pages later (p. 406) he brings in, without comment, a quotation from Nehru which correctly states that secularism does not mean it is something opposed to religion but one which honors all faiths equally and gives them equal opportunities. If we go by his view, there is no secular state at all anywhere in the world. Even in the erstwhile Soviet Russia, the Russian Orthodox Church continued to exist. Our secularist as it comes out bears a close resemblance to Mc-Clay's analysis. Mc-Clay (2001:27) makes one significant observation: "Americans have accepted negative secularism as the essential basis for peaceful co-existence in a largely pluralistic society. Indeed a well considered theological basis for respecting the 'others' which lie outside one's own tradition will be essential to any religion hoping to have a public presence."

Now let us see where things went wrong in India. Certainly there were many omissions and commissions, misuses and miscarriages arising out of opportunistic politics. Political parties, some of them avowedly secularist, have pandered to the religious sentiments of different communities as suited to them from time to time in order to create vote-banks. Every important religious occasion was used by politicians to sidle up with the community concerned. It is one thing if a political leader is a genuine religious devotee and participates in the rituals purely in his private capacity. But the leaders participate as representatives of their parties or, worse, as representatives of the government. This is witnessed at *kumbhamelas*, annual festivals of major temples, *iftar* parties during Ramzan, etc. One may draw a lesson from Japan in this regard. If a Japanese Prime Minister wants to pray at a shrine, he does not use the official transport but goes in his private car. Our leaders should emulate this example and participate in religious functions as private individuals if they genuinely want to do so. Their security can be taken care of by official or unofficial agencies without wearing their badges or uniforms. State funding of Haj pilgrimages is a travesty of secularism. Similarly, *Imams* giving a call to their flocks from the pulpits of *masjids* to vote for a particular party in elections is a mockery of secularism. Governments declaring Friday as weekly holiday in Muslim-majority areas in view of impending election or bye-election (as it happened in Kerala) is a joke both on religion and secularism.

Every agency played ducks and drakes with the Ayodhya issue. Two years after independence, in the wee hours of 23rd December 1949, Ram's idols which were previously being worshiped outside the building were smuggled into Babri Masjid. Then the government took over the place and appointed a receiver. Legal battles followed between the Hindus and the Muslims. In 1984, the Ram Janmabhoomi movement was started, and in 1986, the District Judge ordered the place to be opened to allow the worship of Rama's idols. In protest against it, the Muslims soon formed the Babri Masjid Action Committee. In the same year, *Shilanyas* was performed at the site under the aegis of Rajiv Gandhi. In 1989 all the Ayodhya cases were clubbed together and transferred to Allahabad High Court. It is pertinent to note in this context that the High Court, on a previous occasion, remonstrated with the lower court, saying that such an important matter of public interest should not be kept pending for long. But notwithstanding the pious direction to the lower court, when the matter came up before the High Court itself, it was again kept back in cold storage. On 6th December 1992, the Babri Masjid was pulled down in a mass action in the presence of BJP leaders including Advani, who had earlier performed the *Rath Yatra*. It was a climax of the tragicomedy that the Prime Minister of the day, P.V. Narasimha Rao, makes a reference to the Supreme Court asking the latter to determine whether a temple had existed earlier at the site on which Babri Masjid was built. As expected, the court returned the reference respectfully without any comment. When, after a long wait of 21 years, the High Court delivered its judgement in September 2010, the verdict sounded like the adjudication of a village panchayat, offering to each claimant an equal share in the Babri Masjid site. As expected, the judgement has been challenged and the matter is now pending in the Supreme Court.

Rajiv Gandhi meted out even-handed favours to both the Muslims and the Hindus to please the orthodoxy. When in 1986, the Supreme Court ordered payment of alimony to a Muslim divorcee, Shah Bano, under section 125 of Criminal Procedure Code, Rajiv Gandhi's government promptly passed Muslim women's (protection of Rights after Divorce) Act, making the particular clause of the Criminal Procedure Code inapplicable to Muslims, thus offsetting the benign orders of the Supreme Court. After appeasing the Muslim orthodoxy by this act, the same government saw the building of Babri Masjid opened and the *Shilanya*s performed subsequently in the same year. Of the many pseudo-secular or anti-secular acts witnessed in India, perhaps the worst was the anti-Sikh riots in 1984, engineered and supervised by Congress leaders. Hundreds died and thousands suffered. And as yet the culprits have not met with justice.

Uniform Civil Code

It may be worthwhile to look at the different kinds of views expressed by the members of the Constituent Assembly when the question of Common Civil Code came up. A number of Muslim members harped on the theme that Islam defines the social life of its votaries and their personal laws are a part of their faith. Voicing that view, Mohammad Ismail sought to add a proviso to Section 25 of the Constitution to the effect that any social reform legislation will not affect the personal laws of the minorities. On the other hand, some Muslim members strongly supported reform. Ahmad Ali and Iqbal expressed the view that the personal laws of people should change with the changing times. Jajmal Hussain declared: "I want to tell the house that there is no minority in this country. In a secular state, there is no such thing as a minority." K.M. Munshi's vehement argument for a Common Civil Code reads as follows: "We want to divorce religion from personal laws, from what may be called personal relations or from the rights of inheritance and succession. What have these things got to do with religion, I fail to understand....If in the past, religious practises have been so constructed as to cover the whole field of life, we have reached a point when we must put our foot down and say that matters are not religious and they are purely matters for secular legislation." Realising the need for creating abundant confidence in the minorities that their way of life not be altered against their will, Ambedkar declared that a Common Civil Code would writ and would not be enacted without the consent of the minorities (proceedings of the Constituent Assembly).

Reformers and jurists continue to reflect on this important subject of social reform. Asghar Ali Engineer does not subscribe to the idea of inviolability of *Shariat* or Muslim personal law. The very existence of different schools of Islamic jurisprudence is, according to him, a proof of the fact that Muslim personal laws were interpreted and reinterpreted to suit the ethos of the times. But at the same time he pleads for caution, and says that uniform civil code, even if enacted, should be made optional and that initiative for reform should come from within the community concerned. This is a sage advice from a practising reformer.

M. Chalapati Rau, an eminent journalist and a close confidant of Jawaharlal Nehru, was a staunch advocate of Common Civil Code. In his book "Fragments of a Revolution" he says "Religion should not be a differentiating factor in the exercise of civil and political rights.....There will have to be a Common Civil Code as well as a Common Criminal Code" (1964:22). In his biography of Nehru he reflects on the nature of our constitution and strategies of reform. He says: "It (the Constitution) is obviously a compromise—recognition of the hold of religion on society and the need for a non-religious approach. But the spirit of the Constitution is secular in the sense that the state is above religion. The Hindu code bill was an attempt at secularism ....Muslim law could not be changed without a strong urge among the Muslims", (1973:153). When these hint at an initiative from inside, it should imply an initiative which is long overdue.

I have come across a recent paper on the "Politics of Muslim Personal Law" by Razia Patel (Head of the Minority Education Cell at the Indian Institute of Education, Pune). She deplores the resistance of *Ulemas* to the enactment of uniform civil code on the supposed ground that the Muslim personal laws are based on the received wisdom as enshrined in the Quran. To read her in her own words: "Muslim personal law is not a divine book. It is rather a man-made law. The Muslim personal laws (*Shariat*), Application Act or Act XXVI of 1937 was enacted by the British Government" (2009:45). Before this enactment, each denomination within the Muslim community followed its own customary law leading to a veritable confusion, which made some people demand codification of these laws. While the enactment has given a common code, it has become outmoded. But its regulations still govern civil matters such as marriage, divorce, adoption, succession, inheritance, etc. She points to the paradox involved in the *Ulemas* assenting to a common criminal procedure code but objecting to a uniform civil code. As she points out, Muslim thieves are not having their hands amputated or Muslim women are not being stoned to death for adultery as prescribed by *Shariat*. But the Muslim women are left to suffer oral divorce, lack of proper maintenance, etc. (*Ibid.*: 46). She makes a seething reference to the Muslim women's (Protection of Rights on Divorce) Act of 1986 which according to her, only deprives the Muslim women of the rights offered by the country's Criminal Procedure Code. She sums up saying that the Muslim personal law has moved from colonial politics to vote-bank politics. She approvingly cites the observations of Fyzee and Sathe to the effect that the debate on the Uniform Civil Code is designed not to satisfy Hindu chauvinism or to humiliate non-Hindus but to ensure a rational, humanistic and just law.

A survey she has conducted reveals that 7% of the Muslim households are polygynous, 30% of them include divorced women (mostly based on oral divorce), 44% mention dowry related matters as the main cause of divorce, and 92% have suffered expulsion from homes immediately after divorce. She concludes that communal identity politics is being played out at the cost of Muslim women and that "unless women and progressive organisations succeed in creating a forceful movement, reforms in personal laws remain a distant dream" (*Ibid.* : 49).

The initiatives for social reform may take different forms but they should all finally converge into a Common Civil Code. Women should take lead in this regard. What a paradox, it is if two families living side by side in a village or a town are governed by different laws in regard to marriage, divorce, inheritance and taxation! One should draw inspiration from Indonesia which forbade polygamy as early as 1974. The founder of Pakistan, M.A. Jinnah, can himself be taken as an exemplar of unorthodoxy in all aspects of his personal life, including his marriage, when he was 39, with the daughter of his Parsee friend, Sir Dinshaw. These examples should persuade even the reluctant to welcome a Common Civil Code for the country as a whole.

Radical Secularists

Also entering into this complex equation is the role of intellectuals and media. Mc-Clay in his paper on two concepts of secularism hints at the emergence of a new class of secularists, for whom secularism is a new religion. On the Indian stage, there are quite a few who qualify to be called radical secularists or fundamentalist secularists. Look at the following examples: There is a controversy in regard to the text books on history prepared by the NCERT. The previous set of writers were said to be secular historians and the next set of writers were said to be otherwise. What should be the nature of a text book meant for high school students? It should give only the central message about an historical figure or event and not peripheral frills. Is it necessary that a secular historian should seek to teach the students that Guru Tej Bahadur indulged in rapine and pillage, and that Aurangazeb's innovative taxes like the *jizia* was a signal contribution to the theory and practise of public finance? Romilla Thaper (1996:4) contrasts Hinduism with Islam in the following terms: "The definition of a Muslim community extends to all those who claim adherence to Islam and the adherence is said to be demonstrated by a clearly stated belief and form of worship..............The Hindu community is difficult to define, given the diverse nature of belief and worship. The crystallisation of this perception occurs when erstwhile Vaishnavas, Shaivas, Lingayats and others begin to refer to themselves as Hindus." But does she not see any difference between Sunnis, Shias, Bohars and Ahmadiyas in their beliefs and practises? She ought to have known that Ahmadiyas were declared as non-Muslims by Pakistan.

In an article on Buddhism and Bhakti, Gail Omveldt raises the following question: "Will Kabir who announces himself as the child of Allah-Ram be ever acceptable to Muslim-baiting Hindus?" (The Hindu 23-12-2002). One wonders why she did not pose the question the other way too. In another article she says that there were two versions of secularism in India.......... the Gandhian version and the Nehruvian version and both were wrong (The Hindu 21-01-2003). She however does not offer her own concept of secularism. Deepankar Gupta sums up the results of Gujarat elections in which BJP won, stating that the elections amounted to a referendum; he does not vote in the elections, and expressed that the BJP did not get the support of the majority of the electorate (The Hindu 25-12-2002). The curious logic here is that though the BJP got more than 50 per cent of the votes polled, still the votes they got constitute less than 50 per cent of the total electorate. It means he is very sure that all those who did not cast their votes were against the BJP. Kanchalliah, in an article on OBCs and VHP concludes that the OBCs have been recruited to provide muscle power to the BJP (The Hindu 06-12-2002). Obviously he categorises the OBCs as the modern Samurai.

Such writings will only have a negative effect on the people. Evidently a mistaken notion is developed that if one is to be regarded as progressive, he should express himself against the majority community and in favour of the minority, whatever may be the context. This suggests a kind of secularist fundamentalism. There are also certain media which publish only articles by writers holding that kind of a view. That is perhaps editorial fundamentalism. Having in mind such a species of secularists, Ashis Nandy makes many caustic observations. One of them reads as follows: "Once institutionalised as an official ideology, the concept of secularism helps identify and set up modernised Indians as models of rationality and gives them, seemingly deservedly, a disproportionate access to state power (2004:117)."

Some Recent Events

At this stage I refer to three recent events which are relevant to this theme. One is the *fatwa* issued against the national song, *Vande Mataram*. The 30th general body meeting of *Jamiat Ulema-e-Hind* held at Deoband on 04-11-2009 issued a *fatwa* against Muslims singing the national song, *Vande Mataram*. The reason offered is that it violates their creed of monotheism. It is further explained that while mother is respected, she is not worshiped, whereas the song has overtones of worshiping mother goddess, which is against the Islamic tenet of worshiping only one God. MM Joshi and Muktar Abbas of BJP protested against the *fatwa*, saying that it is violative of the Constitution of the country. Salman Khurshid of the Congress also joined the fray saying that he would himself sing the song and defy the *fatwa*. Malini Seshadri, writing in The Hindu on the next day, adds fuel to fire by saying that the song equates India to Goddess Durga and as it is only a national song and not a national anthem, an injunction against its singing should not reflect on the patriotism of the people who have issued the *fatwa*. Writing in The Times of India 08-11-2009, Swapan Dasgupta first takes the human rights issue, asks why the triple *talaq* is not questioned by anyone. He then suggests very sensibly that *Darul Uloom* could have suggested that the singing of that song be voluntary instead of a flat decree that no Muslim should sing it. It sounded like an unending discord but there came a bright silver lining in the form of a meeting between the ex-chief of RSS, Sudarshan and the leader of Shia Clerics, Maulana Hamud-ul-Hasan to discuss the issue (TOI: 09-11-09). Subsequently the president of the Shia Law Board has written to the President and Prime Minister asking for an authenticated translation of the song. I have presented a few glimpses of the reactions to an event from different sections of people. I shall return to it at the next stage to reflect, on how a detached observer would look at the different facets of the problem.

From Karnataka comes the news that as against Sachar Committee's regret about the low access to bank loans among Muslims, there is now an active drive by the Anjuman organisation to prevent Muslim women from repaying the loans they have taken from micro-credit organisations for their self employment schemes and from having any further dealings with those organisations (TOI 08-11-2009). If this agitation succeeds, the final losers will be the self-employed women; they should stand up to thwart Anjuman's anti-reform drive.

Then there is the news of linguistic chauvinism from Bombay. Raj Thakerey issued a *firman* that the State Bank of India cannot hold tests for the recruitment of clerks unless it is declared that only Maharashtrians are eligible to take the examination (TOI 08-11-09). Some anthropologists should respectfully inform Raj Thakerey that his earliest forefathers came from Africa. Many of them landed directly in Bombay, while some of them came via the Middle East and Europe. Hence, he should not keep all the posts to Maharashtrains but spare a few of them to the non-Maharashtrain descendants of his original ancestors.

When we are speaking of a plural society and its problems, it may be relevant to refer briefly to the concept of civil society or its variant, democratic civility, as formulated by social scientists in recent times. As Hefner (professor of Anthropology at Boston University) explains, the idea of civil society originated in the days of enlightenment, but it lay dormant all along until it was revived in the new international atmosphere of 1989-91. According to him, civil society is realised when the ideas of liberty and quality are extended beyond the political sphere, to home, school, neighborhood and ethnic and linguistic groups. When that happens, plurality comes to the fore to join liberty and quality to form a triad. The balance between the three factors changes when conditions change; a new equilibrium takes the place of the old. While postulating this idea, Hefner strikes a note of caution. To read it in his own words: "Radicalisation of pluralism may revitalise freedom and quality...........Freedom, quality and pluralism come with no guarantee of tripartite compatibility" (1998:10). The sum and substance of this is that when plurality reaches an extreme degree, it may affect equality and freedom, and when equality reaches a high degree, it may affect plurality. Hence a sound equilibrium has to be worked out between the three. In plain words, it amounts to saying that certain matters have to be common even in a plural society; for instance, law, basic human rights, economic opportunities, political participation, etc. Each group can have autonomy in certain matters, say in belief, worship and ethnic customs. It may be useful to keep this in mind when we are talking of a plural society.

What Needs to be Done

I have given a sample of the perennial problems that a plural society has to face. We cannot wish them away. How to tackle them effectively is the crux of the matter. I venture to make a few suggestions aimed at ensuring sound secularist precept and practise in our country. First and foremost, politics should be kept at a little more distance from religion than what it is today. Some clauses in the Constitution need to be amended for this. While Article 27 prohibits the state from utilising state funds or tax proceeds for promotion of any religion or religious establishment, Article 290-A provides for certain customary gifts in cash or kind to be offered by the state to certain temples. This should either stop, or if it cannot be stopped for compulsions of custom, there should still be a bar on ministers and political leaders from personally passing on such gifts in the presence of a large audience. Participation of persons in their capacity as leaders of governments or political parties in religious functions should be strictly avoided. Electoral laws should be modified not only to prohibit organisations championing the cause of a particular religion or a particular religious community from contesting elections but also to prohibit the use of religious symbols and exploitation of religious sentiments in any form by candidates contesting elections. As of now, candidates are allowed to contest and are only required to face legal scrutiny after the elections are over, if there is any breach of regulations. A stricter law to disqualify candidates on secular considerations is necessary.

National Integration Committees consisting of enlightened citizens drawn from different communities should be constituted at the Center and in the states. They should be watchful about any symptoms of communal discord and scotch them immediately. Also it should not be the representatives of the victims of a conflict that should come to the fore demanding redressal, but the leaders of the physical or psychological injury to others. If the known perpetrators of violence belong to one community, the leaders of that community should be the first to condemn them. Active groups of concerned citizens of all communities should work their way to prepare the country for a Common Civil Code; even if it is going to be a slow process and cannot be achieved quickly, but a committee of enlightened members of different communities can draw up a draft code and circulate it for a wider discussion.

Women should take the initiative in this regard. The majority community should take the lead and offer to forego the tax concession they claim as members of Hindu joint family. It is an invidious concession which the members of one community enjoy and others do not. A lead taken by the majority community in this regard will go a long way to change the attitudes of other communities.

Where sensitive or emotional matters are involved, one should not resort to rapier like arguments. In that case, the positions taken by the two sides become more rigid. A gentle plea or a soft suggestion may work better. Take for instance, the *fatwa* against the Muslims singing the national song, *Vande Mataram*. The case of the *Ulemas* is that they do respect a mother but do not worship her. Instead of indulging in a denunciation of their patriotism, it is better for the other party to argue that we only respect our flag or national anthem or national song and we do not worship them. It may also work better if one gently puts it across that even in the case of our anthem, *Jana-gana-mana*, it is addressed to a personified being, Adhinayaka and Bharata Bhagya Vidhata, meaning the supreme arbiter of Bharat's fortunes. In neither case worship is involved: only respect is extended. It may work out to be more effective if the protagonists on both the sides declare that the singing of the national song is optional and voluntary. Also it should be respectfully heeded if the *Ulemas* point out that the context in the novel in which *Vande Mataram* was sung by the monks carried a sectarian connotation. This has to be thoroughly examined.

Hindutva Bhartiyata

Lastly, let us discuss the impact that the campaign for Hindutva has on the interrelations between religious groups. The word Hindu stands for a particular religious community, of course, the largest in the country.

So an inclusive alternative has to be found. In this context, I recall what Atal Behari Vajpayee said in his reply to a no-confidence motion in the parliament. Referring to an accusation that the BJP indulged in Muslim baiting, he said: "yeh bharatiyatarikha nahi." He meant that baiting other religious communities is not the culture of Bharat, or Baharatiyata in short. So a word like Bharatiyata can represent culture more truly than Hindutva.

Ashis Nandy makes a distinction between Hindutva and Hinduism, and according to him, the former differs from the latter. He says that Hinduism is what most of the people in India live by, while Hindutva is the response of some urban, middle-class, westernised, Brahmanic Individuals. He goes on to say: "The growth of Hindutva depended heavily on invented heresies that are organised around themes that have no place in Hindu ideology: the modern state, nationality, etc. It has borrowed almost nothing from existing Hindu ideology in its construction of the non-Hindus.......This is the crucial difference between Hindutva and Hinduism (2004:129)." Nandy also refers to the traditional ways in which the "non-massified" Indians of different ethnic and religious groups lived in harmony, devising their own ways of negotiating across differences. Taking a clue from him, anthropologists and sociologists should bring out, through field studies, how multi-religious villages, towns and neighbourhoods live in peace and harmony, all worshiping at the same shrines and celebrating the same festival without any distinction of caste or creed.

I close with a quotation from that quintessential secularist, Jawaharlal Nehru. Way back in 1930s, he wrote: "Personally I am convinced that nationalism can arise out of the ideological fusion of Hindu, Muslim, Sikh and other groups in India. That does not mean extinction of the culture of any one group, but it does mean a common national outlook (1937:60)." So any label we use should reflect the plurality of our society and the inclusiveness of our national culture. I should think that Bharatiyata fits the bill, not Hindutva.

Integrating different sections into national unity is Indian ethos which is sometimes smudged by time-serving politicians and community leaders. One should realise that any campaign based on hatred for others cannot thrive in India in the long run. As for the majority community, it should stand by what Vivekananda said: "Hinduism sees all religions to be true." That should continue to be the world-view of our national culture.

References

Chalapti Rau, M. 1965, *Fragments of a Revolution*. London: Perganon Press.

Chalapti Rau, M. 1973, *Jawaharlal Nehru : A Biography*. New Delhi: G.O.I. Publication Division,

Gupta, Dipankar 2002, *Times of India* (Editorial Page). December 25, 2002.

Hefner, R.W. 1998, *Civil Society: Cultural Possibility of a Modern Ideal.*

Iliah, Kancha. 2002, *The Hindu* (Editorial Page). December 6, 2002.

Jhingran, Saral. 1995, *Secularism in India*. New Delhi : Har-Anand Publications.

Madan, T.N. 1991, *Religion in India*. New Delhi : Oxford Univ. Press.

Mc-Clay, W.M. 2001, *Two Concepts of Secularsim*. Span. January 2001.

Nandy, Ashis. 2004, *Bonfire of Creeds*. New Delhi : Oxford Univ. Press.

Nehru, J. 1937, *Recent Essays*. Allahabad: Kitabistan.

Omveldt, G. 2002, The Hindu (Editorial page) December 23, 2002.

Patel, Razia. 2009 "Indian Muslim Women, Politics of Muslim Personal Law and Struggle for Life with Dignity and Justice." *Economic and Political Weekly*, 31, October 2009.

Thaper, Romilla. 1996 "Tyranny of Labels." *Social Scientist* Vol. 24, pp. 9-10, Sep.-Oct.

Wilson, B. 1987 "Secularisation" in *Encyclopedia of Religion* (ed.) Mercea Eliade, Vol. 13.

2

Pluralism and Cultural Diversity in India*

Imtiaz Ahmad

Contemporary academic discourse on multiculturalism in India has been centred on a single salient point : There is a fundamental difference between pluralism (and one might as its variant include diversity) and multicultural pluralism. According to most self-proclaimed theorists on the subject, this has characterised societies throughout history, but is silent on the question of the nature of the relationship between the different pluralities. On the other hand, multiculturalism is concerned with the issue of mutual interrelations among the sorts of pluralities that might be found to exist in society. It is concerned with the issue of equality. It asks whether the different pluralities co-exist as equals in the public and political arena.

Thus, having nailed itself down to a fundamental difference between pluralism and multiculturalism, the academic discourse on multiculturalism in India bemoans very deeply that multiculturalism as a theory of democracy and citizenship has received little attention. As one theorist notes, "It appears quite paradoxical that in a country, which was among the first few democracies to endorse the principle quality between groups, there has been no serious attempt to theorise the idea of multicultural democracy."

My own point of departure on this question is that this mode of formulating the difference between pluralism and multiculturalism is seriously flawed and has ignored the difference between the societies where multiculturalism as an ideology of the state and a theory of ensuring democracy evolved. I do not quite deny the relevance of the substantive point that pluralism can be characterised by the presence of

*Key Note Address delivered in the national seminar on "The Cultural Pluralism : The Indian Scenario" from 5-6 December 2009 at Mysore.

diverse groups, communities and cultural orientations or worldviews without being concerned with the nature of the relationship between different cultural pluralities. It is possible that groups or communities may exist in a framework of back-to-back pluralism, that is, within a framework where they exist in relative isolation and independence from one another without coming into interaction except for limited purposes. Or, they may be involved in a daily mutual interaction, but their interrelations may be regulated within a framework of dominance and subordination or hierarchical ordering. However, placing undue emphasis upon the difference between pluralism and multiculturalism ignores the historical differences over how societies have looked at pluralism and in what ways they have legitimised it; this has serious implications for the programmatic design by which they seek to deal with the questions of preservation and sustenance of pluralism within national polities. There is, therefore, no escape from focusing on how these differences have shaped the attitudes of the polities not only towards looking at and handling cultural pluralism, religious as well as other aspects, but also providing for the preservation of pluralism and diversity in the public-political domain.

Even if we recognise that pluralism has been the characteristic of all historical societies (and this point is not denied), at the theoretical as well as empirical level, the two kinds of societies that constitute the point of comparison in the present seminar have historically differed on this substantive dimension. Since the European side of this question will be dealt in the contribution following my own presentation, I would be better advised to limit myself to just a few brief observations. Let me, in order to condense the argument, refer to the concept of nationalism as a means of anchoring the argument central to a discussion of the historical evolution of the concept and theory of multiculturalism. Put in the simplest terms, nationalism proclaims a new political ideal, the nation and a new political structure, the nation-state. It postulates that a nation is in need of its own state and aims to provide states with their inexistent nation from then on operated as a mighty weapon, either to strengthen or weaken, to make or to unmake new and old states. At least in Europe, there existed a bewildering variety of nations: nations without states, self proclaimed new and self confident old nations, nations which had constituted themselves and nations which had been defined by others who stood beside or against each other. Often these nations overlapped and sometimes they mutually denied their very existence.

Gellner has argued that the basic unit of nation is an atomised and autonomous individual and this is arrived at or postulated preceding the destruction of the pre-modern communities, which involves violence. Referring to the formation of nation in the West, Gellner notes that it is: "...... a general imposition of high culture on society, where previously low cultures had taken up the lives of the majority...It is the establishment of an anonymous impersonal society, with mutually substitutable atomised individuals, held together above all by a shared culture of this kind, in place of a previous complex culture of local groups, sustained by old cultures reproduced locally and idiosyncratically by the micro-groups themselves. That is what really happens".

This transformation from the "low culture" to the "high culture" was not smooth, neither governed by sympathy nor understanding of what was being transformed. Again, to quote Gellner, this transformation was not an awakening of an "old, latent dominant force", but "............a period of turbulent re-adjustment, in which either political boundaries, or cultural ones, or both, were modified so as to satisfy the new nationalist imperative which now, for the first time, was making itself felt... (and) this period of transition was bound to be violent and conflict-ridden".

It was this specific historical circumstance that fundamentally instituted the specific nature of nationalism in many societies in the West. Thus, nations in the West were sought to be built by destroying the complex structures of local groups and was built on the foundation of atomised individuals. The theoretical formulation for this was provided by social contact philosophers' notion of "man-in-state of nature" and their notion of "general will"; this embodies the idea of nation. Enlightenment stands towards homogeneity, and pluralism points out that Enlightenment rationality is the "instrumental reason which cannot accept pluralism. Each plurality under pluralism is founded in what AkeelBligrami has called internal reason." However, the reason that is advocated by Enlightened thinkers (with momentary exceptions in Hegel) is not "internal reason" but "instrumental reason", which *per se* rejects pluralism which thrives on cultural differences. Thus, within the social contract theory there is no place envisaged for pluralism; their overriding normativity is bereft of the description of plural instructions. All three social contract theorists have positively rejected natural communities and intermediate natural institutions. Indeed, as Ebenstein noted, Hobbes is vehemently opposed to division of powers or mixed government... (and) to keep the authority of the state strong, Hobbes advised the sovereign not to allow the growth of groups and institutions that intervene between the state and the individual.

Thus, the notion of rationalism in the political philosophy of social contract theorists is not empirical, and without empiricism in politics, democracy is not possible. Even when they talked about democracy, their notion of democracy eventually subscribes majoritarianism.

My limited reading of European history confirms a more cautious interpretation of the historical roots of plurality in Europe. The transition, from a unified Latin Christian tradition to a modern Europe of secularised, multi-confessional states, was not synonymous with the rise of tolerance and the triumph of pluralism. Instead, this transition, which mainly took place between the late 15th and the early 19th century, was more often than not accompanied by intolerance, persecution and religious wars. The ambivalent dialectics of tolerance and intolerance, conformity and plurality become especially evident when we focus on what historians call the early modern period that is the three centuries starting from the Protestant Reformation in the early 16th century to the French Revolution in the late 18th century. At the beginning of the early modern era, a hitherto unified Latin Christian church broke apart, and the 16th and 17th centuries were characterised by the institutionalisation of rivaling Christian churches in a process that has been labeled "confessionalisation."

From the 11th to the early 16th century, secular and ecclesiastical authorities in Europe asserted the unity of the Latin Christian church and used the powers at their disposal to subdue heretical groups. There was a general agreement among late medieval theologians and jurists that heresy the abandonment of the church's teachings constituted a worse crime than heathenism, for religious dissent was constructed as rebellion against the political and social order. The establishment of the inquisition in the early 13th century was the strongest manifestation of the church's determination to enforce religious conformity. What is important to stress here is that the new protestant churches like the old Roman Catholic Church were fundamentally intolerant. Luther, Calvin and their followers initially demanded toleration for themselves, but their belief in the absolute authority of the Bible, their self-perception that instruments and executors of protestant reformers towards the Jews also hardened once they realised that the Jews were unwilling to accept the Gospel's message, which after reformation was now restored to its original purity and true meaning.

The emergence of pluralism is often linked to the process of secularisation, broadly conceived as the abandonment of transcendent religious orientations by individuals, social groups, and whole societies. For Max Weber, secularisation meant the "disenchantment of the world" the replacement of religious dogma and metaphysical worldviews by non-confessional rational principles. According to modern sociological definitions, the concept of secularisation implies that religion as a fundamental, all-encompassing worldview for most people has been replaced by other primary identifications (such as nationalism), while the churches have become specific functional institutions or "sub-systems" in modern states. In this strict sense, secularisation and the growth of plurality were indeed intimately linked. Only when modern states ceased to define themselves as confessional, and when the state's purposes were separated from transcendent religious purposes, did religious toleration and pluralism become possible. If the concept of secularisation is broadened into a general explanatory concept for all the major rationalising and modernising tendencies in Europe over the past three centuries, its relationship to the growth of pluralism appears less clear-cut. Hartmut Lehmann has recently emphasised that the secularisation of modern Europe was hardly a linear process. Instead, a number of Protestant and Catholic religious movements have sought to counter the secularising and rationalising tendencies in modern European societies. The study of these movements has led Lehmann to suggest that the concept of secularisation should be supplemented by the notion of "re-Christianisation", which may well be an ongoing process. Parts of Eastern Europe experienced a period of "re-Christiansation" following the collapse of the Communist regimes in 1989-91; and after the terrorist attacks on New York City and Washington DC on September 11, 2001, the Christian churches in Europe were suddenly reported to be filled with people again. While there is reason to doubt that this was more than a short-lived phenomenon, it nevertheless indicates that the Christian faith continues to remain an important orientation for a great number of Europeans even if only in times of crisis.

I have trespassed into this brief discussion of the tradition of plurality in Europe with two purposes in mind: First, I want to reinforce that there is a basic distinction on this question between Europe and India. Europe, which was historically diverse and plural, underwent a process of establishment of homogeneous nation-states. However, within the special context of India, pluralism and diversity remained a dominant feature of the society until recent times and are today the central concern of the debates about multicultural states. Even the colonial rule, which was in one sense a remarkable source of homogenisation of society and culture, strengthened this concern by reinforcing the already existing cultural pluralism through the instrumentalities of the decennial censuses and the process of legislation whose aim in the initial stages was to create communities and groups. Second, I wish to make the point that multi-cultural discourse in India remains centered on the question of pluralism and diversity of cultures as well as the recognition of these diversities in public and political domains. Echoes of distinctive social identities, aspirations for autonomous states, if not for sovereign national status, and exclusive and inclusive claims to territories characterised as homelands are heard today in the former Soviet Union, Eastern Europe, West Asia, Africa and Canada. However, nowhere are they being articulated as powerfully as in south Asia. Nor have such assertions, aspirations and claims as severely stained the social fabric as in India. This makes a consideration of the Indian situation particularly relevant.

Let us turn now to a consideration of the politics of identity in India. Indian society historically fostered and perpetuated a complex and shifting weave of multiple identities among the diverse people of the subcontinent. Prior to the advent of Western colonialism, these multiple identities were accommodated, if not wholly assimilated, within the loose political arrangements. Considerable body of historical scholarship has shown that sovereign authority vested in a centralised state system co-existed with innumerable identities at regional and local levels. The British not only managed to impose colonial control in India, but also initiated a process of recasting Indian social identities. No doubt, such recasting occurred largely within autonomous cultural settings, and the colonial initiatives were more successful in creating political categories out of local identifications and affiliations, regional, linguistic or religious, rather than fashioning the mental world of the people. Even so, the diversity of social and cultural identities that had historically characterised the Indian society was swamped by the commanding power of the colonial state. The situation was further complicated by the rise of nationalism in a situation where there were many linguistic and cultural indemnities.

Put in the simplest terms, nationalism proclaimed a new political ideal, the nation and the nation-state. Confusion over the form that the nation-state should assume was bound to arise because two mutually incompatible concepts of defining the nation were by this time well entrenched and both concepts gave inconclusive or contradictory answers when they were confronted not with the generalised question "What is the nation?", but with the specific and politically ticklish question "Who is the nation?" These mutually exclusive concepts of the nation were the ideal of the democratic and open nation and the ideal of a closed and "ethnic" nation respectively. Although both concepts normally exist in all modernising societies, it is difficult to disentangle them if one has to understand the nature, form and consequences of nationalism in the case of a society where identities have historically remained diffused and complex.

The concept of an open and democratic nation arose first. This was influenced by liberalism and was necessarily linked to the basic concepts of liberal civil society, the rule of law, and a democratic government. The open and democratic nation comprises, or at least is supposed to comprise, in any given historical context, all those individuals who have lived together under a common social framework and who, as a result of political reforms have acquired the right of democratic self-determination. It is thus the memory of having lived together, whether as one single entity or separately, the existence of a democratic constitution and the constant practise of self-government, which imparts to diverse individuals and groups a common national identity. Such a nation is not only democratic, but also open. Its individuals are not defined by a common social substance, and a singular and exclusive identity, but through a common political relationship.

With this ideal, the open and democratic nation contrasts the closed "ethnic" nation. This nation is not defined through a political, legal or democratic relationship among its vastly different individuals and communities, each with its own distinct identity. It is defined through a common biological, religious, cultural, social or "ethnic" bond, which overrides the various differences among its members, individuals as well as communities. This bond is derived from a common descent, religion, culture, language or history and creates an "ethnic" identity and "ethnic" nation. Commonalities of descent, religion, culture, language and history are no longer seen as separate or incidental or autonomous elements of society. They are instead seen as external manifestations or indicators of an ageless and unique primordial community. The "ethnic" nation is also a closed nation: it is defined by a common substance or social and cultural traits which signify a common descent. Outsiders are either excluded in principle or they have to be completely assimilated.

The three assumptions that underline this concept of the nation have been briefly summarised as follows:

1. Mankind by nature and historical evolution is divided into different and definable "people" communities. These groups have the moral obligation and right to preserve and cultivate their specific identity.
2. The defense and development of a specific identity is only possible inside their own state. This state has, in most circumstances, to be fought for and this collective and heroic understanding implies the transformation of the respective ethnic group from an objective entity into a self-conscious community.
3. It is through this transformation of the people that the ultimate self-realisation of a nation's culture and destiny will be achieved.

These two originally separate concepts of nation and process of nation-building have by now through a global process of colonisation and decolonisation, of increasing modernisation and democratisation have entered the arenas of political completion and ideological debate. In these arenas, proponents of both concepts try to monopolise the term nation and they try to deny this title and ideal to their respective opponents. A liberal nation or nation-state is seen as utopian. An ethnic 'nation' or nation-state is seen as dangerous and fascist. In this battle for semantic monopoly, the partisans of an "ethnic" nation-state are often the most insistent. Having withdrawn from a liberal conception of society, they proceed to "expatriate" their opponents from political debate and start to describe them as "anti-national." Ethnic nationalism advances the claim of one nation its own, against others. It thus discovers and exacerbates arbitrary divisions and acts as an aggressive and intolerant force. It necessarily sets off a chain reaction of counterclaims and of further attempts of "ethnic" nation-building. Widespread "ethnic" conflicts, "ethnic violence" and "ethnic civil wars" such as the ones we witness in India today are thus the consequences of "ethnic" nationalism. To the extent that the liberal concept of nation and nation-state serves "ethnic" nationalism either as a catalyst, a camouflage, or an instrument, it is easy to overwork the fact that these ethnic conflicts and nationalism do not result from the logic and structure of the liberal nation and nation-state. They arise from the cultural context and political constellations which have emerged proportionate to the spread of modernisation and democratisation.

References

Alan O. Ebenstein, *Great Political Thinkers: From Plato to the Present (Great Political Thinkers),* 1999. Wadsworth Publishing.

Ernest Gellner, 1983, *Nations and Nationalism. Cornell* University Press.

Hartmut Lehmann, 2008. "Trade Liberalisation and Employment Effects in Ukraine." *Comparative Economic Studies*. 50 (2), pp. 318-40.

Luther, M. 1957. *The Bondage of the Will. Eds*. J. I. Packer and O.R. Johnson. Old Tappan, N.J.: Revell. OCLC 22724565.

Luther, M., 1955-86, *Luther's Works*, 55 Vols. Eds. H.T. Lehman and J. Pelikan. Pennsylvania: St. Louis Missouri and Philadelphia. Added to my books! Add my review.

3

Plural Societies and Cultures in Modern Nation-States with Reference to India: Anthropological Perspectives

H.K. Bhat

Society and culture are the two most important basic concepts of Anthropology. Historically speaking, the British anthropologist gave more prominence to the concept of society and the American anthropologist considered that culture is the key concept of Anthropology. However, in contemporary Anthropology, although the distinction is maintained between society and culture, they are not considered in dichotomous terms but as an integrated term which is referred as "socio-cultural" system while addressing the various issues related to humans. In some contexts, however, it may be necessary to view them as separate entities.

In this paper an attempt is made to understand the concept of pluralism as it is applied in societal and cultural contexts at various times in the emergence of the discipline of Anthropology and its relevance in the contemporary anthropological discourse. The concept of ethnicity and its relevance in the contemporary nation-states is also discussed with special reference to India.

Society

The term society in its generic sense is applied to all human beings who depend on society for their existence. It is also used at specific levels to refer to the particular ways of life carried out at the group level. European Anthropology, particularly British Anthropology, considered society as the key theoretical concept of Anthropology.

Social life is an important attribute of human nature. Humans are genetically endowed with the ability to live as a member of society. But the focus of anthropological studies has been on human societies in general rather than on particular human societies in the past. At the specific level, a society is identified with the following properties: territory, social institutions which last beyond the life-span of an individual, and a distinctive culture.

The general and specific concepts of society have divided Anthropology into two major areas of research activities: ethnology and ethnography. These two activities are considered as stages of a single process. Ethnographic research on particular societies, leading to theory building at the global level, was developed in the 20th century. Curiously the ethnological perspective dominated the 19th century Anthropology, much before the refinement of ethnographic procedures. Hence, most of the ethnological statements of that period are discarded now.

Since the beginning of the 20th century, society in the specific sense always dominated anthropological writings since it was derived from sound ethnographic research procedures. This is true especially in the case of British Social Anthropology. In this brand of Anthropology, the emphasis was on patterns of relationships among the members of a society. The social anthropologists derived their intellectual inspirations from E. Rurkhain and Max Weber.

At the level of ethnographic research, we do not find much difference between a social anthropologist and a cultural anthropologist. They use the same strategy and techniques. But according to Leach, the outcome of the field work, the monographs of the two look very different because of the difference in the intellectual traditions of the two schools.

Anthropologists of the 19th century wrote about society in singular, but contemporary anthropologists write about society in plural. Whether societies as social units are comparable or not is debated hotly among the anthropologists.

According to Leach, a society means a political unit which is territorially defined, and often a segment of a larger political unit, which is also called a society (1982:40-41). In society, the emphasis is on patterns of relationships among its members. The social anthropologists considered culture as the by-product of these relationships. This view was based on the study of small scale societies like Trobriand and Tikopia. The members of such societies shared a culture.

In the modern nation-states the societies are extremely complex, the segments of which maintain different cultural traditions.

Culture

Culture in its broadest sense refers to a shared way of life that includes values, beliefs, materials and norms, which are transmitted within a particular society from generation to generation. Tylor gave the first scientific definition of culture: "Culture of a civilisation... is that complex whole which includes knowledge, belief, art, morals, law, custom, and any other capabilities and habits acquired by man as a member of society (1871:1). It also includes the word society."

The concept of culture has undergone many transformations since Tylor's days. There is no consensus among the present-day anthropologists about the term. However, as Leach has put it, all of them treat culture as "a kind of clothing which is quite separate from the human beings who are clothed" (1982:39). Many variations are also found among American cultural anthropologists. The cultural materialism of Marivin Harris views all peculiarities of culture with reference to local variations in adaptation to the physical environment (e.g., cannibalism is viewed as an adoptive response to protein deficiency). David Schneider, a pioneer of symbolic Anthropology, looks at culture as "a system of symbols and meanings" and "a language-based process of thought" and undermines the material manifestations of culture (*Ibid.*: 40).

Tylor wrote about culture in the singular. But present day anthropologists are preoccupied with the term in its plurality. Attempts to compare and contrast cultures across the globe was started by Tylor in 1889 and later developed by Murdock under Human Relations Area Files (HRAF) which broke cultures into traits and segments. Leach disapproved this kind of comparison (*Ibid.*:42).

Typologies of Societies and Cultures

Since late 19th century, anthropologists have been attempting to classify societies and cultures, mainly from the evolutionary perspective. L.H. Morgan's division of human societies into savagery (hunting-gathering), barbarism (agriculture) and civilisation (industry and urbanism) was the most popular classification until the early 20th century. He and others believed in the unilinear evolution of human societies, from simple to complex stages, which were considered to be irreversible and predetermined. In line with western thinking of dualism, human societies were placed in dichotomous relationships by various scholars as follows:

Primitive – Civilised (Tylor); Kinship – Territory (Morgan); Status – Contract (Maine); Simple – Complex (Spencer); Community – Association (Tonnies); Gift – Contract (Mouss; Gemeinschaft; Gesellshaft); Mechanical Organic Solidarity – Solidarity (Durkheim); Traditional – Rational (Welber); Non Literate – Literate (Redfield); Holism – Individualism (Dumont); Cold– Hot (Levi -Strauss).

The above dichotomies are based on the nature-culture opposition. The first generally represents a more "natural" state. It also represents the opposition between society and the individual, the group is pre-eminent in the former whereas the individual is pre-eminent in the latter. In the beginning, this dichotomy was used as the theoretical basis for developing Anthropology as a discipline devoted to the study of the so-called primitive societies and Sociology for the study of modern societies. It represented a theoretical division of labour between these two disciplines.

Mainly two theoretical models were used by anthropologists to understand the diversities in human societies in progressive succession and the folk-urban continuum model which placed societies in polar relationships: The classical evolutionary model which was developed in the late 19th century was later abandoned and replaced by the neo-evolutionary model developed independently by Childe, Write and Steward.

Socio-Cultural Systems

Anthropologists generally address the subject of their study by the name of the communities such as Tikopian, Toda, etc. The communities exhibit characteristic behaviours, speak their own languages and distinguish themselves from outsiders. In earlier usages, society generally referred to the group of individuals who maintained characteristic relationships with each other, whereas the term culture referred to their characteristic beliefs and behaviours. The term exhibits all the characteristics of the people whom we may call Tikopian or Toda; since 1950s many anthropologists started using the term socio-cultural system to imply either, society or culture or both (Beals, Hoijen and Beals, 1977:30). It was used as a theoretical concept involving biological, environmental, psychological and historical factors. The major components of this system are (*Ibid.*:30):

1. A group or society affected by decisions and common participation of its members exhibiting characteristic behaviours.
2. An environment where these activities are carried out.

3. A material culture which contains common equipment and artifacts.
4. A cultural tradition to carry on the historically accumulated decisions, artifacts, etc.
5. Characteristic behaviour and activities emerging out of complex interactions among members, with environment, material culture, and cultural tradition.

In these days, most of the anthropologists prefer to use the hybrid term socio-cultural system.

Plurality in Societies and Culture

In 1948, J.S. Fermival described plural society as one in which radically distinct people met only in the market place, a feature of colonial political economy based on ethnicity (quoted from Barnard and Spencer, 2002:425-426).

M.G. Smith was an exponent of plural society theorising in Anthropology (1965). Smith's model was based on race. Other features such as religions and language were ignored; the concept of plural society was dominant in 1950s and 1960s. South Africa had even a Ministry of Pluralism at one time.

Societal pluralism was superceded by cultural pluralism in 1980s. Cultural pluralism theory was advocated by D. Maybury-Lewis (1984).

The theory of cultural pluralism pleads that historical cultural differences should be sanctioned by a legal order and should be given equal rights in the national society. Maybury- Lewis also founded an organisation called "Cultural Survival" to promote cultural pluralism. Leo-Koper is another anthropologist who campaigned for the protection of indigenous peoples at the United Nations.

Ethnicity and Ethnic Group

Ethnicity was introduced as a technical term in Anthropology since 1970s (Sokolovskii and Tishkov). Ethnicity in general, refers to any group of people who claim common descent, language, religion or race. It is also used in the post-colonial context to refer to minority groups in national states. Ethnicity is based on perceived differences in ancestral origins or descent, and shared historical and cultural heritage (Scupin and DeCorse, 2009: 260). 'Ethnicity and ethnic group' are frequently used by anthropologists working in modern industrial societies. Members of an ethnic group believe that they share a common history, culture or ancestry (e.g., The Amish in USA).

Ethnicity takes different shapes in different national and cultural contexts. The meaning of ethnicity also varied from time to time. In early messages of ethnicity, radical characteristics like skin colour, shape of the nose, etc., dominated.

European conquest of large parts of Latin America, North America, Africa and Asia contributed to the emergence of diverse and heterogeneous ethnic groups. In Latin America, three centuries of Portuguese and Spanish rule resulted in the emergence of Mestiozos, a hybrid population, who became a dominant ethnic group representing about 60 percent of the total population (Scupin and DeCorse, 2009: 564).

In Africa, the term tribe is seldom used at present. Instead, the term ethnic group is used to refer to more than 1000 communities spread in more than 50 countries (*Ibid.*: 56). Ethnicity in the Caribbean nations is a complex mixture of imported African slaves, East Indian labourers and various Europeans.

According to Sergey Sokolovskii and Tishkov there are three approaches to the understanding of ethnicity: (a) primordialist views primarily based on biology: a socio-biological approach is used here, also a product of culture and history; (b) instrumentalist approach (also called circumstantialist approach) used ethnicity as a political instrument, exploited by community leaders to attain political goals; (c) constructivist approach is used in specific social and historical contexts as reported by Frederick Barth Barnard and Spencer (2002: 190-191).

Caste and Tribe in Indian Society

The classical Indian society was formed on the principle of *Varnashamadharma* (i.e., dharma of class and stages of life), Basham equates the four *varnas* to four great classes of India, which were flexible in the beginning but later became very rigid (2002:137). Rules of endogamy, commensality, and occupational exclusiveness governed the relations between social groups in later Hinduism. Endogamy was not strictly adhered to by all, especially the wealthy people, who made provisions for hypergamy (*anuloma*) and hypogamy (*pratiloma*). Smaller social groups called *jatis* emerged from the *varnas* which proliferated in larger numbers later. The Portuguese who came to India in the 15th century, named such social groups as *castas* or castes. The four *varnas* remained the same in all parts of India. However, the number of *jatis* under each *varna proliferated* and it varied from region to region and from time to time (Basham, 2002:148). *Jatis rose* and fell in the social scale in the past, but during later years, mobility became more difficult. "Caste is the development of thousands of years, from the association of many different racial and other groups in a single cultured system" (*Ibid.*:148). Further, he states that "The organisation of castes...., was a powerful factor in the survival of Hinduism" (*Ibid.*: 151).

The British divided the Hindu society into castes and tribes. The literate, urbanised and the rural masses which practised agriculture or different crafts were classified as castes and the social groups that lived in isolated places or forest environment were classified as tribes. This classification helped the 'divide and rule policy' of the British. However, even after independence, this policy was continued by the Congress government and incorporated into the Constitution of India. Castes were divided into scheduled and unscheduled. All the social groups which were called tribes in the past were also scheduled. Since independence, many *jatis* also found their way into the scheduled tribe group. The main objections to the caste system have come from the literate, urbanised *jatis* who no longer believe in ritual purity and pollution, caste hierarchy and commensality. At present there are many challenges to this system from a majority of Hindus. Hence, it is appropriate to rename all the social groups in India, irrespective of their religion or race, as ethnic groups. Equality to all ethnic groups should be guaranteed in the Constitution of India.

India is a multi-ethnic society with multi-cultures. India has more than 5000 endogamous social groups with distinctive religions, languages, beliefs and values exhibiting the features of ethnic groups. This would also promote cultural diversity in India which is an essential feature of human life.

Conclusion

We can conceive a richer cultural future for the communities in the world only in a pluralistic form, in which cultures representing the world's diversity connect with one another while sedulously preserving their originality. Throughout cultural history, cultural traditions mingled and fused on many occasions, thus producing a somewhat hybrid form. No doubt, specific contributions were also made at specific cultural levels. That is why diversities continue to exist in human cultures.

Standardisation is danger to the survival of specific cultures. Cultural evolution is inevitable. It is hoped that each culture will preserve the most distinctive features to maintain the uniqueness of each culture

In the Indian situation, thousands of specific cultures have existed for millennia. Division of the Indian society and culture on the basis of religion, race, caste or tribe is detrimental to its plural nature. Since majority of the Indians do not believe in hierarchy of different groups in our society on the basis of traditional criteria, it is necessary to give a new name to our communities. Ethnic group is the most ideal term which is likely to bring the desired changes in the Indian nation-state. All ethnic groups in India must be legally declared as equal in all respects. This may usher an era of harmony in the society.

References

Barnard, A. and J. Spencer. 2002. *Encyclopedia of Social and Cultural Anthropology*. London. Routledge.

Basham, A.L. 2002. *The Wonder that was India*. New Delhi : Roopa and Co.

Beals R.L., H. Hoijer and A.R. Beals. 1977. *An Introduction to Anthropology*. 5th Edition. New York: Macmillan.

Leach E.R. 1982. *Social Anthropology*. Glasgow : A Flontana Paperback.

Maybury-Lewis D. 1984. *The Prospects of Plural Societies*. Washington. American Ethnological Society.

Redfield, R. 1961. *The Little Community and Pleasant Society and Culture*. Chicago. The University of Chicago Press.

Scupin R. and C.R. DeCorse. 2009. *Anthropology: A Global Perspective*. New Delhi. PHI Learning Pvt. Ltd.

Smith, M.G. 1965. *The Plural Society in the British West Indies*. Berkeley. The University of California Press.

Sokolovskii, Sergey and Valery Tishkov. 2002. *Ethnicity : In Encyclopedia of Social and Cultural Anthropologist*. London. Routledge.

UNESCO.1982. Many Voices, One World. International commission for the Study of Communication Problems, UNESCO, New Delhi, Oxford and IBH Publishing Co.

4

Development and Diversity: A Deliberation for Nationalism

Elizabeth Zhakerya

Background

The richness, range and variety of different aspects of most minor societies are often overlooked or considered inferior and substandard. This diversity lends itself in customs, rituals, food habits, language, livelihoods, myths, folklore, etc., evolved over centuries, interacting with specific ecosystems, incorporating rich arrays of tradition, experiences and history. India has the most profuse varieties of all these in the world. Almost all the minor and marginalised groups are usually found living in elemental environments, in isolation, under primitive conditions. It is generally assumed by many that tribal population, especially those living in isolated conditions, should in every sense be brought into the mainstream of development and that these communities should be helped to overcome the seemingly hopeless and dismal conditions. The scale of this task in a country so vast as India is gigantic, and many crores of rupees have been allocated by the government under all the Five Year Plans to address this agenda. When a single agency undertakes such development to uplift a number of under-privileged communities which are all so different, it cannot diversify its programmes to help each community to advance as envisaged and yet retain each one's characteristic features.

No government can cater to the specific needs of all aspects of the huge number of communities that are present here. It is also a tough choice as to resolve how to decide on development, what should constitute development, how, where and for whom this should be implemented, etc. When different cultures come into contact, there are always losses along with many changes. A lot of "uniformisation" occurs when multiple contacts are established, when changes are introduced along identical lines, and when overall development is projected as being a single-lane track. There is a significant percentage of people who believe that diversity cannot really coexist with nationalism, which is true to a certain extent. Because development projects involve a great deal of money, there are plenty of politics, dynamics and strings involved in the programmes planned, the disbursement, and certainly who the beneficiaries should be.

Since the rules and procedures are intricate as well as complicated, it is worsened by all the existing bureaucracy and red-tapism. This debate about development versus preservation of our rich heritage and variety of culture is a continuous one. There are several proponents who assert that when [coordinated] development is absent it leads to resentment, and destructive and divisive forces step in leading to mayhem and chaos. The "deprived" feel betrayed, sidelined and victimised, and at least some sections of them want to hit back at those whom they feel have benefited at their cost. In the name of development, many areas have been depleted of natural resources, or have been destroyed, overexploited; groups of people were displaced without adequate compensations, benefits [and resources] earmarked were siphoned off by, and to, undeserving groups. This added fuel to the resentment and bitterness. Much of these actions have caused untold miseries and wretched poverty, which are claimed to be root causes of uprisings in several places. Many of these situations have also been exploited by unscrupulous persons for their selfish motives. In this context, it seems that this so-called development has achieved little; instead it has created more unrest, and in the process, loss of rich heritage and traditions, which were intriguing, unique and distinct.

Since literacy is perceived as the single major factor hindering improvement of people, development usually implies getting children from these communities to attend conventional school education [an alien concept for most tribes], adapt to "modern" living standards, culture and customs. In this process, traditional practises and way of life of most tribal groups are lost, trampled and/or, unidentifiably altered. Many tribal persons have also in the process imbibed several unwanted habits, learnt vices deplored by even the so-called modern communities. A common belief generally is also that tribal way of life is "below *our* acceptable standards", often disregarding how tribal communities' lives have evolved.

There are many among the marginalised groups who oppose typical development programmes for various reasons and are aware of the short-comings of the government's development programmes to bring them into mainstream advancement. Some of the opposition is due to disagreement regarding losing their inherent culture, values and life-style — a number of people have expressed that it was humiliation to give up a proud tradition for some alien culture and existence. Many insist that it is arrogance on the part of the "developers" to assume that their culture, tradition and life-style are superior to some others. Yet others are hostile to the losses incurred in the process of introducing modern development, and the losses they perceive as being forced upon them instead.

Older persons in particular, often lose their traditional livelihood [the only ones they had ever known], their customary surroundings [when relocated to new places], access to reserves of their long-established supply sources for their various needs, etc. They are often forced to take up unknown [and strange] activities as new livelihood means. Some resent the shabby quality of assets offered to them when they see the better quality of possessions of others around them. Yet others perceive exploitation because of their ignorance, their being subjected to a lot of hardships and being helpless about it all.

Outlined in this paper are some direct observations of such changes that have occurred, or are occurring, during the course of several field visits covering a number of years in [what used to be] predominantly tribal areas of Kerala. [These observations may have been noted by others also through their own experiences.] The author had attempted to verify and analyse most of these assessments to whatever extent possible. Learning from these experiences, I have taken heed to pay as much attention to details in planning and implementations, during my different work assignments in various projects in rural and tribal areas, keeping in mind the many local variations and aspirations of populations where projects were executed.

Education

Education often means attending conventional types of schools conforming to a national syllabus, with learning being imparted in a specified manner. Government officials too subscribe to similar beliefs which actually are in contrast to what tribal communities usually expect education to mean. An often mentioned grievance from many quarters in government departments is the difficulty faced at grass-root levels in rural and tribal areas to get children to attend schools. There are many reasons for this. The chief among these being poverty, alien teaching methods [education process *per se* is not unusual among tribes], inability to cope with strange syllabi and [boring] procedures [which most of their elders feel are nonsense], distances needed to be traversed to reach schools, many dangers inherent in most areas, absence of teachers, lack of basic facilities in schools, dilapidated conditions of most of these buildings, etc. Authorities claim lack of funds, staff [including those disinterested in working in such remote places]. Due to poverty the inputs of children are needed by their families to share work, care for younger children, mind household chores, etc., which many take priority over sending children to school.

The syllabi taught in conventional schools are mostly seen as not of much use to the traditional ways of life of a tribe. I have come across many worried parents who insist that it is more important for their children to learn to make and set traps, important skills, identify and learn about the different flora and fauna in their surroundings [food, medicine, poisonous ones, etc.], to make implements for their day-to-day needs for which they must know where and how to collect the raw materials needed; in short, to learn about the basic business of living [according to their perception]. Many tribal parents were surprised, and expressed bewilderment, that these [important] skills were not being taught in schools [where, they have been told, education will be imparted]. Then, when will their children learn the essential skills needed to survive in their surroundings, if they have to be sent to schools? They ask, "Who will teach them this expertise?" Their judgment about schools, as they see it, is that it is a waste of time learning to "doodle and draw figures." That too with a lot of risks involved.

The risks they perceive about their children going to schools are the long treks through forests, crossing dangerous rivers and cataracts [especially during monsoons], unscrupulous people around that lure kids, especially girls, etc. In our perception, trekking through forests in search of food and for other needs may be "more" dangerous, but according to them, their children are with them, and during the trails, they learn through direct first-hand experiences. Children often help their elders in various tasks and in the process, learn how to perform them.

Very few schools have hostel facilities and even these are only for boys. It is only since a decade that some girls are found to be living in school hostels. During the 1980s most schools in the tribal areas used to be bamboo structures, with no maintenance; they soon collapsed. In the last decade or so, more permanent structures had come up but of very low quality; many in fact pose a risk to the lives of the children and staff attending these schools. Most of these buildings suffer from lack of maintenance and basic amenities like drinking water, toilets, etc. Many schools in such areas do not even have furniture or basic teaching aids like blackboards. Such conditions hardly facilitate any desire for conventional education.

We recommended to government agencies several times about the need to create more awareness about scientific ways of collecting and preserving the produces the tribes collect from the forests [like honey, wax, spices, herbs, bamboo, etc.], about the real economic value of things they exchange/sell/buy, and about the quantities and qualities, which are areas they often get cheated or exploited. Such education can benefit in the immediate sense and is useful until such time that they are convinced about the importance of conventional education.

Government methods of formulating, planning and executing programmes for tribal development often overlook what the tribal people consider education, and the practical difficulties involved, often leading to non-implementation of anything at the ground level. In some places, facts and figures are forged; such falsification leads to the belief that the programmes "being implemented" are good and that these are working! There is also an impression that if a programme has been successful in one area, or among one group, it will be successful among others. Actually, replication of programmes/projects is a false notion. Replication is only possible if the circumstances, beliefs, felt-needs, culture, inherent skills and interest, etc., are all identical. Principles, strategies and techniques can be replicated, but never a curriculum as a whole.

It is a known fact that education is not as easy as it is made out to be; no matter it is important in the modern context; still, several things have to be put in place, and have to come into existence, before education as such can happen. Under the conditions in which most tribal population exists, these ideal conditions are very difficult to achieve. Hence, the absolute necessity to plan the execution of education for tribal and rural population requires time, much forethought and patience —features most government planned and implemented programmes lack.

Despite many of the above-mentioned hurdles, there are a handful of tribal persons who have overcome much impossibilities to get good education and subsequently good jobs. However, an often heard complaint among them was the grudge many non-tribal persons bear against them purportedly because of the special "reservations" and support they receive: people are simply not prepared to accept that their achievements have been through their own enormous efforts also and not just because of reservations alone. They state that the obstacles that they had to surmount were in addition to those faced by students in general. With such feelings of resentment, they claim they do not get the support and comradeship which they feel they would have otherwise received.

Government Programmes versus Tradition Facilities and Life

Housing

Traditional dwelling structures of tribes had been developed over a long time using available local material, keeping in mind the geographical and climatic conditions, considerations like family size, storage, shelter for animals, etc.; hence, they varied accordingly. Most of the tribal areas in Kerala are located in the hilly eastern tracts which are very chilly, especially in the nights and during winter months. Hence, their dwellings are made such that heat is generated from the small fires they make for their basic cooking. In addition to being heat efficient, they also kept away insects and wild animals to some extent. An important aspect was that only a minimal amount of wood and twigs were needed as fuel.

Government funded housing programmes rarely took into consideration family size, local climatic challenges and variations, available building material in the neighbourhood, and the need for periodic maintenance. There was almost a uniform design for housing programmes throughout the state. In the hilly areas of Attapaddy [Palghat District], strong, swirling winds are regular occurrences. The houses provided under the various housing programmes provide tiled roofs, which get blown off by these unpredictable winds. A couple of decades ago, material for replacements were simply not available locally and most houses were seen with missing or broken roof tiles.

The quality of material used and the workmanship [construction on large scale was allocated to contractors] were also poor, and as a result, cement plasters peeled off in large chunks exposing poorly prepared bricks which soon crumbled; floors were pitted, wooden structures rotted, there were also missing windows and doors. As the tribes were unfamiliar with these technologies and also lacking the means to buy material [or because of non-availability] or hire skilled workers, these dwellings got worse each day till they were abandoned, leading to colossal waste all round. In many instances there could be seen traditional huts adjacent to these crumbling and dilapidated structures, which were used to store firewood and straw. They were afraid even to shelter their animals there for fear of falling tiles and crumbling walls! At this point it may be mentioned that in several areas there are still many such houses provided under government schemes that have no window or door shutters — the occupants use sacks, saris or crudely made bamboo/ grass mats instead.

These houses could not be kept warm as the design was not conducive to heating in any way with a wood-fire system. Traditional huts had twigs intertwined and plastered with mud to make them air-tight. Modern houses had [glassed] windows and large doors through which heat got lost. Most people had not much access to warm clothing. Being affected in this way by the severe cold, there were increased and recurring occurrences of respiratory infections, fever, flu, etc., leading to loss of health and inability to work or search for food. In many places, the people actually believed that these "unnatural" houses caused illnesses and were for that reason not good to live in. Such incidences were fertile grounds for new superstitions and much of these were just natural exaggerations of some coincidental occurrences.

Traditional families constituted joint family units and extended family members living nearby. The housing programmes brought along other problems besides those stated above. Since the houses sanctioned were small, joint families broke up [In many instances, even nuclear families could not be accommodated in single units because of large number of children]. Several occurrences had been noted where, under the pretext of large families being catered with houses for their nuclear components, the "extra" houses were only on paper: the whole [joint] family was actually provided with only a single tiny house unit. Space constraints [and therefore, number of houses possible in that area] many times separated families that had been living nearby for years.

Where traditional communities are concerned, particularly tribes, the break-up of joint and extended families posed an array of problems. Small children were earlier left with older members while parents and older children went about their work. Sharing of work and food was more efficient. Their system also catered for things like the aged and ill being provided and cared for, emotional support, sharing of experiences and advices, etc. These advantages suffered due to such family break-ups. Even modern nuclear families face similar problems, but there are other coping mechanisms usually available especially in urban areas, which are absent in government sponsored housing colonies for tribes and other marginalised groups. Drastic changes often created confusion and plunged many people into helplessness. Uniformly, in almost all communities, there have been claims that family fragmentation and disintegration as above is a primary cause for rampant circumstances of vices like alcoholism and drug addiction, besides other sorts of anti-social activities.

Superstitions and Coincidences

Most tribal communities have deep-rooted beliefs about their dwellings. Many associated negative occurrences with some faults or "evil spirits" in their dwellings. For e.g., if a death occurred in a house around a time when a wall had cracked, a roof tile broke, or a window or door shutter fell off a hinge, then the dwelling was abandoned. A parallel may be drawn from the traditional practises of the Cholanaikkan living around the Karulai Ranges [Malappuram District]; this community traditionally lived in caves and under large rock overhangs. If a death occurred during such stay, the whole group abandoned their current dwelling [because according to their belief that place had become uninhabitable or a strong evil spirit had entered there] in search of a new place after burying the dead in the old place. Coincidentally, a portion of the rock wall may have fallen or something similar may have happened [reinforcing their belief]; the people believed that it was due to this that a death occurred. It was also often the same case with accidents, severe injuries, etc.

When some Cholanaikkan families shifted into government housing colonies near Chokkad [Malappuram District], and a death occurred in a family, they were afraid to continue staying in the house, but could not move to a "new" house either. This led to many Cholanaikkan families abandoning the new houses especially in the 1970s and 1980s, and reverting to their old habitations in the remote hill tracts. According to some elders, there were plenty of places to shift to many years ago, but now they were getting lesser, especially due to the many restrictions imposed by Forest Department officials. Therefore, these groups were forced many times to return to old dwelling places. Furthermore, these days they are forced to find alternative burial sites instead of observing their traditional practise.

Many populations have beliefs of similar nature, and with the poor construction quality of government programmes, abandoning of these "modern" dwellings was often seen as incidence hereabouts. With traditional abodes that the tribes and rural people were familiar with, maintenance and materials needed, like coconut leaves, bamboo, brush-grass, mud, cow dung, etc., were locally available [moreover, there were never problems of crumbling cement plaster, falling roof tiles, cracked walls, etc.]. However, with the introduction of tiles, brick, cement, the skills necessary to use them were alien to them. When first introduced, the basic material was not easily available either. Another major lacuna for the new houses was that they rarely took into consideration the practical needs of their daily living, e.g., availability of water, food and livelihood sources, area/means for waste disposal, space for isolation which was compulsory according to custom after child delivery, during menstruation, etc. Many studies had been conducted into the housing woes of tribal areas, but few remedial measures for these anomalies were undertaken.

Traditional Facilities/Practises

The new types of houses constructed under government programmes neither catered to, facilities for storing things the family members collected or produced, nor provided shelter to their animals. Moreover, none of the new houses provided toilets. The houses were constructed closer than customarily spaced, and away from forest covers. Hence, their traditional ablution habits became problematic too [even today these are rarely included — the beneficiaries are expected to construct toilets and bathing facilities on their own]. In a few places where toilets and bathing facilities had been provided these were either not used at all or rarely used, as these people had little idea as to how to use them or, more importantly, the idea of such a facility within or adjacent to their dwelling was highly abhorrent. In many places animals have been observed to be sheltered in the toilets, especially goats and poultry.

A typical tribal *ooru* [hamlet] had a common space for carrying out ritualistic activities and celebrating festivals. There was a commonly accepted code of conduct for most of their activities and needs. Bathing and toilet facilities were also guided by such codes. In fact, traditionally there were well laid rules and regulations governing all aspects of their lives, relationships and conduct. In the new housing colonies such codes became casualties and died out. Even burial customs were affected as already mentioned. Almost all life crises activities got affected likewise — birth and puberty rituals have changed so much, or are not observed so precisely as before. Especially among the older persons, such changes have created resentment and they attribute much of their overall "ruin and decline" to such factors.

Traditional Authority

Traditionally tribal leaders wielded a lot of authority and their rulings were binding on the whole community. A *Moopan* [tribal chief] was a highly respected person, attributed with a lot of experience and wisdom, and numerous rituals and disputes were presided over and decided by him. A community member customarily could not indulge in misconduct and offences without harsh retributions. The traditional authorities of *Moopan*, other leaders and elders have been eroded greatly and youngsters especially, have no respect and pay little or no heed to them. A casualty to this aspect is a rising incidence of alcoholic addiction and other social vices. Conventionally, alcohol was consumed only during special days of festivities and during some rituals. However, alcoholic production and consumption is rampant in most places these days. Alcoholism and drug addiction are the two major vices among many remotely located tribal populations. These have resulted not only in loss of health, but also livelihoods, leading to abject poverty. The situation is most alarming as the youth are horribly entangled in this predicament.

Many tribal leaders have expressed that these are vices of modernity — the lack of respect for authority, excessive consumption and addiction to alcohol and drugs are mostly due to outside influences. They feel that it is excessive exposure to the outside world that has brought about these vices among their youth. Such exposures are also the cause for hankering after a different sort of life, which these leaders claim have led to the erosion of traditional sense of responsibility, values and custom they prefer lives of ease without working. The youth of today are the leaders of tomorrow, but according to them, very poor models for others to emulate.

Health Systems

Before the advent of modern medicine there were several healing and curative practises among the rural and tribal populations. Their medicines depended mostly on herbs, and to some extent on animal parts and products. Although the analyses of traditional medical practitioners regarding underlying causes of diseases were not scientific, their methods for curing were often seen to be focusing on the root cause— this aspect is often missed because of the elaborate rituals involved, especially among tribes. As a tribal doctor had said, "Yes, there is a lot of mumbo-jumbo in the healing practises but these may be seen as being means of protecting trade secrets." Most of these practitioners claim that allopathic medical system focuses on symptoms rather than the causes and the basic problem; rarely is a person treated as a whole being. In fact, many have accused modern medicines of dividing people into body parts rather than providing treatment to the whole individual!

Tribal medical experts [*kuruthala*] and rural practitioners [*vydiar*] are repositories of knowledge of medicinal plants and their uses. However, these days due to various factors they are unable to dispense medication like before. Two major problems are dwindling forest areas due to clearance of land [and therefore, disappearance of many flora], and restrictions and problems of entering forests for collecting herbs and plants. Of course, distance and difficult accessibility to sources are also inconveniences. Most traditional practitioners also blame allopathic system for patients preferring quick and immediate relief for their ailments instead of the traditional restrictions and accompanying difficulties inherent in traditional therapies. It is generally acknowledged that allopathic system of medicine has many side-effects unlike other systems, yet people generally prefer allopathy simply because it is convenient and more easily available. The tribal practitioners opine that people these days are addicted to easy ways, as in other matters.

Several studies on tribal medicine have indicated their efficacy, but instead of encouraging further research into this, they are simply brushed aside as quack medication. The advantageous aspects of this system ought to be encouraged and investigated; the vast knowledge of the concerned people should be recorded and analysed. A small effort was initiated by some institutions a few years ago through promoting tribal medicine, but due to several fake events that mushroomed, the faith in this system is being rapidly eroded.

A number of the tribal people also claim that the foods they traditionally consumed were healthy and these were cultivated naturally without any chemical additions. The vegetables, fruits and animals they consumed were also likewise all "natural." This also, they claim, contributed to good health and general well-being. An analysis into the various kinds of cereals and pulses the people traditionally cultivated and consumed indicates that many of these are not seen these days. There are several ongoing debates on this aspect of agronomy which has become almost defunct of the preservation and promotion of traditional crops and food habits of people.

Commencement of Significant Changes

Conversion and education were claimed to have brought about significant changes with the advent of British missionaries in the 1800s.

But this was restricted to very small pockets of the state, mainly in the Meenachil Taluk [Kottayam District]. The tribe that had apparently made the most amasing transformation is believed to be the Mala Arayans. A startling inconsistency seems to be that despite the presence of many other tribes in this area, these others have not apparently changed so much. From the limited enquiries done it seems that it was mostly the Mala Arayans who had converted and perhaps, for this reason, benefited from the largesse of the British missionaries and education institutions then.

In the 1970s mainly, oppression and exploitation of tribes, low caste and poor people by landlords in many heinous ways in many parts of the state led to extreme collectivist movements in many places [commonly known at that time as the Naxalite movement]. It is believed that it was after this period, when the government machinery kicked in, that significant reforms were introduced and there was transformation and amendments in the abuses inherent in the feudal system. This is not to claim that all atrocities completely disappeared. Ugly incidences, uprising and insurgencies still raise their ugly heads every now and then.

Following the British missionary's educational and health model, many communities opened up similar institutions all over the state, but sadly these have mostly catered to their own [religious] communities; each believing in and promoting their respective culture and creed, and usually in the process, created an "imposition" culture. These have led to powerful segments being able to manipulate socio-political situations using vote banks, often to the disadvantage of the weaker groups. This led to further resentment, divisive forces and crisis of similar nature as outlined above. The government's development schemes are inclined to pursue parallel models, but the basic inputs, especially when first introduced, of other institutions are lacking here, such as the dedication of the institutional organizers, competent and accomplished management, and disbursement of funds, which are not strong points of government programmes. Government rules and procedures do not allow, promote or encourage such qualities.

However, among the marginalised and tribal communities, there are many who believe that in the process of attempting to "absorb" them into the so-called mainstream, these communities are being left deprived and bereft of what they consider a rich tradition and value-based life. As mentioned above, there are many who claim that it is nothing short of arrogance to suppose that their lives are underprivileged and deprived.

Everyone has their own sense of that richness and fulfilled lives amply and a good percentage of their people feel that these sentiments should be respected till such time they are ready to adapt changes labelled as modern or feel the conviction to do so.

The general population has also much to learn and understand from many of these communities. Already several changes have occurred, most of these irreversibly. The debate still continues whether uniform development for all is preferable to strive and bring about a unified and progressive nation, or to preserve variety and diversity as a national treasure, quite unlike most other nations.

PART–II
Cultural Pluralism and Tribes

5

Religious Pluralism and Tribal Identity: An Anthropological Study on the Nicobarese of Katchal, Central Nicobar Islands

D.V. Prasad

Introduction

The concept of "pluralism" is a social phenomenon wherein numerous distinct ethnic, religious, or cultural groups are present and tolerated within a society. Initially this concept was vaguely used for the analysis of ethnic composition in colonial and ex-colonial states by the scholars. Later on, political scientists applied this concept for the analysis of political convulsions that occurred in the newly created nations since their independence. However, anthropologists use "pluralism" to examine the problem of unity and diversity in society and its relationship with the process of cultural change (Leo A. Despres, 1964). The dictionary of Anthropology (1976) states : "*When two or more cultural systems in long continued contact workout a mutual accommodation which allows each to sustain its distinctive way of life, a stabilised cultural pluralism is achieved.*" From this definition, it is clear that many ethnic or cultural groups live together by creating a space wherein each group respects the other's customs and traditions. Whereas, sociologists believe that cultural heterogeneity is a social fact, pluralism has a positive value orientation towards it and supports the dignified coexistence of culturally diverse groups within a polity (Oomman, T.K., 2002). It is evident from the empirical reality in the Indian context, where multi-lingual, cultural and religious groups live peacefully in a given geographical area. The presence of different religious faiths in tribal areas is also testimony to the value orientation of pluralism. Though the external influences are dominant on the traditional life of simple communities, observance of traditional practises by the homogeneous communities are widely observed among the tribal groups of India. The present Nicobarese of Katchal Island, who worshipped objects of nature, have adopted other religious faiths after contact with outsiders. Still this does not restrain them from maintaining their traditional identity, and they continue their customary practises that have been observed by their people for generations.

Conceptual Framework

The term "Cultural Pluralism" was first used by J.S. Furnivall (1939) in his book Netherlands *India,* for the analysis of change in underdeveloped areas. The major finding of his study is that when different cultural groups lived in one common area without much social interaction, lack of integration may destabilize the social order. This situation may be attributed to different ethnic groups brought to Netherlands was not voluntary but by force. Thus he concluded that the plural societies are unsuited for nationalism, and hence democracy. This concept was reformulated by Smith (1955) by testing the phenomenon of pluralism in complex societies. While developing the cultural pluralism model, he stated that institutional differences serve to differentiate cultures and social units. According to his conceptualisation, plural societies in which groups living within a political unit have very different systems of compulsory or basic institutions. The culturally distinct units of the plural society are its cultural sections and they differ in terms of common life, economic and political structures.

But his assumption is not exceptional for criticism on the grounds of "homogeneous society appears to be the exception rather than the rule", and defining the concept of institution from Malinowskian scheme rather than analysing activities in structural functional framework (Braithwaite, 1960). Furthermore, critics opined that it overlooks the minimum core of shared values to achieve integration other than by force. In place of Smith's model, an alternative approach to cultural pluralism was brought forward for the study of complex societies in newly emerging nations. This model held that the unit of study must be the whole society rather than cultural units. While developing this concept, Leo A. Despres (1964) postulated "minimal" and "maximal" cultural sections to distinguish between heterogeneous and plural societies. The institutional activities that serve to integrate culturally differentiated groups at the local level are termed as minimal or local cultural sections and a society contains such sections known as socially or culturally heterogeneous. On the other hand, when institutional activities serve to integrate culturally differentiated groups at societal level they are recognised as maximum or national cultural sections and the existence of such maximal sections is a plural society. The integration of local cultural sections at the societal level is a function of the brokered institutions[1]. They may include markets, corporations, cooperatives, religious associations, public or private school associations, social and civic associations, labour unions, ethnic associations, political parties, and various governmental agencies.

As per the Despres model, if structural activities such as language, family and kinship, work, socialisation, recreation, associations and communal activities are uniformly valid for all groups, then the plural model is not relevant to the analysis of society in question. Hence, the present study limits pluralism to the religious level only, rather than applying at different levels of socio-cultural aspects of the homogeneous community. But, in spite of religious pluralism, the fractured groups of the same community share common structural features such as kinship, family, language, economic and political systems. This hypothesis holds true in the case of the Nicobarese of Katchal. The Nicobarese society is homogeneous in nature and shares similar socio-cultural systems, except their adopted religious faiths. There is not much institutional difference except for the adopted religions in their social system. By adhering to the collective principles, they nurture their central identity, i.e., Nicobarese, rather than multiple identities found in complex societies. The present empirical data on the Nicobarese society strengthens this proposition.

The Study Area

The Nicobar Islands are separated from the Andaman Islands by a distance of 150 kilometers in the north, by a wide ten degree channel; and they are geographically close to South-East Asian countries like Myanmar and Thailand towards the south. The Nicobar Islands are a conglomeration of 22 islands that are clustered in three groups, i.e., Car Nicobar in north; Central Nicobar Islands consisting of Camorta, Nancowry, Trinket, Chowra, Bompuka, Katchal, Terressa, and the southern group of islands consisting of Pulo Milo, Little Nicobar, Kondul and Great Nicobar. Though many comparable cultural traits are observed among the Nicobarese, each island has an identity of its own in terms of local dialect, dwelling pattern and other material culture like racing canoe, beehive community hut, etc.

The present study area, i.e., Katchal Island belongs to Central Nicobar group of Islands. The total area of this island comes to 174.4 km². It is approximately 1600 kilometers away from the mainland and 305 kilometers south to the capital, Port Blair. The Nicobarese are the dominant population in Katchal Island. In Nicobarese parlance, the inhabitants of Katchal Island are known as *Som-Payuh*. Besides Nicobarese, this island is also inhabited by refugees from Sri Lanka, settlers from Ranchi who were brought to work in the Forest Department, working and retired government servants, and Tamil businessmen. The languages mainly spoken in Katchal are Nicobari, Hindi, Tamil, Telugu, and Santhali, and thus it became a "melting pot of different cultural groups."

Methodology and Data Collection

The present work is based on the empirical findings of anthropological fieldwork conducted in November-December 2008 among the Nicobarese of Katchal Island in connection with the research project," People of India: Cultural Diversity, Tangible and Intangible Heritage Exploring Traditional Knowledge", launched by the Anthropological Survey of India. For collection of data, qualitative anthropological techniques like participant observation, extensive case studies, key informant interviews and verbal discussions were employed. For collection of quantitative data, a detailed household census covering socio-economic and demographic details were used to elucidate the existing pluralism in Katchal.

Ethnographic Profile

The Nicobarese belong to the Mongoloid stock and speak Nicobari dialect for communication within family and kin groups. Besides, Hindi is widely used for communication with outsiders, and a few Nicobarese who converted to Islam are conversant in Urdu and Gujarati.

Their traditional dresses like *Ngong* (petticoat) and *Kisat* or *Ning* (loin cloth) are now being replaced by *lungi* or *sarong* and a blouse that resembles the dress pattern of the Burmese, Karen, and Malay women. Among the Nicobari Muslims, the men wear *pyjamas* and round cap and the women wear *lungi,* blouse along with head scarf.

The Nicobarese are non-vegetarian and they eat *kaa* (fish), *kanang* (crab), *pookore* (mutton), *nua* (beef), *ha-un* (pork) and *hayoom* (chicken). Their traditional vegetable foods are *laeom* or *kevidi* (pandanus), *kinreai* (big jackfruit), pampu (small jackfruit), hiloie (otkona fruit), *hipu* or *tayukng* (banana), *uyau* (coconut). They also consume wild tubers like *tahangin, taving, sabudan, kupeng, lechlòng* and wild leaves like *roitakappu, tilfung, vurong, roilong, roihaei*, etc. Further, they also began to consume rice and pulses after contact with non-tribes. *Kavut* or *thuvak* (coconut toddy) is their preferred traditional drink. Eating pork is a religious taboo for Nicobari Muslims. However, rearing of *tuhet's* (lineage) piggery is still practised and the pigs freely roam even in Muslim Nicobarese households. Further, certain foods are prohibited for women during their life-cycle rituals.

The social organisation of the Nicobarese can be understood from its maximal lineage system as it facilitates socio-economic integrity of its members. It is popularly known as *tuhet* in the Nicobar Islands and *Nyi-to-karu* in Katchal Island. Cultivation of coconut, areca nut and other horticultural crops is their main economic activity besides fishing and pig herding. Apart from this, they engage in making pandanus mats, cane and bamboo baskets, outrigger canoes, wooden spears.

Social control among the Nicobarese rests with the Island's Council which consists of Chief Captain, Vice-Chief Captain, Secretary and members who are the headmen of all the villages of that particular island. Inter village and island disputes come under the Island Council's jurisdiction. In turn, each village consists of a Village Council which consists of five captains who deal with dispute resolution and decision making at the village level. It is said that the term "captain" was given by the colonial British to represent the headman of each village, and is being continued even after Independence. At the lineage level, *ma-tuhet* (lineage headman) organises the activities of his particular group, including the plantation.

Though majority of the Nicobarese have converted to new religious faiths, i.e., Christianity and Islam, they still believe in natural powers of the Kareava (fetish human and animal figurine), and *Hentukui* (a fetish wooden board consisting of sketches of their habitat and ecology), and hence, appease them during ceremonial occasions. Elaborate ancestral and spirit worship, magico-religious treatment, and seasonal festivals are integral part in their traditional life and are celebrated in true spirit.

Historical Transect

From the writings of *Ptolemy* (*Circa* A.D. 140) and *I-Tsing* (A.D. 672), the historians found the early traces of outside contacts with the Nicobar Island. The travelogues of those who witnessed these Islands at first instance, referred to them as the land of "*naked people*." The word "*Nicobar*" was thus derived from the corrupted form of South

Indian term *Nakkavaram* (*Land of the Naked*), and the same nomenclature was mentioned in the great Tanjore inscription of A.D. 1050. Later, the term Nicobar came into frequent usage since the time of Marco Polo (A.D. 1292) till now (Whitehead, 1924). The political history of Nicobar Islands reveals that the Portuguese annexed these islands in sixteenth century under the viceroyship of Malacca. From 1756 to 1848, the Danes and the British made several attempts to colonise these islands after the failure of French Missionaries. However, their efforts ended disastrously due to spread of dreadful malaria. From 1807 to 1814 the islands were under British possession and in due course, were handed over back to the Danes by a treaty after the Napoleonic wars. In the meantime, Austrians also tried to form a settlement but miserably failed on account of inclement weather conditions. In 1869 the British Government took formal possession of the islands again and established a penal settlement at Nancowry Harbour which is subordinate to that of Port Blair in the Andaman Islands. In 1885 it was withdrawn on account of long distance from Port Blair and widespread Malaria during the rainy season. As a result of such external interventions, the Nicobarese adopted many cultural traits including food habits, social etiquette and religious beliefs. Due to their trade relations with the British, the Nicobarese were forced to learn English, and its influence can be seen in the adoption of many English names for Nicobari individuals.

Later, Chinese, Indian and Burmese ventured into these Islands for trading coconuts, followed by merchants from Maldives, Laccadives, Ceylon and Madras. During this period, the Nicobarese were persuaded to work in trader's shops for considerable amount of remunerations. Occasionally, they travelled with the traders for several months to cut and collect nuts in interior islands on contractual basis. In this process, due to their prolonged association with the outsiders, some of the Nicobarese showed inclination towards the life-style of the outsiders and started imitating the alien customs and traditions. The Nicobarese travelled with the traders to the islands of Minicoi, Laccadives and Maldives for petty business works. They would stay there for about two to three years, and come back professing Islam. The present Muslim Nicobarese population is a result of such in and out migration.

The forceful annexation of these islands by the Japanese during the Second World War, and the proximity of Myanmar could not succeed, however, in spreading Buddhism into their animistic belief system. This may be due to the oppression of the Japanese and exploitative attitude of the Burmese traders towards the Nicobarese during their stay in these isles.

After Independence, the penetration of Hindu religion took place with the settlement of regional communities from mainland India in search of government service, business, and wage labour. Many of them settled in the islands by marrying the local Nicobarese girls. As a result of this, many Hindu temples were built for the Tamils, Telugus, Bengalis, and settlers from Ranchi in the Central Nicobar Islands, and their festivals are celebrated in a grand manner.

Demographic Scenario

The total population of the Katchal Island is about 5312, including 2847 males and 2465 females (2001 Census). Of these, the Nicobarese population comprises only 2662, including 1372 males and 1290 females. The rest of the population comprises Sri Lankan settlers who were brought to work exclusively in rubber plantations; labour from Ranchi to work in the Forest Department, government servants, and their kith and kin who settled in the Katchal Island long back.

The earthquake and tsunami that hit these islands on 26th December 2004 have had a major impact on the demographic scenario of the Katchal Island. Soon after the tsunami, in 2005, the population enumerated by the administration in relief camps was 1976, as many of the coastal residents, i.e., Marine Jetty, Kapanga and West Bay Katchal lost their lives in the killer waves, while some settlers moved to Kamorta and Port Blair due to fear psychosis. Again in 2008 Census, the total population was found to be 4264 due to the return of the earlier settlers to Katchal. A door to door survey of the Nicobarese during November-December 2009 fieldwork, revealed the exact figures that are stated below to understand the present Nicobarese demographic scenario in Katchal.

Demographic details of the Nicobarese of Katchal, 2009

Sl. No.	*Settlement*	*Male*	*Female*	*Total*
1.	West Bay	64	61	125
2.	Ponda	58	57	115
3.	East Bay	148	128	276
4.	Jhansin	94	76	170
5.	Jhoola	115	103	218
6.	Kapanga	194	214	408
7.	E-wall	98	94	192
	Total	771	733	1504

The present data excludes the dead population in the 2004 earthquake and tsunami. From the demographic analysis, it is revealed that male population is higher compared to the one female and that there would be no problem to find a marriageable life partner in the future (Sinha Roy and Dutta Chaudhuri, 2007).

Religious Pluralism in Katchal

Out of the total Nicobarese population, majority of the population follow Christianity (1486), while a few converted to Islam (98) due to their contacts with the frequently visiting Muslim traders from Maldives and Laccadives. The rest of the population (2680) consists of Hindu non-tribes who belong to groups of Sri Lankan refugees, Ranchi, Tamil and Telugu settlers, etc. A similar religious composition is also widely prevalent in the Central Nicobar Islands.

Religious distribution in Central Nicobar Islands, 2008

Sl. No.	*Island*	*Christian*	*Muslim*	*Hindu*
1.	Terressa	2061	15	—
2.	Katchal	1486	98	2680
3.	Nancowry	1168	75	—
4.	Chowra	1345	—	40
5.	Kamorta	2054	194	1920
	Total	8114	382	4640

Source: Base line Survey for Minority Concentration District Project, Kamorta, 2008.

In Katchal, majority of the Nicobarese follow Christianity and the presence of a Church in each settlement is testimony to this fact. They regularly visit the Church and offer prayers twice a day, i.e., in the morning and evening. Simultaneously they celebrate all Christian festivals like *Tinôt Manak* (All Souls Day), *Inhikoo* (Easter Day), Good Friday, Christmas, *Churchkabada-din* (Church formation day), and life-cycle rituals like *Venoktökui* or Baptism (child initiation and naming ceremony), *Pihoore* (marriage), *Panyapor Kinpaha (death)*, etc. Apart from the Nicobarese, majority of the Ranchi community also follow Christianity and visit the Roman Catholic and Pentecostal Churches located in non-tribal settlements. But unlike the Nicobarese, they visit the Church every Sunday and celebrate only major events of the Church.

The Nicobarese, who were converted to Islam in Katchal follow the *Hanfee* tradition and pray in a temporary Mosque located in Mildera, headquarters of Katchal the *pucca* Mosque was uprooted in the 2004 tsunami and hence, they now visit the non-tribal Mosque. Even among the non-tribal Hindu population, diversity of regional cultural practises like *panginiuttaram* (fire-walking) by the Tamil community, *Saraswatipuja*, *Vinayakachatur,* and that *Ram Navmi*, etc., are also observed by the Telugu and Ranchi settlers in the study area.

Practising Christianity

In the study area, 93.81% of the Nicobarese follow Christianity. On 26th December 2004, the island was wrought by the killer waves of tsunami, including their Church and other physical properties. They are now rehabilitated in new locations far away from the sea coast in temporary shelters. Though they lack proper infrastructural facilities and resources in the post tsunami era, practise of elaborate Christian festivals and activities reinforces their belief towards the great tradition.

One month prior to the Christmas Eve, the Christian Nicobarese are engaged in group carol singing, door to door in each settlement. The Carol programme is decided by the Church's Father in the presence of the heads of the Village Council, Pastorate and Mother's Union in Church. They select convenient dates for the visiting Carol troupe in *tuhet* areas, plantation houses, other villages, and non-tribal settlements. As a part of this, the Carol troupe represented by adolescent boys and girls visits all Nicobarese houses in the village including the houses of non-Christians, and entertains them with Christian songs in English and Nicobari language. During Carol singing, food and other eateries offered by the concerned house to honour the guest are accepted without any hesitation. Even for the inter-village Carol visits, the Muslim Nicobarese offer traditional food to the Carol troupe and voluntarily contribute for grand feasts on the occasion of Christmas. Inter-village feasts are arranged in consultation with the village or *tuhet* headman and the contribution in terms of labour, money, food, etc., are equally distributed between the existing *tuhets* in the village. For example, the contributions of *Changihipoh* house of West Bay Katchal are indicated below:

Family-wise contribution for village feast

Firewood	One bundle
Haradal	One kilo
Pappad	One packet
Sharbat powder	One packet
Mustard oil	One litre
Eggs	One tray
Sugar	One kilo
Fowl	One
Cash	Rs. 100

Apart from the above contribution, each family in a *tuhet* contributes man-power for making temporary guestrooms, Church decoration, cooking, and organisation of community feasts. Along with the grand village feast, the Nicobarese also offer packed gifts in terms of piglets, fowls, tubers, banana, pandanus, sugarcane, soaps, biscuit packets, etc., to the guests by tagging the name of the particular guest or *tuhet* for whom the gift was meant. Interestingly the offerer's name is not mentioned therein.

Further, each Church celebrates its formation day once in a year, which is popularly known as *Church ka bada-din* in Nicobar. As the date approaches, the concerned Nicobarese send formal invitations to their relatives and friends including their Muslim and Hindu friends. On that particular day, a white banner displaying its founder's name and a brass Holy Cross is brought outside the Church and the people walk around the Church singing in a chorus. This is followed by prayer inside the Church and distribution of *Tahet-in-mulkua* (a kind of sweet prepared with wheat flour and sugar) and *Kulah* (red wine). The contributions that the Church receives from different *tuhets* and individuals are announced on the spot. Finally an open auction is held to sell the contributions received in kind, i.e., piglets, coconut oil, cloth, bananas, tubers, fowl, etc. All the settlers including non-Christians participate in such open auctions and purchase whatever they wish. For this event, the Church organisers also collect donations from Nicobari Muslims and non-tribe Hindus.

Apart from the major Christian festivals, the Nicobarese also celebrate important activities of their life like *Venoktökui* or Baptism (child initiation cum naming), *Pihoore* (marriage) as per the Christian Almanac and the Church Father or Presbyter preside over it. He also visits the Nicobarese house during *Panyap* or *Kinpaha (death)* and guides them for a proper Christian funeral. In case of marriage to a non-Christian, it is compulsory for the spouse to convert to Christianity in the presence of Church members.

The Nicobarese who adopt Christianity continue to celebrate their customary practises of life-cycle rituals such as *Vinokonyio* (traditional naming), *In-Hoinyo-Nyio* (child initiation ceremony), *Kinrooka* (after funerals) along with traditional feasting by killing, and slaughtering pigs in the typical Nicobarese manner.

Practising Islam

Unlike the Christian Nicobarese, the Muslim Nicobarese visit the nearby Mosque during Fridays and observe the major festivals of Islam like Ramzan, Bakrid, etc. It is only the non-tribe Muslims who regularly go for *namaz* five times in a day, i.e., *Fazar*, *Zakat*, *Azar*, *Mazgrib*, *Isha*. This may be attributed to their pre-occupation with horticultural works, Arabic version of religious text and lack of awareness about Islamic tenets, etc. To encourage them towards Islam in the true sense, the Muslim seminaries are sincerely working for promoting the cause. *Chalata-Firata Madrasa* is one among them which is operational in Nicobar Islands to spread the tenets of Islam by visiting the different Mosques in the Island.

Chalata-Firata Madrasa (mobile learning seminary)

The main function of this seminary is to facilitate the converted Nicobarese to interact with each other for learning Arabic language and Islamic rules and regulations by visiting various Mosques in Andaman and Nicobar Islands as well as the Mosques located in the mainland. The *Madrasa* troupe consists of five to ten individuals who visit the Mosques after due intimation to the head of the Mosque of the visiting place. The learned persons of the team who visit the Mosques impart training on character, way of living, food habits, etc., to the Nicobarese who converted to Islam. No funding is available for such religious trips. The interested members bear the traveling expenses and the boarding and lodging facilities including food are provided by the concerned Mosque authorities free of cost to the visiting *Madrasa* team.

Despite such efforts, the Muslim Nicobarese still pursue their traditional life-style and participate in the Village Council to express their solidarity for the Nicobarese community life. They also invite the Christian Nicobarese during Ramzan, Bakrid, and other festival feasts and entertain them with festive food and traditional drinks.

Functional Similarities among the Basic Nicobarese Institutions

The present Nicobarese of Katchal Island share a basic institutional framework which has been built into their society for generations together, be it economic or political activities. All the Nicobarese unite and cooperate in maintaining their group solidarity in times of life-cycle and seasonal festivals. They all participate in the below-mentioned social institutions from time to time:

Perpetuation of *Tuhet System*

Social organisation of the Nicobarese can be understood from its maximal lineage system known as *tuhet*. This is a consanguine group related by birth wherein no individual possesses inheritance rights over the land and resources, but it is the *tuhet* as a whole that possesses rights over the resources within their territory. Every *tuhet* has its own beehive community hut in the village to organise its different activities from time to time. For all practical purposes, *tuhet* members collectively celebrate the *Ossuary* feast, its calendrical festivals, and life-cycle rituals, etc., under the banner of their original *tuhet*.

Presently, the converted Nicobarese are living in undivided joint families and pursuing plantation works together. For example, *Altaful* and *Nyihilek* in Kapanga, Katchal comprise Christian as well as Muslim Nicobarese population. When necessary, the *tuhet* headman demands contribution for an ensuing marriage, death or any other ritual purpose, from his *tuhet* members in the form of resources, i.e., *ha-un*, *kevidi*, and processed tubers, as organising a feast is compulsory for its members who gladly contribute.

The practises of inter and intra *tuhet* adoptions (*tayetita* or *haruk*) are the important aspects of the Nicobarese social structure for maintenance of the *tuhet* system. Adoption of a child is not only limited to that settlement or village, but sometimes also crosses the boundaries of the island. Soon after childbirth, the head of the family who wants to adopt the child, supplies food, nuts and other required material to the mother and child as a symbolic act. Continuous supply of essential goods is a proclamation to the rest of the villagers that the child is being considered for adoption. The institution of *tayetita* is instrumental in caring for orphaned children whose parents died in the tsunami. Interestingly, it is observed that inter-religious child adoptions are also pursued by the Nicobarese.

Then there is the practise of *Inlom* (bi-local residence) that facilitates either the groom or the bride to live with the spouse's family after marriage, depending on the requirement of manpower in the family. In case any *tuhet* is not sure of the ability of the man to look after their plantation, they select a groom from another family that possesses sufficient man power. Then the groom has to work for the welfare of his wife's *tuhet* and severe ties with his birth *tuhet*.

Maintenance of Traditional Economic Activities

Economic activities ranging from livestock rearing to cultivation and horticultural works such as reaping coconut, banana, tapioca, pandanus and collection of wild roots, tubers, and leafy vegetables are common to all the Nicobarese. The Katchal Nicobarese still follow

Hinruolo-Kahe (traditional annual calendar) for the initiation of any economic and cultural activity in the village. As a part of this, celebration of seasonal festivals by a particular *tuhet* or village is compulsory during the first fruit collection, first catch of fish or crab, etc. Some of the major seasonal festivals celebrated by the Nicobarese of West Bay Katchal are mentioned below for understanding its significance in maintaining the Nicobarese identity:

Seasonal Festivals of West Bay Katchal

Sl. No.	*Name of the Festival*	*Month*
1.	*Inungoucha*	Oct-Nov
2.	*Fat-Mai*	Sept-Oct
3.	*Kina-Kanang*	July-Sept
4.	*Intah Reev*	May-June
5.	*Kanaichö Ilu*	Feb-Mar

The seasonal festivals are celebrated once every year. For this, the concerned *tuhet* invites the rest of the *tuhets* in the same village for the proposed feast after collective fishing, wherein participation of its *tuhet* members is mandatory. If anyone violates the rule, they are debarred from access to the *tuhet's* plantation.

Adherence to *Manula* (Council)

The present Nicobari Village Council consists of five captains who head the council meetings in the presence of lineage heads for dispute resolution. In case anyone is found guilty, they impose fine depending on the nature of the misconduct. The punishments imposed by the *Manula* of Katchal are binding on all Nicobarese irrespective of their religious association. Some kinds of punishments are discussed below:

Foho: It implies physical beating of the culprit with *Ri-o* (stick or *lati*) ranging from five to ten times the number depending on the nature of the crime committed by the concerned individual.

Yahiyoon: Fine is imposed in the form of feasting with *ha-un* (pig), processed foods of coconut and tubers, etc. In case the concerned individual refuses to do so, the *Manula* snatch the resources forcefully either from his/her stock or from the *tuhet's* property to whom (s)he belongs.

Saacha: In case a defaulter or his/her *tuhet* has exhausted the resources to pay fine, (s)he has to serve as physical labour in the headman's house for one or two years till the *manula is* impressed by the conduct of the concerned individual.

Generally, Council meetings are held in the offender's house. In case of minor disputes, the Council simply fines the offender with grand feast in the offender's house, and gives him/her a warning. If the council disapproves or is dissatisfied with the guilty, they reject the food offered by the concerned house. This is equal to the ex-communication of the concerned family. Feast food is accepted only after an apology from the offender and this is treated as forgiveness from the Council.

Allegiance to the traditional Village Council is mandatory for the Nicobarese, which they cannot deviate at any cost. The case of Henna (Christian) illustrates this point of view in Katchal. She is the daughter of Nyi-hilek *tuhet* headman of Kapanga Village and got married to Mr. Kumar (Hindu), 37 years old, who is an ex-service man of the Tribal Cooperative Society. He migrated from Tamil Nadu and is currently living with his wife's *tuhet.* In due course of time, he mobilised the opinion of the Nicobarese to become the head of the joint family. But this attempt was strongly countered by the wife of the Vice-Chieftain, Tribal Council, who is also a resident of the same village. Then he instigated his wife's sister and attacked the Vice-Chieftain's wife verbally in an intoxicated state late night. Later the council asked its *ma-tuhet*, who is a Muslim Nicobari, to make arrangements for the proposed council meeting at their residence to discuss the issue. As per the village headman's instruction, Mr. Surfuddin made all arrangements for the council meeting at his residence, including the feast. After thorough hearings, the Council and other lineage heads warned Mr. Kumar, the guilty, against the recurrence of such misdeeds in future and they stood for the cause of Nicobari tradition of maintenance and inheritance of property rights within the control of the *tuhet* as a whole rather than an individual.

In another case study, Belinda of Nyi-hi-pool *tuhet* (Christian Nicobari) fell in love with a Ranchi Christian and both agreed for inter-religious marriage. The matter was brought to the notice of the concerned *tuhet* head and later they arranged a Council meeting in the presence of the Church's Father to discuss the issue. Since no objection was raised from girl's side as she liked him, the Church's Father revealed to the Ranchi boy that if he converts from Roman Catholic (RC) faith to Church of North India (CNI) faith, then only the marriage would be possible. The Ranchi boy readily agreed to convert and live with the girl's family. They got married in Church and later it was solemnised through a grand feast for all the villagers.

Traditional Belief Systems

Some of the Nicobarese magical practises relating to malevolent and benevolent spirits are still observed in Katchal's land especially by the Christian Nicobarese. They are mainly:

***Roì Kunhil* (blocking the entry of dead soul):** It is widely believed that soon after a death in the village, the dead soul may enter the houses of the nearest kith and kin of the Nicobarese. To prevent the entry of the dead soul, the Nicobarese of Katchal tie *kutcha* cane twigs in front of the house till the completion of the first funeral rites.

***Hum-ngaicho* (offering of coconut oil):** It refers to the process of smearing ritualised coconut oil on the body, forehead and arms of the relatives of the demised to inform the benevolent spirits about their relationship with the dead and hence request the spirit not to harm them.

***Hinmai* (model out-rigger canoe):** A model *hodi* (canoe) which is made of wood extracted from a wild *papitha* tree is made by the Nicobarese soon after a death in the village. This model canoe is generally kept in front of the house of the demised for upto seven days to send off the malevolent spirit into open sea.

***Intôpö-Nyio* (spirit pacification):** Monthly offerings or *pujas* are performed by the *menlouna* (witch doctor) to appease the *Kareava* and *Intukui* (wooden effigies used for worship). During the appearance of the new moon at the beginning or end of every month, a special *puja* is performed by the *menlouna*, by sacrificing a small pig or cock. Then, he collects the sacrificial blood and applies it to the wooden effigies. Further, he also smears it on the hands and chest of the present gathering. The blood is then mixed with scrapped *kutcha* copra and the resultant paste known as "*laniov*" is also smeared to the spirit affected people. Another paste is made by mixing wild leaves with the blood of the sacrificial pig. The leaves used for this mixture are mainly:

1. *Sih-Oom*
2. *Yeye*
3. *Inhin-anho*
4. *Huklik*
5. *Sin-ail*

This mixture is known as "*kinloomng*" and is dabbed on the body of the *menlouna* and the wooden effigies. At first instance, the "*laniov*" is dabbed by the *menlouna* starting from the right hand to left hand followed by the entire body of the *Intukui*. Thereafter the *kinloomng* is dabbed on it. The container used for preparation of the herbal concoction of the sacrificial blood of the pig/fowl along with coconut milk is known as *kinlong*.

The display of a piece of pork which is extracted from the head to tail of the sacrificial animal is wrapped in a new cloth (yellow) and tied to the roof of the concerned house where the *Intôpö-Nyio* was performed. The Nicobarese believe that this may restrict the entry of evil spirits. Otherwise, the spirits may be attracted to the house and affect the members of the family in the form of diseases such as dysentery, fever, and so on.

Magico-Religious Treatment

Cases of illness, spirit possession, counter magic, etc., are dealt by the Nicobarese by gathering in the affected house and wailing loudly in chorus in the memory of their ancestors and benevolent spirits. For this, a continuous supply of toddy, tobacco, cigar or *beedi for* the wailing troupe is arranged by the concerned house owner. Occasionally, they apply coconut oil on the shoulders of the wailing balladeers. They believe that this would please their ancestors who will rescue them from the clutches of spirits.

During fieldwork, one Neeha Thanuk of Nyi-leh *tuhet* of Upper Katchal visited the house of Mr. Cyril, *menlouna* of Jhoola, for treatment of spirit possession. She feared that spirits of dead persons are running after her to kill, both in dreams as well as during the day. She had developed fear psychosis and began to disturb the family members and villagers with her horrible dreams. As a part of spirit pacification, they invited traditional balladeers and performed the event, in the house of the converted Christian, in memory of their ancestors for not causing harm to Ms. Neeha.

Community Co-operation

The existing social institutions like *Ituo Panam* (*tuhet* unity) and *Manula Panam* (village unity) unites the Nicobarese at the *tuhet* and village level, especially during life-cycle activities, annual rituals, plantation works, construction of *el-panam* (community beehive hut), canoe making, and other economic activities, as and when required by the particular *tuhet* or village. As a part of this, a representative from each family or *tuhet* participates in the major works for the village. Apart from this, there are certain institutional mechanisms that are monitored by the *Manula* to facilitate mutual cooperation during the times of exigency. They are as follows:

Sinyounglose **(Sharing of Plantation):** Due to tsunami, the horticultural plantations of the villagers of West Bay Katchal and Ponda villages were washed out and they had not anyone left at their disposal for subsistence. Hence, they made an arrangement under the Sinyounglose to utilise the coconut plantations of Jhoola Village till their new plantation yield the produce.

Misang **(Sharing of Livestock):** It is an institutional arrangement to facilitate the exchange of scarce resources in the village. During ceremonial occasions, a pig is taken from a *tuhet* that possesses the maximum number. Later this family or *tuhet* has to earmark one small piglet on the Lender's name and rear it to hand over the same when he asks for their *tuhet* festival. It is a prerogative of the Lender's to claim right over such piglet or pig whenever they require one functionally.

Minakren Tavahava **(Cooperation during Illness):** The main intention is to generate voluntary donations in terms of cash or kind to assist the ill person during times of emergency. Under this system, each *tuhet* shares the responsibility of taking care of the ill in the village. As per the instructions of the head of the *tuhet*, they visit the concerned house along with food and drink and entertain them to help them get rid of their seclusion.

Inyakaken ta Kihiyen **(Cooperation during Death):** All the community members extend their possible assistance to a dying person right from shifting the person from residence to death house, taking care during the final stage, and assistance rendered to the concerned family after death. One family from each *tuhet* of the village offers food to the bereaved family members for seven days. Further, it is customary for all the *tuhets* in the village to contribute feast material such as pork, chicken, tubers, banana etc., for funeral feasting. Apart from this, cleaning at the graveyard is also undertaken by the concerned *tuhet* members as per the instructions of their *ma-ku-tuhet* and Captain.

Conclusion

From the above data, it is evident that though the Nicobarese of Katchal follow other religious faiths such as Christianity and Islam, they maintain their central identity, i.e., Nicobarese, by adhering to their kinship, economic, political, and other basic institutions for maintaining community cooperation and unity in times of exigency; this was catalytic during community rehabilitation in the aftermath of the devastation due to tsunami and earthquake in 2004. It is well maintained by expressing solidarity with their birth related kin group during life-cycle and *tuhet* related rituals, living together in the same *ramage*, joint cultivation of *tuhet* plantation, rearing of *tuhet* livestock, adherence to *tuhet* and Village Council, etc. Further, the presence of elaborate traditional practises such as *Roi Kunhil Hum-ngaicho Intôpö-Nyio, etc.*, that are being observed since generations along with their adopted religious traditions, reveal their penchant for maintaining pluralism and identity simultaneously.

Acknowledgement

The author is grateful to Dr. V.R. Rao, the Director-in-Charge, Anthropological Survey of India, Kolkata, for facilitating the logistic support in conducting the fieldwork in Katchal Island. The author also acknowledges the help of Dr. Francis Kulirani, Head of Office, and other scientific colleagues from the Southern Regional Centre, Mysore, in finalising this paper. The views expressed in this paper are those of the author alone.

References

Despres, L.A. 1968. "Anthropological Theory, Cultural Pluralism and the Study of Complex Societies". *Current Anthropology*, Vol. 9, No. 1, pp. 3-26.

Furnivall, J.S. 1939. "Netherlands". *India : A Study of Plural Economy*. London. Cambridge University Press.

Hunter, D.E. and Whitten, P. (1976). *Encyclopedia of Anthropology*. New York: Harper and Row Publishers.

Joseph Tharamangalam. 1989. "Religious Pluralism, the Theory and Practise of Secularism : Reflections on the Indian Experience". *Jr. of Asian and African Studies* Vol. 24, No. 3-3, pp. 199-212.

Justin, A. 1990. The *Nicobarese*. Calcutta. Seagull Books, on behalf of Anthropological Survey of India.

Kaushal Kumar Mathur. 1996. *Nicobar Island* (*India : The Land and People*). New Delhi: National Book Trust.

Oomman, T.K. 2003. *Pluralism, Equality and Identity: Comparative Studies*. New Delhi: Oxford University Press.

Prasad, D.V. 2009. "Cultural Response of Car Nicobarese to Tsunami Disaster". *Journal of Social Anthropology*, Vol. 5, No. 1-2, pp. 107-124.

Sahani, R. and Prasad, D.V. 2007. "Impact Assessment of Tsunami on Car Nicobarese". *Tsunami in South Asia: Studies of Impact on Communities of Andaman and Nicobar Islands* (ed.), pp. 64-89. New Delhi. Allied Publishers on behalf of Anthropological Survey of India, Kolkata.

Guha, S. 1997. "Cultural and Religious Pluralism in India and US". *Economic and Political Weekly*, Vol. XXXII, No. 44-45, November 8-14.

Syamchaudhuri, N.K. 1977. "The Social Structure of Car Nicobar Islanders: An Ethnic Study of Cognition". Kolkata. Anthropological Survey of India.

Whitehead, G. 1924. *In the Nicobar Islands*. London. Seely Service and Company Ltd.

Note

1. Brokered institutions are those institutions that function to link local activities to the wide spheres of societal activity.

6

The Jarawas – Stone-Age People in the 21st Century

B.R. Ghosh* and *S.S. Ghosh

The Jarawas inhabit the western region and coastal belt of south and middle Andaman Islands. There are about 600 to 700 Jarawas who move in bands of 40 to 60 people. The Jarawas of South Andaman do not go to North Andaman and *vice versa,* though there is no formal demarcation. They do not follow any extensive kinship system and rarely remember more than three generations back. Although anthropologists like Bonnigton, Portman, Colebrook, Mann, Radcliffe-Brown and Cipriani mentioned them, only Sarkar gave a comparatively detailed account of the Jarawas, when an accident to a Jarawa boy brought him in close contact with civilisation. After experiencing the benefits of modern medical practises (Sarkar, 2002:20-21) first hand, they agreed to reduce their distance from "civilisation."

In that incident, a Jarawa boy named Enmei, with a fractured leg was brought to Port Blair and painstakingly treated at G.B. Pant hospital. Released after a full recovery with lots of gifts, he carried the message of friendship. Another author reporting that incident states, "Admission of...Enmei... to the G.B. Pant Hospital, Port Blair, on 16th April 1996, marks a major milestone in the history of friendly contact" (Mathews 2002:156). Though all "hostility" did not immediately end, as a consequence of this contact, it made possible to have a detailed anthropological study of the Jarawas. Quite a few anthropologists of the ANRC are today able to converse with them, and a monograph on their language has also been published. The fact that they have only 300 words speaks a lot about their culture. Living on an island and communicating only among themselves, these words were enough for their limited requirement. Since the Andaman Trunk Road (ATR) passes through their territory, they have picked up a few words of broken Hindi, the *lingua franca.*

The Great Andamanese used to refer them as the "Jarawa" meaning "others" or strangers. As the Great Andamanese had more contact with the British administrators, the term stuck. The Jarawas refer to themselves as "Ang" a term, which in their dialect means man. Such a use of the term referring to man for themselves is also present among other "isolated" groups.

Located just to the north of the equator, Andaman is a tropical paradise, with all the basic requirements of life available free of cost. Living very close to nature, the Jarawas have the most rudimentary material culture. These are the all-purpose bow and arrow, a small narrow spade, digging stick, knife, a few baskets and at least one bucket. Today they also use discarded plastic water bottles.

Dress

The first comment of a tourist on seeing Jarawas is their lack of clothing. They realise that in their environment and at their economic level, going stark naked is the healthiest and most practical solution. Wearing clothes involves changing, washing and drying these from time to time, and in the dense tropical forests of Andaman, where the Jarawas live, sunlight enters only for a couple of hours. Wearing perpetually wet clothes is unhygienic and tantamount to inviting various ailments of both respiratory tract and skin. This is what happened when the Jarawas were first exposed to "civilisation" and coaxed/forced to adopt clothing as per its dictates of "decorum." They started suffering from various respiratory ailments and skin diseases. The irony is that since the tribals of Andaman had no resistance against the respiratory ailments introduced by people from the mainland, they suffered extensively. Additionally, the wet clothing not only harboured infections, they also prevented the repeated dips in the sea and drenching in the rain which help to keep their body clean and application of pig fat on the body which keeps their skin supple.

Dwellings

Dwellings of the Jarawas were also developed in response to their specific requirements. As these change from time to time, so do the dwellings which are of three types. Most rudimentary are the lean-tos erected by hunting parties to protect against overnight drizzle. They are made up of fronds of pandanus or coconut interwoven together leaning against a convenient rock or tree. These lean-tos are prepared within half an hour, by a hunting party with material easily available in the jungle, and are abandoned the next day.

More permanent dwellings are of two types, viz. community huts and family huts. They differ in size, the way of construction and decoration. Community huts are bigger. These are semi-cylindrical structures about 4 to 6 metres long and 3 to 4 metres wide, generally located by the side of a rivulet or water channel to ensure water supply. At least three very sturdy colonnades of different heights are used. The central hut is the tallest, of sufficient length, and is raised to about 2 meters above the ground. Others are slightly smaller and are at a height of about 1.5 to 2 metres. Each carries a rafter and a sturdy cross beam which connects all three. Peripheral rafters are made of sturdy cane bent to the required shape over fire. All these are tied together with rattan. Other suitable pieces of cane are used to build the structure of the roof on which a tightly woven thatch made up of fronds of pandanus is fixed. The thatch covers the whole roof and reaches almost to the floor all round. An earthen embankment about ½ metres high is raised all around to prevent water from entering the hut. A gap of about 2 metres serves as the entrance.

Generally, two hearths are maintained. The main one is at the centre and is used to roast the largest game. Its base is lined with round pebbles with channels for firewood. Smaller game, such as fishes and other sea products may be roasted in the smaller hearth, which also serves to keep fire alive. Even today they do not depend on a matchbox to start a fire but use the second hearth for kindling.

A number of conjugal families share these communal huts. Pairs of palisades, each about half a meter high, radiate from the central fireplace. Pandanus leaves are staked to serve as beds. These demarcate the space allotted to every conjugal pair and protect individual members or their mats from getting singed. Skulls of wild boar browned by smoke serving as trophies of the machismo of males hang from the rafters. Spare bows and arrows are kept between the rafters and the thatch for protection from moisture. The smoke coats the hunting equipment with oil making these more supple and durable.

Individual couples make and use family huts. These are smaller in size. Two pairs of pillars make the skeletal frame. The taller pair, about 1.5 meters high stands in front and the shorter, which is about 0.5 meters high, stands at the back. Each pair has a sturdy crosspiece tied with rattan. Over the crosspiece are tied smaller pieces of cane to support the thatch. The eaves on the rear serve as a wall, while the remaining three sides remain open. Palm or Pandanus fronds serve as beds. These fronds are spread on logs about 150 to 160 cm long, 10 to 12 cm thick and are used as beds to protect against centipedes and other similar crawlers. In areas with water logged soil or subject to frequent inundation, like Foul Bay, these log beds are raised about 10 to 15 cm above the ground.

Still being hunter-gatherers like in the past, the Jarawas move from place to place in search of food. Not knowing how to produce fire, they carry fire with them. Even today, when match boxes are common, they continue the practise of carrying fire in the form of a lighted torch that not only lights the jungle tract but also helps start the hearth in the new location. It consists of a stout green branch with a pouch of green leaves in which burn dry leaves soaked in rosin and beeswax. Though the match box has become very common, due to the widespread habit of smoking, starting a hearth with a match stick in that damp surrounding with tinder that is at best semi-dry is a difficult proposition. A flaming torch serves the purpose better.

Hunting equipment

Bows and arrows are possibly one of the earliest technological inventions of man. The Jarawas have not been deprived from this knowledge. The bow of a Jarawa is similar to that of the Onge and the Sentinelese. These are 1 to 1.25 meters long and made of suitable strip of wood or well-matured cane. It is widest in the middle (about 4 cm) and tapers towards the ends, which carry two "necks" for fixing the bowstring which was previously made of pig sinew or plant fibre, but now-a-days synthetic material is being used.

Arrows

Today the Jarawas use two types of arrows. Before the use of iron from shipwrecks, they used plain wooden arrows. These days some arrows have heads made of iron and these are used for hunting pigs and other big game. The simple wooden arrow is a slender, absolutely straight stick, well impregnated with soot. If no iron head is used, one end is sharpened and often fire-hardened. The other end has a notch for catching the bowstring. The advantage of using these for fishing lies in their buoyancy, which makes retrieval of fishes easier.

The iron arrowhead is of three types, viz. needle, dagger and spatula shaped. Needle head is the simplest and is exactly like the wooden arrowhead but for the tip where an iron needle is fixed with the point outwards. These are used for fishing in waters near the shore and occasionally for hunting birds and small game. The shaft is of the same length and thickness as a wooden arrow.

The second type is the flat dagger-like arrowhead. These are of two types, viz. detachable and non-detachable. The butt end of the head is a pointed tang that goes into a hole in the shaft where it is fixed with resin, if it is of the non-detachable variety and only inserted, if it is of the detachable variety. In the latter case, a metre-long piece of plant fibre secures it to the shaft. Both have two backward pointing barbs whose edges are sharp so that after hitting the target it can cut the flesh and enter easily. When the prey tries to dislodge the arrow, the barbs prevent it from coming out. In case of arrows with detachable heads, the shaft dangles and entangles in the surrounding bushes preventing or considerably delaying the prey's escape.

The third variety has a spatula type head fixed firmly to the shaft by tying with plant fibres coated with rosin and reinforced with beeswax. It is not used for hunting but only for shooting down fruits and an occasional beehive from inaccessible palms and trees. This is another example, where Jarawas have successfully modified the traditional time-honoured technology in response to the felt need of a special situation.

Use of iron

Although tribes of Andaman learnt of iron since iron clad ships started coming there, they could use it only from shipwrecks in shallow waters, which had become quite common during the World War II. However, there was a shortage after World War II ended. Hence, the Jarawas started plundering for articles of iron, along with eatables. But getting iron and modifying it into implements are two different propositions. Without basic knowledge of metallurgy they could only shape the iron by rubbing against boulders. No doubt, the process is painstaking and time consuming but results are superb.

Today, their narrow spades, digging sticks and knives have iron heads or blades. Previously, the digging stick was only a fire hardened branch. But now it is a suitable sized fence post with an end sharpened by grinding. Their knife is a flat piece of iron about 15 to 20 cm long and about 2 to 4 cm wide, with one edge sharpened by rubbing on a stone and a point built. Plant fibre is wrapped on the butt end and impregnated with rosin and sealed with beeswax to serve as a grip.

Baskets of cane and fibre, along with a couple of bamboo buckets make up the rest of their material possession. These buckets are a single inter-node of locally growing giant bamboo with the inter-nodal septum at one end cut off and the other intact. Rattan is tied around to make a strap to hang it. These are used almost exclusively for extraction, collection and transportation of honey or honeycombs, which are stored and carried in these buckets. The honey slowly oozes at the start and is later squeezed empty. The empty comb is kept in an old bucket near the hearth to slowly melt and provide beeswax.

Baskets of various types of plant fibre are all multipurpose receptacles. In response to their nomadic mode of life, these have sturdy straps to make carrying easier. Women use a tump line while on a long trek; the basket hangs from the forehead and rests on the back. Netted baskets are used to collect molluscs, oysters, shrimps and other products of the sea from the tidal belt immediately after the tide goes down. Some are eaten raw while others are roasted, grilled or boiled.

Body Adornment

Though the Jarawas move around stark naked, they decorate their bodies with clay. They also use a number of items like the cummerbund, tail-neck-sash, arm-sash and various types of necklaces made of shells, fruits or dried kernels and leaves, often coloured with clay, as ornaments.

Cummerbund is a girdle made of plant fibres wrapped around the waist. From it hang coloured cords about 20 cm long, making a cord curtain half-way to the knee. But as these are few and separated; hence, the private parts are not fully hidden. The tail-neck-sash is made up of yellowish strips of leaves that are discarded when dry and replaced by a fresh one. The arm-sash and head-vault-sash are made of plant fibres. Today these are often interwoven with brightly coloured threads, mostly red, unravelled from cloth pieces given by tourists. As the neck-sash has magico-religious importance, it is made only with interwoven plant leaves.

The Jarawas use a type of white clay or even ash from burnt out log fire for personal decoration. The fat is smeared on the body as protection against insect bites; frequent dips in the sea also act as a base for the clay. Although, the whole body is available for designs consisting of dots and lines, special attention is paid to the face. Unlike the Great Andamanese, the Jarawas never developed the practise of tattooing or other forms of mutilation for decorating the body.

Men wear an abdominal belt made of bark, which might have been protective in the past but is only decorative today. It is a double layer of bark cloth wound around the stomach region and often painted with red line designs. It mainly functions as a pouch. The Jarawa males store tit-bits including various tobacco products between the layers of this belt and his belly. He invariably puts it on when he expects to be outside the hut for more than a couple of hours and tucks the ever-present knife in it.

Transportation

It is not clear why of all the tribes in Andaman, the Jarawas have not developed the technique of canoe-making. They are excellent swimmers. They make rafts by tying up suitable lengths of palm trunks with rattan fibre. Any suitable piece of flat wood serves as a paddle. Rafts become necessary only for transporting game such as the boar, as their meagre possessions can easily be carried on the back.

In fact, there is no reason to presume that the Jarawas have forgotten canoe making as they continue to live in the same environment. The fact is that canoes do not juxtapose well with their way of life. The Jarawas take frequent plunges in the innumerable creeks and channels that criss-cross their habitat. It is difficult to carry a canoe through the dense undergrowth, and if kept on the damp forest floor it is likely to be attacked and destroyed by various fungi and insects in no time. Moreover, canoe building is time consuming, while rafts can be built by just picking up logs from the forest and tying them using the easily available strong lianas. As such they possibly never learnt making small canoes.

The Jarawas select two or three straight logs about 3-5 m long and half metre thick, and tie them securely with lianas to make bigger rafts. Three or four cross-pieces, each of about 1.5 m in length and less than half a metre in diameter are tied at even distances on one side of the raft. Such a raft when floating on reasonably calm sea with cross-pieces at the bottom can support a group of about 6 to 8 Jarawas along with all their worldly possessions. Branches collected from the forest serve as paddles or poles.

Diet

The Jarawas practise subsistence economy. The tropical forest ensures a balanced diet through its variety, though it may appear to be inadequate and unhygienic to the urban people. They secure food by hunting, fishing and gathering various forest products.

The Jarawas relish various types of larvae. The forest floor abounds in fallen timber that harbours innumerable insects. A couple of sharp showers cover these with mushrooms, and soon larvae begin to crawl on them. The Jarawas collect these. Some larvae are eaten raw whereas others and mushrooms are baked by keeping on the edge of the hearth along with caterpillars wrapped in banana or other leaves, and then eaten.

Many marine products are also eaten raw while being collected. Nutritionally all are extremely rich as they are full of protein. The Jarawas can identify which of these can be eaten raw. There is no case of a Jarawa having taken ill by eating a poisonous caterpillar, larva or mushroom, reflecting the knowledge acquired over generations.

Hunting

Though the Jarawas are hunter-gatherers, they do not love or use dogs. They have always been killing dogs on sight while raiding settlements. It may be a relic of the past when the bush-police used dogs to track and hunt the Jarawas.

The main animals hunted by the Jarawas in Andaman are pigs and monitor lizards. Hunting pigs and monitor lizards on foot in the dense forest is time consuming. Living in a community hut with about 20 individuals, the band at any time has 4 to 6 adult males. A Jarawa hunting party consists of at least two males armed with bows and arrows accompanied by adolescent children. Though apparently there is no taboo against women going for hunting or handling bows and arrows, they remain engaged in collecting forest or marine products.

The Jarawas leave their hut at the crack of dawn as tracking pigs takes a long time. They search till adult pigs are within, range as they kill only the adult pigs. With dense undergrowth that deflects the arrows, they must get very close before they attempt to shoot an arrow with a detachable head used for this purpose. If the arrow hits the pig with enough force, the head embeds well. Running of the pig through the undergrowth, detaches the head from the shaft, which dangles outside. The undergrowth, which was initially hampering the hunter, now helps by slowing the progress of the pig with the shaft getting repeatedly entangled in the dense bushes. Soon it becomes tired or gets entangled and is caught. They kill it by slitting the stomach longitudinally. The entrails are removed and mostly thrown away, barring occasional sinews that are kept. Members of the hunting party often consume portions of the liver and heart raw, on the spot. The rest is taken back to the communal hut to be roasted in the central hearth and shared equally by all. Only the denuded skull, if of exceptional size, is displayed as a trophy and as a symbol of the prowess of the hunter.

Deer, which is inimical to cultivation, abounds in the jungles. Although wild life preservation laws protect the deer, settlers hunt these clandestinely to protect standing crops and eat the coveted venison. The Jarawas, however, do not hunt deer, though such restrictions do not apply to them. Their rationale behind abhorrence for venison and preference for pork is that "it (venison) is not tasty." But the real reason is that pork is more suited to their way of roasting than venison.

Fishing

Coastal fishing is done by both sexes. Men use bows and arrows to shoot medium sized fishes through a few feet of seawater. For bigger fish they use arrows with detachable heads to aid its retraction. Women collect molluscs of innumerable varieties, along with crabs and shrimps crawling at the bottom, together with small fishes that move around at these depths, using nets.

Gathered Items

The tropical jungles of Andaman provide honey, kernel of pandanus, plantains, coconut, papaya and mango naturally. Only papaya has been introduced recently. In the past the jungle provided adequate supply of all these items. But as it is easier to raid the settlements and collect the required food, the Jarawas prefer to do so. Though prohibited, there is a clandestine trading of honey between the Jarawas and the settlers.

The Jarawas are always on the look-out for honey-combs. As soon as the beginning of one is spotted, an identifying mark is left either on the tree or rock to demarcate the ownership. They smoke out the bees and smear themselves with plant juices to prevent honeybees from stinging, or at least reduce discomfort from the sting, before attempting to bring down the comb. It is then carried to the permanent hut in the person's bucket, oozing honey all the way. The whole band shares the honey. The empty comb rests near the hearth for the wax to melt; this is used later for various purposes.

Coconut meat is eaten raw after breaking it on a rock. Ripe banana is eaten raw, but raw banana is roasted near the edge of the hearth along with fruits of pandanus. After fully roasting, the outer layers of the fruit fall off and only the central kernel remains. For the Jarawas it is a delicacy.

Cuisine of the Jarawas

In the absence of cooking vessels, roasting is the only cooking method known to them. As already mentioned, the permanent hut has more than one hearth. One of these is about a metre long and half a metre wide and almost equally deep. The base is lined with small rounded pebbles with slots in between to keep firewood. It remains continuously smouldering, controlling mosquitoes and other flying insects. Whenever required, for actual cooking, additional firewood is added.

The killed boar, monitor or fish are laid on the smouldering fire and hot stones after removing the entrails. The dripping fat helps keep the flames alive. The skin and hair get fully burnt and fall off. The process of roasting takes a few hours for a pig. Fishes, being smaller, take lesser time and are often cooked after the bigger game.

Fire is also kept smouldering in a second pit. Raw banana and pandanus may be roasted here. Occasionally these are roasted on the edge of the main hearth along with molluscs, crabs, shrimps, caterpillar, etc., which are put on the edge of the fire pit in shells. Meat of big molluscs such as the nautilus is scooped out with a fine stick and consumed. The shell later serves as a cooking pot for small items. Shells of crabs and shrimps are broken to consume the meat inside. To turn small pieces of meat while being roasted, the Jarawas use fire-tongs. These are made from strips of green bamboo about 30 cm long, 2.5 to 3 cm wide, and are totally flexible after they are allowed to dry.

Until recently, the Jarawas did not use any cooking medium, additional salt or spices. As roasting was their sole method of cooking, they had no way of using condiments or spices. They had no stomach ailments. Today however, the situation is a bit different. Having discarded the extreme "hostility" of the past and becoming more or less amicable, the Jarawas are getting hand-outs from tourists crossing the ATR, mostly "fast-foods" – fried and rich in spices. They have also picked up various types of drugs like tobacco and cannabis and are often found consuming hard liquor. In fact, some Jarawas, both male and female, were found to have already become addicted to tobacco in its various forms, especially, the chewing variety, viz. *jarda.*

Civilised man wants to befriend the Jarawa for their exoticness. Their photographs become conversation pieces in the drawing rooms in the mainland. Another reason is their attire or the lack of it especially of the women. They have now started demanding "modelling charges" in the form of fast food packets, *"jarda" and* other intoxicants. Tourists are also happy to render payment in this "currency" which works out cheaper. Almost all clandestine souvenir shops in Port Blair sell photographs of the Jarawas in their native attire. The administration conducts raids on these shops from time to time and shops selling such photographs are prosecuted. Unfortunately, what is caught in the raids is only the tip of an iceberg.

Sanitation and Health Practises

When the British landed in Andaman, they found it littered with mounds of kitchen-waste. These were accumulations of non-edible wastes discarded for over centuries. Termed as kitchen-middens, these were large when the tribal population was large. A midden of substantial size that is closest to Port Blair is at Chouldary, and its lower strata are more than 500 years old. The size of the midden gives an indication of the tribal population that could have made it over the years. The kitchen-middens being formed today by the Jarawas in middle Andaman are minuscule in proportion.

As the Jarawa bands are small and do not stay long at one place, the tropical climate takes care of their refuse. It does not cause any health problems. Monitor lizards and pigs also serve as scavengers *par excellence* as do other rodents. Their personal hygiene practises also leave much to be desired. They do not have a system of washing their anal region after defecation but just wipe the area with fine sand, leaves or soil available at the nearest water-course. For babies, the mother wipes the area with soft leaf.

The Jarawas do not have the concept of regular bathing. Bathing to them is a natural phenomenon. As it rains almost daily for eight months in a year, in their habitat, it is a common sight to see a group of Jarawas traversing the ATR during light showers. The creeks that they cross by swimming and the coastal fishing that they do, keep them well washed.

The Jarawa-value system

The Jarawas do not recognise individual ownership. It is most effectively exemplified when they spot a honey-comb starting to form on a tree or a rock overhang. The one to spot it first marks the tree or the rock over hang with his mark that everyone recognises. When supposed to be full, it is taken down by him (of course with the help of others if required) and carried to the permanent camp-site in his bucket. He takes the primary share and then distributes the rest. When a pig is spotted during a hunting trip, it is credited to his account whose arrow pierces first though everybody shares equally.

An individual subscribing to such a value system, on seeing bananas hanging in a plantation, simply plucks whichever he craves. Same is the case with coconut plantations. To the Jarawas these are nature's bounty to be enjoyed by everybody. They simply cannot understand why they cannot pluck the coconuts or bananas that they see growing profusely near the huts of settlers. They feel they can take whatever they need. They take not only coconuts, bananas, mangoes and papayas, but also farmyard tools for the iron. They defend themselves by shooting arrows, in case, they are surprised by settlers.

Settlers naturally resent such loss, and hence, there are clashes. These are not clashes for individual interests but clashes of ways of life. Such clashes also took place in the past between the Colonial British and their lackey Indians on the one side and the tribals on the other. The group backed by superior technology triumphed with tragic results for the group with less advanced technology.

Unlike the other tribes, the Jarawas were not purely coast dwellers. As they live in the hills and jungle, they were not fully exposed. Their permanent settlements are all in dense jungles and they only venture to the coast to collect marine bounty. After every skirmish, they return to their jungle fortress which outsiders are afraid to enter. The Jarawas thus get the prefix "hostile" to their name with no fault of theirs (*cf.* Chanda, 1976).

Conclusion

This is a brief account of the life-style of the Jarawas, one of the most technologically backward groups of people today. They have not been subject to intimate extended contact with civilised man like the Great Andamanese, who have now lost their identity and after miscegenation, number around 50 individuals. The Jarawas, considered "hostile" till a couple of decades ago, have a population of about 700. Apparently, their notoriety saved them, as did the undulating terrain and jungle, which, when pursued by the bush-police, provide enough opportunity for them to hide.

Such a situation is not unique in Andaman, but has been repeated time and again. All over the world, the autochthones have suffered whenever they have come in sudden, intimate, prolonged contact with outsiders. It happened when the New World was discovered by

Christopher Columbus in the last decade of the 15th century. The conquistadors devastated the Inca, Aztec and other civilisations. Today only some legends and huge stone structures are found as relics. Later, when the Mayflower landed in 1620 A.D. at what is today known as Plymouth Mass, the white man succeeded in slowly pushing back the populations existing in the Great Plains. Today most of them have vanished.

As brought out by Hutchinson *et al. (1985),* similar are the histories of various isolated tribal groups who had the misfortune of suddenly coming in contact with "civilised" man. Talking of the depopulation of the Australian Aborigines, Hutchinson (1985:51) opines that the government's endeavour to mitigate the grave evils for which the white immigrants were solely responsible was very late. These endeavours only ensured continued tourist traffic to places like Aiyer's Rock that the aborigines considered "sacred."

Margaret Mead was aware of the process when she wrote in her semi-autobiographical book "*Blackberry Winter*", "In the 1920s we knew that primitive societies were vanishing. Today we know that those still remaining are being destroyed even more rapidly by the overpowering impact of our technological society in the far reaches of Latin America by the unchecked ruthless operations of commercial greed, New Guinea by exploitation and by ideological pressures for a form of independence that will make exploitation even more devastating in its effects; in Africa and elsewhere by the acts of young bureaucrats who are determined to make over their new countries in the Euro-American democratic or communist image." Whether one agrees or not with her observations, it is a fact that many tribes and their cultures developed in isolation in Andaman have almost vanished. It is high time that serious efforts are made to save the Jarawas from the same misfortune that befell others.

References

Andaman Adim. Janajati Vikas Samiti "Retrieval from Precipice". 1977, *AAJVS*, Port Blair.

Bhat, V.V. "Hostile Jarawas and Sentinelese of Andaman" in *Island Cultures of India* (ed.), G. Prakash Reddy and V. Sudershan, Secunderabad.

Bonnington, M.C.C. 1931. *Census of India Andaman and Nicobar Islands,* Vol. II Parts 1 and 2, Calcutta. Government of India Publications.

Chanda, Sudhendu 1976. "The Hostile Jarawa of Andaman and Semi Hostile Shompen of Great Nicobar Island", *Journal of Social Research* 19(2): 64-73.

Cipriani, Lido, 1966. *The Andaman Islanders.* London. Weiden Feed and Nicolson.

Hutchinson, H.N., J.W. Gregory and R. Lydekkar (ed.), 1985. *The Living Races of Mankind.* Delhi: Mittal Publications.

Man, E. H., 1902. *Aboriginal Inhabitants of Andaman Islands.* London.

Mann, R.S., 1976. "Depopulation Among Andaman Aborigines : An Analysis". *Journal of Social Research* 19(2). pp. 37-50.

Mead, Margaret 1972. *Blackberry Winter. New* York. Simon and Schuster.

Portman, M.V. 1896. "Notes on the Andamanese" reprinted from the *Journal of Anthropological Institute of Great Britain and Ireland.*

Radcliffe-Brown, A.R. (ed.) 1964. *The Andaman Islanders.* New York. The Free Press.

Sarkar, Jayanta 1987. "Befriending the Jarawa: A Challenging Task" *Human Science,* 36. pp. 1-12.

Mukhopadhyay, K. *et al.* (eds.) 2002. "No More Hostility: A Critical Phase in the Jarawa Society" in Jarawa Contact, Kolkata: Anthropological Survey of India.

Sekhsaria, Pankaj, 2003. *Troubled Islands.* Pune. Kalpavriksh.

Sinha, S.C. 1982. "Report of the Committee of Anthropologists on the Jarawa and Shompen situations", Delhi. Ministry of Home Affairs.

7

Cultural Diaspora : Tribal Migration as a Survival Strategy

Amitabha Sarkar

According to dictionary (Theodorson and Theodorson, 1979) : "Diaspora is a Greek term meaning dispersion or scattering, originally used to refer to the dispersion of the Jews from ancient Palestine. More recently, it has come to be used to refer to any group of persons living in a foreign nation or nations without the protection of their government, e.g., Russian emigres living in Western Europe after the Russian revolution." As per this definition, it is beyond nation, i.e., across different national political boundaries.

The tribals have a specified geographical universe within the nation in which their sustenance activity is roaming; and when due to some reason they are compelled to change or shift to another place for their sustenance, and settle in a different eco-niche, i.e., in a different universe where their world-view is not similar with natal environment, they have adapted to the local cultural elements as a survival strategy in order to cope with the new environ situation. Under this context, the author considers diaspora also within the nation but with different eco-settings, like the present day tribal situation in our country, i.e. India. A vast number of tribal people started to migrate to different eco-settings for their survival. For example, a section of Chotanagpur and adjoining Orissa tribes migrated to Assam, North Bengal tea garden areas, Andaman and Sunderban areas for reclamation work, and even to the coal mining sector and brick-kiln areas. Some of such situations are discussed in this paper.

Before proceeding further, it is important to examine the term "tribe." After the last 32 years' direct empirical experience, among the various tribal groups in the country (except in the NE part of India), a tribe, according to the author, is a group of homogenous people, that is, with a common way of life, having an in-group sentiment of their own that differentiates them from others; and having a common geographical territory with a common dialect, usually in a backward, segmentary society (i.e., specialisation is not rigid and generation-wise), shyness in contact with outsiders, primitiveness lack of access to modern technology, lack of personal ethics in supernaturalism, presence of hierarchic sanction in their world-view, and faith in the transmigration of soul and reincarnation (Sarkar, 1995).

According to the Government's definition, the essential characteristics of a Scheduled Tribe, first laid down by the Lokur Committee for a community that has been identified as ST are:

(i) indication of primitive traits

(ii) distinctive culture

(iii) shyness of contact with the community at large

(iv) geographical isolation and

(v) backwardness

Again, among these there are other distinct groups – Primitive Tribal groups (PTGs) which are 75 in number and their characteristic features are : (i) pre-agricultural level of technology; (ii) stagnant or declining population; (iii) extremely low literacy; and iv) subsistence economy. It has been observed that in each tribal situation, there are some specific economic pursuits which are very much in tune with their immediate environment.

The chief resource in rural economy in India is land-related. Therefore, a number of social/cultural problems cluster around land. For instance, ownership of land in India is complicated. As an effect of the permanent settlement act between the *zamindars* and the *ryots*, some big and small Talukas appeared. The poor tribal peasants' economic condition had become worse in the process of fulfilling the demands of these innumerable *talukdars* and *zamindars*. As a result, there sprouted several types of landholders and many kinds of tenants and eventually, a distinct class – agricultural labourers, appeared.

Situation A: Agricultural Labourers

The enormous growth of population, increasing disintegration of the traditional village industries, injudicious administrative policy, and the development of modern industry and trade accentuated the problems of the agricultural labourers. The large classes of agrarian labourers are creating a huge problem not only for themselves, but also for the overall economic growth of the country. The landless labourers migrate to the urban areas not so much, because they are compelled to do so for a bare living; these labourers are ready to accept any employment, which will enable to have a living comparable to that in the rural areas.

In determining the size of a problem, its definition becomes a matter of considerable significance. For the purpose of population census in 1951, a cultivator was distinguished from a cultivating labourer as a person who takes the responsible decision, which constitutes the direct process of cultivation. On the other hand, agricultural labourers are, broadly speaking, employees of these cultivators. Since, for varying periods, small owners, tenants and artisans find themselves working as cultivating labourers, the line between agricultural labourers and other agricultural groups is subject to marginal shifts. Therefore, agricultural labourers may be described as a residuary group in the rural economy.

The production relation in the ancient and mediaeval agrarian economy was characterised by the self-possessing, self working and self-sufficient cultivators. The villages were almost self sufficient and needed little intercourse with the outside world. During the Muslim rule, this production-relation continued. However, during the British rule in India the ossified shell of the typical village economy was broken. The production-relation changed greatly and the cultivators slowly, but steadily, became separated from the means of production. In pre-British India, crop was produced mainly for meeting the needs of the village population. But this subsistence village agricultural economy was transformed into a market economy during the British regime. The new rulers not only created private property of land but also replaced the traditional rent in kind with rent in the form of money. The land tax progressively increased, resulting in the increasing indebtedness of the cultivators. Owing largely to the necessity for cash for the payment of land tax or rent and debt, the agriculturist, the peasant proprietor, or the tenant was more and more constrained to produce for the market. Thus, village agriculture gradually ceased to produce for direct consumption by the village population and began to produce instead for the national, and subsequently even for the world market. However, the techniques of agricultural production continued to be primitive. Under these techno-economical relations various socio-economical groups, such as serfs, *zamindars*, tenants, peasant proprietors, landless labourers, share-croppers and others grew up.

The key resource in a rural economy, of course, is land. The question of land ownership in India is complicated. It is pointed out that Indian agricultural economy is based on caste that is totally different from the western system. Considering the property structure (i.e., land constitutes the chief basis of productive activity in the rural society, the formation of groups is primarily connected with the differentiation of rights over land; in other words, it is connected with the property structure), the most conspicuous feature was the non-existence of a socially and economically homogenous class of landlords, comparable to the feudal lords of western Europe, in command of large landed estates operated through the labour of unfree peasants. The landowning class in India has a heterogeneous character. As an economic class, it represented an amalgam of three different types, viz. (1) the *zamindars, jagirdars*, and the like; (2) the money-lenders and traders; and (3) the professional middle classes. Further, within each of these types there existed considerable differentiations based on the size of the landed property and the resident character of the landlord, resulting in a diversified pattern of control exercised over landed property. The picture was further complicated by the existence of sub-infeudation, there being a chain of intermediary interests between the actual producer and the master of the land at the top of the land pyramid.

The land-owning class was multi-caste in composition and thus there existed not only significant economic differentiation but also social differentiation. Equally fundamental were the differences in the social and economic position of the direct producers, the mass of the peasants and the labourers. In the Indian context, the social form of labour power was not serf-labour on the owner's land, as under classical feudalism, but labour of self-employed peasants in small plots of cultivation, leased from the landlords under various systems of rental payment.

Again, the direct producers did not constitute a solid undifferentiated economic class subject to uniform mode of exploitation. On the contrary, there existed sharp sartification among the direct producers, a gradation of peasants right in the economic sphere and of social status; and rights and obligations in the non-economic sphere, which did not permit the formation of a well-defined class identity. The direct producers were further divided as (1) peasants who worked only in their own plots of cultivation; and (2) who worked for others.

The peasants themselves were sub-divided into various categories on the basis of the size of land under their cultivation, the security or insecurity of their tenure, mode of rental payment to the landlords, and the extent of freedom or unfreedom characterising the irrelations with the masters of land. Further, the peasants often belonged not to single but to mixed categories. They had security of tenure over a part of the land while they were hired as a tenant-at-will for another part of the land; they paid fixed rent in cash for one part of land, fixed rent in kind for another part, and were share croppers for still another part; or, they were tenants with a small plot under cultivation as well as part-time labourers. At the top there existed big peasants whose economic position was better than that of many landlords and who even leased out parts of their land to others. The big peasants were also often employers of hired labour and some belonged to the class of moneylenders and traders. Apart from the diversity of economic groups among the peasant producers, there was also the diversity of social groups. The peasants had a multi-caste composition, which did not permit a common mode of self-identification also in the social sphere. The mass of peasantry, which was stratified into different types of interpenetrating groups in the economic sphere, was quite often graded into different caste groups in the social sphere. Economic and social forces seldom acquired such strength as to break up the shell of caste and bring about a broader social grouping on non-caste lines.

Those who worked on the fields for others were similarly sub-divided not only between attached and casual labourers, but also between those who were part cultivators and those who were not. Very often these also did not exist as pure, but as mixed types. Equally important was the fact that employment of labour, instead of being concentrated on a small minority of large holdings, was widely diffused over many classes of cultivated holdings. This was because status reasons forced even small landowners from high status groups to employ labourers for agricultural work in their fields.

Before the early fifties, when all the Indian states passed land reform acts designed to eliminate large landholders and intermediaries between the cultivators and the state, there were several kinds of landlords and many kinds of tenants. Before the abolition of large-scale landlords, it was useful to think of three kinds of persons with direct interest in cultivation – the owners of land, permanent tenants, and non-permanent tenants. There was a great variation from state to state in the amount of land owned by the landlords, the rights they had, and the amount of income they enjoyed from their landholdings. Important as the concentration of landholding before the days of land reform was, its social and economic consequences were sometimes misunderstood. The situation was not one of a single landlord and great hordes of tenants at a bare subsistence level under the big landlords. In fact, in the rural social and economic structure, the most important person was not and is not the large landholder, but the small landholder and the permanent tenant. Now one interesting thing in the Indian context was that Indian agrarian economy is based on caste system. According to caste, each group has a recognised occupation, so many among them did not touch the plough or till the land; they employ labourers.

In this situation emerged a class of owners of many lands, though not powerful like the *zamindars*, who did not plough their land. They employed persons who knew the agricultural activities but had no scope to work, i.e., they employed persons in their lands from the landless class of people who worked as labourers on a daily wage basis, job basis or seasonal/annual basis. All these happened due to unequal distribution of land. Hence, a group of people were rendered poor, lived at a bare subsistence level, and migrated to various places in search of work; most of these groups were turned into agricultural labourers.

From land owning cultivators to tenants and from tenants to landless labourers, this has been the plight of a large number of peasants in India. The peasant who mortgages his land to the moneylender sooner or later finds himself dispossessed and has perhaps to work as a tenant under some non-cultivating landowner. His tenancy again may be terminated as soon as somebody else comes up with a higher offer of rent and the proud proprietor of yesterday now falls to the rank of the landless labourer. This process has been going on in India for a long time. The pressure of population in the rural areas and the absence of sufficient opportunities of employment in commerce and industry have compelled people to continue living in the village even without any definite chance of obtaining work on land. The total number of agricultural labourers is believed to have gone up from about 10 million in 1921, to more than 30 million in 1961; a more detailed information in this aspect is not available.

A large landless agricultural population is undesirable for several reasons. Firstly, it creates social unrest in the villages by causing a split between the haves and the have-nots. Secondly, the presence of large labour population in the rural areas presupposes an intensive form of cultivation in large agricultural estates. As the pattern of Indian agriculture is different, so much labour cannot be used and this creates a problem of chronic unemployment among the labourers. Thirdly, the competition among so many labourers drives rural wage rates down to sub-human levels. In some parts of the country, the farm labour is reduced to virtual serfdom, which often descends from father to son (bonded labour like in Palamou District of Jharkhand). The landless agricultural labourer in fact occupies the lowest rung of the social ladder in Indian villages and can never be expected to claim equality of status with the land owning "gentry" of the village. His presence is thus a great hindrance to the emergence of truly democratic institutions in our rural communities.

The study of agricultural labourers is important for theoretical values as well as for applied sense. Anthropology has been concerned with the study of social groups and organisation and paid little attention to the study of economic classes like agricultural labourers, landlords etc. The agricultural labourers have developed some social and religious habits, and norms of their own which are to be observed and understood by the socio-cultural anthropologists. From applied points of view, these studies will help us understand the trend of social and economic changes in rural India.

The Ministry of Labour of the Government of India made a comprehensive enquiry into the conditions of agricultural labourers in India during 1950-51. The enquiry was conducted in about 800 villages selected from all over India on the basis of stratified random sampling. It was estimated on the basis of this sample that out of nearly 58 million rural families in India, 17.6 million families constituted agricultural labour, which were either landless or owned only very small strips of land, and as such had to depend mainly on wage labour for their incomes. More than 8.8 million agricultural labour families thus defined had no land in their possession.

Zone	*Percentage of labourers not employed on wages in any month of the year*	*Average annual unemployment of those employed on wages (number of days)*
North India	4	44
East India	17	73
South India	20	115
West India	14	113
Central India	16	54
Northwest India	17	82
All India	16	82

Source: All India Agricultural Labour Enquiry 1950-51, Essential Statistics.

B. Employment and Unemployment among Casual and attached Agricultural Labourers

Zone	*(Average No. of days) Casual men workers*			*(Average No. of days) Attached men workers*		
	Wage employment	*Self employment*	*Unemployment*	*Wage employment*	*Self employment*	*Unemployment*
North India	280	37	48	345	9	11
East India	215	73	77	323	28	14
South India	173	76	116	301	44	20
West India	171	66	128	340	9	16
Central India	193	99	73	325	24	16
North-west India	141	104	120	288	39	38
All India	200	75	90	326	20	19

Agricultural labourers can be broadly grouped into two categories attached and casual. Those who are more or less permanently attached to particular employers form a small percentage; and the casual labourers suffer from lack of employment almost throughout the year. The extent of self-employment depends on the economic resources available to the household or the individual labourer. Those who have the necessary resources create for themselves adequate avenues for self-employment. Self-employment in case of male workers takes the form of collection of wood, fuel, grass, herbs and other forest produce, fishing, rope making, mat making etc., while the self-employed women take up tending cattle, dairy farming, picking cotton and chilies, grass cutting and a hundred other odd jobs. Thus, the male members of the small cultivator families keep themselves engaged in these odd jobs, which are far from gainful, during the period of unemployment, while the women attend to the household duties and similar other jobs. The implication of self-employment being disguised unemployment, agricultural workers suffer from this malady. Further, it is pointed out that during peak agricultural seasons, all workers cannot secure paid employment and even the employed workers remain idle for some days during such periods. On an average, about 84% of the workers are employed on wages in a month and these employed workers are unemployed for 7 days in a month.

In his book "*Agricultural Labourers in India*", Kamal Kumar Ghosh (1969) pointed out that agriculture is central to Indian economy. Obviously, the agricultural labouring class in India is such a decisive force in comparison with labourers in other segments. Unfortunately however, most of the agricultural labourers are poorly paid, precariously employed and inadequately housed. Poverty is chronic and destitution though rare is not completely absent. He mainly stresses on the economic condition and growth of agricultural labourers from socio-economic and historic points of view. He attempted to reconstruct the economic and social structure of agricultural labourers of the country from the result of a projected research (the first agricultural labour enquiry was conducted in 1950-51 in 800 villages, covering a sample of 11,000 agricultural labour families. The next enquiry was conducted in 1956-57, in 3600 villages and data on employment, unemployment, wage and earnings, income, expenditure and indebtedness were collected from 28560 samples). This study is an endeavor to find out the cause of the growth of agricultural labour class as a distinct group and to observe minutely their economic condition during the long period from 1891 to 1946. An attempt is also made to analyze the recent measures for promoting land use and land management on more efficient lines.

Situation B: Coal Mine Workers

Banerjee (1981) reported in his study from Jharia-Ranigunge coal field areas that the Santal tribe, which is locally referred to as "Manjhee", forms the largest tribal group among the various immigrants in this region. They came from immediate hinterland and had taken up pick mining as their occupation to supplement their income by working as wage earners in this industry. Industrial situation, therefore, places the Santals not only in a new cycle of work but also in a multi-ethnic arena of social interaction. The region has not only provided opportunities for employment to the local people but has also attracted a large number of immigrants from other neighbouring areas who basically in their natal areas were in the rank of surplus labour force.

The table below shows the participation of the Santal workers in the secondary sector (mining category, 1961 Census).

		Total No. of Workers	*Primary Sector*		*Secondary Sector Mining*
			Cultivator	*Labourer*	
Santal	R-102343 U-5901	62059 3447	43478 1344	4681 235	9909 10964

Apart from the Santals, the other important tribal groups involved in this area are the Korwa, Oraon, Munda and Mahali. However, the Santal representation in coal industry constituted the maximum during 1960s.

According to Banerjee (1981) the Santal of Bhowra colliery and Jharia have simplified the process of rituals in response to the demand of a new economy. The ultimate result is that the Santals, without any constraints from their culture, adjusted with the rhythm of work in a more committed manner than their brethren living in the village.

Situation C: Garden Workers

Tea is known as the green gold of India. The plantations are a highly specialised commercial enterprise employing wage labour. The spread of plantation culture must be viewed as a spread of industrialised agriculture (Dasgupta and Khan, 1983). In India tea plantation as an organised industry came up around the middle of the nineteenth century. Tea is cultivated extensively in Assam and its neighbouring districts like Jalpaiguri and Darjeeling in West Bengal and also some pockets of Nilgiri Hills in South India. Large-scale migration of tribal people took place, especially from Chotanagpur and Santal Parganas, to Assam and North Bengal in search of food and livelihood. It is also reported that in Jalpaiguri, such migration started since 1873, and bulk of the immigrants were the Oraon, Munda, and Santal tribes (Census, 1961). In Darjeeling District also there was a phenomenal growth in the population since 1872 and this was primarily due to the growth of employment in the tea industry.

It is known that the bulk of the migrants from Chotanagpur were labourers in the tea gardens of Assam. In 1931, altogether 33000 persons were sent back from Assam as they were speakers of the tribal languages of Chotanagpur. The corresponding figure in 1961 was 195182, assuming that the bulk of the first generation migrants would be speaking their ancestral language.

Situation D : Sunderbans

Sunderbans is the largest delta on globe in the estuarine phase of the River Ganga. It is a unique bioclimatic zone in a tropical geographical situation in the coastal region of the Bay of Bengal. There are altogether 102 islands in Sunderbans, out of which 54 are reclaimed and human inhabited, while the remaining 48 are reserved forests.

The first known attempt of reclamation of Sunderbans was that of Khan Jahan. At the time of the East India Company's acquisition of the civil administration of Bengal in 1765, the forests of Sunderbans extended upto Calcutta. In 1782, Mr. Henekell, Judge and Magistrate of Jessore, inaugurated the system of reclamation between Calcutta and the eastern district. And for such reclamation work, a huge labour force was required : the hired labourers were from the tribal belt of Chotanagpur and Orissa. The present day Scheduled Tribes (STs) of the Sunderbans are mostly the descendants of those few who were once brought over from their original homeland of Bihar and Orissa to this area for clearing the forests and making the land cultivable (Das *et al.*, 1981). The dominant STs in the Sunderbans are Bhumij, Munda, Oraon, Santal, Kora, Mahali, etc. It is also reported that these tribal labourers were brought by the *zamindars* to clear the forests and to raise mud embankments to stop infiltration of brackish water from the tidal rivers. The forefathers of these migrants had left their ancestral villages in Chotanagpur, and Dhenkanal and Mayurbhanjin Orissa because of the pressure due to adverse economic conditions. Their land there was mostly unfertile and it was difficult to raise crop of even minimum requirement to support their families. Apart from the mere economic reasons, there might have been other social reasons, which compelled them to leave their ancestral villages.

It is evident from the empirical data that the factors of human settlement in this part of the country, coupled with the crisis of survival, have brought people together under a common canopy of belief system, which borrows a myth from the twin faiths of Islam and Hinduism. The resultant force of this mythical spread has formed a common folk cult in this part of the Gangetic Delta, which has taken root in all societies, irrespective of their religious faith and occupational pursuits. However, there has been a differential rate of the degree of acceptance of folk deities in different societies, if observed individually, but the uniqueness of this mythical spread is that it lies at the cognitive dimension of the people.

The folk cults that dominate in Sunderbans are *Bonbibi*, *Dakshin Rai*, *Shahjangali*, *Gazi Baba*, *Badar Pir*, *Ola Bibi*, *Pencho-Kencho*, *Panchananda*, *Panchu-thakur*, *Ateshwar*, and so on. The level of acceptance of various local Sunderbans cults by the various ethnic groups in Sunderbans in the study area (like the Gosaba, Basanti and Raidighi) is as follows:

Level of Acceptance of Sunderbans' Folk Deities

Comm-unities	*Bonbibi*	*Dakshin Rai*	*Gazi Baba*	*Badar Pir*	*Tusu*	*Manasa*
Hindu	93%	44%	79%	75%	79%	93%
Muslim	92%	6%	86%	68%	26%	72%
Tribals	100%	36%	82%	74%	100%	100%
Christians	63%	21%	28%	11%	24%	59%

Note: Total respondents were 200 from each community.

Hence, it can be said that due to uncertainty of the life of the people, especially the jungle entrants of the Sunderbans, they depend on various folk deities, who they consider as their rescuers, and assimilated into their own belief system of life for sustainable living.

Situation E: Tribal Women in Unorganised Sector

The structural subordination of women to men becomes more manifested when the phenomenon is considered in the context of working rural women. They work in the scorching sun and in the pouring rain. Away from their homes, they slog, breaking the stones at the quarries and doing all drudgery at the mines, factory premises, construction sites, plantation sites, brick-kilns, etc. They earn on their own and supplement the family income to keep off starvation. Apart from this, they cook and look after children and do almost everything else that the men do, like going around to fetch grass and fodder, all in order to keep the fire of the hearth burning. They also operate the wells to irrigate the land, sow seeds, transplant and harvest crop. This is more or less the common story of women workers in our country. However, enough attention is not paid to the plight of a vast majority of the women working force in the unorganised sector of the economy.

In the tribal world, women contribute to the working force in a more substantial way than in the non-tribal world. Since the tribal economy is largely confined to the primary sector, about 90% female workers are engaged in agriculture as cultivators or wage earners; 2.67% in the pastoralism and hunting, and 0.6% in mining and quarrying (Sachchidananda, 1978).

In the areas where a lot of constructional work is being carried out, the contractors lift tribal women on trucks from the villages and nearby areas, and drop them back in the evening (Sachchidananda, 1978). In some cases, the tribal women even migrate outside their village/district/state for periods ranging from 2 to 6 months for working in the brick-kilns, agricultural fields, etc. For example, many of the tribal labourers left for the Andamans (Vidyarathi, 1971), the tea gardens in NE India (Kar, 1976), and to several other parts of India. The tribal labourers working in the forests of Chotanagpur did not find it much difficult to work in the forests of Andamans. They may be safely termed as the modern builders of the Andamans (Vidyarathi, 1971).

According to Prasad (1988) and Dasgupta (1995) tribal women also feel inclined to go for such short and long term employment because it provides them ready cash, which they prefer to spend on clothes, ornaments and other items of their choice. On the other hand this kind of employment has led to several forms of physical and economic exploitations. The freedom enjoyed by the tribal women in their own social system has been grossly mistaken and misunderstood by the others who utilise them (tribal women labourers) for not only their economic gains but also for sexual exploitation, which ultimately leads to other social problems in their village environment.

The worst victims are tribal women wage earners in the construction industry and brick-kilns who get their employment either through the contractors or directly from the labour centers. These tribal labourer are often subjected to exploitation either at the hands of their contractor or employer's associates. Due to lack of adequate social security and welfare measures, in addition to their fear and sense of insecurity alienation and frustration, they are living in a bi-cultural situation, which leads to psychologically depressing conditions.

The trade of tribal labourers through contractors or agents generally passes through 3-4 tiers. Usually, these labourers are trapped by thei local tribal leaders who command good respect among his fellow members in the village/villages. In view of their poverty-stricken economic conditions and confidence in their leaders, they agree to go with the contractors to work even at distant places; often they have to stay away from their natal village for years together.

Search for New Adjustment

Various conditions have compelled the tribal people to leave thei natal places to other areas for livelihood. In this context it can be sai that infra-nationalism is also found among the tribal people (living i comparatively secluded areas and generally very much reluctant i national developmental programme), who are being drawn into the marke economy. It is an almost instinctive move on the part of the sma communities to expand their identity (Roy Burman, 1980).

According to Oraon (1965), the more acculturated a tribe is, th more severely it feels the thrust of emulation : solidarity in a ran concession syndrome. According to Sarkar *et al.* (2003), the empirica data from Sunderbans clearly suggests that the people from this biospher have contributed to the formation of a syncretic platform through th process of cultural synthesis where all communities (both tribal an non-tribal) contributed to the acceptance of certain deities, ultimatel leading to harmonious co-existence between different social and religiou ethnic groups.

It has also been observed that people of this locale (i.e., Sunderbans) are struggling primarily for survival and then for subsistence; then there are the cure deities all of whom are deeply enmeshed with the local people. The hierarchy of local pantheon is at the first category, the deities associated with survival and subsistence, which is followed by the cure-deities, often cut across and overlapping with the ethnic boundary.

Conclusion

The above empirical situation clearly suggests that survival strategy is the key factor, because in spite of different locales with different occupational opportunities which are altogether different from the natal village situation of the tribals, the migrant tribes are being forced to adapt to local situations and at the same time, they have also incorporated some of the local (i.e., in the new place of their migration) cultural elements as a strategy for survival. This is a kind of diaspora (?) situation in various corners of the country where the tribals are pushed in view of their subsistence. It can also be said that these tribes have been unable to maintain their bare subsistence; hence, pushed to some areas where occupational opportunity is available. These are very alarming signals for planners and administrators because it clearly speaks for the area from where the tribals were/and are migrated, are not fully covered under the government's developmental programmes/schemes. And here lies the root of social disharmony and unrest that is very much common in some pockets of the country.

References

Banerjee, Sukumar, 1981. Impact of Industrialisation on the Tribal Population of Jharia-Ranigunge Coal field Area, Calcutta, Anth. S.I. (Memoir No. 52).

Das, Amal, S. Mukherjee and M.K. Chowdhury 1981. *A focus on Sunderban* Calcutta: Editions Indian.

Dasgupta Samira, 1995. *In search of Alternative: Tribal Women in Desert Scenario*, New Delhi: Gyan Pub. House.

Dasgupta, P.K. and Iar Ali Khan, 1983. Impact of Tea Plantation Industry on the Life of Tribal Labourers, Calcutta. An. S.I. Memoir No. 57.

Ghosh, Kamal Kumar, 1969. *Agricultural Labourers in India*, Calcutta.

Kar, R.K., 1976. "Tribe in the Context of a Tea Industry in India: Some Preliminary observations". *Anthropos,* Vol. 71, pp. 868-77.

Orans, Martin, 1965. *The Santal: A Tribe in Search of a Great Tradition*, Detroit: Wayne State University.

Roy Burman, B.K., 1980. "Demographic and Historical Setting for Ethnic Relations in Chotanagpur with Particular Reference to the Tribals in The Passing Scene of Chotanagpur", ed. P. Dash Sharma, Ranchi, Maitrayee Publication.

Sartorius, J., 1972. *Migration in Chotanagpur*, Massachusetts, Centre for International Studies, MIT.

Sachchidananda, 1978. "Social Structure, Status and Mobility Patterns: The case of Tribal Women." *Man in India,* Vol. 58, No. 1.

Sarkar, Amitabha, A.K. Mukhopadhyay and G.K. Bera, 2003. "Cultural Syncretism in Sunderbans," Xth National Plan Project, Kolkata. Anthropological Survey of India (unpublished).

Sarkar, Amitabha 1995. "Ethnic Conflict: Unrest among Autochthons of Jharkhand", *Social Change*, Vol. 25, No. 4.

Theodorson, G.A. and A.G. Theodorson 1979. *A Modern Dictionary of Sociology*, London. Barnes and Noble Books.

Vidyarathi, L.P. 1971. "The Ranchi Tribal in Andaman and Nicobar Islands" *Jr. of Social Research*, No. XIV, No. 2.

8

Religious Pluralism Among the Khasis

M. Sasi Kumar and *C. Raghu*

A pluralistic society is one where different groups can interact while showing a certain degree of tolerance for one another, where different cultures can coexist without major conflicts, and where minority cultures are encouraged to uphold their customs. India is a pluralistic society and well-known for its socio-cultural, linguistic and religious heterogeneity. It comprises several castes, and social, religious, linguistic and ethnic groups. Though incidence of occasional clashes among them is not very uncommon, they in general tolerate each other when it is a matter of national unity. Several ethnic groups which have been predominantly homogeneous in terms of religion and culture have been influenced by religions which were hitherto alien to them through a process of initial resistance, adjustment, adaptation and tolerance. Each such society evolves certain unique features of its own which, in their entirety and inter-relatedness, constitute its dominant configuration and differentiate it from other societies. An example is the Khasis of Meghalaya. Till the second half of the nineteenth century, the Khasi society was more or less a homogeneous group but subsequently it began to host several streams of religious faiths comprising the major religions of the country such as Hinduism, Islam and Christianity. The focus of this article is not on the pluralism among India's major religions; rather, the paper will examine how an ethnic group with its own traditional belief system and distinctive culture positively ingrained the values of other religious beliefs even though it was often contrary to their traditional social institutions like matrilinial and other customary laws. It analyses how alien religious values were ingrained with the customary law of the Khasis from the perspective of religious pluralism, and how it resolves conflicts in order to discover the reciprocal influences, mixtures and boundaries of religions. Though over years many religious beliefs have influenced the community, the stress here is on Christianity as more than half of the population have already been converted to that religion and the growing movement towards pluralism, relativism and compromise within the community itself.

The Khasis

The Khasi community, more than half-a-million strong, is one of the most advanced tribal communities in India. They are well known in literature as a community practising matrilineal system of descent and inheritance and, though wrongly, often quoted as an example of matriarchal societies in India. They speak a dialect that belongs to Mon-Khmer branch of the Austric family forming a linguistic island amidst Tibeto-Burman speaking communities of North-East (NE) India.

Myth of Origin

Every community has its own stories and folk tales regarding its origin, and the Khasi community is no exception. According to legend, they are the progenies of the people from the original seven huts (*Hynniew Trep)* out of the 16 huts created by God. All of them lived in heaven along with God. Sins were unknown to them at that point of time. God decreed that the Hynniew Trep should populate the world and hence they came down to the earth. But still they maintained their relationship with the rest of the members of the nine huts (Khyndai Trep) and God. A ladder (also said to be a golden bridge) connects the earth with heaven (The golden bridge was believed to be situated in Lumsohpet Bneng near Umroi). Later, one of the members of the Hynniew Trep pulled down the ladder in order to stop the dominance of God over them. God retaliated by plunging the world into darkness. The members of the Hynniew Trep prayed to God and a cock came to the rescue of the Hynniew Trep. The cock mediated between God and the Hynniew Trep. He went to the sun and took upon himself all the blame for the sinful act. The sun was pleased and dispelled the darkness that enveloped the earth and thus re-established the relationship between God and the men on earth but not in the same way, as it was earlier. The cock was since then considered sacred and the most important sacrificial bird (Mathur 1979:62).

Religion

The indigenous Khasi religion was based on the belief of God as the creator (U Blei Nong-thaw) with due respect for the ancestors. "The religion of the Khasis may be described as animism or spirit worship, or rather, the propitiation of spirits both good and evil on certain occasions, principally, in times of trouble" (Gourdon 1907). As far as the Khasis are concerned, religion and worship was a matrilineal family affair performed by the matrilineal male usually the *kni (the* eldest of the maternal uncles) at the *khadduh*'s (youngest daughter of the family) residence. They have a community priest called *lyngdoh* but his services are not normally sought for family/lineage level worships and religious performances.

The Khasis never symbolise their gods as images, their worship being offered to the spirit only. Some such spirits worshipped by them are Uleimuluk, Uleiumtong, Uleilongapah, etc. (Gourdon 1907: 106). The Khasis adore their deceased ancestors by means of periodical offerings. The cock is an important and sacred bird for the Khasis and it is sacrificed as part of their worships. Their Niam Khasi religion has no recorded beliefs, no centrally administered social organisation, but there is a coherent fabric of interwoven socio-cultural practises and beliefs.

Christianity

The Khasis in Meghalaya faced a crisis when the British conquered NE India in the 19 century, encouraging missionary activity to help pacify the areas. The initial attempts to proselytise the Khasis were strongly resisted by them. The first Christian Mission that could make some impact on the Khasis was the Welsh Mission of the Presbyterian denomination. It sent its first missionary under the leadership of the Rev. Thomas Jones and his wife to Cherrapunjee, the then capital of the province, in 1841. It made a humble beginning but its repercussions on the culture of the hill people has been of far reaching consequences. Though initially the Christian missionaries faced acute resistance from the Khasis they later succeeded in converting them into the Christian faith to a great extent. Ka Nabon was the first Khasi woman to be baptised in 1848 (Mathur 1979:16). The Roman Catholic Church started its missionary activities among the Khasis much later in 1890 and the strong spirit of competition among the various denominations helped in intensifying their activities. While the Welsh Mission of the Presbyterian denomination concentrated on primary education, their Roman Catholic counterparts controlled the institutions for higher studies. They opened a number of reputed schools in Shillong like Loreto (1909), St. Mary's (1913), St. Edmund (1905), Don Bosco Training School (1923), and colleges like St. Antony's (1935), St. Mary's (1935) and St. Edmund's (1937). Thus, Shillong became the centre of higher education in the whole of NE India (Mathur 1979:20). Though Christianity has now influenced a fairly large number of Khasis, the structural aspects of the Khasi society remained more or less intact. While earlier a convert had to abandon traditional customs, now-a-days the Christians more pragmatically seek to blend into local cultures.

When Christianity first came, the Khasi family was faced with the question whether a *"Ka Khaduh"* could hold the family property if she converts to the Christianity. In 1918, the Government ruled that Christian converts should be allowed to inherit the ancestral property. Property was thus divorced from religion. Though religion was divorced from the traditional rules, but because of modernisation, such as, educational development along with the spread of Christianity, the traditional systems had somehow changed in many respects.

Role of Christianity in bringing Cultural Change

Christianity entered the scene with its patrilineal values and cultural concepts, and was spread among the Khasis mainly during the British rule, covering more than 50 per cent of the total population at that time. This mainly took place with the help of Christian missionaries, which are found in most of the rural areas in the state besides the urban areas. Christianity is predominantly adopted by the Khasis compared to the other two tribal groups (Garos and Jaintias) of Meghalaya (Office of the Registrar General and Census Commissioner, 1992). The first generation converts completely cut themselves off from practising the traditional religion. Many of them were ostracised and rejected by their '*kur*' or 'clan'.

In the traditional Khasi society, the secular and religious leadership combined in the person, namely Syiem, who in association with the Myntries, Lyngskhors, Basans and Lyngdohs held the Khasi durbar at the regional level. The larger body called *Durbar Bima*, or state assembly, reigned supreme in all judicial matters and was known as *Ka Durbar Blei*, the Assembly of God. This system was adversely affected by the establishment of the British Raj. And now, most of the functions of the traditional political organisation are performed by the District Council and the State Government.

Due to the activity of Christian missionaries during the past century and the development of a dynamic native Christian Church, the culture of the Khasis has been radically altered, and thus, the Khasis have accepted "new lives for old." The main difference caused in the society due to the Christian intervention was the spread of education. This helped them to achieve the goal for providing education to those people who are considered to be isolated or backward group. And as education alters human perception, even among the Khasis, it brought about some changes in the traditional set-up. The challenges of Christianity were met by reorganising traditional Khasis and establishing a formal organisation of the indigenous religion, called Seng Khasi.

Seng Khasi

The modern Seng Khasi movement was started as an attempt to safeguard the essence of Khasi culture, religion and customs from the onslaughts of western and Christian influences. The Seng Khasi was established on the 23 of November 1899 and ever since its establishment, the 23 November of every year is celebrated as the *Seng Kut Snem*. It has won recognition as a distinct religion from the International Association for Religious Freedom (IARF) (An NGO with UN consultative status supporting interfaith cooperation).The SengKhasi is "an association or it includes and stands for all Khasis who follow the tenets and principles of Khasi religion wherever they may be" (Khongphai 1979:142). Late Sri Jeebon Roy and Sibacharan Roy were the prominent among the founding leaders of the modern Seng Khasi movement. "The Seng Khasi plays an important role in revitalising the traditional symbols and aesthetic manifestations through ritual idiom. It organises calendrical festivals like *Shad Suk Mynsiem* and the Nongkremdance which involve mass participation and effective realisation of the Khasi's cultural heritage."

Parallelism and Convergence

Christianity as a religion has strong patrilineal bias and cultural concepts. At the same time matriliny and the cultural complex developed around it is the basic feature of the Khasi social organisation. Initially the converts turned away from Khasi culture, creating a rift between the converts and the Khasi Khasis (The Khasis who follows the original Khasi religion). The converts were forced to abandon their traditional religious rites, rituals and even festivals and increasingly observed the Christian way of celebrations and practises. The animistic way of celebrations associated with funeral ceremonies and ancestor worship were abandoned and they started the Christian way of burial. "In the beginning, Christian missionaries spoke against everything native and pagan and, often, one sect spoke against another even during sermons" (Natarajan 1982:154). It was a Khasi lady, Ka Nabon, who first showed much courage to convert herself to Christianity in the year 1848, in spite of the stiff resistance from the traditional Khasis. Angell Jones described graphically the hardships and tortures perpetrated on Nabon by the traditional Khasis (Natarajan 1982). A sense of intolerance was evident not only between traditional Khasis and converts but even between different denominations of Christians both in approach and practise. The cleavage between the Christians and the Khasi Khasis had initially been frequent, and bitter and feelings of hatred were mutual. Upon the death of Ka Nabon in 1857, members of her family wanted to cremate her following the traditional Khasi practise. A quarrel and minor revolt ensued. Ultimately Nabon was buried (Natarajan 1982:157). The missionaries made rules and regulations about the Christian way of life and instructions were given to dissociate with everything native. According to an instance, as reported by Natarajan (1982), a convert of Mowphlang, who married a traditional Khasi girl through Khasi rites, lost his membership of the Church. Converts to Christianity were even reported to have sold their dance costumes or burnt them (Natarajan 1982:157). A traditional Khasi farmer was reported to have insisted that Catholic helping hands on his farm must work on Sundays also. It was reported that even in the early twentieth century, mutual suspicion and avoidance persisted. "Most issues of the journal *U Nongialam Katholic* over 1880-1919 were a proof of the animosity between the two groups. Some Christian missionaries had started journals mainly for propagating the message of the Church while others were started by the Khasi Khasis to express their views which were generally contrary to those of the missionaries. Among these are *U Naugbit Khupor*, *Ka Pateng Kristan*, *U Nougialam Katholik*, *U Lurshai*, etc. *U Khasi Mynta* was a Khasi cultural journal" (Natarajan 1982:154). Early Khasipractises and rituals and became symbols of acceptance by the traditionalists and points of rejection by the converts. It was quite evident that the traditional Khasis objected to the earlier attempts of Christian missionaries to spread Christianity among them both physically and intellectually. The publication of Khasi cultural journals to counter the Christian missionaries' journal was an example of the resistance at the intellectual level, while the Christian missionaries tried to completely alienate the converts from their traditional culture by framing strict code of conduct for them to observe strictly.

After the initial phase of rift and resistance, both the Christian Khasis and the Khasi Khasis began to rethink. The Christian missionaries soon realised that their intolerance towards the converted Khasis following many of the aspects of their traditional religion including strict adherence to matriliny was not attracting more Khasis into their fold. When the missionaries interfered in sacred customs' violation which amounted to a taboo, the rate of conversions declined. For example, when they encouraged inter-*kur* marriages, i.e., marriage within members of the same clan (it is unthinkable to a Khasi), the rate of conversions declined in many villages. This has made them rethink and tolerate certain degrees of aberrations. On the other hand, the children of traditional Khasis were influenced by the western system of education imparted by the Christian missionary institutions, which were opened throughout the Khasi areas especially in and around Shillong. They did not want to close the doors of higher education, opened before them and enjoyed by their Christian counterparts. They also did not want to restrain the fruits of modern health care facilities extended by the Christian missionaries. Both sections of the Khasis were thus confronted with similar problems and compelled to seek solutions. This has ultimately made them to tolerate each other to a certain extent, bridging their initial phase of rift and resistance. The relatively homogenous ethnic base of the Khasi society to which all the Khasis belonged and the absorptive capacity of the Khasi society facilitated the smooth assimilation while retaining their cultural homogeneity. The corporate nature of the early Khasi life helped them to retain their distinct identity as a unit. Even the Christians found it difficult to break away from this bond. The catholic denomination then adopted a cautious approach; they began to show a practical approach and tolerance towards Khasi culture.

Influx of outsiders in large numbers, leading to varied and more inter-ethnic marriages, upsurge in the economy, greater social capillarity, improvements in the prospects of trade, etc., made them rise and adjust to the new ways and methods, yet maintaining continuity; what mattered most was being a Khasi, whether Christian or traditional. Their historic experience of exploitation by the outsiders, who came to their land during different historical periods had inculcated among them a feeling of insecurity and apprehended against internal fights; they realised that these would weaken their social solidarity, creating scope for outsiders to interfere in their affairs more easily. The Khasis became more unified than ever, wanting to combine the old and the new cultural values, and in their search for a collective identity. Knowledge of a wide horizon further awakened an in-group consciousness. The plainsmen were looked upon as strangers. But the Khasi society was tolerant and accepted an outsider when he adopted their way of life. Similarly, the Christians accepted some aspects of the Khasi culture and the traditional Khasis began to emulate the Christians in certain ways, for example the way of living.

The Khasis, both Christians and non-Christians adjusted themselves quickly to the new cultural and economic environment ushered in by Christianity and western style of education. In some affairs the Christian Khasis found it prudent to come to a compromise with their tribal brethren. For instance, the Christian Khasis not only participate but even take a prominent part in the Nongkrem dance festival held at Smith. At the initial stages, any Christian Khasi who attended or participated in the traditional dance was liable to be excommunicated by the denominational Church to which he belonged. The participation of the Christian Khasis in the traditional dances and religious ceremonies is a recent development and is tolerated by the Christians without any stigma. A number of Muslims from different parts of India and abroad also entered into marital relations with the Khasis, which led to the growth of a small section of Muslim Khasis, the members of which are regarded as Muslims in religion but are, for all other purposes, treated as Khasis. The Muslim Khasis mostly born of Muslim fathers and Khasi mothers have fully retained their tribal heritage. The Khasis, both tribal and Christian, are keen on preserving their traditional political institutions and associated religious practises.

Now-a-days there are a number of socio-cultural institutions formed among the Khasis to reinstate the Khasi solidarity, the memberships in which are given to all irrespective of their religious affiliations. For example, the Khasis of Shillong irrespective of their religious association joined hands and formed a number of clan societies for the revitalisation of Khasi heritage. It helped to bring all members of the clan together irrespective of their religious affiliation. In the gatherings of such associations the clan members belonging to different religious groups never show any type of intolerance towards each other; rather they often show some type of kinship bonds. This was not the situation earlier in the initial phase of conversion. Due to the increased communication, social events such as marriages, death ceremonies, etc., brought relatives together, who were otherwise on the polar ends on account of religion. Now-a-days no stigma is attached with a Khasi Khasi marrying a Christian Khasi, though they usually try to avoid it. The Christian Khasis in rural areas are still found following the traditional Khasi cult called *U Thlen* and they also resort to divination during crisis. Many of the first generation Khasis retained some of their old rituals in order to foster the Khasi solidarity. Even though Christianity has made deep inroads into Khasi religion and culture, the Khasis irrespective of their religious faiths continue to maintain a sentimental attachment in following the traditional customary practices and matrilineal systems. It is this sentimental attachment to their traditional culture that unites them to identify as a group irrespective of the peripheral differences in the religious identities.

Conclusion

The Khasis have been a tradition-bound society, which often persuaded its members to cling to their age old customs and traditions by enforcing various kinds of sanctions on deviants. In a close-knit society no one can live as a social isolate and hence they observe the traditional norms and values as strictly as possible. It is this deep-rooted sentiment of the Khasi society towards their tradition and culture, together with the Christian missionaries' rigid attitude that the converts should give up everything native, that resulted in the initial rift between the converts and the Khasi Khasis. But the Christian missionaries soon realised that their rigid attitude distanced a major section of the Khasis from embracing Christianity. This has made them rethink and tolerate certain degrees of aberrations. While earlier a convert had to abandon the traditional customs, now-a-days Christians more pragmatically seek to blend into local cultures. The traditional Khasis, on the other hand, were attracted by the economic liberties and the facilities for modern health care and higher education created by the missionaries. Gradually both the sides restrained themselves from direct confrontation and compromised on certain respects. It can be seen that though a considerable section of the Khasis embraced Christianity, and it brought considerable changes in the socio-religious and economic life of the Khasis, they still follow the matrilineal system of descent and inheritance pattern. The close link of matrilineal system with their traditional social life and culture helped them tolerate each other in spite of religious differences.

References

Gourdon, P.R.T. 1975 (Reprint). *The Khasis*. Delhi. Cosmos Publications.

Gassah. Ed. 1997. *The Autonomous District Councils*. New Delhi: Cosmo Publications.

Khongphai. 1979. "Seng Khasi", B.B. Goswami. Ed. "Cultural Profile of Shillong". Calcutta. Anthropological Survey of India.

Mathur, P.R.G. 1979. *The Khasis of Meghalaya*. New Delhi. Cosmo Publications.

Natarajan, N. 1982. "Cultural Revivalism among the Christian Khasis of Meghalaya" in *Tribal Movements in India*. Ed. By Singh K.S. New Delhi. Manohar Publications.

Sasi Kumar M., 2005. *Matriliny and Masculinity among the Khasis : A Study in Retrospect and Prospect*. Unpublished Report.

9

The Idea of Health: Medical Pluralism and Management of Treatment Among the Jenu Kurubas of Karnataka

B.R. Vijayendra

General Introduction

The relationship between Anthropology, Medicine and medical practise goes back a long way and is well documented (Comelles and Martínez, 1993). A large number of contributors to the 20 century Medical Anthropology had their primary training in medicine, nursing, psychology or psychiatry, including W.H.R. Rivers, Abram Kardiner, Robert I. Levy, Jean Benoist, Gonzalo Aguirre Beltrán and Arthur Klein Man. Some of them share clinical and anthropological roles. Others are from Anthropology or Social Sciences, like George Foster, William Caudill, Byron Good, Gilles Bibeau, Luis Mallart, Andres, Gilbert Lewis, Ronald Frankenberg and Eduardo Menéndez. A recent book by Saillant and Genest (General references), describes a large international panorama of the development of Medical Anthropology, along with some of the actual main theoretical and intellectual debates. Much of the 20 century concept of popular medicine or folk medicine is familiar to both doctors as well as anthropologists. Doctors, anthropologists and medical anthropologists used these terms to describe the resources, other than the help of health professionals.

The major goal of Medical Anthropology in the latter half of the 20 century was to document and describe the various medical systems of the non-western world. But towards the end of the 20 century, a few medical anthropologists focused on some critical issues such as access to various medical systems. Since the colonial and industrial era began, political economy became a crucial component of health care because illness, disease and treatment occur within the context of the capitalist world. This critical perspective has been mainly drawn from the writings of Karl Marx, Engels, Mills, etc. According to this view, ideologies and patterns of health care are shaped by forces outside the field of medicine. The critical approach defines health as follows: "access to and control over the basic material and non-material resources that sustain and promote life at a high level of satisfaction (Baer *et al.*, 1986). Medical system is an integral part of any cultural system. It consists of beliefs and practises consciously directed at promoting health and alleviating disease. Every medical system mainly includes three major components, viz. conceptions of health, etiology of illness or disease and treatment. In complex societies, more than one medical system generally co-exists. Hence, persons suffering from illness or disease can make choices among the medical systems.

Introduction of the Tribe

The Jenu Kuruba are a Scheduled Tribe community inhabiting the southern districts of Karnataka. The Ministry of Home Affairs, Government of India, identified the community as a Primitive Tribal Group (PTG) in 1977, as the members of this community subsist mainly on hunting and gathering. According to the Census of 1981, the population of Jenu Kurubas was 34,747 out of which 17,867 were males and 16,880 were females. They are distributed mainly in H.D. Kote, Hunsur and Periyapatna, taluks of Mysore District, Gundlupet Taluk of Chamarajanagara District and in Virajpet, Somavarpet and Madikeritaluks of Kodagu District. The Jenu Kuruba settlements (haadis) are concentrated in and around forest areas. About 5,000 people continue to live in the Rajiv Gandhi National Park, even after rehabilitation of the residing tribals. They speak Jenunudi, a dialect of Kannada. They also use standard Kannada, when they communicate with others.

The Nagarahole game sanctuary, the traditional habitat of the Jenu Kurubas, was declared as a National Park on 1st April 1983 (and later renamed as Rajiv Gandhi National Park in 1992). The park comes under the control of the Forest Department, Government of Karnataka, and as per the rules of the wildlife sanctuary, human beings are not permitted to reside within the park. However, about 1,000 tribal families (most of them Jenu Kurubas) still reside inside the National Park. Since 1999, tribal families are being shifted to rehabilitation centres just outside the National Park. The first batch of 50 families volunteered to shift in 1995 to Nagapura rehabilitation centre. At present, there are 250 families in the centre; and a majority of them are Jenu Kurubas.

Area of Study

The present study was conducted in a modem Jenu Kuruba settlement known as Basavige (pseudo name), situated 24 km from Hunsur, the taluk headquarters. The place is 72 km from Mysore, the district headquarters. There are 66 Jenu Kuruba families living in this new settlement, which was established about 20 years ago. Their total population is 331 (171 males and 160 females), and the literacy rate is about 50%. However, all the literates had only a few years of school education.

The settlement is about 1 km away from the road, which connects the place to the taluk and district headquarters. The settlement is outside the National Park. Out of the 66 houses, 65 have tiled roofs and the remaining one house has a thatched roof. The Lakshmana Theertha River (a tributary of Cauvery) flows about half a kilometer away from the settlement. The river is the main source of water for drinking, washing, cooking, bathing, etc. The settlement also has five bore wells with hand-pumps, out of which only one was found to be in working condition during the field work. The village is electrified and 25 houses have electrical connections. One ashram school is situated in the settlement. One Primary Health Unit is situated about 3 km away from the settlement.

Ethno-Medicine

Anthropologists have been involved in the study of ethno-medical systems since the last quarter of 19 century. Tylor, Saligman and Frazer have described healing, shamanism, witchcraft, magic, etc., and related them to the concept of illness in preliterate societies. In the early part of the 20 century, Rivers, Ackernecht and Clements provided elaborate descriptions and analyses of ethno-medical systems. Leslie and Dunn discussed ethno-medical systems in a comparative perspective during the second half of the 20 century and encouraged scholars to undertake ethno-medical studies in different continents. Earlier studies of ethno-medicine focused more on mentalistic aspects of illness and virtually neglected the biological components, as pointed out by Horacio Fabrega (1974:40). Hence, the ethno-medical studies did not have much impact on cosmopolitan medicine. A major contribution of the mentalistic perspective was broadening the horizon of Western Psychiatric categories.

The term ethno-medicine is generally applied to the study of traditional medical systems of the non-western societies (Foster and Anderson 1978:51). Later, the meaning of the term was broadened to include all medical systems, including biomedicine, viewed within the framework of their respective cultures (Lock and Scheper Hughes, 1990: 47-72; Rhodes, 1990:159-173). Fabrega applied the term more broadly to include all "culturally oriented studies of illness" (1974:39-43).

In this study an attempt is made to provide a broad outline of the traditional health beliefs and practises of a tribal community.

The Jenu Kurubas

The Jenu Kurubas prefer to be lean and medium or short statured, and such persons are considered strong and healthy. This type of body build enables them to work hard and run faster to avoid the attacks of wild animals. Such persons are also considered to be more intelligent.

The Jenu Kurubas do not have elaborate knowledge about the internal structure of the body. They believe that food goes to the liver and is converted into blood. Red blood is considered as a sign of the healthy body, usually a characteristic feature of young people. It is said that as the person grows old, red blood turns to blackish red and the quantity of blood decreases, thereby indicating lesser strength and decreased health status. Since the Jenu Kurubas' traditional habitat is forest, this environment seems to have influenced certain health beliefs of the people. Sitting in front of the fire, especially during the rainy and winter seasons, is a common sight in the Jenu Kuruba settlement. They believe that this practise, in addition to providing warmth, increases the thickness of blood and decreases the fatness of the body. An individual's good health and activity is also linked to the thickness of blood. Youngsters are believed to have thin blood, which flows fast in the body and makes the individual healthy and active, whereas the aged people are believed to possess thick and blackish-red blood, which makes them less healthy and active.

An ill person is easily identified by his indifferent behaviour, dull face and non-participation in routine work. Usually all members of the family go for routine work and only elderly persons remain in the settlement. Hence, the diseased person prefers to take rest in the *haadi* (settlement). Each person in the *haadi* tries to give his opinion regarding treatment and it becomes a topic for discussion for the day. The ill person keeps all the views in mind and waits for one or two days. If the illness does not come down, then he chooses one among the several suggestions given by his people; and if the condition still persists, then he approaches a diviner to find out the cause.

The Jenu Kurubas, whose traditional occupation is honey collection and hunting in the wild forest, believe in greater body movement. They do not sit idle even for a moment in one place. They think that body movement is required for proper blood circulation, which in turn promotes good health. Circulation of blood is believed to stop while one is in sleep. Weakness and illness are attributed to decrease in the quantity of blood.

The Jenu Kurubas consider honey, a variety of yams and green leafy vegetables available in the forest as healthy food items. Of late, *ragi* (a type of millet) is also considered as a good food item. Worship of several deities in the forest is also considered necessary to keep one's health in good condition. The Jenu Kurubas are very suspicious in nature due to their strong belief in sorcery. They hesitate to eat food in the houses of their neighbours and even kinsmen. In any case of illness sorcery is suspected.

Classification of Illness

The illnesses identified by the Jenu Kurubas may be classified into four categories on the basis of etiological factors, viz. body-linked illnesses (*shariladakayile*), deity-linked illnesses (*daivadakayile*), spirit-linked illnesses (*galiyetu*) and sorcery-linked illnesses (*matadakayile*).

The causative factors for body-linked illnesses are defective diet, bad water, worm infestation and other environmental conditions. Illnesses linked to this causative factor roughly include stomach-ache, cough, cold, headache, giddiness, dysentery, body itching, fever, eczema, scabies, etc. Naturalistic causative factors are mainly linked to diet and the qualities of various food items. Food items are classified into hot, cold, *vayu* (air), *paithale* (bile) and *thonte* (phlegm). Consumption of food items is made on the basis of their qualities in terms of the above-mentioned categories. Persons also inherit these qualities since birth, and proper matching of these qualities are made before consumption. This is a clear case of interaction between the 'little' and 'great' health traditions in the Indian subcontinent. Ayurvedic concepts and practises have been in constant contact with the local cultural traditions in the historical period.

Several illnesses are also linked to the pantheon of the Jenu Kurubas. The female deity Maramma is worshipped every year by all the residents by sacrificing fowls. Failure to perform this ceremony is believed to cause measles, chicken pox and small pox. If a person suddenly falls sick or a sick person does not respond to other types of treatment, it is suspected that the cause of the illness is a deity. Family deities are also worshipped at the family level. The authors have recorded 12 family deities in the Basavige settlement.

Another common causative factor of illnesses is the spirits of the dead. The spirit of any dead person residing in the habitation area may cause illness to a person of the opposite sex who passes through that area, especially in the evening or at night. Any physical symptom or illness is generally attributed to a spirit, if it does not respond to other forms of therapy. If the spirit is that of an ancestor or ancestress, they are addressed by using kin terms such as grandfather or grandmother.

The last but important cause of illness is sorcery (*mala*). Sorcerers among the Jenu Kurubas employ different techniques to cause illness to the victims. Some of the common techniques are as follows:

1. The sorcerer puts spell-cast thorns and glass pieces inside a lemon and calls the name of the victim. The lemon is then buried on the path of the victim. If the victim passes through the path he will suffer from acute pain, swelling of a body part and ultimately loses that body part. This type of sorcery is known as *datu (i.e.,* crossing).
2. Another type of sorcery known as *chilluhodevuvudu.* The sorcerer inserts certain objects such as seeds, frogs or ants into the body of the victim. The victim experiences the movement of the object inside his body. The victim becomes restless and cannot perform his daily activities and can't even sleep at night.
3. Poisoning (*madduhakuvudu*) is another form of sorcery. A poisonous substance is put into coffee, tea or some liquid food and is offered to the victim. The victim becomes weak and looses appetite. The victim's stomach may swell and work-efficiency may reduce. He also develops vomiting sensation at the sight of the food or drink through which the poison was administered.
4. In yet another method, the sorcerer buries a spell-cast hen's head covered in a coconut shell in a pit dug near the victim's house. Due to the ill-effects of this sorcery, the entire family suffers from sickness.
5. The sorcerer sometimes may cast a spell on a plant in the name of a victim. This plant is supposed to dry and die within a

specified period. In a similar way, the victim is also believed to suffer from weakness and die, coinciding with the death of the plant. Sorcerers may also cast evil spells on any part or object which once belonged to or is in contact with victim such as spittle, urine, faeces, hair, foot dust, menstrual clothes, clothes used during the delivery of a child, etc. The Jenu Kurubas avoid urinating, defecating or spitting in the presence of other people in order to avoid the evil effects of sorcery.

The belief in the evil eye is also strong among Jenu Kurubas. Some individuals in the society are identified as having this quality.

Diagnosis of Illness

There are mainly five types of diagnostic procedures among the Jenu Kurubas, viz. *bundekarevuvudu (summoning* their deity by the diviner), *allushastra (cowrie* shell method), *kayileguruthu (*diagnosis based on physical signs and symptoms), *peedekadevuvudu (spirit* exorcism) and *kempuneeru (red* water method).

Divining is considered as the perfect method of diagnosis for most illnesses. A diviner does this. There are six diviners in Basavige. All of them are part-time specialists. The patient and his family members visit the house of the diviner with a coconut, incense sticks, millets, areca nuts, betel leaves, bananas, etc. These materials are used by the diviner to worship the tutelary deity, who guides the diviner in the diagnostic session. The diviner chants a verse known as *bundepada* and is possessed by the deity. At this time, the patient and his family members pose several questions regarding the identity and cause of the illness and the appropriate method of treatment to be followed. There is no fixed payment in cash for the services of the diviner.

In the second method of diagnosis, the expert (*allupanditha*) throws a few cowrie shells on the mat, and looking at the number and position of the shells (dorsal or ventral) decides the cause of illness. The diviner actually thinks about a particular cause and then throws the cowrie shells. He repeats the same act five times and if he gets an even number of ventral positions up, the cause of the illness is confirmed. He repeats it again thinking about the actual cause. This procedure sometimes may take hours. The expert relies on the blessings of his tutelary deity for his success.

The third method is symptomatic diagnosis. The specialists who rely on this method are herbalists. Internal and external symptoms are considered in diagnosing an illness. The internal signs are pain, burning sensation, loss of taste, thirst, loss of appetite, and movement of an ant or frog inside the body. The common external symptoms are swelling, colour of eyes/urine, etc., wounds, blisters, vomiting, coughing, patches on the skin, itching, facial expression, etc. The herbalist examines these symptoms in association with each other and arrives at a diagnosis. The herbalist is known as *maddukoduvavaru (medicine* giver). They are part-time practitioners, and their knowledge is generally passed down the family line. The herbalists collect their medicines alone on auspicious days like Sundays, Thursday and new-moon days. There is no fixed payment for the services of the herbalist.

Identification of the spirit is another form of diagnostic procedure. The exorcists are known as *peedekadeyuvavaru.* This specialisation is also generally passed down the family line. The exorcist is consulted on Sundays and Tuesdays to identify the spirit and expel it. Three types of spirits (*gali*) are identified by the commoners as well as the exorcists. They are *sannagali (*small spirit), *doddagali (*big spirit) and *valadagali.* The *Sannagali*is the spirit of an individual who dies without fulfilling his desires. It can be driven out after satisfying his desires. Generally, these spirits ask for a particular type of food.

Doddagali refers to the spirits of individuals who had unnatural death like suicide, accident or murder. The spirits of the dead bodies, which did not undergo proper death rituals, also belong to this category. The third category of spirits is those of psychotic patients who met with unnatural deaths. The exorcists find it difficult to expel the third category of spirits since they do not obey the orders of the exorcist.

The last method of diagnosis known as *kempuneeru (*reddish water) is used to diagnose a culture-specific illness called *soku.* This illness generally affects children. An elderly woman does this diagnosis by putting turmeric and lime on water contained in a small plate. The plate is waved in front of the patient and a piece of burning charcoal is put on it. If the water turns red, the illness is confirmed as *soku.* Children generally suffer from *soku.* This is marked by symptoms such as crying, restlessness and refusal to eat food or drink breast milk.

Treatment of Illnesses

The pattern of treatment given by the Jenu Kurubas can be categorised into two types, viz. magico-religious and herbal. Magico-religious treatment is opted when the cause of illness is attributed to some "personalistic agents" (Foster, 1978) such as sorcerers, spirits or supernatural deities like Maramma. The healing rituals are performed either by the family members (as in the case of *soku*) or by the specialists such as spirit exorcists (as in the case of *peede*) or by the sorcerers (as in the case of *datu*).

The Jenu Kurubas have a rich heritage of herbal medicines. Herbal treatment is opted when the cause of the illness is identified as a natural substance or phenomena. Certain foods are restricted for the patients during the treatment. The herbalists claim that they can cure most of the illnesses except cancer, cholera, tuberculosis and diarrhea. Herbal medicines are used to treat headache, dysentery, sores on body parts, stomach ache, snake-bite, scorpion-sting, measles, eczema, body swelling, tooth ache, migraine, mouth sores, sprain, asthma, etc.

Conclusion

Ethno-medicines have to be interpreted in both biological and behavioural frameworks, as both have substantial impact. The use of plant or material medicine may be found to influence the human physiology. Diet and medicines are not strictly separated in the Jenu Kurubas' ethno-medicine. Diet may be a medicine, or vice-versa at different contexts and times. Laboratory analysis is required to assess the impact of various medicines on the human body. Pharmacologic interpretations of the *materia medica* will advance the knowledge of ethno-medicine of the Jenu Kurubas.

The behavioural interpretations of ethno-medicine show that the Jenu Kuruba society and culture have a unique theme of socio-cultural integration. This theme revolves around suspicion and distrust. The traditional ecological and economic conditions of the tribe promoted this kind of integration of the society. The Jenu Kurubas who lived in the dense forest always struggled for their livelihood, which includes collection of honey and various kinds of tubers, leaves and animals. The struggle for the limited resources made them suspect each other. The scarce and difficult conditions of forest life seem to have contributed to the development of ideas related to sorcery and other magical practises. The Jenu Kuruba ethno-medicine (a little tradition) is also linked to the Ayurvedic tradition (a great tradition) as illustrated in these concepts of three humours.

References

Dhar, U., Manjkhola, S., Joshi, M., Bhatt, A. and Joshi, M. *Current Science*, Vol. 92, No. 12, 25 June 2007, and 2002, 83, 956-964.

Foster, G.M. and B.G. Anderson, 1978. *Medical Anthropology*, New York. Wiley.

Iyer, L.K.A. (reprint 1988). *The Mysore Tribes and Castes*, Vol. IV, Delhi. Mittal Publications.

Lock, M. and N. Scheper Hughes 1990. "A Critical-Interpretive Approach to Medical Anthropology: Rituals and Routines of Discipline and Dissent" in T.M. Johnson and C.F. Sargent, (Ed.), Medical *Anthropology: Contemporary Theory and Method.* New York. Praeger.

Luiz, A.A.D. 1963. Tribes of Mysore, 180-186, Bangalore: Govt. Press.

Misra, P.K. 1969. "The Jenu Kuruba", *Bulletin Anthropological Survey of India*, Calcutta.

Ruebel, A.I. and M.R. Hass 1990. "Ethno medicine" in T.M. Johnson and C.F. Sargent. (Ed.). *Medical Anthropology: Contemporary Theory and Method*, New York. Praeger.

Vijayendra, B.R. 1997. "Ethno Medical Study among the Selected Tribal Communities of Southern Karnataka", Unpublished Ph.D. thesis submitted to University of Mysore.

Rhodes, L.A. 1990. "Studying Biomedicine as a Cultural System" in T.M. Johnson and C.F. Sargent, (Ed.) *Medical Anthropology: Contemporary Theory and Method.* New York: Praeger.

World Health Organisation, "Traditional Medicine Strategy", 2002–2005.

10

Disease and Health Care Among the Kamar Tribe : Ecological and Demographic Perspectives

Nilanjan Khatua

Medical anthropologists distinguish between illness and disease and these two concepts are again distinguished from sickness. Illness is viewed as the subjective experience of the patient and immediate members of his family, friends and neighbours. This is an emic perspective of the reality. Disease, on the other hand, is an etic perspective which refers the clinical manifestation of abnormality of physical function or infection by a pathogen in an individual or host. Arthur Kleinman uses a generic term "sickness" to include both illness and disease. The disease is considered a biological phenomenon, while illness includes psychological and social dimensions as well.

The distinction between disease and illness begs the question what is "health", a concept that is notoriously difficult to define. Health is the most precious possessions of human beings. It is the solid foundation on which man's happiness rests. According to Carter from the WHO (1948), "Health is a state of complete physical, mental and social well-being and not merely an absence of disease or infirmity." The ecological approach in Medical Anthropology focuses on how human cultural and behavioural patterns shape the complex interactions of the pathogen, the environment, and the human host, and produce both infectious and non-infectious diseases. (Inhornand Brown, 1997).

In the context of the tribes of India, health problems need special attention. This is because many tribal communities live in isolated and inaccessible areas where modern health care facilities are not available. Besides, the health problem of the tribal communities is not an isolated phenomenon, but part of a national problem among the weaker sections. Like other disciplines such as Sociology, Geography and Economics, Demography is also closely linked with Anthropology. The relationship is so close that in the Oxford Dictionary (1955), it is defined as" Demography is a part of Anthropology which treats the statistics of the birth, deaths and diseases, etc." Both subjects are concerned with the study of inbreeding, assortative mating and breeding, mutations and gene flow.

The present paper deals with the concept of health, disease pattern and factors associated with causes of disease and health care, prevalent among the primitive tribal community, namely the Kamar Tribe of Chhattisgarh. The demographic information has been collected through structured schedules from 188 households of the Kamar Tribe during 1997 and 1998. The present paper is based on a fieldwork carried out in seven villages of Gariaband Block in Raipur District, Chhattisgarh. Out of total population, 421 are male and 458 are female; and 278 individuals (31.63%) are literate. Previously, the Kamars were engaged in shifting cultivation. However, they do not practise shifting cultivation now as it is prohibited by the Government. Basketry and selling of minor forest produce are their everlasting economic activities. Agriculture, and agricultural and forest labour sustain the Kamar economy to a great extent. Data have been collected by cross-checking, using the same questions for several informants. It was observed that the tribal people are trying to explain their culture in terms of the culture of their neighbouring dominant community. To avoid such circumstances, interviews were conducted with informants from isolated villages as well as from the villages which are more exposed.

Fieldwork was carried out in two phases for about six months. The household census and couple of information have invariably been obtained from the head of the households; even married women were personally interviewed about their reproductive life, viz. the number, age and sex of the children : dead or surviving, and abortion and still birth, if any. Care was taken to record proper ages of the young as well as the old; in the latter case, age was estimated with the help of past local events of importance and by comparison. For the reproductive life of women, a sample of 100 married women from each tribe was considered for the present study, which represents women from all the villages studied. The ages were cross checked from the information of marriage duration, age at marriage, gap between age at marriage and first child maternity. The ages of children were taken sometimes from school and physical examination from the various phases and special events in their lives : the eruption and exfoliation of deciduous teeth, eruption of permanent teeth, onset of menstruation cycle, and whether they have started to work outside the house, such as rearing of animals, ploughing, harvesting, etc.

The People and Ecological Settings

The Kamar is the dominant Scheduled Tribe in Raipur District. Some of their major tribes are Binjhwar, Gonds, Kawars, Halwa, etc. The total population of Kamars in Raipur is 14,922 as per the survey in 1995 by the Kamar Development Agency, Gariaband, Raipur. According to the Census of 1981, the total population of the Kamarswas 17,517 in Madhya Pradesh and 5,939 in Maharashtra.

Raipur District is divided into two major physical divisions, viz. the Chhattisgarh plain and the hilly areas. To the east of the Chhattisgarh plain, the hilly areas cover the southern part of Dhamtari Tahsil, the south-eastern part of Baloda Bazar Tahsil, and the bulk of Mahasamund and Bindranawagarh (now Gariaband) Tahsils. The Mahanadi and its important tributaries like the Pairi, Seonath and Jonk are in Raipur District. The principle hills are Gauragarh, Milcowa, Doratti, Deodonga, Atang, Kanda and Shringi. Of these, Gouragarh is the longest plateau which runs length-wise on the western border of Gariaband Tahsil. There are some Kamar villages on these plateaus, which are difficult to reach and deserve special treatment for development. Gariaband Block covers an area of about 660.73 sq km. The area under forest is 372.86 sq km, i.e., nearly 40% of the Kamar area is under forest. The area is mostly undulated and hilly, and rich in flora and fauna. In the past, the Kamar habitat was full of wild carnivorous and herbivorous animals : tiger, sambhar, cheetal, deer and wild bear are still present in the forest though their numbers are reduced. The climate of the area is temperate. Winter is generally cool and the summer is considerably hot. About 90% of the annual rainfall is received during the monsoon. The mean maximum temperature in May is 41.9°C. The relative humidity is high (75%) during the south-west monsoon season.

Concept of Health and Disease

To the Kamars, when a man is able to do work s/he possesses good health. It is their common belief that if one drinks cold water after leaving bed in the early morning his/her health remains sound and s/he feels less thirsty for the whole day. Generally, the Kamars relate their health status with age. In young age, the blood is warm and red in colour. This warm blood is full of strength and thus the young possess good health. As one grows older, then s/he has to face many health problems like joint-pains, constipation, loss of hearing, loss of eye sight, etc. During illness one loses energy to work and feels pain in the body. According to them, "*Bimarmekamkarebarichchhanehihote, god-hath pirathekhunkamjor ho jathe, is liyekhunkojanchkaranapadthe*" : disease occurs when one's blood becomes weak and that is why, the blood is sent for pathological test.

During conversation regarding health concept, one cited that when it is necessary to walk in the mid-day sun, then hot boiled rice with *pasia (left* over water after boiling rice) is a must for anybody. As a consequence of this type of precaution one remains safe from sunstroke. Further, Naleshram of Bamhni Village opined that un-boiled egg and honey makes a man healthy if he takes it in the morning on an empty stomach continuously for one month.

Causes for Illness

According to the Kamars, the causes for illness are classified into the various categories: wrath of deities, spirit intrusion, magical practises, wrong or less nutritive food, and environmental effects.

Wrath of Deities

Among the Kamars certain illnesses are thought to be due to the wrath of deities. Illnesses like vomiting with loose motions, stomach ache, unwillingness to take food for a period of two and half days, occur when particular deities are dissatisfied. This is also known as *mataathe* or *devtadhamidharlethe.* According to them, these diseases are not curable by modern medicine or herbal medicine given by their own village medicine man. Instead, the Kamars worship different Goddesses who are all generically called *Mata* to avoid such illnesses. For example, *Mai* is the goddess of small pox, and *Devi* is the goddess of cholera. *Thakurdeo, Dulhadeo* and *Mahadeo* are also worshipped by the Kamars, who are believed to save them from the disastrous effects caused by malevolent spirits.

Spirit Intrusion

Besides the deities, some evil spirits cause similar afflictions on the people. If one is affected by evil spirit (*buraatma*) he is surely attacked with continuous fever. Illness such as chest pain, and clumsiness for a period of two or more days, are common due to intrusion of evil spirit.

Magical Practises

In this category, illness is believed to be caused by human beings who practise black magic. This category is sub-divided according to the type of causative agent recognised by the Kamars, which include witches, evil mouth and evil eye.

Witches

A Witch is a female who has magical powers to do evil. A female becomes a witch *(tonhi)* after possessing some magical powers given by her Guru. Only the *baiga* can undo their evils. Dube mentioned, "Witchcraft originally belongs to *Savara*, *Dhobi*, *Chamar*, *Lohar* and *Kewat* women. A witch from one of these tribes/castes may initiate a Kamar woman into the mysteries of witchcraft. Very few Kamar women have this evil reputation. Constant efforts of the Kamar *Baigas* save the tribe from the mischief of witches belonging to other tribes and castes.

Evil Mouth

The practise of sorcery (*jadutona*) is common amongst the Kamars. Sorceresses are those who are believed to practise magic with the help of evil spirits. They cause evils by casting some spells on a person. To cause harm by casting magical spells in the Kamar society is known as *Ban Marna.*

- ***(a) Dhur-ban***: *Tonhi* is responsible for this type of evils. She casts magical spell on dust or a stone and throws it on the person whom she wants to harm; or these charmed objects are kept beside the door or the house of the intended victim. When the person crosses this place the magical power goes inside the body through his leg, causing unbearable pain.
- ***(b) Kosa-ban***: If a boil develops in one's body, the Kamars believe that s/he is affected by *Kosa-ban. They* believe that some harmful object through some magical power is leading to an elevation in the body.
- ***(c) Garva-ban***: Sterility among women is believed to be caused due to the intrusion of magical spell by a sorceress. This is also responsible for unbearable pain in the neck and stomach.
- ***(d) Raksa-ban***: The effect of *Raksa-ban*is so ferocious that all the members of a family die one by one. The sorceress with the help of evil spirits casts spell on the person whom she hates. The *Baiga* can hardly save the life of the affected family members

unless the whole family shifts to another village, as they believe that a sorceress's evil effect is confined to a particular area/ territory.

Evil Eye

It is believed that the eyes of the sorceresses are so powerful that as soon as she looks at any person, s/he feels some sort of trouble. The evil eye is so effective that food is not properly digested in one's stomach and s/he will usually suffer from loose motions and stomach pain. Somaru Ram Kamar said that white cowries and white bangles prevent the bad effects of evil eye and evil mouth. So their children are made to wear white bangles; they also wear stringed white cowries around the neck or waist.

Wrong and Less Nutritive Food

According to the Kamars, if one consumes excess food then s/he will surely be out of order. If one takes nutritious food with vitamins, nothing will be wrong with health. If one takes food frequently and if this food is not properly digested then there is a chance to store air in stomach, as a result stomachache occurs. Consumption of vegetables like pumpkin, (*Cucurbita maxima*), bottle gourd (*Langenria vulgaris*), and *kundru* (*Cocciniacordifolia*) leads to diseases like malaria. Salty food is easily digestible and so good for health; whereas sweet dishes make a man clumsy and inactive. Foods with bitter taste, like neem (*Azardirachtaindica*) and *karela* (*Momordicacharantia)* are also good for health and act as a medicine. They believe that persons, who eat more bitter foods, are hardly affected by snake-bites.

Environmental Effects

Environmental effect is one of the causes of illness among the Kamars. Certain illnesses are "hot" illnesses and are believed to be a result of over-exposure to sun or from ingesting "hot" foods or beverages. Heat strokes occur due to excessive heat of the sun. This type of illness is treated by the ingestion of "cold" foods or by "hot treatment", such as drinking of hot boiled rice water (*pasia*) before getting exposed to the sunlight. Both pregnancy and menstruation are considered to be "hot" states, so women are not allowed to consume mahua (*Bassialatifolia*)liquor during these periods.

Local Name	*English Version*
Telgi	Pneumonia
Ulti-tatti	Diarrhea
Bukhar	Fever
Khunki kami	Anaemia
Pet me kida	Worm infection
Malaria	Malaria
Khujli	Skin disease
T.B.	Tuberculosis
Mattijhir	Typhoid
Sudki	Rickets
Yaj	Yaws

Common Childhood Diseases

It has been rightly said that the diseases responsible for the heavy mortality rate among children living in the tropics are preventable. In many countries of the western world, where similar mortality occurred not so very long ago, these diseases have been eradicated. Hospital records show that the commonest causes of death among children in the tropics are malnutrition, gastro-enteritis and respiratory infection. Of these, protein-caloric malnutrition is the most widespread; by lowering the body's resistance, this not only facilitates infection, but also allows the infection to spread unchecked and become severe, resulting in early death. Thus, malnourished children easily become gravely ill and do not respond well to treatment. Besides the above-mentioned three main causes of death, the other common causes of death are malaria, anaemia, tuberculosis, infectious childhood diseases, such as measles and whooping cough, hookworm and other parasitic infestations, and accidents, mainly burns (Ebrahim, 1991).

The common health problems found among the children of Kamars are respiratory infections, pneumonia, common cough and cold, loose motions, worm infection, stomach ache, typhoid, malnutrition, etc. These common illnesses of children are usually diagnosed and treated quickly.

Respiratory infections : These constitute more than half of all acute episodes of illness during childhood. Many are viral infections, which are usually self-limiting in a well-nourished child. Bacterial infections occur if there is overcrowding at home. These can result in bronchopneumonia. Most such infections respond to modern medical treatments. Sometimes, it is also observed that they try to make a scar around the belly with the help of a hot iron sickle (the pointed part), as they believe that stomach pain can be checked by applying pain : they apply the isopathy method of treatment, i.e., curing pain by applying pain.

Worm infection: Hookworm and other parasitic infestations are common among the Kamar children. This problem is more common among children aged between 3-4 months to 1 year. Generally, the yolk from the hen's egg, when applied on the head of a newborn baby, is believed to destroy the worms in the belly.

Loose motions: The mother of a newborn baby observes certain restrictions in diet up to 6-7 months of childbirth. It is believed that any irregularities in the mother's diet will have effect on the child's health. If the mother eats new rice, and vegetables like bottle gourd, pumpkin, and *kundru*, there is a chance that the child will suffer from loose motions. As a remedy, the mother applies yolk from a hen's egg on her baby's head.

Stomach ache: This is common among the children of all ages. Home remedies are prescribed with hot baking. A commonly used home remedy is mustard oil boiled with camphor, which is then cooled and rubbed on the belly. And then to make the body warm, the mother puts a warm cloth on the body of the child.

Diarrhea: Dehydration, due to loss of water and electrolytes from the body during diarrhea causes many deaths among children. A recent research has demonstrated that in such children, rehydration is possible through the oral route, especially when a solution containing glucose (sugar) and electrolytes is used. Glucose stimulates the mechanism in the gut epithelium for rapid absorption of water and salt. The efficacy of a solution containing 20 gm of glucose, 3.5 gm of sodium chloride, 2.5 gm of sodium bicarbonate and 1.5 gm of potassium chloride in one litre of water has been demonstrated in all forms of mild/moderate dehydration, including cases of cholera. Experience in many clinics has shown that the use of such oral electrolyte solutions has reduced mortality from diarrhea and has cut down the number of referrals to hospitals for intravenous infusions (Ebrahim, 1991). It was observed that a newborn baby is not allowed to drink water upto 8 or 9 months. This may be one of the causes of dehydration, which leads to diarrhea among the Kamar children.

Malnutrition: The health status of the people depends mostly on their nutritional status. Food is the primary requisite of life and the quantity and quality of food consumed by the people determines their nutritional status (Gopal, 1987). On the basis of caloric intake, it is noticed that most of the Kamar population is affected by malnutrition. This is due to fact that most of them belong to the low-income groups. Malnutrition and poverty are concomitant to each other and have been the hallmark of the Indian population during the last several centuries. The local doctors admit that malnutrition also affects the health of children and women.

Malaria: Malaria is one of the major causes of child mortality among the Kamars. Malaria is a disease caused by protozoa of the genus plasmodium. Nearly 120 species of plasmodium exist of which 22 species are found in primates. Only four species of plasmodium, viz. P. *malaria*, *P. vivax*, *P.falciparum* and *P. Ovale* inflict human beings. Malaria is characterised by fever, anemia, headache, body ache, splenomegaly and a wide variety of other anomalies. The definite host of this parasite is the mosquito in which sexual development takes place.

Some host factors that provoke the prevalence of malaria:

1. Ill-ventilated and ill-lighted houses of tribals provide ideal indoor resting places for mosquitoes.
2. Habits of sleeping in the verandah increases man-vector contact.
3. Factors such as accumulation of sewage water, lack of drainage, the habitation site, cattle sheds being attached to their main house, etc., influence the spread of malaria.

Environmental Factors : Heavy rain generally provides opportunity for the breeding of mosquitoes. "Rain increases the humidity which does not have any effect on parasites (plasmodium) but is necessary for the survival of the mosquitoes. Generally 60% humidity is suitable for the longevity for the voracious feeding of the mosquitoes" (Pandey, 1999). Lesser rain also provides opportunities for the spread of mosquitoes, as it leads to the formation of small pools of water in forest places, which serve as active breeding places for the vector.

Causes of Child Mortality						
Cause of Death	*Hill Korwas*		*Kamars*		*Baigas*	
	No.	**%**	**No.**	**%**	**No.**	**%**
Fever	43	39.45	5	6.25	28	26.17
Diarrhea	7	6.42	7	8.75	15	14.03
Fever with body swelling	3	2.75	1	1.25	10	9.34
Asthma	3	2.75	0	4 3.74	0	0
Pneumonia (*Telgi*)	0	32	40.00	0	0	0
Gastro-enteritis	1	0.92	0	0	0	0
Rickets (due to malnutrition)	3	2.75	4	5.00	2	1.87
Malaria	3	2.75	17	21.25	8	7.48
Measles (*Khasra*)	1	0.92	0	0	0	0
Small Pox (*Chechak*)	2	1.83	1 1.25	0	0	0
Chicken Pox (*Chhoti Mata*)	0	6 7.50	0	0	0	0
Dysentery (*Patchis*)	10	9.17	0	10	9.34	0
Premature Birth	1	0.02	0	0	0	0
Convulsions/Fits (*Darra*)	6	5.51	0	3	2.80	0
Snake Bite/Dog Bite	1	0.92	2 2.50	4	3.74	0
Bronchitis	5	4.59	0	4 3.74	0	0
Stomach Pain	3	2.75	0	3 2.80	0	0
Not Specified	17	15.60	5	6.25	16	14.95
Total	109	100.00	80	100.00	107	100.00

The above table clearly shows that the main cause of deaths reported among the Kamars' children was pneumonia or upper respiratory infection (*Telgi*), followed by malaria fever. Diarrhea and Dysentery (*Patchis*) are also observed to be common. In case of Hill Korwas, water-borne diseases, various skin diseases and diseases related to liver and stomach are observed to be common; this is due to lack of hygienic drinking water. Among the Baiga Tribe, *Falciparum* Malaria is common due to the heavy rains in the hilly and forest areas. Malnutrition is the chief factor which causes affliction of various diseases like dysentery, thyroid, goitre, rickets, etc. Unhygienic living conditions are also responsible for their various types of skin diseases. "In the contemporary world, the ecological approach is basic to the study of epidemiological problems" (Foster, 1978). This is examined in three ecological zones inhabited by the three tribes. The Hill Korwas inhabit high altitudes of the hilly areas with denuded forested zones. The Kamars live in rain forests with plain habitation. And the Baigas live in hilly and dense forest areas. An attempt has been made here to highlight the disease distribution among three different tribal groups in the three different ecological zones.

Food during Pregnancy

No special care is taken to meet the increased nutritional requirements of the pregnant mother. They eat well-cooked and hot food during pregnancy and prefer to eat food that is sour in taste like pickle, chutney, sour vegetables, etc. Among the Kamars it is a general belief that pregnant women should be fed with her desired dishes to ensure the birth of a healthy and proper child, without any physical deformity. In their words, "Jelalalchiathe, *olakhojkedenaparthe*." They strictly practise this custom. However, she should not eat black brinjal. It is believed that if she eats so, her child will develop cold and cough at the time of birth. During pregnancy, they also do not drink mahua liquor.

Antenatal Care

Majority of the Kamar's pregnant woman never consult health workers or visit the Health Centre. Based on the intensity of the immunisation programmes, tetanus injections and iron tablets are given to expectant mothers during their gestation period. It is important to mention here that the MCH programme in India recommends two doses of TT (between the 4 and 9 months of pregnancy) and 100 folic acid iron tablets to each expectant mother. Tetanus injections are received only by those pregnant women who are literate and aware of the benefits of the immunisation programme. Iron tablets are rarely consumed though they are supplied by the health workers. During the advanced stages of pregnancy, a woman is cared by both the family members of the husband and her own. The pregnant woman's sister or her mother helps her in household works.

Post-Natal Care

After delivery, the Kamar women don't use any modern medicine unless they face a critical problem. The birth attendants try to heal the labour pain by means of heating process. Cold water is prohibited for three continuous days; instead she is given hot water for drinking. Soon after child birth, the mother drinks mahua (*Bassialatifolia*) liquor to get relief from stomach pain. The new mothers are given herbal medicine by their own medicine man (*vaidh*). Bark of *kanke* (*Flacourtiaramantchi*) and roots of *chhind (Phoenix acaulis*), after cutting in suitable size, are boiled with water; sometimes they mix jaggery while boiling. This liquid dose is given to the new mother for a period of three days, which gives them relief from stomach pain. To regain energy, the new mother takes *pej* (rice with boiled rice water). The mother is treated hot water baths for upto 2 to 3 weeks after delivery.

Tribe	*State*	*IMR*	*References*
Bhattras	Chhattisgarh	148.56	Basu, 1986
Murias	-do-	123.35	-do-
Halbas	-do-	92.78	-do-
Marias	-do-	85.44	-do-
Hill Korwas	-do-	162.16	Present study, 1998
Kamars	-do-	121.00	-do-
Baigas	Madhya Pradesh	125.00	-do-

Figures Related to Reproductive and Child Health among the Kamars

1. Mean menarcheal age - 13.86
2. Mean marital age - 14.75
3. Age at first maternity - 14-15
4. Total Pregnancy (in 100 mothers) - 440
5. Total live births (in 100 mothers) - 405
6. Total still births (in 100 mothers) - 35

7. Total child mortality - 115
8. Death below 15 years - 80
9. Total fertility rate - 7.84
10. Infant mortality rate (per 1000 live births) - 121
11. Maternal mortality rate (per 1000 live births) - 6-7

Infant Mortality Rate (IMR) shows a higher trend among the tribes. The table shows that the Kamars have had 121 deaths per 1000 live births. IMR is quite high among the Kamars as compared with the national average of 80 (1991-92 Census). Further, Park (1974) recorded 111 IMR in Madhya Pradesh. This indicates the deteriorating health conditions among the Kamar children. Maternal mortality rate is found alarmingly high, i.e., 3 per 405 live births among the Kamars which is much more than that of the national average which is 4 to 5 per 1000 live births (1993 Census). As majority of the Kamar women get married between 13 to 17 years, child bearing begins shortly after that. About 7% women have reported their first child at the age of 14 years, while 21% women had experienced their first childbirth at the age of 15 years.

Health Care by Worshiping Deities

Some diseases are attributed to supernatural causes : they are considered as a divine punishment for man's sins. Such diseases are generally treated by the village priest or *dih-baiga*. To appease these deities, the village priest generally worships them and offers animal or bird sacrifice. Cholera, small pox and measles are the common diseases, cured by this method. The Kamars worship different Gods and Goddesses who are generically called *Deo* and *Mata* or *Mai* respectively.

Types of Deities	*Name of the Deity*	*Abode*	*Sacrificing/Offering Objects*
Universal Deities	*Bhima-deo*	in the shape of round stone under the *sarai* (*Shorearobusta*) tree.	Goat/pig
	Gata-Dooma	ancestor spirits of inner room	
	Dharti-mata	cooking room	
	Murmati	particular place (*mati*) from where the clan originates	

[contd...]

Types of Deities	*Name of the Deity*	*Abode*	*Sacrificing/Offering Objects*
Family Deities	*Budharaja*	inner room	Reddish goat
	Dulha-Deo	cooking room	
Village Deities	*Chhotemata (Hinglajin)*	small pox	Goat
	Badimata/ Budhi ma	chicken pox	Hen/goat
	Kankalin/ Kalipat	vomiting with loose motions	Black hen/goat
	Debi	cholera (outside the house but within the tribal settlement)	Goat
Territorial Cults	*Bamhni Mai*	top of the hill	One flag and white goat
	KachnaDhurwa	top of the hill	Coconut goat/hen
	Bhalgarh-mai	top of the hill	Coconut goat/hen

Health Care by Herbal Medicine

The Kamars have good faith in their village medicine man (*vaidh*) who gives them herbal medicines collected from the various medicinal plants. They may be roots, leaves, barks, tubers, flowers, fruits of some plants, etc. The medicine man collects the same from the hillside and forests, and preserves them carefully for future use. This curative health care system was invented by them in order to adjust and survive in their ecological niche. It is believed that in the past they learnt this art of curing the ailments through experience, and by trial and error method, and this knowledge is passed on orally and practically from generation to generation.

Modern Health Care Services

In Gariaband Block, the Community Health Centre is also known as the First Referral Unit. This health centre has a maternity centre, pathological laboratory, x-ray centre, eye department, leprosy unit, malaria unit, and TB unit, along with a 30-bedded indoor patient capacity. A total of 142 villages are covered under this PHC. Out of the 142,74 villages are Kamar tribal villages, having a total population of 5373. There are 42 sub-centres under this health centre and 54 Multi-Purpose Health Workers (MPHW) work in them. It is also found that two sub-centres are assigned to one health worker, who has to visit atleast 6-7 villages.

It is observed that the medicines supplied by the health centre in Gariaband PHC are expired. One health worker has reported that the PHC suppiied medicines (pills, capsules, etc.) only once in a year. However, after 4-5 months of disbursement the medicines expire. So, for the rest months of the year she purchases medicine from her own pocket for the health care of the villagers.

Institution	*Officials and Staff*
Primary Health Centre One PHC, Gariaband	One Block Medical Officer (BMO) Three Assistant Doctors One Block Extension Educator (BEE) They are assisted by nurses, ward boys, health attendants, sweepers, lab technician, midwives
One Additional PHC	No doctor It is headed by a health supervisor
4 Sectors	Each sector is supervised by two health supervisors (one male and one female)
42 Sub-centres	In each sub-centre, there is provision for two MPHW, one male and one female

It is observed that the Kamars visit the health centre only when the cause of the diseases is not understood or they do not get relief from their own medical system. They have strong faith in injections as they give immediate relief from pain, fever and wounds. However, parents avoid immunisation of their children as they get swelling and fever due to the introduction of the foreign liquid.

Conclusion

It is observed that health problems and health care practises of the Kamar Tribe are very closely associated with their environment : the forest and the hills. They depend mostly on the various plants and animals for the treatment of their illnesses and for their daily consumption;

they also use clay, black soot, charcoal and cow dung ash for personal hygiene and sanitary habits. Besides the magico-religious practises for the health care, treatment by medicinal plants is also common among the Kamars. Most of their illnesses are believed to be caused due to wrath of supernatural beings or by some magical means. Climatic change and wrong/excessive food are also responsible for illness. They generally perform rituals and sacrifice birds and animals to appease the supernatural being that is believed to have caused their illness. They also have adopted some herbal medicines in their indigenous methods of treatment. For the treatment of various illnesses, local medicine men are consulted. They generally visit the PHCs or health workers only when the cause of the diseases is not understood or there is no relief from their own medical system. Due to the cold climate, diseases related to infection of the upper respiratory tract such as, pneumonia (locally known as *Telgi*) are more common among the Kamars. Heavy rainfall provides opportunities for breeding of mosquitoes : frequent rains lead to the formation of small pools of water in forest places which serve as active breeding places for mosquitoes. So malaria is a common disease. Accumulation of sewage water, lack of drainage, and having cattle sheds attached to the main house, further influence the spread of malaria; further, diseases like yaws prove to be fatal among them : during the author's fieldwork, the Government doctors were able to identify a total of 41 such cases in Mainpur Block and one case in Gariaband Block in Raipur District.

The common health problems among the children of Kamars include respiratory infections, such as, pneumonia, and fever, malaria, malnutrition etc. Lack of access to safe and effective contraceptives, inadequate obstetric care during pregnancy and childbirth, maternal malnutrition, early marriage and child bearing, poor sanitation, lack of safe drinking water, and ignorance of causes of diseases are the factors responsible for the health problems among the Kamar women.

References

Basu, S. 1994. *Tribal Health in India*, (ed.) New Delhi: Manak Publications Pvt. Ltd.

Chaudhuri, B.D. 1986. "Tribal Health : Socio-Cultural Dimensions", Inter India Publications, New Delhi.

Chauhan, D. and Sangita Kamdar 1997. "Social Sector and Development: Focus on Health Care", in *Yojana*, Vol. 41, No. 4, New Delhi.

Dube, S.C. 1951. *The Kamar*, Lucknow: Universal Publishers.

Ebrahim, G.J. 1991. *Practical Mother and Child Health in Developing Countries*, London. EL. BS. Macmillan Education Ltd.

Foster G.M. and Anderson, B.G. 1978. *Medical Anthropology*, New York: Wiley.

Gopal, K. Rani, 1987. *Economics of Health and Nutrition,* Some Aspects of Growth and Welfare, Allahabad. Chugh Publications.

Inhorn, M. and Brown, J. Peter 1997. "The Anthropology of Infectious Diseases: International Health Perspectives". Gordon and Breach.

Joshi, P.C. 1988. "Traditional Medical System in the Central Himalayas" in *Eastern Anthropologist*, Vol. 41(I) pp. 77-96.

Mukharjee, B.M. and N. Khatua 1998. "Exchange and Reciprocity in the Kamar Tribe" in *Man in India,* Vol. 78, No. 3 and 4, pp. 349-354.

Pandey, B.N. *et al.* 1999. "Impact of Industrialisation on Socio-Cultural and Health Aspects of Tribal groups of South Bihar, India" in *Jr. of Human Ecology*, Vol. 10 (I), pp. 15-28.

Park, J.E. 1974. *Test Book of Preventive and Social Medicine*, Jabalpur, M.P. Banarasidar Bhanot Publishers.

United Nations 1994. Report of the International Conference on Population and Development, Cairo, Egypt. September, 1994 (preliminary version) U.N. New York, pp. 25-54.

World Health Organisation 1994. Health Population and Development, WHO position paper for International Conference on Population and Development, Cairo 1994 WHO, Geneva.

PART–III
Religious Pluralism

11

Syncretism in India : Shared Traditions Among the Lingayats in Karnataka

S.A. Azeez Saheb

Syncretism has gained momentum all over the world in recent years, emphasising the importance of composite culture in building national character. Of course religious faith is a matter of belief, but at the same time its boundaries do not limit the people from following other religious practises. Obviously, the phenomenon of assimilation is possible only with the help of cultural homogeneity rather than religious heterogeneity. Hence syncretism has gained popularity in developing countries like India as an instrument to develop peaceful coexistence among divergent faiths. Either through a conscious effort or an unconscious process, social realities can be understood in a complex social structure. In the process of encounters between various processes of changing materialism, formal and mechanical social interactions, and other varied social phenomena, syncretism has become significant in most developed societies. It has become a conscious effort among the political and academic circles to look into the social realities of the toiling masses, which permits a peaceful social coexistence of discrete entities. This discourse on religious syncretism in the academia led to the need for micro-level studies on the nature of syncretism that is presently prevalent in developing countries.

Syncretism has been receiving a rather step-motherly treatment so far as its study in Anthropology is concerned. The word itself has been maligned; if not by the anthropologists, by the Church. Thus, according to the Church, syncretism gives credence to idol worship, something that god is supposedly have thoroughly and roundly condemned in the scriptures. Broadly speaking, syncretism refers to fusion or blending of religious beliefs and practises either through the identification of gods, taking over of observances or selection, and reinterpretation of traits of one culture by the other. Obviously this cannot happen unless at least two cultures are in regular, day-to-day contact. There are certain factors that facilitate the mutual acceptance or respect of each other's traits, such as beliefs and practises. These may be through trade, invasion, migration, political role of the state, inter marriages, drive for independence, missionary activity of the mystics and mendicants, impact of master-disciple relationships, role of local traditions, and so on. Though syncretism has been studied by many anthropologists and sociologists, its field was mainly restricted to the tribals. Consequently, various dimensions of syncretism among civilisational religions have been largely overlooked, besides, a review of literature on religion *per se.*

In all religions, God bestows *pavadagalu* (miracles) to His people only through suffering. These people are either the prophets or the saints (Saheb, 2005). In South India, the *Gaddige* (tomb of a Lingayat Jangama) is considered as a pilgrim centre by the Lingayats. However, it is open to followers of other faiths also. Thus the Lingayat devotees of all sub-groups in the society treat the Jangama Mutts as sacred centres. In this article, a modest attempt is made to analyze syncretism in the ambit of the functioning of Hindu-Muslim syncretism in general and Hindu-Muslim-Lingayat syncretism in Karnataka in particular. In the light of the same, the possible syncretic dimensions of Shri Adi Jagadguruji at Suttur and Shri Guru Malleshwara at Devnur, Nanjanagud Taluk, Mysore District, and Kodekal Basavanna of Kodekal Village, Surpur Taluk, Bagalkot District, Karnataka have been discussed.

It is necessary to mention that a picture purporting to be that of Kodekal Basavanna, a recent addition, is placed at the entrance of the Kodekal shrine. He appears as a *Sadhu* (sage) draped in a tiger's skin. On one foot he wears a Hindu style wooden sandal *padarakshe* and on the other, a Muslim style leather shoe *kausi*, this suggests his dual identity, his mission of bringing Hindus and Muslims together. His grave is housed in a Muslim style domed structure with slender minarets topped with the Islamic symbol of the crescent and the star. His grave is constructed in Muslim fashion, covered with a green cloth *galf* decorated with the insignia of the crescent and star, along with embossed words that say there is no God but Allah and Prophet Muhammad is His messenger. His grave is a *Mazar* for the Muslim devotees and referred by them as Mohammed Sarvar. So his grave is a common shrine for the Muslims as well as the Lingayats in the region.

The Meaning and Scope of Syncretism

It is believed that the word syncretism has been derived from Greek root words : "*syn" which* means "with"; and "*krasis" which* means "mixture." When combined as "*synkrasis", they* mean" a mixing together", or" compound." (Shaw, 1994). It refers to the mutual acceptance of elements of two religions, their textual or other practises (Roy Burman, 2002). The Dictionary of Sociology (1994) defines syncretism as a "union of distinct elements drawn from different systems into a new whole or system." Cultural syncretism has been the fusion of distinctive beliefs and practises of one culture into another. The Encyclopedia of Social and Cultural Anthropology mentions that "syncretism refers to the hybridisation or amalgamation of two or more cultural traditions".

According to Smith (1986:274) the term syncretism is usually applied to religious phenomena or movements, though it may be applied to cultural change in general. The present study of Lingayatism, protest religious reformist movement in Karnataka started by Basavanna, supports the statement made by Smith. Basavanna wanted to make religion a mass movement and to achieve this he founded the religious parliament *Anubhava Mantapa. Till* the Saranas (preachers of Lingayatism) entered the scene, religious matters were considered sacred, and confined to the high born and learned. Contrary to this, the discussions that transpired in his parliament were neither discourses nor sermons, and never directed by a religious head; instead it was moderated by a chairman, *Allamaprabhu*, who was a householder and a musical drummer in a temple by profession. Till then such positions were graced only by heads of religious institutions (*Mathadhikari*) and conducted as a one-way activity.

Basavanna wanted to do away with the priestly class. He told that in his religion, everyone should follow a vocation and earn a living, instead of depending on charity and alms. With this he also wanted to do away with the Hindu noble act of giving (*dana*), which according to him encouraged idling and exploitation of the ignorance of the masses. Furthermore, he wanted to give everyone a right to worship God personally and not through a priest. His argument was that if someone is hungry he should satisfy it himself, and not through a middleman. To facilitate the devotees in fulfilling this need, and since all were not allowed into the temple to worship the idol there, Basavanna introduced the concept of *Istalinga* personal emblem of Siva, which is different from the static form of *Shivalinga* (*Stavaralinga*) worshipped in Hindu

Shiva temples. This *Istalinga*is always worn on the person and regularly worshipped. With this he wanted to prevent the devotees from going to temples where the static form of *Shivalinga* is worshipped and the priestly classes, who established themselves as the agents of God, were patronised. The cult itself was based on the concept of a formless god. The phallic symbol *lingam*. In place of the *lingam*, they worship the scripture *Vachana* of Kodekal Basavanna, which they consider as their *atmalingam* (the *lingam* of the soul).

Basavanna also wanted to remove the importance given to the five kinds of pollution: *jati, janana, preta, udhista* and *rajasa* (caste, birth, death, spittle and menstruation of a girl), advocating that by wearing the *Istalinga* always on one's person, the physical body, which comes in continuous contact with God, not only the body is purified, but also the mind. In this sense, according to Saranas, the human body becomes the abode of Shiva temple and heaven (*Kayakave Kailasa*). This has been illustrated in many of the *Vachanas*.

Basavanna's teachings were meant to liberate the devotees from the clutches of temples and priests. These ideas were novel and dynamic and the whole society was charged with action for change, away from Brahminical religious order. These discussions later transformed into action and the Saranas, including Basavanna who was a Brahmin by birth and a minister, started mingling and inter-dining even with unclean scheduled castes; they also stopped going to temples and inviting Brahmin priests for their rituals. This angered the Brahminical groups and they complained to the King about these unreligious activities. But Basavanna convinced the King that the laws of Manu do not apply to the Lingayats who are outside the purview of Hinduism.

The Village Society-Population Composition, Caste Structure and Social Hierarchy

Devirammanahalli (village) is multi-caste in nature and consists of the Lingayat sub-castes like Jangama, Aradhya, Vokkaliga, Viswakarma and Achari. In Mysore District, the Jangamas and Aradhya Brahmins are regarded as priests. Life cycle rituals such as childbirth, naming ritual, puberty of a girl, marriage and death of the Lingayats are performed by either of these, while in northern Karnataka only the Jangamas are the priests for most of the castes except the Brahmins.

Vysyas (Shetty), also known as Komatis, are a trading community and they are distributed throughout the state. Besides their traditional occupation of trade, and merchandise, a few are also occupied in white-collar jobs such as clerks, teachers and doctors. The Vokkaliga are traditionally agriculturists. They affix titles like Gowda/Gowder (head man), to their names and the women are called Gowdthi or Vokkalagatti. They are distributed in Mysore, Mandya, Bangalore, Tumkur, Hassan, Shimoga and Chikkamagalur districts. The Viswakarma, also known as Panchalas, Akkasale, Achari, Viswa Brahmin, Sutar and Gajjegar, are traditional artisans and distributed in Mysore, South Kanara, Bangalore, Raichur and Dharwad districts. In Devirammanahalli Village there are two sub-groups among the Viswakarmas. They are Marakelasada Achari (Carpenter) and Kabbinakelasa Achari (Blacksmith).

The sub-caste Lingayatas are endogamous in nature and follow the social hierarchy, just like the Hindus. In arranging the sub-castes of the Lingayats in hierarchical order, the ritual status, opinion of the people and the rules of commensality are taken into consideration. The Lingayat Jangama claims the highest position among other sub-caste Lingayats. Aradhyas come next in order although they claim themselves to be superior to the Jangamas. Third in social order is Vokkaliga Lingayats followed by Vysya (Shetty) Lingayats. The Marakelasada Acharis (Carpenters) and Kabbinakelasa Acharis (Blacksmiths) occupy the lowest position although they too vie with each other over their respective position in social hierarchy. Finally, the blacksmiths were placed in the sixth position. Thus, the invisible social hierarchy is observed among the Lingayats in Devirammanahalli Village.

Traditional social hierarchy of sub-caste Lingayats in Devirammanahalli village is as follows:

I. Jangama Lingayats

↓

II. Aradhya Lingayats

↓

III. Vokkaliga Lingayats

↓

IV. Vysya (Shetty) Lingayats

↓

V. Marakelasada Achari Lingayats (Carpenter)

↓

VI. Kabbinakelasa Achari Lingayats (Blacksmith)

Table 1 : Types of Sacred Performances and Secular Activities Conducted at the Suttur Jatre Festival of the Pontiff of Sri Adi Jagadguru Shivarathreeshwara Swamiji

Jatre Festival Days	*Date and Month*	*Time and Place*	*Types of Sacred Performances*	*Time and Place*	*Types of Secular Activities*
1st day	05/02/2005	6.00 a.m. Suttur Mutt	*Maharudrabhisheka, Mahamangalarathi*	5.00 p.m. *Jatre* campus	Inauguration of 13th JSS Inter-Institution Sports Meet by Shri M. Kharge, Minister for Water Resources and Transport
		10.00 a.m. SutturVillage	Ceremonial procession of idol of Sri Adi Jagadguru Shivaratheeshwara Mahaswamji left from the Suttur Mutt.	7.00 p.m. *Gaddige* Premises	Magic Show by Shri S.N. Guru Swamy, Someshwarapura
		4.30 p.m. Sri Kshetra Shrine Premises	Arrival of ceremonial procession of idol of Sri Adi Jagadguruji at the shrine of Sri Kshethra	8.00 p.m. *Gaddige* Premises	Comedy one act play, **Kattale Rajya** by Suttur Free Education School Children
				9.00 p.m. Bridge Premises	**Tiruneelakantha Charite** (Devotional Songs) by Shri Shivakumara Shastri, Badanavalu

contd...

contd...

2nd day	06/02/2005	6.00 a.m. *Gaddige* Premises	*Maharudrabhisheka.* beginning of *Laksha Bilvarchana, Mahamangalarathi*	7.00 a.m. SutturVillage	*Prabhat Peri, Sadbhavana Yatra,* Hoisting of *Shatsthala* Flag, *Dharma Sandesha* by Shri Sadashiva Swamiji of Sri Virakta Mutt, Madapattana
		8.30 a.m. *Gaddige* Premises	*Shata Kumbhabhisheka* to Shri Someshwara Swamiji, *Mahamangalarathi*	10.00 a.m. Exhibition Premises	Inauguration of Cultural Programmes like *Rangoli* and Art Competitions by Shri H.D. Deve Gowda, Ex. P.M. of India
		10.30 a.m. *Gaddige* Premises	*Maharudrabhisheka*	10.00 a.m. Exhibition Premises	Inauguration of Agricultural Quiz Competition by Shri V. Shrinivas Prasad, Former Union Minister
		11.30 a.m. *Gaddige* Premises	Shri Someshwara Swamy Procession, *Sahasra Kumbhabhishek, Halaharavi* Procession.	10.00 a.m. Bridge Premises	Inauguration of Boating by Shri J. Shettar, BJP State President
				4.30 p.m. Exhibition Premises	Valedictory function of Agricultural Quiz, *Rangoli* and Art competitions by Smt. Bhagirathi, Minister for Women and Child Development
		12.00 p.m. *Gaddige* Premises	*Mahamangalarathi*	6.00 p.m. Exhibition Premises	**Thunta Robin** (drama) by Natana, Mysore

contd...

contd...

		6.00 p.m. *Gaddige* Premises	*Maharudrabhisheka, Ksheerabhisheka, HasiruvaniAlankara*	6.30 p.m. *Gaddige* Premises	**Bellakki Hindu Bedaravyu** (Dance-drama) by Smt. Lalitha Srinivas, Mysore
		6.30 p.m. *Gaddige* Premises	Mahamangalarathi, Registration of names for *Shivadeekshe* ritual	10.00 p.m. *Jatre* Campus	**Kurukshetra** (drama) by Ambedkar Sangha, Mysore
				10.00 p.m. Bridge Premises	**Kurukshetra** (drama) by Rotary Kalakshetra, Bangalore
3rd day	07/02/2005	6.00 a.m. *Gaddige* Premises	*Maharudrabhisheka, Mahamangalarathi*	7.00 a.m. AlatturVillage	*Prabhat Peri*, *Sadbhavana Yatra*, Hoisting of *Shatsthala* Flag, *Dharma Sandesha* by Shri Chandramouleshwara Swamiji of Chandramouleshwara Mutt, Madapura
		6.30 a.m. *Gaddige* Premises	*Shivadeekshe* Ritual	11.00 a.m. *Jatre* Campus	Inauguration of Religious Conference by Shri S. Bangarappa, Ex. C.M. of Karnataka

contd...

contd...

		8.00 a.m. *Gaddige* Premises	*Phalalankara Pooja*, *Vibhuthi Pooja*, *Samsmaranotsava* of Sri Mutt Guru *Parampare*: *Mantra*, *Maharshi* Shri Shivaratheeshwara, 38th Annual Commemoration of *Mantra Lekhane*	11.00 a.m. Exhibition Premises	Unveiling of the statue of Shri Dr. Rajendra Swamiji, Releasing of JSS Calendar by Shri Somashekhar, MLA
		9.30 a.m. *Gaddige* Premises	*Rajopachara*, *Mahamangalarathi*	11.00 a.m. Exhibition Premises	Inauguration of 14th Bhajana Mela by Shri M. Veerappa Mohili, Ex. CM of Karnataka. Releasing of Brochures of *Jatre* festival in Kannada version by Shri H.D. Kumaraswamy, JD(s) President
		10.30 a.m. *Gaddige* Premises	Car Festival	11.00 a.m. Exhibition Premises	Releasing of Brochures of *Jatre* festival in English by Shri N. Cheluvarayaswamy, Minister of Health and Family Welfare, Hindi version by Shri Sathyanarayana, Minister for Resource Water Supply

contd...

contd...

		11.00 a.m. *Gaddige* Premises	*Maharudrabhisheka*	12.30 p.m. *Jatre* Campus	Veeramakkala Kunitha Dance Competition, Releasing of Brochures on JSS Mahavidya Peetha and Sri Suttur Mutt in Kannada, English and Hindi version by State Minister
		2.00 p.m. *Gaddige* Premises	*Shivakatha Keerthane*, *Jagajyothi* Shri Basaveshwara by Shri Gana Murthy, Kolar	6.00 p.m. *Jatre* Campus	**Mukmal Topi** (drama) by Master Hirannayya, Bangalore
		6.00 p.m. *Gaddige* Premises	*Maharudrabhisheka*, *Masashivarathri*	6.30 p.m. *Gaddige* Premises	Humour Programme inaugurated by Shri M.D. Ramanashree Groups, Bangalore, participated by Shri Krishnegowda and Shri Anand, Mysore and Mruthyunjaya, Tumkur
		7.30 p.m. *Gaddige* Premises	*Mahamangalarathi*	10.00 p.m. *Jatre* Campus	**Shivajalandara** (drama) by Basaveshwara Krupaposhitha Nataka Mandali, Bilikere

contd...

	8.00 p.m. *Gaddige* Premises	Procession of the Portraits of *Shivayogi* Shri Adi Jagadguruji and Dr. Rajendra Swamiji in Silver Palanquin, Procession of Shri Shivalingeshwara and Shri Basaveshwara	10.00 p.m. Bridge Premises	**Siddappaji Pavada** (drama) by Ambedkara Sangha, Bannahalli Hundi
08/02/2005	6.00 a.m. *Gaddige* Premises	*Maharudrabhisheka, Narikela, Phalalankara, Navaneethalankara, Vishwaroopalankara, Mahamangalarathi*	7.00 a.m. Hoskote Village	*Prabhat Peri*, *Sadbhavana Yatra*, Hoisting of *Shatsthala* Flag, *Dharma Sandesha* by Shri Shadakshara Desikendra Swamiji of Sri Suttur Muttbranch, Halawara
	9.00 a.m. Bridge Premises	*Ashtottara*, *Sahasra Kumbabhisheka* on the banks of the River Kapila	4.00 p.m. Exhibition Premises	Valedictory function of 13th JSS Inter-Institutional Sports Meet by Shri Honnahalli, Minister for Minorities, Prize Distribution by Shri Mahadevu, Ex-Minister of State
	10.30 a.m. *Gaddige* Premises	*Maharudrabhisheka*	6.00 p.m. *Jatre* Campus	**Sri Krishna Sandhana** (drama) by Ananthu, Bangalore

contd...

contd...

contd...

		6.00 p.m. *Gaddige* Premises	*Kondotsava* (sacred fire walking) by the Suttur, Alattur, Hoskote villagers, Devotees of Shri Adi Jagadguruji	6.30 p.m. *Jatre* Campus	**Bhuvana Deepike** (dance-drama) one-act play based on the lineage of the Pontiffs of Sri Suttur Mutt by Smt. Sangeetha Bharathi, Bangalore
		6.30 p.m. *Gaddige* Premises	*Maharudrabhisheka, Mahamangalarathi*	10.00 p.m. *Jatre* Campus	**Daksha Yagna** (drama) by Sri Basaveshwara Kiriya Kala Sangha, Kurubur
		10.00 p.m. *Gaddige* Premises	Procession of Sri Malai Mahadeshwara Swamy in Pearl Palanquin, *Guru Brahmotsava* and *Jangamotsava*	10.00 p.m. Near Bridge Premises	**Adarsha Vivaha** (drama) by Sri Gavi Rudreshwara Nataka Mandali, Belavadi
5th day	09/02/2005	6.00 a.m. *Gaddige* Premises	*Maharudrabhisheka, Mahamangalarathi*	7.00 a.m. Kalamahalli Village	*Prabhat Peri, Sadbhavana Yatra.* Hoisting of *Shatsthala* Flag, *Dharma Sandesha* by Shri Chandrashekhara Swamiji of Sri Jangama Mutt, Karpooravalli
		8.00 a.m. *Gaddige* Premises	*Samsmaranotsava* Ritual of Dr. Rajendra Deshikendra Shivaratheeshwara	3.00 a.m. Exhibition Premises	Inauguration of Wrestling Competition by Shri Y. Nagappa, Minister for Social Welfare

contd...

contd...

		9.45 a.m. Suttur Village	Procession of the Village Deity (*Gramadevathe*) Mariamma in Suttur Village	4.00 p.m. *Jatre* Campus	Valedictory Function of 14th Bhajana Mela by Shri Krishna, Speaker, Karnataka *Vidhana Soudha*, Bangalore
		10. 00 a.m. *Gaddige* Premises	*Maharudrabhisheka*, *PhalalankaraPooja*, *Uyyalotsava*	6.30 p.m. Exhibition Premises	**Rama Ravana Yudda** (drama) by Janamana, Mysore
		12.00 p.m. *Gaddige* Premises	*Mahamangalarathi*	10.00 p.m. *Jatre* Campus	**Mohini Bhasmasura** (drama) by Sri Shivaratheeshwara Kala Sangha, Suttur
		6.00 p.m. *Gaddige* Premises	*Maharudrabhisheka*, Devotional Songs by Smt. Vani Jayaram, Chennai	10.00 p.m. Bridge Premises	**Kurukshethra** (drama) by Ambedkara Sangha, Sonahalli
		7.30 p.m. *Gaddige* Premises	*Mahamangalarathi*		
		8.00 p.m. Bridge Premises	*Laksha Deepotsava* on the banks of the River Kapila, *Teppotsava*	9.00 p.m. Bridge Premises	Display of Fire Crackers

contd...

contd...

6th day	10/02/2005	6.00 a.m. *Gaddige* Premises	*Maharudrabhisheka, Mahamangalarathi*	7.00 a.m. Geemarahalli Village	*Prabhat Peri, Sadbhavana Yatra*, Hoisting of *Shatsthala* Flag, *Dharma Sandesha* by Shri Sambasadashiva Sadashiva Swamiji of Sri Ukkeri Kanthe Matha, Maddahalli.
		9.00 a.m. *Gaddige* Premises	*Ashtottara, Sahasra Kumbabhisheka* on the banks of the River Kapila and *Pancham Rudrabhisheka*	10.30 a.m. *Jatre* Campus	Mass Marriage inaugurated by Shri S. Jarkohalli, Minister for Textiles
		10.30 a.m. *Gaddige* Premises	*Maharudrabhisheka*	3.00 p.m. Exhibition Premises	Valedictory Function of Wrestling Competition by Shri Chinnigappa, Minister for Seri Culture, Prize Distribution by Shri S. Dakshina Murthy, Ex-Mayor, Mysore City Corporation
		12.00 noon *Gaddige* Premises	*Mahamangalarathi*	4.00 p.m. *Jatre* Campus	Quiz Competition on Suttur ***Darshana*** by JSS Gurukula, Suttur and Mysore
		6.30 p.m. *Gaddige* Premises	*Maharudrabhisheka*	6.30 p.m. Exhibition Premises	Magic Show by Shri Prahallad, Bangalore

contd...

contd...

		7.30 p.m. *Gaddige* Premises	*Mahamangalarathi*	10.00 p.m. *Jatre* Campus	**Shivajalandara** (drama) by Shri Basaveshwara Kala Sangha, Komaranapura
		8.30 p.m. *Gaddige* Premises	Folklore evening by Appagere, Bangalore	10.00 p.m. Near Bridge Premises	**Shri Shanidevara Mahime** by Sri Veerabhadra Nataka Mandali, Kadukottamahalli
7th day	11/02/2005	6.00 a.m. *Gaddige* Premises	*Maharudrabhisheka*, *Mahamangalarathi*	7.00 a.m. Bilugalli Village	Prabhat Peri, *Sadbhavana Yatra*, Hoisting of *Shatsthala* Flag, *Dharma Sandesha* by Shri Sharpabhooshana Swamiji of Sri Virakta Mutt, Harave
		9.00 a.m. *Gaddige* Premises	Renovated Sri Someshwara Temple and *Kumbhabhisheka*	10.00 a.m. *Jatre* Campus	Inauguration of Religious Conference by Basavaraj Horatti, Minister for Small Savings
		10.00 a.m. *Gaddige* Premises	Renovated Sri Veerabhadra Temple and *Kumbhabhisheka*	10.30 a.m. *Jatre* Campus	One Day State level Workshop on Comprehensive Rural Development Strategies Partnership for 4 chief sectors ? government, industries, NGOs and media inaugurated by Shri P.G. R. Sindhya Minister for Small Scale Industries

contd...

contd...

		12.30 p.m. *Gaddige* Premises	Sri Someshwara Temple –*Mahamangalarathi*	4.00 p.m. *Jatre* Campus	Valedictory function of State Level Workshop by Shri M.V. Rajashekhara Murthy, Union Minister for State Planning
		1.00 p.m. *Gaddige* Premises	Sri Veerabhadra Temple –*Mahamangalarathi*	6.00 p.m. Exhibition Premises	**Gokula Nirgama** (drama) by Binaka Troupe, Bangalore
		6.00 p.m. Sri Kshetra Premises	Taking back the idol of Shri Adi Jagadguruji in Procession to Sri Suttur Mutt	6.30 p.m. Bridge Premises	**Poli Kitti** (drama) by Raganna, Mysore
				10.00 p.m. *Jatre* Campus	**Daksha Yagna** (drama) by Kanakadasa Yuka Mandali, Kirugunda
8th day	12/02/2005			10.00 a.m. *Jatre* Campus	Inauguration of **Dasoha Bhavan** by Shri Dr. Manmohan Singh, Hon'ble Prime Minister of India

Quantification and Analysis of the Data

Of the total population of 871 in Devirammanahalli Village, 472 (54.19%) are men and 399 (45.80%) are women (Table 2). Almost all Lingayats in the village visit the *Gramadevathe* (village deity, Mariamma). The local people in the village call the village deity as Deviramma. Hence, the village is called Devirammanahalli.

Devotee's contribution to village deity/Mutt is shown in Table 3, which shows that cash contribution is more among Vokkaligas (12.06) when compared to the Marakelasada Acharis (1.26) followed by the Aradhyas and Shettys who contribute equally. Their contribution of service to the *Gramadevathe* in kind is also significant. Voluntary services like offering bell (0.11) by the Acharis and (0.80) Vokkaligas, offering goat (1.15) and chicken (2.64), clothes to the deity (8.04), cleaning the temple (2.64), and paddy to the deity (1.84) shows their attachment to the village deity and their sentiment, as considering the deity as their *Gramadevathe*. Mutt teachings of the Jangamas have influenced the (2.41) males among the Vokkaliga, which is negligible, when compared to the impact of the village deity. The data suggest that the villagers offer animals like goats or chicken to the village deity, through the washerman. After offering the animals, the sacrificed goat or chicken is given to the Adi Karnataka people, because the Lingayats are vegetarians. This incidence shows that the Lingayats have not given up their pre-religious practises even after converting to Lingayatism. Everybody in the village believes in the miracles of the village deity. The data in Table 4 show that 4.59% males and 5.74% females believe in miracles. They take vows for curing of diseases, economic hardships, failure of crops or household problems. About 7.58% males and 12.63% females visit the Mutt for fulfillment of their vows and 4.59% males and 5.62% females visit the Mutt to overcome their household problems.

Lingayat Mutts (Monasteries)

The Lingayat Mutts are of two types: the *Virakta* Mutt and the *Pattada* Mutt. The Lingayat Viraktas are celibate, and they preside over their own monasteries. They are not necessarily always recruited from the Jangama sub-caste. The second category is further divided into *Parampara* (hereditary) Mutt and *Guru-Shishya Parampare* (teacher-disciple relationship) Mutt. The Suttur Mutt falls under the former category whereas the Devnur Mutt falls in the latter category.

Suttur *Jatre*

Jatre (fair) is a very old religious institution, generally centered

Table 2 : Caste-wise Population and Marital Status in Devirammanahalli Village, Mysore

Sl. No.	*Name of the Sub-Caste of the Lingayats*	*Population*		*Un-Married*		*Married*		*Widower*	*Widow*	*Total*	
		Male	*Female*	*Male*	*Female*	*Male*	*Female*			*Male*	*Female*
1	Jang-ama	1 (0.11)	-	1 (0.11)	-	-	-	-	-	1 (0.11)	-
2	Aradhya	4 (0.46)	2 (0.23)	2 (0.23)	-	2 (0.23)	2 (0.23)	-	-	4 (0.46)	2 (0.23)
3	Shetty	5 (0.57)	3 (0.34)	3 (0.24)	1 (0.11)	2 (0.23)	2 (0.23)	-	-	5 (0.57)	3 (0.34)
4	Marakelas-ada Achari	55 (6.31)	40 (4.59)	32 (3.67)	17 (1.95)	22 (2.53)	22 (2.53)	1 (0.11)	1 (0.11)	55 (6.32)	40 (4.59)
5	Kabbinak-elasa Achari	25 (2.87)	8 (0.92)	18 (2.07)	1 (0.11)	6 (0.69)	5 (0.57)	1 (0.11)	2 (0.23)	25 (2.87)	8 (0.92)
6	Vokkaliga Gowda	382 (43.86)	346 (39.72)	190 (21.70)	151 (17.34)	188 (21.58)	174 (19.98)	5 (0.57)	21 (2.41)	382 (43.86)	346 (39.73)
	Total	**472 (54.19)**	**399 (45.80)**	**245 (28.13)**	**170 (19.51)**	**220 (25.26)**	**205 (23.54)**	**7 (0.80)**	**24 (2.76)**	**472 (54.19)**	**399 (45.80)**

Table 3 : Contribution to the Village Deity by Household Members in Devirammanahalli Village, Mysore

Sl. No.	*Name of the Sub-Caste of the Lingayats*	*Cash*	*Offering Bell to the Deity*	*Offering Paddy to the Deity*	*Cleaning the Temple*	*Offering Clothes to the Deity*	*Offering Goat*	*Offering Chicken*	*Mutt's teaching*
1	Jangama	-	-	-	-	-	-	-	-
2	Aradhya	1 (0.11)	-	-	-	1 (0.11)	-	-	-
3	Shetty	-	-	-	-	1 (0.11)	-	-	-
4	Marakelas-ada Achari	11 (1.26)	-	3 (0.34)	2 (0.23)	-	-	-	7 (0.80)
5	Kabbinak-elasa Achari	3 (0.34)	1 (0.11)	-	1 (0.11)	-	-	1 (0.11)	3 (0.34)
6	Vokkaliga Gowda	105 (12.06)	7 (0.80)	13 (1.49)	95 (10.90)	21 (2.41)	10 (1.15)	22 (2.53)	60 (6.89)
	Total	**120** **(13.78)**	**8** **(0.92)**	**16** **(1.84)**	**98** **(11.25)**	**23** **(2.64)**	**10** **(1.15)**	**23** **(2.64)**	**70** **(8.04)**

Table 4: Purpose of Visiting Temples by Household Members in Devirammanahalli Village, Mysore

Sl. No.	*Name of the Sub-Caste of the Lingayats*	*Belief in Miracles of Gurugalu*		*Fulfillment of Vows*		*Curing of Diseases*		*During Economic Hardships*		*Failure of Crops*		*Household Problems*	
		Male	*Female*	*Male*	*Female*	*Male*	*Female*	*Male*	*Female*	*Male*	*Female*	*Male*	*Female*
1	Jangama	1 (0.11)	-	-	-	-	-	-	-	-	-	-	-
2	Aradhya	-	-	2* (0.23)	2 (0.23)	-	-	-	-	-	-	2 (0.23)	2 (0.23)
3	Shetty	-	-	1 (0.11)	1 (011)	-	-	-	-	-	-	-	-
4	Marakela-sada Achari	10 (1.15)	12 (1.38)	10 (1.15)	16 (1.84)	2 (0.23)	3 (0.34)	6 (0.69)	3 (0.34)	2 (0.23)	4 (0.46)	10 (1.15)	11 (1.26)

contd...

Sl. No.	Name of the Sub-Caste of the Lingayats	Belief in Miracles of Gurugalu		Fulfillment of Vows		Curing of Diseases		During Economic Hardships		Failure of Crops		Household Problems	
		Male	Female	Male	Female	Male	Female	Male	Female	Male	Female	Male	Female
5	Kabbinak-elasa Achari	5 (0.57)	6 (0.69)	2 (0.23)	2** (0.23)	1 (0.11)	1 (0.11)			-	-	3 (0.34)	3 (0.34)
6	Vokkaliga Gowda	24 (2.76)	32 (3.67)	50* (5.74)	89** (10.22)	26 (2.99)	20 (2.30)	15 (1.72)	19 (2.18)	12 (1.38)	19 (2.18)	25 (2.87)	33 (3.79)
	Total **	**40 (4.59)**	**50 (5.74)**	**66 (7.58)**	**110 (12.63)**	**29 (3.33)**	**24 (2.76)**	**21 (2.41)**	**22 (2.53)**	**14 (1.61)**	**23 (2.64)**	**40 (4.59)**	**49 (5.62)**

** - Binne – for arranging food (Dasoha) on Unname (Poornimaday).

round a deity or a religious saint, and takes place annually. Though a religious institution, *Jatre* is also socio-cultural in character, providing recreation and merriment. *Jatre* also has economic importance when associated with cattle fairs. In good old days they were major venues where people brought vessels, bangles, clothes and other items. They fulfilled the aspirations of the people, and provide a way out to vent the emotions of the participants through cultural activities and activities for fun and frolic;

Such is the *jatre* of Suttur Adi Jagadguruji that was held from 05/02/2005 to 12/02/2005 for 8 days, depicting the syncretic elements of Hinduism and Lingayatism.

The Suttur *Jatre* festivities can be broadly categorised into two groups, i.e., sacred performances and secular activities. The former were conducted at the *Gaddige* premises of the shrine of Suttur and on the banks of the River Kapila. For the convenience of the tens of the thousands of the devotees attending the *jatre* and the cattle fair customers, cultural programmes were held at both the exhibition and *jatre* premises. For the convenience of the Suttur villagers, the cultural activities were conducted near the bridge premises.

On 05/02/2005, the first day of the *jatre,* the inauguration started around 6.00 a.m. and the rituals of *Maharudrabhisheka* and *Mahamangalarathi* were performed to the idol of Shri Adi Jagadguruji, and these rituals were continued till the completion of the fair. The idol procession of Shri Adi Jagadguruji started from the Suttur Sri Mutt and reached to the shrine of Sri Kshetra at 4.30 p.m.; it was received ceremonially by the present Pontiff Shri Shivarathri Deshikendra Mahaswamiji. Various troupes from the regional level that participated in the procession including Nandidwaja (Suttur), Veerabhadra Kunitha (Nagamangala), Veeragase-Dolu Kunita (Holaluru), Karadi Mela and Pooja Kunitha (Mysore), Nadaswara Garudi Garudigombe, Kombu Kahale and Donnevarase (Suttur), and Beesu Kamsale and Maragalu Kunita (Halepura). Folklore troupes such as Karagattam from Tamil Nadu, Mayura Theyyam Dance from Kerala and Jaan Pathak from Maharashtra also participated in the *jatre* and added colour to the procession. In addition to the above troupes, the JSS institutions contributed tableaus of religious, educational and economic themes based on the *Vachana Sahithya* of Shri Basavanna, the founder of Lingayatism. The local people of Suttur Village and tens of thousands of devotees of Shri Adi Jagadguruji witnessed the procession. The cattle fair was declared open after receiving the idol procession of Shri Adi Jagadguruji, and kept open throughout, till the completion of the *jatre* festival; the customers were busy even during the nights. In the evening, cultural programmes like Magic Show, Kattale Rajya, a comedy one act play, and *Thiruneelakantha Charithe Rangageethe (devotional* songs) were arranged to entertain the cattle fair customers and devotees of the Pontiff of Suttur Mutt at the *Gaddige* premises.

On 06/02/2005, the second day of the *jatre*, rituals like *Maharudrabhisheka* and *Mahamangalarathi* were conducted to the idol of Shri Adi Jagadguruji at 6.00 a.m. After the completion of the ritual of *Sahsra Kumbhabhisheka* to Shri Someshwara Swamiji, the ceremonial procession started at 11.30 a.m. at the *Gaddige* premises. In the evening, rituals like *Maharudrabhisheka* and *Hasiruvani Alankara* were held. Besides the sacred performances, secular activities like *Prabhat Peri*, *Sadbhavana Yatra* and hoisting of the *Shatsthala* flag were arranged regularly till the completion of the *jatre*, followed by *Dharma Sandesha*. In the afternoon, cultural programmes such as *rangoli*, drawing, boating and agricultural quiz competitions were conducted. In the evening, entertainments like Thunta Robin, Bellakki Hindu Bedaravyu and Kurukshetra (dramas) were held.

On the third day, i.e., 07/02/2005, the regular rituals were performed as usual at 6.00 a.m. followed by special rites of *Samsmaranothsava Mantra* of Shri Shivadeekshe, i.e., 38 annual commemoration of *Mantra Lekhane* of Shri Adi Jagadguruji at the *Gaddige* premises. In the evening at 8.00 p.m. the portraits of the Pontiffs of Shri Adi Jagadguruji and Dr. Shivarathri Deshikendra Rajendra Swamiji were taken in procession in the silver palanquin along with the procession of Shri Shivalingeshwara and Shri Basaveshwara. Secular activities such as one-day religious conference, humour programme, and one act plays like Makmal Topi, Shivajalandara and Siddappaji Pavada were arranged.

On the fourth day, i.e., 08/02/2005, at 6.00 a.m. rituals such as *Narikela Phalalankara*, *Navaneethalankara*, *Vishwaroopalankara* were conducted at the *Gaddige* premises and *Ashtottara* and *Sahasra Kumbhabhisheka* were conducted on the banks of the River Kapila. At 6.00 p.m. *Kondotsava (sacred* fire walking) was conducted at the *Gaddige* premises and the devotees from Hindu castes such as Vokkaliga, Kumbara, Agasa, and Kuruba from Suttur, Halattur, Hoskote and Karpooravalli villages, participated and expressed their devotion to Saint Adi Jagdguruji. This ritual is a Hindu custom adopted by the Suttur Mutt. At 10.00 p.m. *Guru Brahmotsava* and *Jangamotsava* were held, followed by the procession of Sri Male Mahadeshwara Swamy in a pearl paianquin. In the evening secular activities such as the JSS Inter-Institutions' Sports Meet, a one act play Bhuvana Deepika based on the theme of the lineage of the Pontiffs of the Suttur Mutt, and other dramas like Shri Krishna Sandhana, Daksha Yagna and Adarsha Vivaha were held.

On the fifth day, i.e., 09/02/2005, besides regular rituals, the meditation prayers of *Samsmaranotsava* were conducted to Dr. Rajendra Swamji at the *Gaddige* premises. The procession of the *Gramadevathe,* the village deity Mariamma, which is a unique ritual, was conducted by the pontiff of the Suttur Mutt. This shows the sentiments and beliefs of the pontiff. In the evening *laksha deepotsava* and *teppotsava* rituals were conducted on the banks of the River Kapila to Shri Adi Jagadguruji. Finally firecrackers were displayed. These rituals express the age-old traditional practise and accommodation of Hindu rituals in the *jatre* festival. This is the real syncretic aspect shared both the Hindus and Lingayats. Secular activities like educating the villagers about communal harmony, unity and integrity, *bhajanamela,* wrestling competitions, and dramas such as Rama Ravana Yudda, Mohini Bhasmasura and Kurukshetra were held.

On 10/02/2005, the 6 day of the *jatre*, in addition to the regular rituals, *Shata Kumbhabhisheka* and *Pancham Rudrabhisheka* were held at the *Gaddige* premises. At 10.30 a.m. mass marriages were arranged, irrespective of caste and creed, and the new bridal pairs were blessed by the present Pontiff Shri Deshikendra Swamiji. In the evening, Suttur *Darshana* quiz competition, magic show and one act plays like Shivajalandara and Shri Shanidevara Mahime, were held at the exhibition premises, *jatre* campus, and bridge premises respectively.

On the seventh day, i.e., 11/02/2005, prayers started at 6.00 a.m., at the temples of Shri Veerabhadreshwara and Shri Someshwara, which were renovated by the Suttur Pontiff, followed by *Kumbhabhisheka* conducted according to the Hindu tradition at the *Gaddige* premises. This aspect also expresses the Pontiff's attachment to Hinduism. In the evening at 6.00 p.m. the idol of Shri Adi Jagadguruji was taken in a procession from the Sri Kshetra *Gaddige* premises, back to the Suttur Sri Mutt. A one-day state-level workshop was conducted on the theme of Comprehensive Rural Development Strategies involving the four chief sectors, government industries, NGOs and media. In the evening, one act plays, namely, Poli Kitti and Daksha Yagna were enacted.

On 12/02/2005, the final day of the *jatre,* at 10.00 a.m., the Hon'ble Prime Minister of India Dr. Manmohan Singh was welcomed to inaugurate the Dasoha Bhavana, which was built with a cost Rs. 2

crores, for the welfare and free education of poor children. This was one of the prime themes of Shri Basavanna, the founder of the Lingayatism, to uplift the down-trodden in the society; this was truly implemented by the present pontiff of Suttur Mutt.

Kodekal Basavanna *Jatre*

Living together for centuries, many Hindus, Lingayats, Dalits and Muslims in northern Karnataka inevitably came to share, to a considerable extent, a common cultural world. Though at the local level, they maintain a sense of a separate identity, they often worshipped together at the shrines of Sufi saints. The situation at Kodekal Basavanna is different. His grave is a *Mazar* for Muslims, temple for the Hindus and Mutt for the Lingayats; and the annual fair is celebrated collectively. The Hindus and Lingayats call it a *jatre* whereas the Muslims call it *urs*.

All castes in the village are assigned different responsibilities during the *jatre*. The Viswakarmas (blacksmiths) clean the *Kalasa* and the *ghee*/oil lamp stands. The Nekar Lingayats, the followers of the saint traditionally conduct the daily worship at the shrine. The Agasa (washerman) clean the flags and umbrellas used during the *jatre*. The Muslim Chowdhary caste people take the responsibility of white-washing the shrine and make the arrangements for the *galf*, green cloth, which is covered on the grave of the saint. The Holeya (Scheduled Caste people) fetch water from the Krishna River, which is received by the Lingayats to make the sandal wood paste.

The *Mathadhikari* who is a descendent of Kodekal Basavanna and belongs to Sudda Saiva Lingayat caste, adopts the dress pattern of a Sufi saint, i.e., green turban and white shirt. He does not wear the saffron dress and *Istalinga* like the traditional Lingayats; instead he recites the *Vachanas* of Kodekal Basavanna. Traditionally the *Mathadhikari* observes fasting, goes to the Krishna River on a horseback in a ceremonial procession accompanied by musical pipes and drums to take a ritual bath, and returns to the Mutt where he performs the ritual of plastering the grave of Kodekal Basavanna with a fresh coat of sandal wood paste and covers it with the *galf*, a custom associated with most of the Sufi shrines in India. He then prays, after a Muslim *faqir* recites the *Fatiha* and asks for blessings of God and Prophet Muhammad.

It is interesting to note how this apparent incongruity between the tenets of Islam on the one hand and the age old culture and tradition of the followers of Kodekal Basavanna on the other come to the Mutt for his blessings, is settled. Although at the outset the problem may appear to be insurmountable, the down to earth people of Kodekal in particular have solved it in general. Thus in Kodekal, Lingayatism and Sufism traditions go hand in hand to bring communal harmony in the region.

Syncretic Elements in Lingayatism

Whenever two or more cultures come in contact, whatever may be the situation, traits are always exchanged between both cultures. In the present study also the Hindu, the Lingayats and the Muslim cultures have accepted traits from each other. We will now take up one example of each trait of Hindu and Muslim cultures that have been adopted by the Lingayat culture and vice versa.

Performing *Sashtanga pradashinam* (prostration) in temples is observed in South India. This tradition is performed by the Lingayats at the *Gaddige*, in the form of *uruluseve* of their respective affiliated *Gurugalu*. Even *karthika deepam*, the festival of lights, which is an important festival of the Hindus is adopted by the Lingayats as *Unname* ritual and celebrated on the full moon day in every Lingayat Mutt.

The Lingayats consider *amavasya* (new moon day), as a pious day. Hence special prayers are offered to the Malai Mahadeshwara Swamy and to their respective *Gurugalu*. *Poornima* (full moon day) is considered as auspicious by the Devirammanahalli Mutt, and *dasoha* (feeding of the poor) is arranged on this day by the *Mathadikari* for the local devotees. These rituals are condemned by the founder of the Lingayat religion, but still followed by the Lingayats.

The Hindus perform the first tonsure ceremony for the male child at their respective family deity. Similarly, the Lingayats also perform the same kind of rituals to the male child at their affiliated Mutt. Coconut breaking at temples is a Hindu tradition. Though the founder rejected this tradition, the Lingayats continue this practise even today, when they visit the *Gaddige* of their respective *Gurugalu*, to fulfill their desires.

In rural areas of southern Karnataka, the Lingayats follow the tradition of conducting *Kondotsva* (sacred fire walking) at their respective affiliated Mutts. This is an adoption of Hindu tradition performed at the temples, and shows their continuation of pre-religious practise. This Hindu tradition is allowed by the pontiff (head of the *Mutt*) of the Suttur to accommodate the Hindu castes like Banjigara, Holeya, and Vokkaliga in the annual *jatre*. This is one of the best examples of syncretism in Lingayatism in Karnataka.

Construction of temples and priest culture is against the principles of Basavanna. But after Basavanna's *Lingaikya* (death), the *Mathadikaris* allowed the pre-religious practises such as construction of the sacred places like *Gaddige*, and started performing daily rituals similar to the daily worship at temples by the Hindus. In the present context, the Suttur *Jatre* highlights that the pontiff not only renovated the temples, but the rituals are conducted according to the Hindu tradition. Even the village deity's procession is conducted during the *jatre*. The Lingayats are vegetarians, but the data suggested that they do not give up the practise of sacrificing animals to the village deity. All these religious practises show the shared tradition of Hinduism by the Lingayats.

Jangama is considered as a priest by the Lingayats. He conducts life cycle rituals like birth, marriage and death. The purity and pollution concept of Brahminical ideology also continues with the Lingayats and purification ceremonies such as post delivery rituals and cremation rituals are performed with the help of Jangama. Carrying umbrellas and flags during the procession of a village deity is a Hindu tradition. This tradition is adopted by the Lingayats and observed at the time of the *jatre* of Shri Adi Jagadguruji at Suttur and Shri Guru Malleshwara at Devanur Mutts.

The *Pir-Murid* (master-disciple relationship) practise of the Sufism is adopted by the Lingayats in the name of the *Guru-Shishya Parampare* (teacher-disciple relationship). As a mark of respect and identification, the disciples suffix the name of their masters to their personal names. For instance, at Basaveshwara Muttin Gulbarga, the disciples suffix their spiritual guide's name to their personal names. For example, Sarana Basappa Appa Appa, in which Sarana Basappa is the personal name and Appa Appa is the spiritual teacher's name (Saheb, 2004:44). A similar type of naming pattern is found among the followers of Kodekal Basavanna.

Traditionally the Lingayats bury the dead. The body is seated against a wall, cross-legged, and then carried to the grave in the same posture, in an ornamental, decorated bier, chanting the *Vachana Bhajane*, and buried in the sitting posture. But the followers of Kodekal Basavanna bury the dead body in the lying posture. They follow the Lingayat and Sufi religious practises because Kodekal Basavanna was a follower of Sufism. Even the death rites of his followers are performed according to the Lingayat and Sufi traditions. However, the recent converts such as the Shetty Lingayats cremate the dead. A feast called *Shivaganaradhane* is given to the relatives on the eleventh day. This is a sentiment of pre-conversion religious practise. Even the auspicious occasions like marriages are not performed till the completion of the annual death ceremony (*tidhi*). Thus the pre-conversion religious practises are still prevalent among the Lingayat sub-castes of Devirammanahalli Village in Mysore District, Karnataka.

Dasoha is commonly found in every Lingayat Mutt. This is one of the unique ways of sharing the food with the fellow men, irrespective of their caste affiliation. But contrary to this some interesting facts are noticed during the *jatre* at the Devnur Mutt. The data suggest that the Devnur Mutt maintains the social distance between the Lingayats and the Hindus, including the Brahmins. Furthermore, the Adi of Karnataka are neither allowed inside the Mutt premises nor is food provided to them at par with other devotees. Instead they are given food outside the Mutt premises. Thus, discrimination is still maintained at Devirammanahalli Village Mutt, which is against to the tenets of Lingayatism.

The practise at the Kodekal Basavanna Mutt is, however, unique. The dalit Holeya Scheduled Caste people are not only honoured but the water brought by them is received by the Lingayats at the Mutt, and the same water is used by them to make the sandal wood to paste which is used by the *Mathadhikari* to plaster the grave of the saint. This tradition is continued till today showing that the dalits are not discriminated in the society.

Summary and Conclusion

Basavanna's philosophy was based on the belief that everyone is equal and should have the same rights and opportunities. The new faith, Lingayatism, which he founded, was opened to one and all, both high and low in social hierarchy. Through his charisma and his sacrifices in life, he could attract people hailing from the highest as well as the lowest castes in the social hierarchy.

Thus, Basavanna was able to do away with most of the cultural differences between the highest as well as lowest castes in the social hierarchy, and their individual ritualistic traditions, and mould them into one single faith. However, in course of time, the Lingayat adherents succumbed to the age old principles of purity and pollution belonging to the Hindu ideologies, though all major rituals survived among them in a syncretistic style.

It is observed that though Lingayatism tried to carve out a new path for itself, it fell in line with traditional Hinduism. Over a period of time, it equated ritual status with social status and conformed to the traditional ranking of castes based on birth, and occupational differences. Notwithstanding these drawbacks, Lingayatism is a notable example of a syncretic movement, which introduced many revolutionary changes, and an ideology based on anti-Brahmanism.

References

Bhat, H.K., 1975. "A Formal Analysis of Lingayat Kinship Terminology", *Bulletin of the Anthropological Survey of India*, Vol. 24, Nos. 1-2, pp. 24-29.

Bradford, N.J., (N.D.). "The Indian Renouncer: Structure and Transformation in the Lingayat Community", in R. Burghart and A. Cantlie (eds.), *Indian Religion*, London: Curzon Press.

Bradford, N.J., 1985. "From Bride Wealth to Groom Fee: Transformed Marriage Customs and Socio-economic Polarisation amongst Lingayats", *Contributions to Indian Sociology*. Vol. 19, No. 2; N.S., pp. 269-302.

Chekhi, D.A., 1968. "Some Aspects of Marriage among the Lingayats", *Man in India*, Vol. 48.

Chekhi, D.A., 1968. "Mate Selection, Age at Marriage and Propinquity among the Lingayats of India", *Journal of Marriage and family*, 30 (4), pp. 707-711.

Hutton, J.H., 1946. *Caste in India: Its Nature, Function and Origin*, London. Oxford University Press.

Gurumurthy, K.G., 1976. *Kallapura: A South Indian Village*. Dharwad. Karnataka University Press.

Gurumurthy, K.G., 2005. "Death in Lingayatism", in B.N. Saraswathi (ed.), *Voice of Death*, New Delhi. Manohar Publications.

Ishwarom, K., 1982. *Religion and Society among the Lingayats of South India*, New Delhi. Vikas Publishing Company.

Singh, K.S., (ed.) 2005. *People of India: Karnataka*, Vols. 1-3, Delhi. Oxford University Press.

Mccormack, 1963. "Lingayat as a Sect", *The Journal of Royal Anthropological Institute*; 93 (1) ; pp. 59-71.

Farquhar, J.N., (ed.), 1998. *Lingayats: Modern Religions Movements*, New Delhi. Munshiram Manoharlal Publishers, pp. 301-302.

Manohar, J., 1977. "The Evolution of Political Arenas and Units of Social Organisation: The Lingayats and Vokkaligas of Princely Mysore", in Srinivas, M.N., S. Sheshaiah, N.S. Parthasarathy (eds.), *Dimensions of Social Change in India*, Bombay. Allied Publishers, pp. 169-187.

Havanur, L.D., 1984. Report of the 2 Backward Class and Castes Commission, Submitted to Government of Karnataka, Bangalore.

Nandimatha, S.C., 1979. *Hand Book of Veerasaivism*. New Delhi. Motilal Banarasidas (reprint).

Parvathamm, C., 1977. "Religion and Social Change: A Study of Tradition and Change in Veerasaivism", in Srinivas, M.N., S. Sheshaiah, N.S. Parthasarathy (eds.), *Dimensions of Social Change in India*. Bombay: Allied Publications, pp. 243-252.

Srinivas, M.N., 1952. *Religion and Society among the Coorgs of South India*. Oxford. Daredon Press.

Tipperudraswamy, H., 1990. "Veerasaivism", in Nayak, H.M. and B.R. Gopal (ed.), *South Indian Studies*, Mysore. Geetha Book House.

Venugopal, C.N., 1980. "Some Aspects of Lingayat Ideology and Monastic Organisations", *The Eastern Anthropologist*, 33(4).

James Hastings (ed.), 1921. *Encyclopedia of Religion and Ethnics*, Edenburgh T. and T. Clark.

Oxford University Press, 1971. *The Compact Edition of the Oxford English Dictionary*, Vol. II, p. 18, London.

Syedshah Khusro Hussaini, 1986. *The Life, Works and Teachings of Khwajah Bandahnawaz Gisudiraj*, Gulbarga. Sayyid Muhammod Gisudirag Research Society.

Smith, C.S., 1986, *Macmillan Dictionary of Anthropology*, Macmillan Reference Books, p. 274.

Suryanath, U. Kamath, (ed.), 1988. Gazetteer of India, Karnataka State Gazetteer, Mysore District, Bangalore. Government Press.

Saheb, S.A.A., 1998. "A festival of Flags: Hindu-Muslim Devotion and the Sacralising of Localism at the Shrine of Nagore-e-Sharif in Tamil Nadu", in Pnina werbner and Helene Basu (eds.), *Embodying Charisma*, London. Routledge.

Saheb, S.A.A., 2009. "Sufism in India", in N.K. Das and V.R. Rao (eds.), *Identity, Cultural Pluralism and State South Asia in Perspective*, New Delhi. Macmillan.

Saheb, S.A.A., 2010. "Ethnic Identity and Islamisation among the Borewale Muslims of Andhra Pradesh", in Vinod K. Jairath (ed.), Frontiers of Embedded Muslim Communities in India, London, New York and New Delhi. Routledge.

12

Communal Harmony in India: The Role of Mystics and Saints

B. Krishna Reddy

Communal harmony is *sine quanon* for national integration, peace and prosperity, particularly in a vast country like India inhabited by people following variety of religions, speaking numerous languages and dialects and observing cultural pluralism. In addition, the issue of communal harmony is quite relevant and significant under the present circumstances in which communalism, fundamentalism, religious bigotry and social turmoil have been posing serious threat and danger to our national unity. It is saddening to note that even after six decades of independence, the country requires more and more peace committees, and increasing deployment of police force during communal riots, rather than tracing the root cause of the problem and finding a solution to it.

The problem of communal harmony is to be addressed from different angles. It is often understood that it is basically a religious problem; however, it is not so. This fact can be demonstrated by depicting the socio-religious conduct of saints and Sufis. Even historically, the country is, by and large, known for religious tolerance of different faiths. Both Hindu and Muslim Kings exhibited a great deal of tolerance towards "the other" faiths, though during the Islamic rule some Muslim rulers had adopted the policy of destroying Hindu temples, spreading Islam (Islamisation) and converting Hindus to their faith (proselytisation). The latter two processes posed a major challenge to Hinduism during the medieval period. Various factors such as continuous defeats in the hands of foreign invaders, loss of political power and the domination of alien religions accentuated the degree of frustration. Islamic principles such as monism, simple worship, social equality and *nirguna* (belief in god without any forms and attributes) greatly influenced the Hindu religious thinkers. As a result, the age of *Bhakti*[1] (religious devotion) and self-surrender to god was ushered in. It resulted in the emergence of many mystics and saints[2] who devoted their lives in pursuit of the Truth.

The *Bhakti* cult cut across distinctions of high and low births, the learned and the unlettered, the haves and the have-nots, and opened the gateway of spiritual realisation to all and sundry. The mystics and saints of the age, both in the North and in the South, were unconventional and anti-ritualistic, ignored the age-old restrictions of caste and creed, and presented their teachings in the language of common people. In addition, they belonged to different castes and had among their disciples, men of all professions and religions. They also belonged to both *saguna* (belief in god with many forms and attributes) and *nirguna* schools of thought. Their basic approach was by no means alien to Hindu Vedantic philosophy, but there is no doubt that Islamic thought gave it a new form and strength. Thus, there was much in common between the *Bhakti* movement and Sufism.

The middle ages also witnessed the emergence of the Sufi[3] (Chisti) and the Shattari saints, who reflected the *Bhakti* movement, which had gained great strength among the Hindus. Many Hindus had great reverence for the Sufi saints among whom Muinuid-din-chisti, Baba Farid and Nizamuddin Auliya, are among the most important. They never advocated conversion of Hindus to Islam ; "Teach people the method of remembering God (*dhikr*); don't be after formal conversion" was the advice that Shah Kalimulla of Delhi gave his *Khalifahs*. The Chisties were opposed to any discrimination between Hindus and Muslims in matters of government, and advocated a common policy. Further, the Sufis adopted several spiritual practises of the Hindus and were believers in pantheistic monism (*wahdat-ul-wajud*), unity of being which had its earliest exposition in the *Upanishads*. By adopting this, they established an ideological relationship with the core of Hindu religious thought. As a working idea in social life, it insisted on equality of all men, the essential unity of all religions and freedom from all religious prejudices.

The *Bhakti* movement as one of the unifying forces of Indian masses continues to exert its influence for many a century. In spite of the differences between the textual values of Islamic culture and that of Hindus, both have shown several contextual features of assimilation and adaptation of cultural elements from each other, which they have absorbed into their socio-cultural fabric (Zubeeda Banu, 1977). This sort of cultural syncretism can be seen from several borrowed customs of the wider society such as following Sufi institutions, cult of *pirism* (religious pedagogy), breaking coconuts, lighting lamps, naming ceremony, tonsuring ceremony, puberty ceremony, betrothal, *nikkha* (marriage), fire-walking ceremony at the time of Muharam celebrations, and consulting the *Panchangam* (almanac). Similarly, Islamic cultural traditions influenced the Indian society in such a way that many non-Islamic communities in India borrowed Muslim cultural patterns ranging from food habits, style of dress, art, architecture, and language (Persian) to even visiting *dargahs* (religion pedagogy) and participating in Muharam celebrations.

Role of Shirdi Sai Baba in Communal Harmony

Cultural syncretism continues to exhibit its influence in pre and post independent India. In this context, the role of Shirdi Sai Baba, in addition to that of Gorakhnath, Swamy Ramanand, Kabirdas, Ramakrishna Mission, Ayyappan cult, and the ISKCON (International Society for Krishna Consciousness) movement, is highly commendable and noteworthy in paving the way for an emotional and cultural integration among the Hindus, Muslims, Christians and Parsees. Sri Sai Baba of Shirdi, the universally revered *Avatar* (incarnation of God), during his mortal appearance (1838-1918) in the State of Maharashtra of India, taught the basics of morality and spirituality in addition to granting mundane benefits. He promised a unique kind of unity and integration among the Hindus, Muslims and members of all other communities through his simple, yet powerful teachings of *atomic* unity, love, compassion, *saburi* (patience), *shradda* (faith), *samabhava* (equanimity), *vairagya* (detachment), etc. He is regarded as the universal Master whose message transcends all traditional religions and cults, and unites and elevates all people morally and spiritually.

Sai Baba was born, according to Swami Sai Sharan Anand, at Pathri in a family of Yajurvedi Deshastha Brahmins. Sai Baba himself had told him that he left his household at a tender age of eight and traveled in the company of a *fakir* (Muslim monk) along the banks of the River Godavari. The history of the Medieval Deccan reveals that the *fakir* whom Sai Baba accompanied must have been a Sufi. From the age of eight to about thirty, Sai Baba spent wandering in the process of realising the Supreme Being. During his wanderings and in the many years that he passed in and around Aurangabad, he interacted with Sufis and holy men of other orders. Prominent among them were Shamsuddin Mia to whom four months prior to his (Sai's) *Mahasamadhi*[4], Sai Baba sent Kasim, the son of Bade Baba with an amount Rs. 250 for performing *maulu* or *nat* (singing prophet Mohammad's praises), kavvalis (devotional songs of Muslims), and *nyas* or *langar* (preparation and distribution of food, i.e., *annadana)*. At the same time, Kasim was also directed by Sai Baba to meet *fakir Banne* Mia with the message," Navdinnavtarikh, *Allah Mia apnadhuniya le jayega*", and a garland. Banne Mia had close interaction with Sai Baba. It was the latter who had enabled Banne Mia to realise God and stationed him at Aurangabad. Sai Baba also knew *fakir Amiruddin* of Nanded who was asked in a dream by Sai Baba to send his *shagird* (servitor) Abdul to him. Thus, Abdul came to Shirdi in 1889.

Abdul became a staunch devote and servitor of Sai Baba and had an opportunity to remain in close contact with him. From the beginning, Sai Baba initiated Abdul in the task of service. It was the responsibility of Abdul to keep lamps burning perpetually at five places in Shirdi, viz. *Lendi*, *Masjid*, *Chavadi*, etc., when Sai Baba would make offerings of water in different directions. Abdul was also assigned many other duties such as sweeping all the roads near the *Masjid* and *Chavadi*, washing Sai Baba's clothes at the stream near the northern boundary, fetching water, etc. As Abdul would clear the human refuse on the streets, Sai Baba would lovingly call him a scavenger. For all the services rendered by Abdul, Sai Baba undertook the responsibility for his spiritual progress. Abdul would read the *Quran* sitting near Sai Baba. At times, Sai Baba would open the pages of the *Quran* at random and ask Abdul to read. Sai Baba himself often would recite the *suras* from the *Quran*. He would also ask Abdul occasionally to remàin awake the whole night and go on reading the *Quran*. Sai Baba had strongly urged him to remain satisfied with only one or two dishes in his food and to observe restraint and moderation in eating and sleeping. Abdul would abide by Sai Baba's exhortation (Kher, 2001).

There is yet another *fakir* commonly known as Bade Baba or Fakir Baba whose real name was Peer Mohammad. He first came to Shirdi in 1909 and put up in the new *chavadi*[5]. Initially he was not permitted to enter the *masjid*. He was directed by Sai Baba to remain in the *Chavadi* and read the *Quran*. After a lapse of some months he was allowed to enter the *masjid*. Subsequently he shifted his residence to Neemgaon. He would come to Shirdi in the morning and spend time up to the meal at noon time in the *masjid* in the company of Sai Baba. He enjoyed a place of honour in Sai Baba's *darbar*[6], he occupied the seat on the right side of Baba. Sai Baba would smoke the *chillum* (clay pipe used for smoking tobacco, etc.) after Bade Baba had passed it. The former would not take a single step without Bade Baba, who daily received any amount ranging between Rs. 15 and Rs. 50 from Sai Baba.

Devotees of Sai Baba are aware of his omniscience. Sai Baba had profound knowledge of the Islamic religion and civilisation including Sufism, the *Quran sira* (the life of Muhammad), *Sunna* (his code of conduct), *Hadith* (the traditions), *Fakah* (*dharmashastra*), *Shariat, Tarikat,* etc., like any learned Muslim divine or *Suri Shaikh*. Sai Baba could also explain, elaborate and comment with insight into the deeper meaning of various Hindu scriptures including the *Vedas*, the *Upanishads*, the *Bhagavad Gita,* the *Jnaneshwari*, and the *Eknath Bhagavat*. Similarly, he was at equal ease with all the Muslim religious works and traditions including works of Sufi Shaikhs, and of orders like Kadaria, Chistia, Suhrawardiya, Nakshbandi, etc. Infact, his range of knowledge was superb, fantastic and incredible, surpassing all comprehension. Testimony to this effect is found in several accounts of his devotees as well as the work of Abdul in Urdu, now available in Marathi and English.

The *darbar* of Sai Baba was open to all, irrespective of any distinction such as the rich and the poor, good and wicked, healthy and sick, men and women. People of diverse religions and sects, from varied professions and fields came to Shirdi to register their presence. Hari Sitaram alias Kakasahab Dikshit, solicitor, Member of the Bombay Legislative Council, and a colleague of Sir Pherozshah Mehta; Ganesh Srikrishna alias Dadasaheb Khaparde, Member of the Council of the State and colleague of Lokamanya Tilak; and Swami Sai Sharan Anand (formerly Vaman Pramgovind Patel, solicitor), have recorded their experiences in Shri Sai Leela, diary, and in the biography of Sai Baba. Similarly, Govind Raghunath alias Annasaheb Dabholkar and Das Ganu have sung the leelas (miracles) and described the teachings of Sai Baba. In addition, many other Hindu devotees like Nanasaheb Chandorkar, Chidambar Kesav Gadgil, Madhav Rao Deshpande, Rao Bahaddur Dhumal, Mahalsapati, Raghuvir Purandhare, Hari Vinyak Sathe, Balwant Nachne, Damodar Rasne, Moreswar Pradhan, Narke, Bayyaji Appaji Patil, Mrs. Tharkad, Radhakrishna Ayi, Meghashyam, Krishna Sastri Jogeswara Bheeshma, Saptanekar, Rege Saheb, Janardhan Galvankar, Hari Sitaram Dabholkar, B.V. Dev, Mahajani, Nanasaheb Nimonkar, Somnath Shankar Pande, Smt. Chandrabai Borkar, Ramgir Bua, Lakshman Nulkar, Tatya Patil, Pilaj Gurav, Sagunmeru Nayak, Gopalrao, Booti, Madha Phasle, P.R. Avasthe, Prof. G.G. Narke, Bala Saheb Dev, Balgangadhar Tilak, etc., came into contact with Sai Baba. Similarly, Muslim devotees like

Imambhai Chotekhan, Abdul Rahim Rangari, Abdul Karim Khan Saheb, Nuruddin, Abdul Khadar, Shalik Abjulla, Anwar Khan, Muhammad Khan, etc., and Parsee devotees like Jahangir Patil, etc., were attracted to Sai Baba, and most of them benefited in their mundane life with his blessings. It is also to be noted in this context that after the *Mahasamadhi* of Sai Baba, according to Arthur Osborne (1957), Miss Dutton, a British Catholic nun became an ardent worshipper of Baba. Similarly, a 30 year old black American, Christine has settled in Shirdi for eight years now (Rangaswamy Parthasarathy, 1996).

Baba was above all religions. To describe him as a Muslim by his external appearance is contrary to the established facts. It has been proved beyond doubt that he was born of Brahmin parents and there is no evidence to show that he changed his faith in the course of his saintly life. He also discouraged conversions and asked his devotees to stick to their faith. While dissuading people from changing their religion, Baba asked them not to bother about external conversion but conversion of the heart which made a man lose his sinful and bestial nature and climb up to Godhood. His vision was that all people should be really converted and should have God in their hearts. Thus, Baba held all religions in reverence.

A close perusal of literature on Sri Shirdi Sai Baba reveals that the contemporary devotees of Baba did not exhibit any undesirable competition, conflict or any other kind of disintegrative tendency, lack of mutual regard, or superiority or inferiority complexes, although the devotees represented diverse socio-economic, religious and cultural backgrounds. "A great deal of accommodation, adjustment, co-operation and integration was found operative in them and there always was a tendency to respect and co-operation like among brothers and sisters. Baba controlled and guided all of them in his direct and indirect ways. The fatherhood of Baba as their common living God, and the brotherhood of all the children of Baba was the matchless reality in those days. Baba's Dwaraka Mai Masjid was a unique spiritual university which taught secularism *par excellence* to Hindus, Muslims and others" (Ruhela, 1994). He allowed both Hindu and Muslim devotees to pray to him as *Iswar* or *Allah*, encouraging them to follow their own religious and spiritual beliefs and modes of worship apart from reading of religious scriptures like the *Yoga Vashsitha*, the *Vishnu Sahasranama*, the *Ramayana*, the *Gita*, the *Bhagavatha*, the *Jnaneshwari*, the *Vithal Pothi*, the *Quran*, etc.

Further, though Baba was a Hindu, he looked like a *yavan* (Muslim).

The name of *Allah* was always on his lips. He usually described himself as "*fakir*" or "*Allah's* servant." From 1895 onwards he started the annual Rama Navami-Urs Utsava (celebrations) in order to forge Hindu-Muslim unity in Shirdi and influence human values and spirituality among all people who participated in these celebrations. The Hindus worshiped Baba with all their rituals as observed in Hindu temples. The Mohammadans present there, enjoyed all this and freely shared the offerings distributed by the Hindu devotees. Similarly, the latter used to witness the reciting of *fatia* (Muslim prayers) and partook the lump of sugar as well pieces of coconut with pleasure and joy. Thus, Sri Sai Baba of Shirdi assimilated the characteristics of both Hindu and Muslim saints which formed his composite and universalistic personality.

Further, all the best in the world's religions had been assimilated by Sai Baba of Shirdi in thought, word and deed. Perceiving all religions objectively and dispassionately, he had blended into his life every acceptable feature of all faiths. For him there were no barriers of religion, sect, race, sex, caste, creed, language and nation. He founded no new religion but confirmed each devotee who came to him in his/her own faith and spiritual practise suited to his/her level of development. He exhorted all by precept and example to be tolerant and charitable towards others who were not of their faith and followed practises and ways appearing strange to them. Though some Muslim fundamentalists disliked his staying in the *masjid* and yet allowing him to be worshipped according to Hindu practises, they were overpowered by his spiritual experience, fearlessness, courage and other divine qualities of an *Aulia* of the highest order. Today, his shrine is a place of pilgrimage for lakhs of devotees of diverse faiths. A majority of them are no doubt Hindus including Jains, Sikhs and Buddhists, but there is also a good proportion of Zoroastrians, Muslims and Christians among them (Kher, 2001).

Recommendations for Communal Harmony

Despite the role played by the *Bhakti* movement in achieving communal harmony, an important issue that stands as a formidable block on the path of India's unity is the incidence of violent clashes among the different religious groups. There have been serious inter-religious misconceptions and misunderstandings with a lot of history full of conflict. However, the *Bhakti* movement has still relevance for communal harmony which is a continuous process.

The following recommendations would enhance the degree of relevance of the *Bhakti* movement:

1. To bring about harmonious relationship among the different religious groups, Harijans and non-harijans, religious organisations such as the Arya Samaj, the Ramakrishna Mission, and heads of various *mathas,* etc., should intensify their activities on a massive scale to propagate the spiritual aspects of religion, including the lives of mystic saints, as majority people usually follow the outer shell or ritual aspects of religion without understanding the meaning, purpose and essence of religion.
2. With regard to the need for awakening the people for achieving communal unity, like in the South and South-East Asian countries, efforts should be made for inter-religious understanding through interfaith dialogue, though it is not absolutely possible to have an empirically harmonious society, as communal and ethnic tensions are a world-wide phenomenon today. Those intellectuals, writers and theologians, who have no political axes to grind, should come forward and stress what is common between the two. There is a great need to revive the rich tradition of dialogue between Hinduism and Islam. We must remind all the rich synthesising cultural heritage of Nizamuddin Chisti and of Kabir and Dara Shikoh. Though we cannot revive the *Bhakti* and the Sufi traditions mechanically in our modern context, we can certainly borrow from their spirit. The increasing gap between the communities must be brought to a halt, if the foundations of multi-religious and multi-ethnic society are to be strengthened. However, this is not the only aspect requiring our attention; other aspects, political, economic and cultural in nature, are also very important.
3. Efforts should be intensified to build temples/mosques/churches on the model of the Behai temple in Delhi; and Shirdi Sai Baba temple (in Chittoor) and the Cathedral Church (in Kadapa) in Andhra Pradesh, symbolising the spirit and symbols of all religions. We may even initiate the tradition of everybody making a bow passing by a religious place of whatever community and organising different festivals of all religions, involving the people of all communities.
4. To achieve appropriate enculturisation or socialisation, the educational system must be re-oriented, especially at the primary stage, to instill in the children pride in their individual religion, mutual esteem for each other's religion and cognition of the universal values that are contained in all the religions. Appropriate text books for the said purpose should constitute a part of compulsory reading and should be accompanied by songs, plays,

and other audio-visual aids that depict the "unity in diversity" that is, the essence of positive secularism (Rao, 1982).

5. Inter-religious boards should be set up at various territorial levels with the object of promoting inter-religious understanding, mutual esteem, and inter-communal harmony, apart from promoting an understanding and appreciation of the composite culture, that is, the heritage of India.

6. The common elements in all major religions, the need for the upliftment of the poor and downtrodden, plea for avoidance of conspicuous consumption, limitation of property and simple living, equality of all human beings before the Almighty, and the need for materialisation of this noble value into the conditions of living should be brought out clearly and emphasised. An attempt should be made to educate the people of common religious inheritance for a just and egalitarian society in the country (Rao, 1982).

Notes

1. The Bhakti movement may be said to have originated in the South in the teachings of Tamilian mystic saints in the 7 - 9 centuries A.D. It was systematised by Ramanuja in the 12 century A.D., and propagated throughout India. It was spread in the North by Ramananda who was greatly influenced by the teachings of Ramanuja.
2. In the Indian context, the mystics and the saints are those who are supposed to have a direct experience of the transcendental truths of the spiritual world. When they experience the Highest Truth, they identify with the supreme self and unity of all existence and are called "realised" souls. In the western context, mystics and saints are distinguished. The latter need not have any mystical experiences. Salvation can be obtained merely through faith, sacraments and obedience to the Commandments of the Lord.
3. The seekers after Truth or the ultimate reality in Islam are known as Sufis. The Sufi movement originated, emphasising liberal theology and freedom of expression, in the areas of Basra and Kufa of the present Iraq. A Sufi saint is required to give up all worldly temptations, bid farewell to all natural urges and subdue them, to adhere to spiritual qualities, to ascend by means of divine knowledge, to give wise counsel to all people, and to observe the truth. A Sufi seeker of the Truth has to repeat the name of *Allah* for a fixed number of times in the prescribed posture. He also has to repeat the name of *Allah* silently by practising *pranayama* (breath control exercises) and meditation. Repentance, celibacy, patience, poverty, belief in God, contentment, equanimity, love, compassion, etc., are some of the other qualities of a Sufi saint.

4. A sacred expression signifying the death of a pious one.
5. A rural assembly : a hall where elders of the village gather to discuss matters related to public interest.
6. The word, *darbar* literally refers to a royal court. Here it is used for the congregation of devotees.

References

Asgar Ali Engineer (ed.). 2002. "Sufism and Communal Harmony". Jaipur. Printwell.

Balakrishna, V.V. 1998. Sree Sadguru Sai Smaranam (Tel.). Sowmya, H.No. 18-86-5 Sreelakshmi Nagar, B Camp. Kurnool-518 002, Andhra Pradesh, pp. 316-321.

Zubeeda Banu, 1977. "Cultural Syncretism : A Study of Muslims in Madras city". *South Indian Folklorist*, Vol. 1, No. 1, pp. 85-100.

Kher, V.B. 2001. *Sai Baba: His Divine Glimpses*. New Delhi. Sterling Publishers Pvt. Ltd., pp. 63-64.

Arthur, Osborne 1957. *The Incredible Sai Baba: The Life and Miracles of a Modern Saint*. Bombay. Orient Longman.

Rangaswamy Parthasarathy 1996. God who walked on Earth: The Life and Times of Shirdi Sai Baba. New Delhi: Sterling Publishers Pvt. Ltd., p. 224.

Ruhela, S.P. 1994. *Sri Shirdi Sai Baba: The Universal Master.* New Delhi: Sterling Publishers Pvt. Ltd., p. 75.

Rao, V.K.R.V. 1982 "The Role of Religion", in National Integration and Communal Harmony New Delhi. Gandhi Darshan Samithi, Rajghat, p. 109.

13

The Indian Christians : Regional Ethnic Formations and Denominational Pluralities

B. Francis Kulirani

The Indian Christians in general have been described as "Hindu in culture and Christian in Religion." The acceptance of this religion has not distanced them from their socio-cultural milieu. At the same time they have also been subjected to the ramifications of Christianity that occurred in the western countries and got transported to India by the missionaries who carried the cross after the sword especially during the 18th and 19th centuries.

The Doctrinal Diversity

The emergence of the Roman Empire and its patronage of Christianity gave it a dominant position among world religions. The original Christianity developed with East and West distinctions, as the Roman Empire was divided into East and West during the end of fourth century. There was a long drawn-out schism between the Church of Rome (Western) and Constantinople (Eastern) which ended with the heads of Western and Eastern sections excommunicating each other. The Western Church became the Roman Catholic Church and the Eastern Church, the Byzantine or Eastern Orthodox Church. The major differences between Roman Catholicism and the Orthodox churches are as follows:

The trinity dogma called Filioque adopted by the Roman Catholics in 579 A.D holds that the Holy Ghost proceeds from God the Father to God the son. Whereas, the Orthodoxy holds that the Holy Ghost proceeds only from God the Father, which was mutually agreed in the

Constantinople Council (1381 A.D.) and Nicene Council (325 A.D.). The Catholics believe in the concept of hell for sinners, and by virtue of saints, the indulgence is granted. Catholicism has the dogma of infallibility of the Pope, while Orthodoxy does not attach much importance to the ecclesiastical hierarchy. The Catholics distinguish the clergy from believers sharply. Celibacy is not enforced in Orthodoxy, while celibacy is legalised in the Catholic Church. The Catholics use unleavened bread for the Eucharist while the Orthodox use leavened bread.

The Orthodoxy again has two major branches: the Oriental Orthodox Church and the Byzantine Orthodox Church. This occurred after the Council of Chalcedon (451 A.D.) which was at variance with Nicene (325 A.D.), Constantinople (381 A.D.), and Ephesus (431 A.D.) creeds. After the Chalcedon Council, the Oriental Orthodox Churches (the Orthodox Coptic Church of Egypt, and the Armenian Orthodox Church of Syria, India, and Ethiopia) came to hold the Monophysitic (single nature of Christ) view, as against the Diophysitic (dual nature of Christ) view held by the Byzantine.

The next phase of changes occurred in the Roman Catholic Church during the 16th century, spearheaded by Martin Luther who called for reformation. The movement led to the formation of Protestantism which the Catholics called heresy, while for Orthodox it was a schism. Protestantism has four major branches : Lutheranism, Calvinism, Anglicanism and Independents or Radicals.

The Catholics and Protestants share a spiritual outlook which looks beyond material things to spiritual values, and which reminds man to live for entirety as well as for time. They share a belief in God and loyalty to the person of Jesus Christ. They accept the same Ten Commandments as a rule of conduct, acknowledge that a fallen man cannot attain his own salvation unaided, and needs a savior; they honour and read essentially the same Bible, recite the same Apostolic and Nicene creeds, and pray the same Lord's Prayer. According to Catholic teaching, both are admitted to the list of grace through the sacrament of baptism, which may be administered by a priest, minister, laymen, or even a Jew/Muslim. Bride and groom, whether baptised catholic or protestant bestow the sacrament of matrimony on each other which brings necessary space to their houses, and makes their marriage a truly sacramental union. The feasts of Christmas and Easter, the writings of the Fathers of the Church and devotional literature and hymns form a common heritage.

However, there are fundamental (dogmatic), and accidental differences. The Catholics enforce clerical celibacy : a common (approved) liturgy and communion under one species, which is opposed by the Protestants. On the question of man's nature after fall, the Catholics hold that man's natural and religious endowments were weakened, but man has graces of the supernatural, and prefer natural quality; however, the Protestants view man's nature as totally corrupted by fall and believe that purification is possible only by faith. Faith is an act of the will and emotions for the Protestants, while it is an act of intellect for the Catholics. The supreme religious authority from the Protestant point of view is found not in man or institution, but in book, "The Bible", which is the sole rule of faith; while from the Catholic angle, the Bible itself claimed no supreme authority. It is the sole rule of faith that the Church had compiled, translated and preserved the Bible. The concept of Church also varies for the Protestants, Christ is the head of the invisible Church and Pope is "anti-Christ"; whereas the Catholics hold that there is one Holy. The Catholic and Apostolic Church was founded by Christ, whose visible head is the Pope-Vicar of Christ, the successor to St. Peter, the Holy Father or the Bishop of Rome. The Protestants believe that baptism and Lord's Supper were specifically enjoined by Christ and would be observed as an act of obedience to his will; on the contrary, their sacramental meanings are denied by the Catholics, but were retained as ceremonies of Church. Preaching the word of God is the central feature of Protestant worship, while predestination of men (salvation and damnation) is flatly denied by the Catholics, which is also disowned by modern Protestants. The Protestants believe in consubstantiation and spiritual presence, while the Catholics believe in transubstantiation and the real presence of Christ.

The Calvinists consider that even after consecration, the bread and wine remain. The Methodists, Baptists, Mennonites and Brethrens consider the Lord's Supper as a simple memorial service. The Anglicans encompass a variety of views. The Quakers and Salvationists do not observe a communion service. Other Protestant teachings are principles of total depravity, justification by faith alone, private interpretation of scriptures, and the priesthood of all believers. The existence of purgatory was denied : after death, the soul was assigned to either heaven or hell. Prayers for the dead are considered useless and non-scriptural. Devotion to Mary as the mother of God and intercession of the saints were abandoned.

Indian Context

Christians form the second largest minority of India; their population was 16,174,498 which was 2.43% of the total population during the 2001 Census. The states in South India account for about 60% of the total Christians; and there is a considerable proportion of Christians in Goa-Diu (29.28%), Andaman and Nicobar Islands (25.28%), Kerala (20.56%), Tamil Nadu (5.76%), Andhra Pradesh (2.68%), Sikkim (2.22%), and Karnataka (2.08%). However, the highest proportion of Christians in comparison to total population is found in the north eastern states of Mizoram (83.81%), Nagaland (80.21%), Meghalaya (52.62%), and Manipur (29.68%). Kerala has registered a proliferation of denominations, and the missionaries and evangelists from Kerala, Mangalore, Goa and Bombay are working in all parts of the country.

Early Traditions

The earlier tradition of Christianity in India is a combination of Malabar, Mylapore or Coromandel and other Chaldean traditions which claim their origin from Apostle Thomas in 52 A.D., or even by two Apostles, the second Apostle being St. Bartholomew, according to western traditions. The evidence in support of origin from Apostle Thomas put forward by Church historians (Medlycott, 1962; Mundadan, 1978; Perumalil, 1971; Hambye, 1952; Podipara, 1970) is the New Testament apocryphal "Acts of Apostle Thomas" written in Syriac in the Edessa Circle around third century A.D. Those scholars who oppose the apostolic origin negate the historicity of the Acts of Thomas and deny the Indian Apostle St. Thomas. However, another group asserts the Apostleonly to North Western India (Mundadan, 1982; Joseph, 1955). The Indian tradition is a living oral tradition of the St. Thomas Christians (The Nasarani Mappila or Syrian Christians) of Kerala, and the tomb at Mylapore (Coromandel also had a flourishing St. Thomas tradition) is believed to be that of St. Thomas (Mundadan, 1982:5 in George Menachery, Ed.). The association of a second Apostle, St. Bartholomew, with India is also controversial. "Those who argue against this, attribute him to Arabia Flex or Ethiopia and those who are positive, to Bombay region after the ancient town of Kalyan-India or Felix-India", known as the happy (*ibid.*: 5). The Indian tradition of St. Bartholomew, however, has disappeared.

The migration of a community of Chaldean Christians, East Syrians (400 in number) to the Malabar Coast, was led by Thomas of Kana or Cana, Jerusalem, who is variously described as a merchant, a traveller and pilgrim (along with Bishop Mar Joseph according to oral traditions) in 345 A.D. (the date is disputed) (*ibid.*: 7), under the direction of the Patriarch of the Persian Church, otherwise called Catholico of the East (Babylon). This migrant community settled in Maliankara or Cranganore and constituted the early Christians of the Malabar Coast. The Perumal (native ruler) conferred many royal honours upon them (as evidenced by the Christian copper plates of 56 A.D.). The community of migrants and native Christians settled in Kodungallore and Cranganore, and were visited by Syrian Bishops of Mar Saper and Mar Parut, and priests (*ibid.*). The native Christians, the Nasrani Mapillas and the migrant Chaldean Christians maintained their separate identities and did not inter-marry. Among themselves, they differentiated as the *Vadakkumbhagar* (northists) and the *Thekkumbhagar* (southists) respectively. The former came to be known as the Syrian Christians, because Syrian Language was used in their Liturgical services; and the latter as Knananya Christian after the Thomas of Kana. According to Jussey (1990), the former chose to reside in the northern portion of the Kodungallore, while the latter in the southern portion (Mundadan, 1984:8). He holds the view that the original community, whether it consisted of Kerala elements only or of both Kerala and Coromandel elements, came into existence as a result of the evangelisation of St. Thomas, the Apostle who introduced into their composition a new element group of East-Syrian colonisers." According to Tisserant (1957:11-13), by far, the most important testimony of this early period is of the traveller Cosmas Indicopleustes.

"The Christian Topography"

Cosmas Indicopleustes visited India between 520 A.D. and 525 A.D. and reported about the Christians of Male (Malabar Coast), Kalliana (Kalyan near Bombay, probably the Christians of St. Bartholomew origin) under the Bishop ordained in Persia, indicating the connections with the Persian Church. The Tarisapally copper plates of 9th century are another early documentation about Christians in Kerala (Jussey, 1990). There are sporadic references about Christians in Kerala after the 10th century, till the arrival of the Portuguese (Friar John of Monte Corvino, 13th century and Jordan Catalani, 14th century).

The Portuguese voyages to the Malabar Coast starting in 1498 had three main aims: (1) Political (expansion of the empire); (2) Economic (expansion of trade and commerce); and (3) Religious (evangelisation of "pagan" lands). For the last-mentioned aim, the Kings of Portugal were granted special powers and privileges by the Pope of Rome, known as Padroado, to make ecclesiastical appointments. They immediately took up the patronage of the native Christians. It also became an economic and political expediency for the Portuguese to gain monopoly over the Malabar Coast, and the Persian connection of the Syrian Christians had to be terminated, branding it as Nestorian in character (two distinct, divine and human characters of Christ as against the Catholic doctrine that Christ was at once God and man). So the Portuguese missionaries set about Latinising the Syrian Christians, by removing and destroying the Syriac liturgical texts. This objective was achieved by confining a Synod at Diamper (Udayamperur) during June 1599 by Archbishop de Meneses of Goa, initiating a Latinisation phase of the Indian Syrian Church. The Portuguese maritime monopoly over the sea prevented the Persian prelates from reaching Malabar. The Portuguese missionaries (mostly of Society of Jesus order) under the treaty of Padroado even prevented the Persian Prelate (Mar Ahathalla) to take charge of the Syrians who were annoyed with the Portuguese inquisition. The Prelate was not permitted to disembark at Cochin, and the people revolted. Holding on to a rope tied to the cross in front of Mattancherry Church, they vowed not to submit to the Bishop of Angamali and to the Portuguese Missionaries. This event in 1653, popularly known as the *Koonankurisusathyam* (the oath of *koonan* + kurisu, meaning slanting cross), and the Archdeacon (the administrator of the Malabar Church under the Persian Prelate was under an Indian priest known as the Archdeacon). Thus the split of ancient Syrian Church of Kerala was complete. The new group came to be known as the *Purthenkootukar* (new party) and those who remained loyal to the Church of Rome were known as the old party or the *Pazhayakootukar*, who later came to be known as the Syro-Malabar Church, or Catholic Syrians, or Romo-Syrians, and they continued to use East Persian liturgy. A new Vicariate was erected for them in 1656 (*cf.* Meersman, 1982:16). The new party finally came under the West Syrian Church of Antioch, known as the Jacobite Church or the Malankara Orthodox Syrian Church. The split of Syrians into two also affected the already existing community (northists and southists) division. Differences, cleavages and reunions continued in this community after the 1653 incident.

The present day Roman Catholic Church in Kerala comprises of three groups having a common Syrian Christian tradition:1) The Latin Church (excluding a large community of fisher folk converts; the

Mukkuvar Christians and others who were converted later) who completely follow the Roman Catholic Latin liturgy. A separate hierarchy of Latin Bishops was established in the year 1534 at Goa comprising Malabar, and for Kerala, in Cochin in the year 1558 (Christian, 1982); 2) Syro-Malabar hierarchy established in the year 1923 (Mundadan, 1984:91) with Ernakulam as Archdiocese. They partially follow the East Syrian tradition except for leavened bread, married clergy, etc.; 3) the Syro-Malankara hierarchy which was formed by a reunion with a break away group from the *Purthenkootukar* (Malankara Jacobite rejoining the Roman Catholics). This re-union occurred in the year 1930, and the hierarchy of Syro-Malankara Church was established in 1932. Their particular identities are the Oriental Church, which retains many pre-16th century Malabar customs and practises (giving up many of the 16th century liturgy), and the church discipline patterned after the West-Syrian/Antiochian Church guided by the customs and practises of Latin derivation.

The former Malankara Syrian Orthodox Church of Kerala which formed the *Purthenkootukar* section after the 1653 division further got fragmented. The Christians who revolted against Latinisation under the leadership of Archdeacon (Thomas of Angamali who was ordained Bishop Thomas I) gradually accepted Jacobitism and the Syro-Anthiochian Rite in 1665 during the visit of Jacobite Bishop Mar Gregorious (Punnen, 1973:45; Vattkuzhi, *ibid.*:54). From then onwards, Syrian practises in their oriental form (use of leavened bread for celebration of mass and a wooden altar for mass, ways of keeping fasts and abstinence, and important Syrian feasts, etc.), were restored in the Malankara Church. The first fragmentation occurred after the consecration of Mar Thomas VI who had a rival Mar Kunilose (he was exiled to Anjoor). He founded a Church at Thozhiyur and the Malabar independent Jacobite Church of Malabar in 1772 which is popularly known as Thozhiyur Sabha. Interaction of the Jacobite Church with the Anglican Church Missionaries from England induced reform activities like removal of invocation of the Virgin Mary and saints, prayers for dead and a change in the concept of Holy Qurbana (mass) from sacrifice. The excommunication of the reformist was led by Mathew Mar Athanasius in 1875 by the Antiochian Patriarch (Mundadan, 1984). The Travancore Royal Court's judgement of 1888 against the reform party (Christian Encyclopaedia, 1973:90) resulted in the formation of the Marthomite Church with the help of London Missionary Society. The Marthomite Church itself underwent a split in the year 1961 (Mundadan, 1984:122), as a result of the demand for drastic changes in its liturgy and even the doctrine. They formed a new Church under the name St. Thomas Evangelical Church of India and discontinued the historical episcopacy. A splinter was the formation of what is locally known as "Surayi" or the Church of the East in India. The origin of the Church was traced to 1812 and stabilised during the early 1900s at Thrissoor. They recognise Nestorian views and Nicene Creed, follow Adhar and Mari liturgy for worship, and pray for departed souls. Memorials of saints are observed but without using statues or icons. Episcopal celibacy is practised. They do not practise confession and use leavened bread and wine in communion.

What remained of the *Purthenkootukar* section (Jacobite Syrian Orthodox) again underwent a split in 1909 during the visit of the Patriarch of Antioch Mar Gregorious Abdulla (St. Thomas Christian Encyclopaedia, 1973:76). The Metropolitan Mar Geevarghese Dionysius VI refused the Patriarch to "execute a document pledging complete obedience to the Antioch Patriarch, on the ground that the Church of India was always autonomous. This led to the excommunication of Mar Dionysius VI and the enthroning of Mar Koorilos as metropolitan. In a counter move, Mar Dionysius invited a deposed Syrian Patriarch Mar Abdal Messih who reinstated Mar Dionysius and consecrated the senior most Bishop, Mar Dionysius, as "Catholicos of the East" with the title Mar Baselinel in 1912. Abdal-Messih also bestowed on the Catholicos the rights to consecrated Holy Chrism (holy oil) and bishops of their own. Prolonged legal battle followed, as the laity also took sides and controversy broke out about sharing of churches and institutions.

Thus, today the Jacobites of India are divided into two autonomous groups : (1) The Metrankakshi or those who sided with the Metropolitan of Malankara Mar Dionysibs and the Catholicos Mar baselines (or the Metran party) calling itself the "Syrian Orthodox Church of India" and (2) The Babakakshi, who adhered to the Antiochian Patriarch, calling, itself the "Jacobite Syrian Orthodox Church (of India). The Syro-Malankara (Roman Catholics) was formed by the unification of a section comprising two Bishops, Mar Ivanios of Thiruvananthapuram and Mar Theophilos of Thiruvella and the congregations of Bethany sisters and Bethany brothers of the "Metrankakshi" with the Roman Catholics in 1930. (*cf.* Mundadan, 1984:109-112; St. Thomas Encyclopaedia, 1913:76-77). The term Orthodox Christianity indicates (*orthos*, straight correct, true; and *doxa*, glory) a community which worships or glorifies god in the true, straight or correct spirit. The Armenian presence in the coasts of India is reported in the 16th and 17th centuries and organised into independent Armenian Apostolic Church in Kolkata, Chennai and

Mumbai. Through inter-marriages the Armenians left their ancestral Church to join the Catholic, Anglican, or other Protestant churches (*cf.* St. Thomas Christian Encyclopaedia, 1982:12). This group also came under oriental orthodox tradition. The Greek Orthodox Church is also represented in India by the presence at Kolkata and building a Church there in 1779 (*cf. ibid.*:12). They belong either to the Byzantine Orthodox Church or the Eastern Orthodox Church. This small community in India is controlled by six ecumenical patriarchs through the Australian Archbishopric.

The Early Expansion

The Christians of St. Thomas tradition were present in different parts of India and Ceylon (Sri Lanka) before the arrival of the Portuguese, but were bound by tradition and native affiliations. The earliest and most large scale expansion of Christianity started with the Portuguese occupation of the Konkan, Malabar and Coromandel coastal pockets, which were then under their control. "The territories comprised of Vasai (Bassin), Goa and the coastal tract extending from Cranganore to Cape Comorin and from there to the island of Pambam to such isolated towns or settlements such as Diu, Chaul, Nagapattinam, San Thome (Mylapore) and Hoogly (Thekkdath, 1982:3). This expansion was financed and administered by the "Padroado" treaty (referred earlier). The setting up of Goa diocese in 1534 was a first step towards the formation of an "autonomous" Latin Church in India under the Padroado. St. Francis Xavier (at present, Spanish missionary) who arrived at the Goan coast in the year 1542 carried out large scale evangelisation in Travancore (Mukkuvar fisher folk) pearl fishery coast (Bharathar or Paravar). In 1558 the Cochin diocese was formed under Suffragan to the sea of Go a (*cf.* Thekkdath, 1982:130), whose jurisdiction was over South India and Bengal. In spite of the achievement of St. Francis Xavier, Christianity still remained at large *parangimargam* (religion of the *parangis* = Portuguese, implying a greedy and immoral person). In the seventeenth century, Fr. Robertde Nobili, another Jesuit Missionary, adopted the Hindu way of life and reformulated Christianity in accordance with Indian culture. His mission field was Madurai in Tamil Nadu. The monopoly of Christian missionary activity was in the hands of the Padroado (1681 to 1774) Mission, comprising of religious orders of the Franciscans, the Dominicans, and the Augustinians (who had colleges and novitiate in Goa). The Carmelites, the Theatines and the Jesuits were broken when Portugal lost the monopoly over India to the Dutch, who in turn, lost to the British, Portugal could no longer support the existing missions. The need for monitoring the mission directly by the Pope himself led to the formation of the Propaganda in the year 1622 (*cf.* St. Thomas Christian Encyclopaedia, 1982: 27). Rome by-passed the authority of the Padroado by appointing Vicars Apostolic who were ordained Bishops. They took full charge of pastoral and missionary work in regions under the Padroado. The Propaganda missionaries belonged to the Capuchin, Theatines, Discarded Carmelites and the French Mission. The vicar apostolate functioned in Karwar Bombay, Madras, Malabar, Kanara, Suratand Pondicherry. The purpose of the Propaganda mission was to propagate and indigenise the functions of the Church as well as to Latinise the Oriental Christians, which was met with lot of opposition from the missionaries. The efforts of the Roman Catholic Church to Indianise the Church was a slow process (*cf.* Mundadan, 1984:158); though it was started in 17th century, it could not be achieved until before the early 20th century, by establishing Indian hierarchies for Latin, Syro-Malabar and Syro-Malankara and Knananya (Syro-Malabar).

The Catholic Community Comprises the Following Elements

(1) A section of Syrian Christians; (2) Converts of Portuguese missionaries from 1500 onwards in Goa, Southern Peninsula, West Coast and Bengal; (3) Descendents of European origin (Anglo-Indians); and (4) Modern converts from the Hindu Tribal sections. As on 2011, the organisational hierarchy consists of 30 Archbishop-Metropolitans (including one Archbishop-Patriarch), 125 Diocesan Bishops, one Coadjutor Archbishop, two coadjutor Bishops, 12 Auxiliary Bishops and three Diocesan Administrators, who, at the national level, have a coordination committee of Catholic Bishops Conference of India (CBCI).

Entry and Expansion of Protestant Christianity

During the 17th century, European powers that were Protestant in faith, established hold in different parts of the country. In 1600, the English East India Company established control over Surat, Bombay, Masulipatnam, Madras and Calcutta. The Dutch East India Company (1601) held Pulikad, Thuthukudi, Nagapatnam, Chinsena, Cochin and Malaka. The Danish also held sway over Serampur (near Kolkata) and Tanjore. The above places became centres of Protestant missionary activity since the 18th century (*cf.* Koodapuzha, 1980:606; Mundadan, 1984:161; Menacherry, 1982:212). The pioneering Protestant Missions in India were: (1) Lutherans, from Halle in Germany, who started the Tranquebar Mission in 1706 with the help of SPCK (Society for

Propagation of Gospel); (2) The Serampur Mission founded by William Carrey (Baptist Missionary Society, 1792) with two other Englishmen; and (3) The mission movement started by Alexander Duff in Calcutta during 1830. Unlike the early Catholic missions, the Protestants stressed on the spread of Bible and translated it to several Indian languages. English education was encouraged.

American, European and English Protestant denominations began to operate in India in the nineteenth century. Their break-up was as given below:

British

Church Missionary Society (1813), Wesleyan Methodist Missionary Society (1819), General Baptist Missionary Society (1821), Church of Scotland (1829), Plymouth Brethren (1833), Welsh Calvinistic Methodists (1840), Irish Presbyterians (1841), and Free Church of Scotland (1843).

American

American Board of Commissioners (1812), American Presbyterians (1833), American Baptists (1835), Dutch Reformed Churches of America (1836), and Methodist Episcopal-Church (1856).

European

Basel Mission (1818), Gossamer Mission (1839), Berlin Missionary Society (1842), North German Missionary Society (1843), Leipzig Missionary Society (1840), and Swedish Lutherans and Moravian Brethren (source: St. Thomas Christian Encyclopaedia, Vol. I, 1982:78).

Major Protestant Churches

1. Anglican Church

The Church Mission Society of Anglican Church carries out evangelistic work in the north, south, central and western parts of the country along with medical and educational missions. The Oxford Mission of Calcutta (Kolkata), the Scottish Episcopal Church at Nagpur, and the Palampur Mission also come under the Anglican Mission (*Ibid.* 49).

2. Lutheran Churches

Missionaries of this reformed society established many mission centres, including the Tranquebar Mission in Tamil Nadu (Tanjavur, Tiruchirapalli, Cuddalore), and later branched into the Tamil Evangelical Lutheran Church and the Arcot Evangelical Lutheran Church. Other centres include Andhra Evangelical Lutheran Church (1842) in Guntur,

Rajahmundry, the Krishna Delta of South Andhra Lutheran Church (Tirupati), the Jeypore Evangelical Lutheran Church (Orissa), and the Gossamer Evangelical Lutheran Church (Chotanagpur, 1845), which is divided into five *Anchals* (Tribal zones) with its headquarters in Ranchi. Their activities are spread across Bihar, Bengal, Assam, Orissa Madhya Pradesh and Andaman Islands. In MP again, the Swedish Lutheran Church started a mission (1877) comprising areas of Sagar, Betul, Bhopal Chindwara, Shadol and Surguja districts (*cf.* Gafe*ibid.* 65 to 68).

3. Baptist Churches

Major areas of concentration of Baptist Congregations in India start with Andhra and extend through Orissa, and from Bengal to Assam, Meghalaya, Nagaland, Manipur and Tripura. The mission was established in 1800 at Serampore by William Carey who is hailed as the father of protestant missions in India. They grew rapidly in Andhra and Orissa.

The Baptists had an overwhelming response in the north-eastern states. The Christian movement in the hills was indigenous in nature and their political organisations promoted the growth of local congregations which were self-supporting. According to 2001 Census, Nagaland has the highest percentage (89.96%) of Christians in the country and most of these are Baptists. The Baptists Churches have an all Indian organisation called the Baptist Union of India, having denominational or regional grouping: (1) the *Semavesam* of Telugu Baptist Churches; (2) Convention of Baptist Churches of the Northern Circars in Andhra; (3) The Council of Baptist Churches in North-East India (*cf.* Frederick. S. Downs, *Ibid.*: 69); (4) Council of Baptist Churches in Northern India; (5) Central India Baptist Mission; and others.

4. Assemblies of God

This denomination is of American origin. Most of the followers are in the South. They have two regional assemblies South India and North India. The assemblies (*Jehova Shammath*) are also called Brother Bakht Singh group, comprising Chaubra/Sikh converts.

5. Bible Mission

Formed in 1938, it is a group of independent Lutherans distributed in Andhra Pradesh, especially Guntur with main centre at Railpet.

6. Church of North India (CNI)

The world missionary conference held in 1910 at Edinburgh developed into a great ecumenical movement and finally culminated in the formation of the World Council of Churches (WCC) in the year 1948. Simultaneously in 1924, efforts were launched by various

Presbyterian and congregational churches to form the United Church of North India who invited other churches to form a wider union. The churches which joined this movement were the Australian churches of Christ Mission, the Australian Methodist Church, the Wesleyan Methodist Church, the Methodist Episcopal Church, the Church of Brethren, and a few others. Negotiations went on for many years until finally in 1970 at Nagapur the Church of North India was inaugurated with a Presbyterian minister. The area of activities extended from parts of Andhra Pradesh to Kashmir and from Gujarat to Assam comprising seven Synods headed by secretaries.

7. Church of South India (CSI)

This union of churches in South India consisted of the Anglican Church, the Methodist Church and the South India United Church (SIUC), which was formed in 1908 as a result of the union of Congregationalists (Presbyterians). The CSI came into existence in the year 1947. As per the plan of union, all the ordained ministers of the different uniting churches, whether Episcopal or non-Episcopal, were accepted as ordained ministers of the new church, and future ordinations were to be held by Episcopal laying of hands. The CSI union fundamental principles recognise the Holy Scriptures (Old and New Testaments), the Apostles creed and Nicene Creed sacrament of Baptism, Lord's supper and the Episcopate.

8. India Mennonite Brethren Church

Established by missionaries sent by the Mennonite Brethren Church of North America in 1899, they evangelised Telugu people. They had a three-pronged approach, "preach teach and heal." Their centres are located in Nagarkurnool, Devarkonda, Hughestown, Shamshabad, Mahabubnagar, Jamenpet, Narayanpet, Malakpet, etc. The Mennonite Church of India is also operating in Madhya Pradesh with Dhamtari as centre.

9. Jehovah's Witnesses

The Jehovah's witnesses draw their name from scriptural account of the psalm where "Jehovah" is referred as most high. It was moved by Charles Taze Russel in Pennsylvania, USA in early 1884 and incorporated as Watch Tower Bible Tract Society. Their activities started in India during 1905 and had followings in Bombay, Goa, Kerala and Karnataka, who were mostly Roman Catholics. The old and new testaments are taken literally except for figurative and symbolic expressions.

10. Methodist Church

It started activities in India as Methodist Episcopal Church in the year 1956. The Church was started by American missionaries. The regional division of the Methodist Churches are called Annual conferences and are present in Agra (Chamars, Mazhabi Sikhs), Bengal (Bengalis, Santals, Orans and Mundas), Bombay (cosmopolitan), Delhi (Chubra and artisans of Rajasthan), Gujarat (Dherds), Hyderabad (Madiga, Sudra), Lucknow (Chamars and Doms), Madhya Pradesh (Lal Begis, Bhils and other tribes), Moradabad (Chamars and Doms), and South India (Sudra and Madiga) (World Christian Encyclopedia, 1982).

11. Presbyterian Church of North-East India

It was established in the year 1812 and has many followers among the Mizos and Khasis. They stood away from CNI.

12. Pentecostal Churches

The Pentecostal Churches in India have proliferated rapidly. The term is applied to all those churches in the reformation tradition, which held that the "charismatic" gifts experienced on the day of Pentecost (Acts 2:4) are still operative in the present day...... and is directly related to revival movements of the 19th century (St. Thomas Christian Encyclopaedia, 1982:76). They believe that the Bible is inspired; that Christ will visibly return to the earth; and that the Church and believers are led by the Holy Spirit; they also believe in simple worship; in the holiness of life; and in baptism (*ibid.*). There are many groupings among them including the Indian Assemblies of God (1918, in Saharampur), the Indian Pentecostal Church (1924, Kerala), The Pentecostal Church of God (1936, AP), the Ceylon Pentecostal Church, and the Revival Church of Nagaland.

13. Salvation Army/Muktifauj

"It is a Christian movement, international, multi-racial, non-political and combines a fervent, joyous. religious faith with practical and worldwide social services" (*ibid.*:71). It was founded by William and his wife Catherine in 1865 in England, and the name was adopted in 1878. It adopted a military plan of organisation; the mission station became corps, members became soldiers, evangelists became officers with uniforms and ranks; and flag as crest. They do not believe sacraments to be essential for salvation and therefore, do not observe them. This arrived in India in 1882, and they have five "Territorial Commanders."

14. Seventh Day Adventist Church

They observe "sabbath", also known as *Shanivarthlis,* on Saturday. They originated in New York, America, founded by Elan Herman, and were established in India in 1895. "Preach, teach and heal" is their missionary approach as well. Their mission centres are in central, south and north-eastern India.

Other important denominations are Evangelical Congregationalists Church of God (Anderson), in council of Baptist churches in North-East India and the Baptist Church of Mizoram that refused to join the CNI.

The Protestant Church in India grew and expanded in terms of members and area during the 19th century. The ecumenical movement of the Protestant Church of 20th century and the vigorous national movement of India during the early part of the century paved way for indigenisation and Indianisation of the Protestant Church. The National Christian Council of India (NCCI) became an Indian affair since the 1940s. It strongly supported the National Movement and protested against the denominationalism of western Protestantism. The Protestant Churches in India have made great contributions to the field of education and medical care in remote areas of the country, including tribal areas.

References

David Daniel. 1972. "The Orthodox Church of India", Vol. I, *History*, New Delhi. Print Aid.

Hambye, E.R. 1952 "Saint Thomas and India", *Clergy Monthly,* Vol. 16, pp. 363-75.

Joseph, T.K. 1955. *Six St. Thomas of South India*, Chengannur.

Jussey, P.M. 1990. "Christians of Kerala" (Communication).

Koodapuzha, Xavier, 1980. *Bharatha Sabha Chariteam* (Malayalam), Kottayam St. Thomas Apostolic Seminary.

Mayhew, Arthur, 1988. *Christianity in India*, Delhi. Gyan Publishing House.

Medlycott, A.E. 1905. *India and the Apostle St. Thomas*, London. Oxford University Press.

Menacherry George (ed.) 1988. *Trichur St. Thomas Christian Encyclopaedia of India*, Vol. I.

Mundadan A.M. 1984a. *History of Christianity in India*, Vol. I, Bangalore. Theological Publication in India.

________1984b. *Indian Christians: Search for Autonomy*, Bangalore. Dharmaram Publications.

National Christian Council of India 1959. *The Christian Handbook*, Nagpur, NCCI.

Perumalil, A.L. 1971. *The Apostels India: Facts and Fiction*, Patna (Revised Edition).

Pidipara, P.T. 1970. *The Thomas Christians*, London and Bombay. Oxford University Press.

Thekkedath, Joseph, 1982. *History of Christianity in India*, Vol. II, Bangalore.

Whalen, William J. 1958. *Separated Brethren: A Survey of Non-Catholic Christian Denomination in the United States*, Milwaukee. Bruce Publishing Company.

World Christians Encyclopaedia (ed.) David B. Barrett 1982. *A Comparative Study of Churches and Religions of Modern World*. New York, Oxford University Press. pp. 370-80.

14

Multiculturalism in the Ritual Performance of Kerala: A Study on Teyyam

V. Jayarajan

Andrew Heywood distinguishes between two overall forms of multiculturalism: descriptive and normative. "The term 'multiculturalism' has been used in a variety of ways, both descriptive and normative. As a descriptive term, it has been taken to refer to cultural diversity ... As a normative term, multiculturalism implies a positive endorsement, even celebration, of communal diversity, typically based on either the right of different groups to respect and recognition, or to the alleged benefits to the larger society of moral and cultural diversity" (Heywood, Political Ideologies, 4th edition, Palgrave Macmillan, 2007: 313).

The northern part of Kerala, to be more precise, the small stretch between Korapuzha in Kozhikode District and Chandragiri River in the present Kasargod District is the region where the age-old culture of Teyyam still prevails. Kozhikodòe and the surrounding regions were ruled by the Zamorins and the Northern tip was ruled by Kolattiri and thus known as Kolattunadòu. In fact, though the whole region was once a part of erstwhile Malabar, as it was in the five northern districts of the present day Kerala State (viz. Kasargod, Kannur, Waynad, Kozhikode, Malappuram and some parts of Thrissur and Palakkad districts), especially with the commencement of British rule. Almost a similar ritual form can be seen in Kozhikode and southern parts of Kannur District but there it is known as Tira. In the two districts of Dakshina Kannada and Kodagu in the neighbouring State of Karnataka, it is known as Bhutakola.

As mentioned earlier, Teyyam or Tira (as it is considered the synonym of Teyyam) or another ritual performance such as Putan along with Tira found in Malappuram, and Palakkad districts of Malabar with slight variations, even now appears as an annual ritualistic festival. All these performances require ritualistic arrangements as also the involvement of the traditional performing community. Therefore, it is considered as a ritual performance, and not as merely a performing art.

If a rich form of folk culture sprouts from the Dravidian region and also from the caste-based composition of the society, it is the Teyyam, a ritualistic performance, which can be described as the most visible, spectacular art form of Malabar, associated with myths and legends. Other major folk forms, which are inseparable from the dominant culture of the region, include Kolkali[1], Bhuta[2], Purakalti[3], Kummatti[4], Tirpputan[5], Kanyarkali[6], Arabanamuttu and Daphmuttu[7], Oppana[8].

Tidambu Trittam[9], etc. Folklorists agree that Tira, Putan and Bhuta strike a similar chord with Teyyam in terms of their ritual and performative aspects. Also, these three forms including Teyyam, command religious fervour for the underlying divinity and for the belief that they are Gods, Goddesses and divine spirits, while most other folk forms are devoid of the aspect of divinity. A few find their places in the folk culture as entertainers. Some folk-arts like Kanyarkali and Purakalialso provide religious solace for the believers who propitiate Gods and Goddesses. The ritual dances and the connected art forms in Northern Kerala can be related to the more vibrant Dravidian culture of South India.

As mentioned earlier, this region was called Kolattunadòu, the land ruled by Kolattiri. The unique form of worshipping Gods, Goddesses, dead ancestors, deceased heroes, victimised personalities, terrific animals and serpents, devils, etc., is based on a rather simple concept, that, after suitable propitiatory rituals, a God or Goddess belonging to a pantheon of hundreds of deities becomes temporally manifest in the body of an empowered man, thereby elevating him to a divine status.

Ceremonies usually take place either within the precincts of a small shrine or in the yard of an ancestral house, or in an open space with a temporary shrine called *Pati*[10]. The first stage of almost all Teyyam performances is either a *Tottam Pattuu*[11], in which a performer with simple costume and minimal make up comes before the shrine and recites the invocatory songs or tales of the deity, or comes before the shrine wearing a more elaborate costume and make-up as *Vellattam*[12] to perform an energetic dance as usually associated with vigorous war heroes. Some Teyyam do not have *Tottam Pattuu*, as its origin is confined to the invocatory songs. On the other hand, some Teyyams have an elaborate *Tottam Pattuu* which lasts for several hours. The authors of these songs are not known, but for a few exceptions. Generally songs are composed in local language but Sanskrit verses drawn from epics are also sung as *Tottam Pattuufor* some Teyyam*s*. Similar *Tottam Pattuuare* performed, with slight variations, for several Teyyam*s*.

After these rituals, the performer retires to prepare for the actual Teyyam performance, a process beginning with the application of intricate facial make-up, whose every line is symbolic, and ending with the donning of the elaborate costume. The most sacred part of the costume, the head-dress, is put on before the shrine's sanctum after which, as drum beats, the performer looks at his reflection in a small hand-mirror. This is one of Teyyam's most conceptually crucial and intimate moments as what he sees in the mirror is not his own image, but the powerful divine being which he represents.

While the Teyyam ritual proceeds, the performer with the striking costumes and head gear, circumambulates the shrine, dances, runs and walks through the shrine's compound to the tune of the *Cenda. Towards* the end of the performance he blesses devotees, receives offerings and speaks in a dialect alien from the general parlance, creating a divine atmosphere.

Dance is one of the earliest forms of human worship (Kurup, 1977:5[13]), and has its roots in the primitive life of the tribes, as they have adopted dance as a mode to worship the divine power or the spirits. It is the propitiation of Gods, Goddesses and spirits. The divine dancer achieves identification with the deity, and the movements of his body represent a religious rite associated with the mysterious divinity (*ibid.*).

Generally, Teyyam is not performed in the Brahminical temples, but in small village shrines. A shrine is a worshipping place of one family or one community and in a few cases it is a common worshiping place for all castes where one or more Teyyams are performed.

Teyyam can be described as a form of worship consisting of a special combination of symbols, rituals and art forms, particularly dance, through which the ghosts, good and evil spirits, in the manifestation of sub-human, animate beings, ancestor spirits of legendary figures of great valour, extraordinary powers, and endowments and Gods and

Goddesses: *Shiva, Sakti,* and *Vishnu* are appeased and honoured (Pallath, 1995:60[14]).

The origin of Teyyam is traced to tribal living and culture. As a cult, its origin can be related to rituals and practises of primitive society. The elaborate accounts of *Velan Veriyatal* available in the Sangam literature may have some connection with the Teyyam cult (Kurup, 2000:16[15]). But the impact made by Brahminism widened it into almost a religion, more appropriately a folk religion. The influence of Brahminism cannot be ignored, because the dominant castes found Teyyam quite close to divinity and provided patronage. The Brahminical religion casts its influence on Teyyam and in the process new rituals came into being within the framework of the tradition. There are both male and female deities. In fact, Goddesses outnumber gods in *Teyyattam*. We can find that most of these Goddesses are either called Bhagavatis or Camundis. It is true that the Brahminical religious philosophies such as Saktism, Vaishnavism and Shaivismhave made their impact on Teyyam. However, the tribal character has not much altered and hence, it is still the most powerful and vibrant folk/tribal form of the region. Later, the perceptions and practises of Buddhism, Jainism and Brahminism have also had their effect on the evolution of Teyyam. A significant incorporation into Teyyam and associated rituals is that of earmarking a separate space for offerings of blood and other edible items, and toddy in the northern part of the shrine known as *Vadakkenvatil*[16]. In the shrines where the main deity does not require such sacrifices, space for *Vadakkenvatil* can be seen outside the main compound, where sacrifices will be offered for subordinate deities.

Further, Lord Vishnu did not appeal much to the imagination of the people of Malabar, because the influence of Vaishnavism on Teyyam is minimal. Likewise, with Lord Shiva and Lord Ayyappa; although many people go for pilgrimage to Sabarimala (famous for Lord Ayyappa temple in Kerala) and Lord Subramanya, they are not worshipped as Teyyam. Instead people are more inclined to worship different forms of Mother Goddess for fertility and warding off ills. In spite of this, there are at least two Teyyam*s* which emerged out of the minimal impact made by Vaishnavism: one is Vishnumurty and the other is Palot Daivam. However, Lord Shiva's son (Vettakorumakan) and his incarnations are performed as Teyyams.

As in some other societies in India, the caste system has dominant influence on the evolution of the Teyyam cult in Kerala. It would be impossible to perform Teyyam in a ritualistic manner if we ignore the caste hierarchies. The link between Teyyam and the Gods/Goddesses of the Hindu pantheon is unmistakable. But sometimes, in actual practise, ancestors, heroes and heroines, village Gods and victimised persons are also found worshipped as Teyyam (a detailed classification of Teyyam*s* can be seen elsewhere in this book).

Teyyam is believed to be a corrupt form of a Sanskrit word *Daivam*, which means God/Goddess. Worship of Teyyam can be considered one of the earliest forms of worshipping village Gods in Malabar. Irrespective of caste and religion, people attend Teyyam performances seeking blessings, warding off evil spirits, demanding prosperity in their agricultural activities, and for settling disputes.

Earlier, many colonialists (both missionaries and administrators), considered Teyyam as spirit worship, or devil dance. The Bhuta cult, which is seen in Tulunad (present-day Southern Karnataka), was also sometimes described by some British as devil worship due to their ignorance of its deeper meaning. "The spirits worshipped in this cult are not to be identified with devils, nor is the ritual associated with them to be equated with witchcraft, black magic or propitiation of ghosts" (Upadhyaya and Upadhyaya, 2002:2[17]). Some foreign scholars misinterpreted this as devil dance (Innes and Ivans, in their Malabar Gazetteer; and Hammerton[18] in his edited work, *The Customs and Manners of Mankind* described *Teyyattam* as a devil dance). Penny[19] also misunderstood this dance as propitiating evil spirits in Southern India. But Herman Gundert, in his famous Malayalam-English Dictionary[20] defines Teyyam as *Daivam (God)*. Later, it became very much a part of the social life of the northern part of Kerala, and still exists with all its pomp and passion along with all its visual beauty in Malabar.

There are various theories about the origin of Teyyam. A few argue that it is a continuation of hero-worship. Yet another theory is that it is a relic of tribal worship. It is very difficult to find out the exact period of the origin of Teyyam. At the same time, none can refute its antiquity.

The Teyyam tradition acquires double significance when we observe that it becomes a meeting point for the Hindus and Muslims. Kerala, especially the Malabar area, had a strong relationship with Islam, and trade links existed with the Arabs even during olden times. It is also a fact that Malabar has always had a considerable Muslim population compared to other parts of Kerala. This is well reflected in the Teyyam cult. Though the Muslim Teyyams are all performed by the Hindus in Hindu shrines, their religion is clearly stated and they are duly respected (Seth, 2000:7)[21].

There are a few Muslims who have been deified as Teyyams. Some of these are bereft of individuality as they are performed along with other deities. For example, the Ankakaran Teyyam (Hindu Deity) has a Muslim assistant namely Bappuran or Bappiriyan. This Teyyam narrates his forays along the Mosques of Kerala; and also into the rituals. But still Ankakaran allows him to accept the offerings on his behalf. Some Muslim characters stand apart as Teyyams with their own individuality. For example, Ali Bhutha or Ali Camundi worshipped in Kumbala and Babbirayar in several shrines of Kasargod. These are victimised Muslims who were killed by none other than the Goddess. Mapila Teyyam in Kamballur Kottayilveedu is a typical example of victims attaining divinity.

Community Symbiosis in *Teyyam*

Irrespective of castes, all people worship Teyyam. But the right to don the Teyyam outfit and dance as a divine being is restricted to a few castes. Even among the performers there are geographical restrictions for their movements. Each performing community will have its own right-holding geographical areas and shrines to perform. They should don the Teyyamin accordance with the customary rules. This right to perform Teyyam is called *Cherujanmavakasam*[22]. Some performers have the jurisdiction of a village while others have a larger jurisdiction comprised of several villages.

Another notable aspect of Teyyam is that all Teyyam-performing communities are considered to be lower in social status. According to the Government of Kerala, all of them belong to Scheduled Castes and Scheduled Tribes. Malayan, Vannan, Velan, Koppalan, Mavilan, Pulayan, Paravan, Pampathan, and Chinkathan are the main communities that perform Teyyam.

While the above communities are performers of Teyyam, other communities are also involved either directly or indirectly in it. The Tiyya community supplies toddy and palm leaves to the Teyyam. Kollan is engaged in making or sharpening the swords and spikes of Teyyam, the Asari (the carpenter) is responsible for wooden works such as making the Peedom (Pedestal); and the Kidaran (astrologer), for painting the shrines. The Kanisan supplies umbrellas and also predicts the success of the festival, while the Veluthedan (washer man) supplies fresh clothes to the higher castes and the Vannathi (female folk of Vannan community) to the lower castes. The Brahmins involve in purification functions, and installation of idols. Generally, patronisation of a shrine is the responsibility of the Nair, Nambiar, and Poduval communities. The

Mukkuvans/Mugayas offer fish to some places. The Mogayas on the other hand, work as the *kodikkoora* bearers in the northern areas of Kasargod. In some shrines, the Pulayas are engaged to remove weeds and also to bring mats in connection with the *Perumkaliyattam*. The Kusavansare engaged in supplying the earthen vessels. Thus, the entire community in a village has a role in the Teyyam performance. It is interesting to note that even Muslims offer salt, sugar, jaggery and other provisions for the successful conduct of the festival in some shrines.

The study of any cultural practise cannot be taken in isolation; rather, it has to be studied along with the society. Teyyam of North Kerala has evolved over a period of time and adopted several changes along with the society. Kurup (1977:1) is of the opinion that Aryan and Dravidian cultural complexes constituted the cultural tradition of Kerala. He uses these terms for two distinct socio-linguistic groups. He also states that Aryan stands for Brahminical culture and Dravidian denotes the tribal and indigenous groups. However, the author prefers to use the terms Brahminisation and Sanskritisation interchangeably, as the term Aryan is more controversial and vague in the present context. The cultural tradition of the Hindus in Kerala is a mixture of "great" and "little" traditions of Hinduism.

A deep study on the *Kavus*, where the popular cult of Teyyam or *Teyyattam* is maintained, will help us understand the above phenomenon. Although the *Kavu* is a center of worship for lower communities, it is not a temple as prescribed under the Brahminical religious concepts. It is a Dravidian institution which has its own folk-deities and rituals. However, under the process of Sanskritisation, these shrines house some prominent Brahminical Gods and Goddesses among their innumerable folk-deities. The Kuruvanthatta *Kalakam* in Ramanthali, the Ramavilyam *Kalakam* in Trikaripur, Nilamangalam *Kalakam* in Thuruthi near Cheruvathur and Palakunnu *Kalakam* in Kottikulam are the centers of Tiyya socio-religious life. Kuruvanthatta *Kalakam* and Ramavilyam *Kalakam* are situated just 5 km to the west and 6 km to the north of Payyanur, one of the northern most, and therefore, the earliest, Brahmin settlement in Kerala (Logan, 1993:236)[23]. The northern region of Kannur District was the earliest region in Kerala to be affected by the wave of Brahmin immigration and colonisation. According to legend, Parasurama brought Brahmins from Aryapuram (i.e., North India) and helped them settle in 32 different villages of Kerala. These villages were grouped under four *Kalakams* or administrative units. William Logan described the old system of administration in his manual (1887) as the social organisation of the Brahmin community which was based on clustering of villages. *Teras* was the basic unit of the Nairs and the *Cheri* was the basic unit of the Tiyyas (*ibid.*:122).

Following the Brahmin practise of organising the settlements into *Kalakams*, the Tiyyas of North Kerala between the rivers Chandragiri and Perumba also organised their society into four *Kalakams.*

The influence of Brahminic tradition on Tiyyas can be seen in the organisation of their shrines. Earlier, the Tiyya shrines under the control of a *Kalakam*, known as *Mundya* or *Arai*. The Tiyyas of the locality were controlled by the community leaders from these centers. Later, such shrines also came to be known as *Tanam* (*Stanam*, i.e., sacred place) following the Brahminic tradition. The Tiyyas, as well as the lower castes, started imitating the Brahminic cultural traditions in many ways. However, the priests in *Kalakam* shrines continued to be Tiyyas. Now almost all the shrines including the *kalakams* have become temples. Even the Andallur Kavu of Thalasseri, which was one of the ancient worshipping centres of the Tiyya community, has become Andallur Kshetram (temple). Like-wise Muchilott Kavus of the Vaniya community have been renamed as Muchilott Bhagavati Kshetram. It is also a fact that after the re-installation ceremonies, even the patrons of the shrines are considering to rename it as a temple. When we observe those shrines very closely, we can see that the changes have taken place not only in the names, but also in the day-to-day affairs.

Among those Kavus, who belong to the lower castes, a few of them have started daily pujas, which was not in practise during the olden days. And among the four Kalakams of Tiyyas of North Kerala, two of them have started daily pujas to the tune of Brahminical rites. They are Kuruvantatta *kalakam* in Ramanthali and Palakkunnu *kalakam* in Kottikulam (Jayarajan, unpublished PhD thesis, 2006). Installation of mike-sets and playing of devotional songs in the morning and evening is also common in the shrines. *Annadanam* (serving food to all the devotees) has also become a usual practise during the Teyyam season.

Barbosa had described in his Manual that the Tiyyas worshipped separate idols kept in their shrines. Probably, the idols referred by Barbosa are the Teyyam deities of the Tiyyas. The shrines of the Tiyyas consist of deities which may be classified into two categories: indigenous (non-Sanskritic), and Sanskritised. Even Palanytayi Kannan, a common man was deified after his death. But the deity is named after Vishnumurti and performed in accordance with the myth of Narasimha *Avatar* of

Lord Vishnu (fourth *Avatar*). Shrines such as Andallur Kavu, Kappad Kavu, Paduvilayi Kavu and Mavila Kavu, with Daivattar as main deity, have been Sanskritised with the stories of Ramayana, and the Daivattar became Sree Rama; Ankakkaran became Lakshmana and another local deity, Athiralan became Seeta. The depiction of local fight became the fight between Bali and Sugrivain the great epic Ramayana.

The legend of Ramavilyam is further related to the Parasurama tradition. It is believed that on the occasion of erecting the image of Lord Vishnu at Chakrapani Temple at Trikkarippur, Parasurama was obstructed by a local *Asura* or demon. This *Asura* was defeated and killed by a Goddess of battle, called Patakkatti Bhagavati, who is now propitiated in the northern shrine of Araiin Ramavilyam. Another legend is that Parasurama himself had placed his bow at the place of the present shrine. Thus this *Kalakam*, a Dravidian institution, claims superiority by linking its legends with the popular Aryan tradition and mythology of Parasurama (Kurup K.K.N, 1977).

It is interesting to examine how the Dravidian institution of worship differs in rituals and customs from that of a Brahminical temple. The priests and officiants of the *Kalakams* and shrines are members of the corresponding community and/or elders. The Brahmins have no priesthood in these shrines. But it has become a practise in many places that the Brahmins' presence is required for the purificatory rituals prior to the *Teyyattam.* Ganapati *homa* by Brahmin priests (puja to please Lord Ganapati in order to avert obstacles) was introduced in several shrines.

Due to the influence of the Brahmins, a hierarchical caste structure was formulated and the natives were given a subordinate position. According to the legendary *Keralolpatti,* Parasurama sanctioned festivals like *Kaliyattam, Puravela* and *Daivattam* or *Teyyattam* to the people of Kerala. The native communities like Panan, Velan and Vannan were allotted the profession of Teyyamdance. He installed shrines like Camundi for the prosperity of the Keralites. He also established Goddess Durga on the sea coast. These traditions explain how indigenous cults were tolerated and metamorphosed under the religious supremacy of the Brahmins (Kurup, 1977:4). Thus, the Dravidian shrines owed their allegiance to the Brahminical temples. Simultaneously, as a process of Brahminisation, a few Brahminic Gods and Goddesses were incorporated among the folk deities of the indigenous people.

Thus, we find an assimilation of both Brahminic and non-Brahminic cultural complexes, the process described by Mac Kim Marriott as universalisation and parochialisation. Redfield called these cultural complexes as "great" and "little" traditions. Srinivas had called the process of interaction between great and little tradition as Sanskritisation. This process is very much prevalent and is described in relation to different aspects of social life of North Kerala. In this respect, the institutions of *Kalakam* and Teyyam are highlighted.

The migration of the Brahmins into this region brought several new practises which also got integrated into the local customs. For example, deities like Vishnu, Shiva, Kamadeva, etc., were borrowed from the Sanskritic traditions. Different branches or sects of Brahminic traditions such as Saktism and Vaishnavism dominated the process of integration of diverse cultural practises. The Teyyam shrines may be owned and managed by individual families, particular castes or the village community, but Brahminism has had its own influence on this local custom as can be seen in its integration of many cultural elements. Moreover, the rising trends of purification and installation ceremonies by the Brahmin priests, clearly shows the influence of Brahminism in Teyyam cult. It is estimated that during the last five years about 378 (survey reports of folkland) shrines were subjected to installation ceremonies by Brahmin priests.

There are both male and female Teyyam deities, but the female Teyyams outnumber the male Teyyams. This shows the influence of matriliny in Kerala. Most of the female Teyyams are called Bhagavatis or Camundis which are interpreted as the incarnations of deities of great tradition like Parvathi. Another important factor is that Teyyam is also related to Shiva (of the great tradition) and they outnumber the Teyyams related to Vishnu. This shows the dominance of Shaivism and Shakitism in North Kerala. The Brahminic traditions in the region are also dominated by Shaivism.

The Teyyam cult also has the effect of integrating the society. Though Teyyam may be celebrated by people of any Hindu community, its participants include various communities who occupy different positions in the caste hierarchy. The participation of the members of castes like Tiyya, Maniyani, Vannan, Kollan, Asari, Thattam, Pulayan, etc., are absolutely necessary for the performance of Teyyam. The authorities of the shrines have to observe many formalities before the commencement of a *mega* Teyyam festival. We find the influence of feudalism and Brahminism in such practises. Before the commencement of *Perumkaliyattam*, Shrine officials approach the local Landlords and Brahmin priests for seeking their permission.

At the time of big festivals like *Perumkaliyattam,* permission is obtained from the priests, such as Tarananellur Nambudirippad (*tantri*), who has supreme authority over all rituals of temples as the right derived from Lord Parasurama. They also have the right to conduct other ceremonies like *Naveekarana* (renovation) or *Punaprathishta* (re-installation of idols) ceremonies. There are several other such *tantriks* in this area who have the authority to conduct purificatory, installation and re-installation, or consecration ceremonies of the shrines. Further, the shrine officials make the traditional offerings of betel leaves along with coins at the nearest temples where Brahminical pujas are conducted regularly prior to the functions of the shrine. The sacred fire for lighting the lamps at the *Kalakam* or the shrines is commonly brought from the nearest Brahminical temple to mark the commencement of the ceremonies. All these formalities reveal the supremacy of the Brahminical deities over the local deities. Furthermore, *Teyyattam* is prohibited in the jusrisdiction of Brahminical deities at the time of their temple festival; Muttappan Teyyam cannot be performed in the areas where brahminical deities dominate.

The *Koyma* (supervisor) and *Matambi* (chief authority) of the shrines belong to the higher castes such as the Nairs and Poduvals. Caste hierarchy is strictly observed in the organisation of worshipping centers in Malabar. The shrines belonging to the Tiyyas or other lower castes are also under the supervision of higher castes. During ceremonies the traditional presents of betel leaves along with cash are usually made by tenants to their landlords in Kerala. The *Kalakams* and other shrines of North Kerala not only recognise the supremacy of the Brahmin priests in ritual matters but also respect the Brahminical temples in the locality. The purification ceremony generally known as the *Kalakam* of the shrines is performed by the chief Brahmin priest. The right of consecration of idols also rests with these priests. Through these formalities, the supremacy of the Brahminic Gods and Goddesses and Brahmins are established over these institutions.

Celebration of *Perumkaliyattam*, the great festival of Teyyam illustrates several aspects of the evolution of the present cultural traditions of North Kerala, including the cultural traditions of the Tiyyas and Vanyas. Evolution of deities like Bhagavati can be traced to local traditions like the cult of Mother Goddess and matrilineal system of descent of several communities in North Kerala. Ramavilyam *Kalakam* is in the forefront in the organisation of Teyyams and hence contributes to the development of a vibrant cultural tradition in this region. The dominance of Ramavilyam *Kalakam* over other *Kalakams* is also due to the fact that this *Kalakam* directly relates itself to Lord Parasurama (a Brahmin).

The Bhagavati and chamundi cults are related to the cult of Kali or Durga, according to prominent scholars who have written on the cultural traditions of Kerala (Kurup, 1977). Regarding the popularity of the Mother Goddess cult, Menon states that "there is hardly a Hindu community or a village in Malabar that does not worship Kali in one form or another, or own a shrine dedicated to the Mother Goddess" (1943). The *Kuladevata* (family deity) of many royal families in Kerala is a Mother Goddess in the name of Bhagavati, chamundi or some other form of Kali or Durga. A Bhagavati of a particular locality is known after the place. Generally, the Goddess is situated in a *Kavu* (sacred grove) which may be located by the side of a village settlement or a few kilometers away from the forest. The term *Kavu* is used to denote the shrines of Bhagavati, serpent god, Ayyappa and Kurumba. There are no idols in these shrines; this indicates an indigenous origin. The deity is generally represented by a weapon such as a trident (*trishul*) or a spear which is associated with the deity. The weapons may be made of wood or some metal like brass or iron. These shrines differ from the *stanams* or temples constructed according to the *Vastushastra* by expert masons under the guidance of Brahmins and astrologers.

Sanskritisation of the indigenous deities like Mother Goddesses may be explained by referring to some processes. First of all, these indigenous deities are linked to Brahminic deities, and to some Hindu religious texts in Sanskrit like Devi Mahatma, Markandaya Purana, Bhagavatha or Mahabharata. Secondly, the deities are linked to certain mythological characters like Parasurama. The people of Malabar strongly believe that Parasurama had granted them several shrines and the festivals associated with them.

Members of the Tiyya community and the cult of Teyyam have played an important role in the Sanskritisation of Hindu cultural traditions in North Kerala. A *Kalakam* is a socio-religious centre of the Tiyya community. Most of the rituals and festivals of the Tiyyas and other communities are conducted under the patronage and management of the *Kalakam* officials. The *Kalakam* maintains a record of all the activities of the community, and also plays an important role in bringing members of various Hindu communities together to organise the religious events.

Sanskritisation is a process which is very much present in the contemporary society in Kerala. Although the Brahmin communities are insignificant in the political and economic life of Kerala, they still wield enormous influence in the religious sphere. High level of political awareness among the people of Kerala does not affect their religious traditions. However, parallel democratic structures like committees, clubs, trusts, registered societies, etc., have come into existence in the recent past. This change is due to the spread and strengthening of modern education, and the strengthening of democratic institutions both at the village and state level. This change may be called modernisation, following Srinivas (1952). However, people do not find any contradiction in Sanskritisation and modernisation. In fact, these two processes are reinforcing each other. Tradition and modern practises may be considered as the two faces of the general social processes, which have made the society in Kerala very vibrant.

Notes

1. Rhythmic stick dance has its origin in mythology. Though it is prevalent all over India, the Kolkai of Malabar is unique. Muslim Kolkai is distinct from the other Kolkai. It has several regional variations in mythology, and the steps and moments.
2. Legend has it that this dance is drawn from the dance of 18 *Apsara-Kanyas* (celestial beauties). It became a vigorous dance of the men folk in Northern Kerala during the Puram festival, which is celebrated during February-March. The performing communities are Tiyya, Maniyani, Mugaya, Mukkuva, Chaliya and Kammalas.
3. *Kummatti* is a form of entertainment in Thrissur and Palakkad districts. During the Onam season, the so-called *Butaganòas* of Lord Shiva visit the houses in costumes made of matted grass and masks to ward off the evil spirits. People from all religions take part in this performance, especially in Thrissur.
4. Putanand Tiraare performed in Malappuram, Thrissur and Palakkad districts. Male dancers in accordance with their traditional make-up dance in tune with the drum beats. The headgears and costume of Putan and Tira are excellent, quite elaborate and colourful. Mannan and Parayan are the main communities that perform Putanand Tira.
5. Male Muslim folk of Malabar sing and dance rhythmically on festival occasions in accordance with the beating of small drums called *daphu.* Arabanamuttu, another dance form of the Muslim community, uses a different drum called *Arabanòa.*
6. Oppana is a bridal dance of the Muslim community in the Malabar Region. It usually takes place on the eve of a marriage. Girls, including the bride, put henna on their hands and sing and dance.
7. Kanyarkali is a form of ritualistic entertainment of Palakkad District. Male folk from the Nair community stand around a burning lamp and dance vigorously to commemorate a mythological fight.

8. Male Muslim folk of Malabar sing and dance rhythmically on festival occasions in accordance with the beating of small drums called *daphu. Arabanòamuttu* another dance form of the Muslim community using a different drum called *Arabanòa.*
9. Oppana is a bridal dance of the Muslim community in the Malabar region. It usually takes place on the eve of a marriage. Girls, including the bride, put henna on their hands and sing and dance.
10. This is a temple dance associated with temple festivals, performed by the Brahmins, who carry the decorated idol on their head and dance around the temple in accordance with four different rhythms played on the *Cenda* by the Maran community. It is performed only in the Kasargod and Kannur districts.
11. A temporary abode of gods. It can be a shed made of dry coconut leaves or a raised platform on which an oil lamp and weapons of Teyyam are placed.
12. A corrupt form of the word *Stotram* which means invocation.
13. An introductory dance associated with male characters.
14. Kurup K.K.N., "Aryan and Dravidian Elements in Malabar Folklore" (Trivandrum, 1977).
15. J.J. Pallath, "Teyyam: An Analytical Study of the Folk Culture, Wisdom and Personality" (New Delhi, 1995).
16. Kurup K.K.N., "The Cult of Teyyam and Hero Worship in Kerala" (Calicut, 2000).
17. It means northern door, this is a place where symbolic sacrifice is performed
18. U.P. Upadhyaya and Susheela. P. Upadhyaya, "Folk Rituals of the Tuluva Region of Coastal Karnataka" (Udupi, 2002).
19. Cited in Kurup K.K.N., "The Cult of Teyyam and Hero Worship" (Calicut, 2000).

20 *Ibid.*

21 *Malayalam-English Dictionary* by Herman Gundert (Kottayam, 1991).

22 Pepita Seth, "Reflections of the Spirit 2000", Dilectica Gallery, New York.

23 The traditional right to perform Teyyam in a particular territory was conferred to a family.

References

Kurup K.K.N. 1977. *Aryan and Dravidian Elements in Malabar Folklore*, Trivandrum.

J.J. Pallath 1995. *Teyyam: An Analytical Study of the Folk Culture*, Wisdom and Personality, New Delhi.

Kurup K.K.N. 2000. *The Cult of Teyyam and Hero Worship in Kerala*, Calicut.

U.P. Upadhyaya and Susheela. P. Upadhyaya 2002. *Folk Rituals of the Tuluva Region of Coastal Karnataka*, Udupi.

Herman Gundert 1991. *Malayalam-English Dictionary*, Kottayam.

Pepita Seth 2000. *Reflections of the Spirit*, Dilectica Gallery, New York.

15

Persistence and Change Among Sacred Specialists at Nagore Andavar's *Dargah* in Tamil Nadu

K.G. Gurumurthy* and *S.A. Azeez Saheb

Indian Muslims have the tradition of observing Islamic rituals and religious festivals besides their reverence towards the Sufi saints. Along with saint worship, it is found that constant efforts have been made in Nagore, Tamil Nadu, to Islamise the *dargah* by constructing Mosques using the patronage of royal houses. At Nagore, the Sufi saint Hazarat Sahul Hameed, the subject of the present paper, is being propitiated by the Hindus as a presiding god. The Hindu sage Shivananda, while praising the healing powers of the saint, described Hazarat Sahul Hameed as Nagore Andavar[1] (Hameed, 1986:12). Since then, the Nagore saint is locally known by this name by which he will henceforth be referred to here.

Sufi saint shrines were recorded in the earlier Gazetteers as *pallis* (mosques), but the term, in fact, denotes a *dargah* (shrine) of a Sufi saint. Even today, the Tamils, refer to the *dargah* of a Sufi saint as a *palli*. Hence, records grant the sacred merit of a Mosque to a *dargah*, to be regarded as a religious place of prayer for orthodox Muslims (Hemingway, 1906:890; Sharieff, 1921:121). Yet *dargah*s are places of veneration for all religious faiths. They not only fuse architectural styles and motifs, but create a fusion of local customary ritual practises shared by Muslims and Hindus; this is vividly evident in the performance of the Kanduri[2] festival of the saint of Nagore; these are the modes of incorporating and sacralising an inter-religious community and its spaces, joined in celebrating the anniversary of the saint's death (Saheb; 1998:56). Accordingly an attempt has been made to understand the role of the sacred specialists and the Islamisation process which is going on in the Nagore Andavar's *dargah* in Tamil Nadu.

The Problem

The identity of Nagore Andavar's *dargah* sacred complex in Tamil Nadu is maintained in many ways. There are several ritual specialists such as *muthawalli* and *peshmam* (sacred specialists of the classical Islamic tradition), *khalifah* and *muzawars* (lineal descendants of the saint), *faqirs* (spiritual descendants of the saint), followers, and devotees of the saint; who cultivate, preserve, and promote the classical and Folk-Islamic[3] cultural traditions. How these elements are spread to the masses and in turn help them in giving the perception of sacredness of the *dargah*, and also interpret in a more scientific way in relation to the Islam, are discussed in the present paper.

Methodology

The data needed for the present study of the *dargah* were collected by conducting extensive six-month field-work in two spells during 1992 and 1993. Participant observation, interviews at individual and group level, and case studies were the other techniques employed for data collection.

The Legend of the Sufi Saint

It is said that the parents of the saint of Nagore, Syed Hassan Kuthos and Bibi Fathima, migrated from Baghdad during the rule of Sultan Feroz Shah Thugluk of Delhi and settled in the small town of Manikupur in Pratapgarh District of Uttar Pradesh. The saint was a true Sayyid, who claimed direct descent in the 21st generation from the Prophet of Islam, and in the 7th generation from Sayyid Abdul Qadir Jilani of Baghdad (He was also related to this saint, founder of the *Qadiriya* order, by a spiritual genealogy of Sufi masters and disciple (Appendix No. 2). Nagore is situated nine kilometers from the district headquarters of Nagapatnam, on the banks of the River Vettar, on the coast at the confluence of the Bay of Bengal.

The Sacred Specialists

At the contextual level, the sacred complex in Nagore Andavar's *dargah* has both classical Islamic and Folk-Islamic components. The Folk-Islamic (Sufi) component as taught by Sufi tradition is orally handed down from generation to generation. According to Vidyarthi (1978:59), sacred specialists are those who wholly or partially depend on ritual activities for their livelihood. In the Sufi tradition there will be a set of mediatories between the saint and his devotees. They plead, recommend or negotiate with god for the benefit of the devotees. In this connection, the lineal and spiritual descendents of the saint are discussed here. Their duties for the convenience of analysis of the data may be categorised into two groups as follows:

1. *Muthawalli* and *peshmam* of the Mosque of the classical Islamic tradition.
2. Sacred specialists of the *dargah* of the Folk-Islamic (Sufi) tradition.

Besides the above two principal categories of sacred specialists, there are persons who are associated with the performance of rituals directly or indirectly and have peripheral role in the performance of rituals and hence, cannot be called sacred specialists. Rather, they are treated as ritual associates, such as barbers, musicians and sellers of sacred objects and materials that are offered to the saint by the devotees on fulfillment of their vows.

(I) *The Sacred Specialists of the Classical Islamic Tradition*

Muthawalli and *peshmam* are the only sacred specialists, who come under the classical Islamic tradition. *Muthawalli* is the clergy of the mosque and conducts the sermons and prayers on *Zuma* (Friday) and on festival days of *Ramzan* and *Bakrid*. Next to *muthawalli* in the ritual order is the *peshmam*, who is unique to the mosque and leads the daily prayer at his respective mosque. In the absence of *muthawalli*, he conducts prayer on Fridays and festival days. At Nagore Andavar *dargah* four mosques are located. They are Arcot Nawab Mosque, Diwan Saheb Mosque, Madarasa Palli Mosque and Maraikkar Mosque. Except the last one, the other three mosques are visited by the pilgrims and local devotees for their daily prayers. All the three mosques have a *mouzin* (care taker); in the absence of *peshmam*, he leads the regular prayers at the mosque. This is a hereditary post and is paid by the mosque authorities. During the Kanduri (anniversary of the saint's death), which lasts for 14 days, starting from the 1st day of *jamathulakhir* (the sixth month of the Muslim calendar), for 14 nights *mould-sharif* (audition) is conducted at the mosque. At the time of Kanduri these three mosques serve as shelters to the male pilgrims during the night. Since the female pilgrims are not allowed into the mosque, they stay outside the Mosque in the *dargah* premises.

(II) The Sacred Specialists of the Folk-Islamic (Sufi) Tradition

1. Sacred Specialists: Orthodox Type

The saint of Nagore had adopted Yusuf Saheb as his son. He also had six sons and two daughters. Their lineal descendants are known as *adhinams* (the custodians) of the *dargah* of Nagore Andavar. Since they are genealogically related to the saint, the local people respectfully address them as *Sabus*. As all the descendants of the saint get equal share in the income of the *dargah*; hence, they are also known as *pungudars* (share holders). The lineal descendants such as *khalifah* (the supervisor of the ritual activities) and *muzawars* (the ritual functionaries) are treated as the sacred specialists.

The next group of sacred specialists at the *dargah* includes the *faqir jamas* (mendicant functionaries) who are considered as the spiritual descendants of the saint. Their duty is to preach and promote the teachings of the saint among the devotees by visiting them in their villages and towns. They also maintain a distinct way of life and transmit certain elements of the great tradition to masses with the little tradition by popularising certain texts through organising pilgrimages and officiating over the *dargah* rituals (Redfield, 1953). The role of the lineal descendants is to tell the devotees that the saint is alive, while the mendicants prove it using their mystical powers by organising a *faqirpir* (ritual saint)[4] during the time of Kanduri festival of the saint.

The lineal descendants have two clear functions: (1) attending to the sacred performances of the *dargah*; and (2) attending to the devotees. Daily ritual duties such as the ceremonial opening of the gates of the *dargah* at the specified time, lighting the lamps, cleaning the *sanctum sanctorum* of the Nagore Andavar and the shrine premises, and closing the gates of the *dargah* at a specific time everyday, are also attended by them. After completing all these duties alone, the gates of the *dargah* are kept open for the devotees. Then the *fatiha*[5] (the ritual reading of Quran) is conducted and the *phoolkichadar* (flower shawl) is placed on the tomb of the saint. While opening the *dargah* gates, *thop* (cannon) is fired and musical instruments like the *nadaswaram* and *nawbath* are played. Traditionally, this was done as a mark of respect to the saint only. In due course of time, however, the cannon is also fired also as a mark of respect to the *faqirjama s*on their arrival (saint's disciples), and when a political leader such as a Chief Minister, Prime Minister or Governor visits the shrine, this is a change introduced by the *dargah* authorities to please the VIPs.

Besides, the number of cannons fired may vary from one occasion to another and from one dignitary to another. Traditionally, the cannon is fired twice every morning, once at 4.30 a.m. when the gates of the shrine are opened and again at 7.30 a.m. when the gates of the shrine are closed for the day. It is customary that on hearing the cannon, pilgrims, devotees and others including the non-Muslim, who live in the vicinity of the shrine, symbolically express their respect to the saint. The gates of the shrine are opened again for the second time in the evening at 5 p.m. and closed at 8 p.m. The cannon is fired both times and holy musical instruments are played. In this manner, on normal days, the gates of the shrine are kept open for the devotees, twice a day.

Thursdays are venerated as auspicious and local devotees visit the shrine in big numbers. On these days, to facilitate the pilgrims, the doors of the shrine are kept open till 9 p.m. On Fridays, the local Muslims attend the sermon and the afternoon prayers, so the cannon is fired at 12 noon, and as a special case the shrine is also kept open till 2 p.m. After the Friday noon prayers are completed, two rounds of cannon are fired. During the 14-day Kanduri festival at the shrine, there is a slight change in the time of closing of the *dargah* gates : they are closed at 11 p.m. Besides, the cannon is fired every hour, starting from 4.30 a.m. to 11 p.m. Two rounds of cannon are also fired while hoisting the sacred flags on the minarets. On the 14th day, when flags are removed from the minarets, once again four rounds of cannon are fired as a mark of completion of the Kanduri festival of the saint of Nagore.

The *muzawar's* primary duty is to attend to the *dargah* rituals and to help the devotees who visit the saint's tomb. The main attraction of the anniversary of the saint's death is the hoisting and carrying of the flags in procession, in an unself conscious fusion of Hindu as well as Islamic rituals (Table No.1). The Islamic rites include recitation of Quranic verses and observance of the *fatiha*, whereas the procession with its models and floats is reminiscent of other Hindu processions in Tamil Nadu (Saheb, 2000:42).

Another important ritual performed at the *dargah* is *sandanakoodu*, a chariot containing sandal paste is pulled by the pilgrims, preceded by an aloe-wood cart and musicians of the *dargah*, from Nagapatnam town to Nagore, to bestow the blessings of the *Andavar* on the people of the area. The two pots of *sandanam* which have been carried through the towns in procession are received by the *muzawars* (saint's lineal descendants) at the *dargah*; they take them inside the *sanctum sanctorum* of the *dargah*, where the *khalifah* (the supervisor of the ritual activities) of the *dargah* anoints the *rowlasharif* (tomb) of the saint with the sandal paste. He first utters the *fatiha* and then recites the *Silsila-e-Quadaria* (spiritual genealogy) of the saint.

Table 1 : The types of sacred performances conducted at the Nagapatnam and Nagore sacred centres during the Kanduri festival of the saint Sahul Hameed Nagore Andavar

Day and Month as per Muslim Calendar	*Time and Place*	*Types of Sacred Performance*
26th *Jamathul Avval* (the 5th month of the Muslim calendar) AH 1413	2.00 p.m. Nagore	Erection of flagpoles on the five minarets of the Nagore Andavar's *dargah*
30th *Jamathul Avval* (the 6th month of the Muslim calendar) AH 1413	11.00 a.m. Nagapatnam	Reception of *kodi*. Installation of the *iradam* (car) in the *usimaram* (chariot) for the flag procession ceremony
30th *Jamathul Avval* AH 1413	8.30 p.m. Nagapatnam	Display of firecrackers at the *iradam* place
1st *Jamathul Akhir* AH 1413	8.30 a.m. Nagore	Reception of *faqirjama* (mendicants) during Kanduri festival
1st *Jamathul Akhir* AH 1413	12.00 p.m. Nagapatnama and Nagore	Procession of *kodi* followed by devotee offerings such as boats, minarets and palanquin models along with aloe-wood cart and musicians of the *dargah*
1st *Jamathul Akhir* AH 1413	8.30 p.m. Nagore	*Thuvajarohanam* (flag-hoisting ceremony)
8th *Jamathul Akhir* AH 1413	8.30 a.m. Nagore	*Vanavedeke* (display of firecrackers ceremony)
9th *Jamathul Akhir* AH 1413	8.00 a.m. Nagapatnam	Installation of *sandanakoodu* (sandal paste) in the *usimaram* (chariot)
9th *Jamathul Akhir* AH 1413	10.00 p.m. Nagore	Installation of *faqirpir* (Nagore Andavar's disciple's fasting ceremony)
10th *Jamathul Akhir* AH 1413	7.00 p.m. Nagore	Reception of Nagore Andavar's *rowlasharif* (*sanctum sanctorum*) *chadar* (Shawl)

contd...

contd...

Day and Month as per Muslim Calendar	*Time and Place*	*Types of Sacred Performance*
10th *Jamathul Akhir* AH 1413	8.30 p.m. Nagapatnam Nagore	Procession of *sandanakoodu* (sandal paste)
11th *Jamathul Avval* AH 1413	4.30 a.m. Nagore	Anointment ceremony of *rowlasharif* with *sandanakoodu* (sandal paste)
12th *Jamathul Akhir* AH 1413	5.00 p.m. Nagore and Chilladi	*Faqirpir* proceeds to seashore to break his fast
14th *Jamathul Akhir* AH 1413	8.30 p.m. Nagore	*Thuvajaavarohanam* (flag-lowering) ceremony

Following the prayers and ritual smearing, the shawl, presented by the descendants of Palaniandi Pillai, an ardent devotee of the saint, imbued symbolically and metonymically with the spaces of the towns, through which the chariot has moved, is spread over the saint's tomb. After the anointment ritual, the *dargah* gates are opened to the pilgrims and public.

2. *Sacred Specialists: Extension*

In the previous section, it has been shown that the *muzawars* as a community of sacred specialists have their own orthodox style of performing rituals at the Nagore Andavar's *dargah*. Further, depending upon the *muzawars*' interaction with outsiders in their socio-economic life, two types of relationships emerge: (1) *piri-muridi* (mentor-disciple) and (2) *muzawar-bhaktharga* (sacred specialists-devotee) relationships. Each of these is discussed below:

Piri *(Mentor)*-Muridi *(Disciple) Relationship*

The *piri-muridi* (mystical movement) in Islam was started by both men and women, who devoted themselves exclusively to Allah (God) and His service. This tradition went hand in hand and has become a practise even today. The first of its kind was initiated by Hazarat Syed Abdul Quadir Jeelani of Baghdad in Iraq. His spiritual descendants claimed the status of *Quadiri* title after his death. The saint of Nagore is not only related by descent but also as a follower of his order. Hence, he is also referred to as *Quadiri*. This tradition continues even today by the saint's adopted son's descendants and the five *faqir jamas* (mendicant functionaries) who attend to the Kanduri festival of the saint.

The first *piri-muridi* relationship was between the saint Nagore Andavar and his disciples. It is said that the saint had 404 disciples in his "spiritual" team. They were divided into four groups, each of which consists of 100 members along with a headman. The four groups are the Banwa, Malang, Mondal and Jalali. Since the tomb of the saint Nagore Andavar was first erected, these saintly followers visited the Kanduri festival annually, to pay their homage to their spiritual master. In due course, the local mendicants : the *Rafai Jama*, were added to the earlier four mendicant groups of the saint. At present five mendicant groups attend the saint's Kanduri festival to observe the rituals. These five *jamas (groups)* are welcomed to the saint's Kanduri festival by the lineal descendants, who perform the *chilla* (40 days meditation) at Nagore Andavar's *dargah*. The main duty of the five *jamas* is to conduct the rituals at the saint's anniversary and to perform *ziarat*[6] (ceremonial visit) in the evening, during their stay on the *dargah* premises. According to Banwa Jama, there are four *pirs* (spiritual masters) and 14 *kanwade* (households). They claim that the saint of Nagore Andavar belongs to their group. Hence, they claim superiority of rank over the other groups. That is why at the time of Kanduri festival, they are received first. Besides, they perform the *ziarat* prior to the other groups.

The hierarchical arrangement of the five *faqirjamas* is as follows:

Banwa Jama

↓

Malang Jama

↓

Mandal Jama

↓

Jalali Jama

↓

Rafai Jama

Each group is endogamous in nature and has a separate social organisation. The social organisation of a *faqirjama* is as follows:

Sarguru

↓

Bandari

Ukkari

↓

Kothuwal

↓

Nakliban Aulia

Sarguru is the headman of the *faqirjama*. He initiates persons who wish to become a *murid* (disciple of a *faqir*) of the Sufi religious order. To enter into the *faqir* order, one should be 12 years or older. The novice is called *Nakliban Aulia*. Usually, the novice *faqir* must be an unmarried person. The customary possession of a *faqir* are a *kishthi* (bowl), *bisthar* (bed), *chotta* (walking stick), *kanta* (beads), *kafan* (unsewn cloth of upper garment), *lungi* (the lower garment) and *duppata* (headgear). A *faqir* carries a "Y" shaped *chotta*, which represents the symbolic image of the *faqir* tradition. In religious teachings he leads his team. After completing two years of ritual service, he becomes a *kothuwal* and starts performing his duties of attending to the *sarguru*. He reaches the next position, i.e., *ukkari*, after completing another two years of service. As the *ukkari*, he should work for 12 years to become a *bandari* : the next rank in the *jama* social organisation. During this stage, he acts as the in-charge person of the *jama*, during the absence of his *sarguru*. After serving another 8 years as *bandari* he reaches the final stage of *sarguru*.

While customarily visiting the shrine, a *sarguru* wears a green dress, while the rest of the *jamas* of the lower order wear a yellow dress. This shows the hierarchical pattern of the *faqir* order. The visit is performed in the morning, after the *azan* (morning prayer call), i.e., at 5 a.m.; and in the evening after the evening prayer call, i.e., at 6 p.m. Before circumambulating the saint's tomb in a clockwise direction, they perform the *fatiha*. Later they visit their own mendicant group headman's tomb, perform the *fatiha* and take their seats. This routine continues for nine days till the starting of the "*faqirpir* ritual." During this ritual, a disciple from the *malangfaqirjama* is selected to be the "ritual saint", which is referred to as "the installation of the *faqirpir*." It is performed at the place where the *janazekenamaz* (funerary prayers) over the saint's body are originally offered, by members of the *malang faqirjama*, whose founder is one of the saint's original disciples who followed him during his travels, and preached the divine message of Allah.

In the evening all *muzawars*, the *khalifah* of the *dargah*, members of the five *faqirjamas*, and the rest of the pilgrims assemble near the *faqirpirmandapam* (ritual saint place). The *fatiha* is conducted and the *faqirpir's* toes are tied with a fine thread. It is believed that the thread should remain in this position for three days. The "ritual saint", during this period, observes *zikr* (meditation) by constantly reciting the name of god. During this meditation he throws lemons to the crowd. There is a popular belief that a lemon thrown by the *faqirpir* has miraculous powers. The pilgrims believe that these lemons, are auspicious, and will bring good luck to anyone who catches them, since all their desires will be fulfilled by the Nagore Andavar. The women particularly believe that if a barren woman catches a lemon, she will be blessed with offspring. So people stand before the *faqirpir*, day and night, in the hope of catching a lemon. They do not mind bearing the scorching heat of the sun or being soaked by the rain. Their sole desire is to catch one of the lemons and with it the blessings of the Nagore Andavar. This ritual proves that the *faqirs* (mendicants) are the intermediaries between the "Great and Little Traditions", by telling the masses about the saint and his powers. Since they move in society they spread this message among the devotees; thus, they become a link between the saint and the devotees. Before leaving the shrine, the *faqirjamas* take the permission from the saint, their spiritual master, and continue their mission in the places where the saint had visited during his lifetime. They again visit the *dargah before* the commencement of the next Kanduri festival. During their stay at the shrine, their lodging and boarding facilities are provided free of cost by the *dargah muzawars*.

It is observed that the *faqirs* do not perform the prescribed five times prayer as per the classical Islamic tradition. They believe that their *dekhana* (visiting the tomb of the saint) is their *ibadat* (prayer or worship), and *yadkarna* (remembering the god) is their way of life. Thus, their *ziarat* (visiting of the tomb) is considered equal to that of the worship of Allah (god); and thus, they uphold the Sufi cult. When the Saint Nagore Andavar was alive, he visited the devotees personally and there was a direct spiritual contact between them. With his death the devotees lost this contact and also the benefits. So, as per the tradition, the two have no direct spiritual contact. But the *faqirs* who go into the society to preach and also to collect alms are a link between the devotees and the Sufi tradition.

The tradition is also continued by the lineal descendants who tell the devotees that the saint is alive; while the mendicants prove it, through their mystical powers which were bestowed on them by the saint by way of installing a *faqirpir* (ritual saint) during the time of the Kanduri festival. In the eyes of the supplicants and devotees, the ritual saint possesses a higher spiritual rank than ordinary human beings. The sanctity maintained in the *dargah*, and the aggregation of people of different faiths and classes itself embodies this sacredness of the ritual saint. It is believed that the saint's intercession can bring success in love, and can damage the property and life of rivals; in love, they can resolve marital conflict, bring about the returning home of a lost child, or the reform of a wayward husband or son. Thus every wish, right or wrong, good or bad, moral or otherwise is placed before the saint. Supplicants sit before the saint's tomb for hours at a time until they feel that their prayers are heard.

Levels of relations between Saint, *muzawars*, *faqirjamas* and Devotees

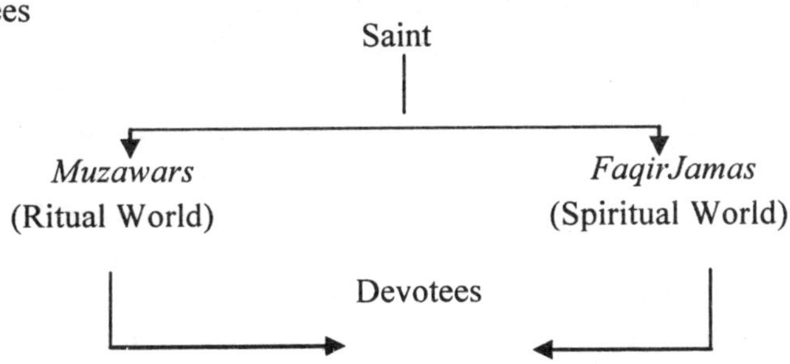

The above diagram shows that the saint is the spiritual head of the *faqirs* and the ritual link to his lineal descendants who are also genealogically related to him. The disciples are linked to him spiritually and not lineally. They are integrated in the spiritual and eternal world of Allah. Thus, they propagate the saint's teachings in the society and have kept him active and alive. The lineal descendants attached to the material world. In due course, the mendicants meet devotees, spread the message of the saint and collect alms to make a living.

Muzawar (Sacred Specialist)-Bhakthargal (Devotee) Relationship

This is the second category of relationship between the saint's lineal descendants and the devotees of the *dargah*. The *muzawars* are grouped into two categories: (1) those who are attached to the *dargah*; and (2) those who attend and perform the ritual services of the devotees voluntarily and also act as local guides to the visiting devotees. One category of *muzawars* at the sacred centres such as *Ghee dan*, *Uddan*, *Uyir-Ku-Uyir* and *Ashare Sharif*, never go out to the devotees; instead the devotees come to them to get their blessings. They stay near the main door of the *dargah* and attend to the service of the devotees. The second category of *muzawars* goes in search of devotees to the bus stand and railway station; they bring them to the *dargah* and help them perform the *fatiha.* Sometimes they even provide food and accommodation to the pilgrims, and accept whatever amount is given by the pilgrims. They also perform the duty of local guide, accompanying the devotees to the various sacred centers such as Chilladi Dargah, Mela Nagore Dargah and the Meerapalli Mosque, and attend to the ritual activities, thus maintaining the Sufi tradition at Nagore Andavar's *dargah.*

Sometimes the *muzawars* establish rapport by way of communicating the date of the Kanduri festival, sending pamphlets and blank money order forms in the regional language to the devotees, with a request to convey the message to their relatives and friends. The devotees are asked to inform their *ziarat* programme in advance so that the *muzawars* can make proper arrangements. In case, the devotees send the message and cash by post, the *muzawars* pray for the devotees at the *dargah* on their behalf and send the *tabruk* (*prasadam*), which contains rose petals and *malida* (sweet meats) after the Kanduri festival. A few *muzawars* are reported to have visited foreign countries like Burma, Singapore, Malaysia, Sri Lanka and Maldives, to spread the message of the saint of Nagore and his miracles, and to collect funds for the development of the shrine. They maintain their network with the devotees by dispatching books and other publicity material.

Thus, the lineal descendants of the saint and the spiritual descendants exhibit their persistence with the devotees at the Nagore Andavar's *dargah.*

3. Sacred Specialists: Persistence and Change

The sacred specialists who have taken up secular occupations have not been able to cultivate Arabic learning to perform the prescribed ritual observances. As Milton Signer (1959:176) states .... "they (the Brahmans of Madras) found in their new preoccupations less time for the cultivation of Sanskrit learning and performance of the scripturally prescribed ritual observances, the two activities for which as Brahmans they have had an ancient professional responsibility. They have not, however, completely abandoned these activities and to some extent they have developed compensatory activities which have kept them from becoming de-Sanskritised and cut-off from traditional culture." Similarly, one by one many *muzawars* (sacred specialists) are walking out of their traditional profession leaving just the old ones along with those who were either forced into it or were unable to do anything else. The *muzawars who* make enormous income continue to claim the rights without performing their duties as strictly as tradition demands, and their life-style has significantly changed; but those whose income is small, have discarded their hereditary posts, migrated to other places and taken up other occupations.

Earlier, when people were prosperous and living was easy, the sacred specialists had a secure and comfortable world of their own. They had enough lands (Appendix No. 3), patronage, money and honours, and they devoted their entire time to the service of the *dargah*. After the Indian Abolition Act of 1970, the government took over the lands due to which a substantial income was lost to the *dargah*. Next, The land Reforms Act, 1974 transferred the ownership of the land to the tiller. The government fixed compensation at the rate of Rs. 250 per acre, per year for wet crops and Rs.100 for dry crops. The compensation was fixed, but it was forthcoming. This deprived the *muzawars* of their *inam* (gift) and other lands.

In addition to the Indian Abolition Act of 1970, from time to time strong movements were launched against saint worship in the religious history of Islam, the latest of them being the Wahabi Movement which, among other things, strongly condemned grave and ancestor worship in all forms, including the most innocent and harmless of forms. Even the latest movements such as the *Al-Quaida* Islamic movement discourage the worship of Sufi saints. Such new trends have compelled the *muzawars* to give up their traditional occupation and take up government or private service.

The dressing pattern has also changed from traditional to modern, and a certain amount of loss of respect for the priestly profession is observed. None of the elderly people wish their children to carry out their traditional priestly profession. "It is only when I am in the *dargah* that I have any feelings of *bhakti (*devotion), once outside, I am like any other man on the road. It is the *punya (virtue* or holiness) of my previous life that I am a *muzawar now*. I have the chance to serve the saint and I pray that I may be born as a *muzawar* in my other lives too", says a 78 year old *muzawar*.

However, Mr. Khasim *Sabu*, for whom a life of hardship and deprivation is nothing compared to the satisfaction he gets from serving the saint, when asked whether he would allow his sons to continue in this profession, replied in the negative. "In my heart I feel this is my best profession. My desire is that this should continue, but in these days of hardship what can I do? In this profession survival is very difficult. Tell me, if the son suffers, can the parents watch silently? So, I would rather ask my son to choose some other work, so that if he cannot live a life of luxury, he would atleast be able to make both ends meet."

The profession of the sacred specialists is thus one that is gradually fading and losing its social esteem. Desertion is so rampant and complete that the sons of sacred specialists are prepared to do anything else, but circumstances force them to persist in their father's profession.

Conclusion

As stated by Vidyarthi (1979), the combined functioning of the three components of a sacred centre reflects classical as well as Folk-Islam (Sufi) tradition. The sacred specialists of a place of pilgrimage maintain a distinct style of life and transmit certain texts, organising pilgrimages and officiating as the *dargah muzawars*. Further, the sacred complex in general and the sacred specialists in particular undergo modification and transformation as a result of general development in the larger universe of Islamic civilisation, of which they are a part. The position and the status of *faqirjamas* that are peculiar have not received the attention of the scholars so far; this enables them to persist in their occupation of saint worship. The people derive faith from their concrete relation to the *dargah* and its *muzawars*, rather than a direct relation to the distant and metaphysical God.

As a unit of study of the role of sacred specialists and the spiritual descendants of the saint of Nagore Andavar *dargah*, which encompasses Folk-Islamic (Sufi) traditional aspects with the classical Islamic civilisational content, not only integrates the two cultural traditions but also opens up a new vista in understanding the basic resilience of two different civilisations juxtaposed, proving that there exists unity in diversity in Indian culture, which is unique to multi-ethnic, multi-linguistic and multi-religious traditions.

Notes

1. In Tamil vernacular, *Andavar* means God. The Sufi Saint Sahul Hameed of Nagore Sharief is called Nagore Andavar because of his degree of spiritual excellence and power to fulfill the material needs and vows of his devotees. He was honoured with this title in 1966 by the Hindu sage Shivananda for his remarkable miraculous acts. Since then, the saint of Nagore is referred to as Nagore Andavar by the local people.
2. In South India, the term Kanduri is used for the annual festival of a *dargah*. It is stated that the term is derived from Persian where it means "covering a table." The new Royal Persian English Dictionary (1932:336) states that Kanduri means a feast or ceremony observed in honour of

Holy Personages. The Tamil Lexicon and Jubilee Tamil Dictionary (1935:718) specifically explain that Kanduri is the festival held at Nagore in honour of the Holy Saint of Nagore.

3. The word Folk-Islam is used in the same sense as used by Eliade, M. (1987) in The Encyclopedia of Religion, Macmillan and Free Press, London. In this study, we have examined the non-Islamic practises such as worshipping the Sufi saint's tombs, observance of death anniversaries of the Sufi saints and the rituals associated with them. The supernatural beliefs and practises, vow-taking rituals and also the local traditions in accordance with the Sufi saint's teachings and preachings are also covered under this category of Sufism. It is clearly stated here that Sufism is not a separate religion, it refers only to the Sufi practises and the Islam observed at folk level. Hence, it is clearly stated as the Folk-Islam or Sufism.
4. *Pir* literally means a spiritual mentor; one who initiates the novices into the spiritual line of Sufism. He is also called *shaikh* or *murshid*. But in present study, the word *faqirpir* denotes the mendicant disciples of the saint who attend to the traditional Kanduri festival of Sahul Hameed Nagore Andavar. One of the mendicant disciples performs as a "ritual saint" and symbolises the spiritual exercises of the saint of Nagore.
5. *Fatiha* indicates a single recitation of the *surafatiha* (the first verse of the holy text in Quran) and the *suraiklas* (three times), a chapter that occurs in the daily prayer and reads thus; He is God, the one and only God, the Eternal, Absolute. He begetteth not nor is He begotten, and there is none like unto Him (Abdullah, 1979). Usually this ritual is conducted by the Muslims before making an offering in the name of Allah, and to *Aulia Allah* (Sufi saints) at the beginning of auspicious occasions as a mark of respect to God or saints.
6. Traditionally, a visit to the tomb of Prophet Mohammad, at Madina, in Saudi Arabia is known as *ziarat*. The place of *ziarat* is called *ziaratgarh* or *dargah*. It also indicates a Sufi saint's residence or resting place. In ordinary usage, the burial place of an ordinary person is referred to as *kabar* (grave), and for the graves of Arabic scholars the term *zazar* is used. For the graves of the Sufi saints the term *dargah* is used. Thus, at the regional level there is a distinct style of usage of words for the graves of Muslims in South India. But the *dargah* has a specific denotation, a sacred centre.

References

Abdullah, Y.A.A. 1979. *Holy Quran*, Vol. I and II (English translation), Delhi: Khutub Khana Ishayat-ul-Islam.

Eliade, M. (ed.). 1987. *The Encyclopedia of Religion*. Vols. 1-15. London. Macmillan and Free Press.

Gurumurthy, K.G. 1992. "Ritual Mendicants of a Shakti shrine." In N.K. Behura and K.C. Tripati (eds.) *Science, Culture and Development*. Felicitation Volume in Honour of Dr. L.K. Mahapatra. Bhubaneswar. Paragon Publications.

Goswami, B.B. and S.G. Morab 1968. "Study of Chamundi Temple in Mysore. Calcutta." Anthropological Survey of India.

Hameed, S. 1986. "Nagore: The City of *Dargah* Cult and Communal Harmony. Proceedings of the Seminar on Facets of Temple Cities." Tanjore. Tamil University Press (Unpublished Paper).

Hemingway, F.R. 1906. Madras District Gazetteer Records: Madras and Salem. Madras. Government Printing Press, p. 890.

Redfield, R. 1953. *The Little Community and Peasant Society and Culture*. Chicago. Chicago University Press, p. 890.

Saheb, S.A.A. 1997. "A Festival of Flags: Hindu-Muslim Devotion and Sacralising of Localism at the Shrine of Nagore-Sharief in Tamil Nadu" Pnena Webner and Helene Basu (eds.) Embodying Charisma. London: Routledge, p. 56.

Saheb, S.A.A. 2009. "Sufism in South India" N.K. Das and V.R. Rao (eds.) *Identity, Cultural Pluralism and State South Asian Perspective*. Macmillan. New Delhi, p. 333.

Saheb, S.A.A. 2000. "Study of Nagore-e-Sharief: A Sacred Complex in Chennai." *Journal of Anthropological Survey of India,* 49, pp. 41-54.

Sharieff, J. 1921. "Islam in India: The Customs of Musalmans of India" (G.A. Herkolts translated, rearranged and edited with additions by W. Crooke). London: Curzon Press.

Singer Miltton (ed.). 1959. *Traditional India : Structure and Change*. Philadelphia. American Folklore Society.

Tamil Lexicon 1932. *The New Royal Persian English Dictionary*. Vol. 1 Madras. Madras University Publication, p. 336.

Tamil Lexicon 1935. *Tamil Lexicon and Jubilee Tamil Dictionary*. Vol. I and Vol. II. Madras. Madras University Publication, p. 718.

Vidyarthi, L.P. 1961. *The Sacred Complex of Hindu Gaya*. Delhi. Concept Publication.

Vidyarthi, L.P 1978. *The Sacred Complex of Khasi : A Microcosm of Indian Civilisation*. Delhi. Concept Publication.

16

Religious and Ritual Practises among the *Arundhathiyar* : A Socio-Religious Perspective

V. Pragati* and *C. Raghu

India is a confluence and agglomeration of all religious beliefs in the world. The followers of Zoroaster, a very small but slightly intellectual, wealthy, enterprising, charitable group of Parsi people have had their home in the western part of the country for about ten centuries. The ancient colony of Jews in Cochin is well-known to all. Tradition says that St. Thomas, one of the 12 Apostles, came and planted the seed of Christianity shortly after the passing away of Jesus. We all know that India is the birth place of Hinduism, Jainism, Buddhism, Sikhism, etc. Nowhere else in the world religion has been made the object of such vast experimentation as in India. There have been strenuous endeavours of spiritualism, spread over the entire country.

With such an enriched background, when we talk of religion in India or Hindu religion, some kind of sacredness, piousness and the concept of purity and honesty automatically creep into our minds. But the religious attitude or behaviour of the people in villages of India towards Hinduism varies from the religious scriptures, classical and modern text books. The great tradition of Hinduism and the local little tradition marked by a continuous process of Sanskritisation comprise the village Hindu religion. Religiosity is more pronounced among the people living in the rural areas than among those in the urban areas. The degree of variation in religiosity is caused due to several factors, including the individual, caste, creed, sect and community.

Religion is a part of culture. The views and attitude of anthropologists on religion are quite different. Anthropologists are more keen to view religion in the social perspective and cultural setting. They give importance to the congregational, functional and the societal aspects of religion. To them, religion is, in short, faith in supernatural or spiritual beings, and includes beliefs and rites. Religion is the human response, expression and relation to the uncompromising, uncontrollable phenomena and forces of nature that are related to the cultural aspect of the people of a particular region. It varies from region to region, place to place, and caste to caste. Thence, religion is a part and parcel of the cultural pluralism.

There are various theories of religion, and under each category of theory, different scholars like Tylor, Malinowski, Marett, Codrington, Max-Muller, Frazer, Durkheim, Freud, Herbert-Spencer, Paul Radin and George Simmel, have tried to interpret the origin of religion on the basis of conjectural arguments, on the basis of gathered experiences in life, the relationship between the male and female, on the foundation of study of particular phenomenon or happenings of nature, or on the specific religion of a society or group. These scholarly studies on religion guided many Indian and European anthropologists towards research on various aspects of religious and belief practises of rural and tribal people. Scholars like Jacob-Pandian (1975); Babb (1975); Wadley (1975); Appadurai and Breckenridge (1976); Inden (1976); Clothey (1978); Ostor (1980); Fuller (1982, 1992); Kjaerholm (1984, 1992); Dumont (1986); Thurston (1987, 1909); Whitehead (1988, 1921); Raheja (1988); and Nobokov (1995) have also shown that such fusions are accomplished by other sorts of reciprocal relations.

This paper presents a socio-religious perspective of the religion of the *Arundhathiyar* of Puducherry in village settings, and in terms of their religious beliefs and practises. In the Union Territory of Puducherry there are about 15 groups of Scheduled Castes; and *Arundhathiyar* is one among them. In the census list of the Scheduled Caste population in Puducherry, the *Arundhathiyar* are identified by the names of *Adhi-Andhra*, *Madiga* and *Chakkiliyan*.

They are a Telugu speaking community that migrated from the Andhra Pradesh in the 16th century. They are now bilinguals, as they are good in both Telugu and Tamil. The *Chakkiliyan* of Puducherry have changed their name to *Arundhathiyar*, as this name is considered more respectable than their original names, and it gives them a relatively better status among the other depressed communities. Traditionally, the *Arundhathiyar* of Puducherry are tanners and leather workers. But they also do menial jobs and are supposed to remove all dead animals from the village. Even now some of them hold the traditional occupations.

Religion among the *Arundhathiyar* plays an important role in people's life and unites them in belief and ritual activity. They believe in the Gods and Goddesses of both great and little traditions. They are highly religious and are very afraid of supernatural powers.

The two major deities, Siva and Vishnu, have been the faces of metaphysical arguments as the two main streams of Hindu religion, i.e., Siva, the school of Saivism and Vishnu, the school of Vaishnavism, are also found among *Arundhathiyars*. The entire *jati* of Puducherry *Arundhathiyars* is divided into two major *vamsams*, namely *bujakoolu* and *namakoolu*. These two divisions are based on the Saivite (*bujakoolu*) and Vaishnaivite (*namakoolu*) divisions.

The *Arundhathiyar* of Puducherry believe that their community has originated from two different Gods; one from Lord Siva and the other from Lord Vishnu. They follow two different customs while performing the rites and rituals. The two *vamsams*, i.e., *bujakoolu* and *namakoolu*, are sub-divided into five *gotrams*, which are further classified to several *kulams*.

God Worship

The *Arundhathiyars* are strong believers in simple devotion to Gods and Goddesses. Their devotion is expressed through the worship of various Gods. Their main figures, who have inspired as well as animated their souls through the ages, and still do, are Siva and Vishnu. They value both as equally capable of giving supernatural rewards.

The three-fold marks, visible on the forehead of *Arundhathiyars*, are the symbols of the popular Gods : horizontal lines marked with ashes represent their devotion to Siva and those who wear such a mark are known as *bujakoolu*. The *bujakoolu* are divided into three *gotrams*, namely, *bujakoolu*, *pandibujakoolu*, and *lingabujakoolu*. The *bujakoolu* are worshippers of Lord Siva. The *pandibujakoolu* are worshippers of Lord Madurai-Viiranand they sacrifice a pig to their God on all occasions. The *lingabujakoolu* worship a *lingam* during all important ceremonies and festivals.

The vertical single line in white signifies faith in Vishnu and people wearing such mark on their forehead are known as *naamakoolu*. In *naamakoolu*, there are again two types of *gotrams* : *padamleininaamakoolu* and *padampetinanaamakoolu*.

Padamleininamakoolu wear only a single vertical line with white chalk on their forehead, while the *padampetinanamakoolu* wear a single vertical line with white chalk that ends in a red horizontal line at the bottom. There is slight variation in the rites and rituals of these two divisions at the time of marriage, birth, and death ceremonies and during the celebration of festivals.

Goddess Worship

Goddesses have great importance and ineffacable impact on the religious life of the *Arundhathiyars*. They are worshipped occasionally during ear-boring, tonsuring, marriage and other religious occasions. The *Arundhathiyars* worship *devatai* (Goddesses) in order to achieve their different ends in life. Lord Brahma's wife Saraswati is the Goddess of learning; and Lord Vishnu's wife Lakshmi is the Goddess of wealth and prosperity.

Along with these Goddesses of the great tradition, they also worship Goddesses of the little tradition such as Mariamman, Ankalamman, and Paaliriciyamman. Belief in the Goddesses is very strong and they are worshipped elaborately by all the community members, as this act of worshipping protects the village from sickness, epidemics and evil spirits. Mariamman, Ankalamman, and Paaliriciyamman are represented by a black-stone; and an iron-rod spear is placed next to the statue. In Mariamman temples, a snake hood is also placed.

Village Gods

Aiyanaar

This god is regarded as the son of Siva and Vishnu. Actually, he is an old Dravidian divinity. The Aiyanaar temple is located in the outskirts of the village. He is guardian of the fields and the armed protector of the village's territory. Many *Arundhathiyar* families have Aiyanaar as their family deity and their children are named after him.

Madurai-Viiran:

He is a secondary divinity, and a fearsome, carnivorous and alcohol-drinking God. They usually offer a pig in sacrifice to this village God. They say that Madurai-Viiran is "our God", and many *pandibujakoolu* have him as their family deity.

Kulatyvam *(Family Deity):*

Among the *Arundhathiyars*, there are deities (inherited) which are referred to as *Kulatyvam* (family deity), and are enshrined in a corner of the house. Worshipping the family deity is mandatory at the time of life-cycle ceremonies and religious occasions. The entire lineage members are involved during such worship. Failure to perform worship brings harm to members of the family who have a family deity. *Paerattanai* (vows) are made to them for redressing problems, and if the vows are not fulfilled the family deities are supposed to cause harm. The family deities can also harm the enemy, either by inflicting physical harm, or causing death, if the ritual of "burning incense" is performed.

Ancestral Spirits

At the family level, every *Arundhathiyar* worships his own ancestors who are enshrined in the *nattuvittu.* In the *nattuvittu*, underneath the photos of deities, a circle is drawn with turmeric and three horizontal lines are drawn in the centre of the circle with vermilion. During life-cycle rituals like child birth and marriage, ancestor worship is obligatory. If there occurs any negligence in the offerings and sacrifices or any polluted person enters into the *nattuvittu*, the ancestral spirits may harm the family members.

Hence, it is the duty of the head of the family to keep the ancestors pleased and favourable by worshipping them on several occasions during the year, viz., *diwali, nattukaritikai, mattu-ponkal*, child-birth and marriage. In other words, when they observe any festivities and happy occasions, they worship the ancestors through suitable offerings and sacrifices.

Malevolent Spirits

Spirits which are evil in character and cause harm to human beings on malicious whims are termed as the *pey-picacu* (evil-spirits), and *kattu-karuppu* (wind-spirits), which are so powerful that they might kill human beings. The *pey-picacu* and *kattu-karuppu* are supposed to dwell in the grave-yard or in the old temples.

In almost all parts of mountains and forests, some kind of malefic spirits are believed to exist. Therefore, they are propitiated at the time of worship of trees and plants. Giant trees like palm trees or neem trees, are the habitat of the spirits known as *muni* or *muniswaran.* These spirits are supposed to be invisible and cause diseases or death if any one unknowingly passes by such a tree alone.

Temple Worship

Besides these informal worships, they offer *puccai* to different deities or Gods, installing them in a temple. Temples of Lord Siva and

Perumaal are widely spread in the area. Almost all the villages have a Siva temple where *puccai* is offered every day.

Sun and Moon Worship

The worship of the sun and moon is also popular among the *Arundhathiyars*, generally on Tuesdays and Fridays, and particularly on lunar junctures of *amavacai* (new moon) and *paurnami* (full moon) nights. *Amavacai* is celebrated in the honour of ancestors, specifically in the months of *Adi, Purattaci,* and *Tai.*

Animal Worship

The cow and cobra occupy an important place in the *Arundhathiyar* community. The cow is worshipped in natural/normal death anniversaries. The cobra is better understood as human procreation and the fertility. God and Goddess, i.e., *Nagappa-Nagamma,* who are seen as bestowers of fertility. The *Arundhathiyar* women who believe themselves to be infertile, pray to their idols depicted in sexual embrace, hoping to conceive.

Tree Worship

The neem, banyan and peepal trees are planted in the backyard and courtyards of the *Arundhathiyar* households. These trees and plants occupy an important place in magic and medicine, in which they believe and apply accordingly. The *Arundhathiyar* women worship the neem tree on Fridays and Tuesdays by smearing it with turmeric and vermillion; they regard it as Goddess Mariamman.

The Sacred Specialists

The ritual functionaries who perform various sacred performances are known as the "sacred specialists." Among the *Arundhathiyar*, the sacred specialists are found at two levels: The family level and the village level. The head of the family acts as the sacred specialist while performing the family level religious functions. There are certain taboos such as observance of strict fast on the day of the worship, and abstinence on the previous night. The sacred specialist cannot perform the function if his wife is menstruating, and also if there was accrual of ritual impurity due to a death or birth in the house. The sacred specialist decides the dates of sacred performances only after considering all these factors, and also the convenience of the members of his lineage group who are co-sharers of such worship.

The other important sacred specialist is the village temple priest. Usually each settlement of the *Arundhathiyar* has one or two shrines and also the priests for worshipping them. While the village temple priest performs the sacred rituals in a shrine, he also functions as a seer, cures diseases and wards off spirits which possess individuals, etc. There are some priests who are also diviners.

Sacred Performances

Sacred performances can also be similarly categorised into those which are performed at the family level and village level; and as festivals and magical performances. They are invoked and propitiated by performing several rituals such as worship, prayer, making vows, offering vegetarian and non-vegetarian food and sacrifices; such offerings and sacrifices are made to ensure the health, happiness, prosperity and plenty of food supply for the people. These various rituals can be considered as sacred performances.

The objectives of such sacred performances are clear: The Gods and Goddesses give their blessings only if they are appeased by elaborate rituals. Even spirits are to be satisfied, and failure to do so incurs their wrath and leads to harmful consequences. The benevolent spirits may not cause much harm if one fails to perform a particular ritual, but if evil spirits are not satisfied, disease or death are likely effects for the defaulters.

Offerings made to the Deities

The worshipping, propitiation and celebration of deities consists of two types of offerings : animals and articles such as cooked rice, coconuts, camphor, incense, flowers, vermilion and turmeric. The animals sacrificed to the deities are he-goats, he-pigs and cocks. The kind of offerings made to the deities depends upon the occasion, ritual and the food habits of the deity receiving the offerings. The animal offerings are made by individual families and collectively by the entire community.

Conclusion

The beliefs and practises of the *Arundhathiyar* regarding supernatural beings show the devotion and anxiety the people at the level of socio-cultural integration. The religious life of *Arundhathiyars* analysed with the help of three methodological terms, viz., sacred centers, sacred specialists and sacred performances, if conceived together may be termed as a "Sacred-Complex". The sacred centers of the *Arundhathiyars* are located at a number of places, viz., in the house, courtyard, cattle shed, within the settlement, in the outskirts of the village, and in neighbouring areas. These sacred centers or deities enshrined there are represented by stones or rocks of different colours, trees, spears, iron rods and the trident.

Practically no significant change is perceptible in the religious and ritualistic behaviour of the *Arundhathiyars*. The impact of technological and modern materialistic culture has not been as powerful on the *Arundhathiyars* as the religious culture. Worship and other religious acts form part of their daily life. However, the so-called modern and sophisticated youngsters do not generally conform to these ideals, though the old and the aged still live up to them. Hence, it is concluded that the *Arundhathiyars*, like most other castes in Puducherry, attach prime importance to religious practises in every walk of life. Human life as perceived by them is full of hazards; and they believe that they should seek the help of the supernatural beings. Moreover, even in the day-to-day life of *Arundhathiyars*, religion is incorporated in the pluralistic sense.

References

Appadurai, Arajun, and Carol Breckenridge, 1976. "The South Indian Temple Authority, Honor, and Redistribution". *Contributions to Indian Sociology. n.s.* 10.

Babb, L.A. 1975. *The Divine Hierarchy: Popular Hinduism in Central India.* New York. Columbia University Press.

Clothey, F.W. 1978. "The Many Faces of Murkan : The History and Meaning of a South Indian God." The Hague. Mouton.

Dumont, Louis. 1986. "A South Indian Subcaste : Social Organisation and Religion of the Pramalai Kallars". Delhi. Oxford University Press.

Fuller, Christopher, J. 1992. "The Camphor Flame: Popular Hinduism and Society in India". Princeton. N.J. Princeton University Press.

Inden, Ronald, B. 1976. "Marriage and Rank in Bengali Culture". Berkeley. University of California Press.

Jacob, Pandian, E.T. 1975. "Nadu Veedu Rituals and Family Shamanism in Tamil Society: A Cult Institution of Hinduism". *Man in India*, 55(1).

Kjaerholm, Lars. 1984. "Aiyanar and Aiyappan in Tamil Nadu : Change and Continuity in South Indian Hinduism." *Folk*, 26 (Copenhagen).

Nobokov, Isabelle. 1995. *"Who are You?" Spirit Discourse in a Tamil World.* PhD. Dissertation, Berkeley. University of California Press.

Ostor, Akos. 1980. *"The Play of the Gods: Locality, Ideology, Structure, and Time in the Festivals of a Bengali Town"*. Chicago. University of Chicago Press.

Raheja, Gloria, Goodwin, J. 1988. "The Poison in the Gift: Ritual, Presentation and the Dominant Caste in a North India Village". Chicago. The University of Chicago Press.

Thurston, E.B. 1909. *Castes and Tribes of Southern India*. Vol. 5. Madras Government Press.

Wadley, Susan Snow. 1975. "Shakti: Power in the Conceptual Structure of Karimpur Religion". Chicago. University of Chicago Press.

Whitehead, Henry. 1921. *The Village Gods of South India*. Second Edition. Calcutta. Association Press and London. Oxford University Press.

17

The Sacred Complex of Vailankanni: A Study in Cultural Pluralism

R. Rajendra Prasad

Pluralism

(a) A condition or system in which two or more states, groups, principles, sources of authority, etc., coexist.

(b) A form of society in which the members of minority groups maintain their independent cultural traditions.

(c) A theory or system of devolution and autonomy for individual bodies in preference to monolithic state control.

Visits to places of interest of one's own religion or those of others, pilgrimages, and religious assemblies, have been a dominating motive in the minds of men of various religious affiliations. The practise of traveling for religious reasons, i.e., going on a pilgrimage, became a well-established custom in many parts of the world. By the end of the middle ages large numbers of pilgrims were travelling to the main shrines in Europe. Likewise, the adoption and spread of Christianity subsequently led to numerous pilgrims making their way to the Holy Land. So deep and strong was the hold of faith that the ritual of pilgrimage flourished over the centuries in which religion was a great unifying force; and pilgrimages strengthened religious bonds.

India is a religious country with deep religious sentiments among its adherents. It is the cradle of many ancient religions in the world, such as Hinduism, Buddhism, Jainism and Sikhism, and it is aptly said that India is a land of temples and places of various pilgrimage centres belonging to various religions of the world. India is dotted with places of religious importance from the north to the south, and from the east to the west. In the north places like Kashi, Badrinath, Mathura, and Sikh Gurudwarass such as, the golden temple in Amritsar are important pilgrimage centres. In Tamil Nadu too there are a lot of temples specially built for various Hindu Gods including Lord Murugan, Shiva, Vishnu and Vinayaka.

Religion is considered to be an important element of culture. Social groups are expected to be parthy religious, and are thus, divided. For example, the Christians are not a homogeneous population. They belong to different denominations like Roman Catholic, Protestant, etc. The unifying forces of such groups can be understood through syncretism.

The present study in Vailankanni aims to understand the social groups from their religious ideas and ideals. Whether religion is static or dynamic, it will be a study to understand human beings, in their religious domain, be it a single largest source or a confluence of different sources.

The primary sources of intermingling of religions have been the religious pilgrimage centres, be it that of the Hindus, Muslims, Sikhs, Christians, Jains or Buddhists. It is to be noted that the Buddhist pilgrimage centres in India, such as Bodh Gaya, Sarnath, etc., attract pilgrims and non-pilgrims worldwide and more so from the Buddhist circuit, of East Asian countries.

The Hindus have a plethora of pilgrimage centres; similarly, the Christians too have a few pilgrimage centres which have been developed according to the local beliefs and customs based on the grace and power of the local deities. One such pilgrimage centre of the Christians in South India is the 17th century shrine at Vailankanni (the Lourdes of India), which also attracts non-Christians.

Tradition recounts that the "*Mother of God*", Mary of Nazareth, appeared holding the Infant Jesus in this small hamlet around the end of the 16th or the early 17th century. Ever since, Vailankanni is the most important destination and almost the synthesis of all Marian sanctuaries for the pilgrims of the world. For the Catholics in India, it is one of the most popular and sacred pilgrimage centres.

Marian Apparitions in Vailankanni

Apparition

Apparition is the concept assigned to certain kinds of supernatural visions, either bodily or visibly, and is the term most frequently applied to the various visions of Mary. The teaching of the Church regarding apparitions is comparable to her teaching about miracles, which frequently occur from these apparitions.

There are many visions, apparitions and locutions; even today, extraordinary apparitions are reported all over the world. The Vatican is unable to process the unprecedented number of reports of private revelations that it receives daily. As the second Vatican council states "Such gifts of grace, whether they be of special enlightenment or whether they are spread more simply and generally, must be accepted with gratefulness and consolation as they are suited to and useful for the needs of the Church" (Vatican II, Lumen Gentium. 12).

Although the apparitions here in Vailankanni were not well documented as in the case of Lourdes, Fatima and Guadalupe, the *Vailankanni Matha* apparitions have been proved to be of divine origin, simply because millions of people today have gone beyond the surface of history and to the depths of the mystery. Countless persons from many different religions believe in the gentle presence of the Blessed Mother here and honour her.

The people who flock to venerate our lady of good health may not know her name other than *Arokia Matha.*

Apparitions are the sense-perceptible visions or appearances of Christ, the Blessed Virgin, angels, or saints. Many apparitions are recorded in the scriptures, e.g., Tobias 3:16-17; Genesis 26:24; Luke 1:11, 26. The authenticity of the apparitions is, however, a matter for investigation and evaluation of the Church. The Church's approval is always regarded when a popular cult arises in response to alleged apparitions.

Mary to the Milk Boy

In this tiny village on the east coast of the Bay of Bengal, Mary appeared to a boy who was selling milk for his livelihood. It is believed that this took place towards the end of the 16th century, under a banyan tree near the pond in Anna Pillai Street. The shade of the tree and the water of the pond attracted passersby to rest a while. The boy who was fetching milk for a rich man in Nagapattanam similarly rested under the tree and fell into a sweet slumber. Suddenly, he was startled by a bright vision of a lady with a child standing before him. Since he never had seen such a countenance, he was fascinated by this extraordinary phenomenon and was filled with a sense of awe. The lady took milk for the child in her arms from the boy. Since then, the people called this pond as "*Matha Kulam*" (our lady's pond), and thousands of people pour in to pray at the place where the Blessed Mother appeared.

Blessed Mother to the Buttermilk Vendor

Some years after the first appearance, Mother Mary appeared to another lame boy whose widowed mother, in order to make a living, sold buttermilk near Naduthittu, which is not very far from *Matha Kulam*. The Blessed Mother took whey for her child and told the boy to inform a certain rich Christian in the area to build a Church in Vailankanni. When he expressed his inability to do so, due to his lameness, the Mother of God cured the boy's handicap. He went on to fulfill what had been asked of him by the Blessed Mother. He reported the apparition as well as the miracle of his healing to the wealthy man in Nagapattanam, who had already seen the Blessed Virgin with the Infant Jesus in a dream the previous night. Hence, he could easily believe the apparition and the message. He built a small Chapel with walls of clay mud and a thatched roof. He made a statue of the lady holding Infant Jesus in the same form and figure that he had seen in his dream and placed it in the Chapel.

Miraculous Escape of the Portuguese from the Sea Storm

In the middle of the 18th century, the Portuguese had a flourishing trade with the East. It was a great privilege that the port of Macao in China was in their custody and under their control. During a voyage from Macao to Portugal, their ship was caught in a terrible storm and the sailors prayed beseechingly to the Blessed Mother. The Mother safely guided them to land on the shore of Vailankanni. As a token of gratitude, the Portuguese sailors built a 24 feet to 12 feet Chapel, with a dome overhead. In their possible subsequent visits, perhaps they also brought porcelain plates, which can be seen even now, illustrating scenes from the Bible and other cultural arts of the time, to beautify the Church they had earlier built. The main statue that they had brought to the altar of the shrine was our lady holding the Baby Jesus, standing majestically on the Globe; this was how the Blessed Mother had also appeared to the two boys in Vailankanni (*Source*: The Shrine History, published in the year 1997 edited by Fr. Gabriel).

The peculiar character of the visions at Vailankanni is the selection of the two Hindu visionaries. The large number of Hindu pilgrims visiting this shrine is often attributed to this choice of visionaries. The obvious innocence of the chosen children, untainted by worldly experience or influence, combined with their simple, unpretentious and poor background rendered them capable of relating to or being identified with a great majority of people of all regions and religions, who could accept without questioning the simplicity, purity and truth of what the children said they had seen and heard. Unlike in other apparitions, there was no message given at Vailankanni except the request for building a Chapel for the Blessed Virgin.

The Church authorities slowly approved the promptness and generosity of the faithful in discerning the sign of the apparitions. Official recognition of the authenticity of the apparitions at Vailankanni saw the throng of people at the shrine as an argument in favour of the authenticity of the apparitions.

Eight Great Appearances of Mother Mary in Modern Times:

1. Our lady of Guadalupe in Mexico – 1531
2. The lady of the Miraculous Medal – Paris, 1830
3. The lady in Tears – La Salette, 1846
4. Bernadette and our lady of Lourdes – Lourdes in France, 1858
5. Our lady of silence – Knock, 1879
6. The lady of the Rosary – Fatima, 1917 in Portugal
7. The virgin with the Golden heart – Beauraing, 1932-33
8. The virgin of the Poor – Banneux, 1933.

The above eight great apparitions of Mother Mary have been properly documented by the local clergy of the respective places, and all the apparitions of Mother Mary have been authenticated and approved by the Pope in Vatican. The apparitions have been documented after thorough interrogation and investigation of the witnesses who claimed to have experienced the apparition. Often a committee probed and concluded the authenticity of the apparitions. Later, many publications were brought out relating to the above apparitions. However, the Marian apparitions in Vailankanni have been retained only in the popular consciousness of the people. Since Christianity was not so strongly established in the late 16th century in India, as such the apparitions in Vailankanni couldn't be documented and authenticated as they were done in Europe and elsewhere. Hence, the apparitions in Vailankanni have only the authority of tradition and legend.

Categories of Worship

The worship offered in the shrine has been divided into three categories, depending on the liturgical and non-liturgical aspects of worship of the devotees:

Formal worship
Informal worship

Popular devotion

Formal Worship:

Formal worship hinges on the theological part of the religion: reciting the rosary, reading the Bible, and conducting masses at prescribed hours of the day intermittently in different languages of Southern India, i.e., in Tamil, Telugu, Malayalam, Kannada, Marathi and Hindi. The choir that sings the Biblical hymns on the public audio interrupts the readings of the Bible. The visitors or pilgrims, who visit the shrine, after making their offerings in the main shrine, invariably attend the mass adjacent to the extended basilica of the shrine. The reading of the Bible is subsequently interpreted by the sermons explained in plain and simple language to the august gathering that attends the mass.

Formal worship includes attending mass, reading the Bible, followed by sermons and Holy Communion, administering of the Blessed Sacrament to the congregation, anointment of the holy oil, lighting the candles, and sacraments of the texts. Normally it is the local populace who take part in the mass, apart from the visitors and pilgrims. In formal worship, the liturgical and theological aspects of the religion have to be strictly adhered to and no dilution or deviation of any kind is allowed and observed in the said doctrinal practises.

Informal Worship

People coming from long distances visit the shrine to make their offerings, and attend the mass at the prescribed hours if they find time before they return. Most of the people who come from long distances usually do so to offer thanks-giving prayers to the shrine.

Informal worship under Roman Catholicism, on the other hand, altogether assumes a different form as its adherents are allowed to practise their own indigenous ways of offering worship; the informal way of worship is specific to the ethnic and cultural background of its adherents. One may observe that the practises of the local indigenous customs and practises hinge on the Hindu mode of worship in temples, and the ritual substances offered like coconuts, garlands, flowers, incense, coconut saplings, etc., draw many parallels and similarities to the Hindu mode of worship. In informal worship, the pilgrims or visitors visit the shrine at any hour of the day, and after making their offerings of flowers, garlands, coconuts and candles and incense, etc., kneel down in silent prayer with the rosary in their palms; some visitors/pilgrims even carry a small Bible along with them during their worship. It is usually the occasional tourists, casual visitors and pilgrims who comprise the informal worshippers. The non-liturgical aspects in the form of various offerings dominate the informal way of worship.

Popular Devotion

Popular devotion encompasses the practises of majority of the people who make their offerings by following the popular practises of the Church, irrespective of their religion and denomination. Popular devotion also includes practises like the annual feast of the *Matha*, where people congregate in large numbers to take part in the festivities like hoisting the flag, pulling the chariot, carrying of the statue in the weekly Novenas observed during the evenings every Saturday; certain calendrical events like Christmas, New Year, Lent, and Good Friday followed by Easter, during which people throng the shrine in large numbers to take part in the events, irrespective of their religious and ethnic background; and the liturgical as well non-liturgical aspects followed in the Church.The liturgical aspects constitute the annual feasts and events found in the Christian liturgy, while the non-liturgical aspects constitute the various offerings that are made to the presiding deity of the shrine. Besides, it is popular devotion, due to which the local indigenous traditional practises form part of the observations both inside and outside the shrine.

Mary in Popular Devotion

Apart from the worship of Mary in Catholic devotion, by and large, popular devotion to Mary assumes a cultic phenomenon of addressing her as the *Matha*, which in itself entails a comprehension of different viewpoints expressed by her devotees who do not attach much importance to the immaculate conception of Mary in the Christian liturgy of the New Testament.

Mary in popular devotion assumes the role of a divine mother if not a Goddess but much more than a Goddess; a divine mother is the nourisher, the provider, and care-giver. The omnipotent part of the divine mother assumes great significance among the non-Christian believers especially the Hindus who ascribe to her all the qualities associated with a mother, who is not propitiated and to whom no sacrifices are made for invocation. She is venerated and worshipped as the benevolent *Matha*; devotion to the *Matha* is through prayer, petition and penance. Popular devotion to Mary also encompasses those practises by her devotees who make their offerings such as garlands—some of which are made of roses—incense, coconut and flowers, and lighting of camphor in front of the image or statue of Mary.

It is commonly seen that the followers of different faiths and religions visit the Roman Catholic Churches, especially those of St. Mary and Infant Jesus. Mary is worshipped across religions : some worship her as a Goddess while some worship her as a divine mother. The popular devotion to Mary cuts across boundaries of religion, caste and nationality as is seen in Vailankanni and other places. The reason for this is the easy adaptability of Roman Catholicism to Hinduism where we can find a lot of commonalities and similarities in the mode of worship and offerings, and an inherent belief that the Holy Mother answers the prayers and petitions of her faithful devotees.

As Mary assumes the role of a mother, offerings to her indicate more of personal piety than of liturgical observations, such as reading the Novena and reciting the rosary. Pilgrims and devotees, both Catholics and Hindus, can be seen in silent prayer sitting on the benches and squatting on the floor, and sometimes kneeling down with hands raised; practises, such as these are not found in the formal liturgical services of the shrine where emphasis is more on the liturgical aspects of prayer than on the devotional aspects.

The veneration and devotion to Mary by the Hindus is more of an act of self-seeking : either in seeking some favours or an act of thanksgiving for the favours already received; the process is more invocational for their material benefits than for understanding the spiritual merits of devotion. In the popular devotion, Mary assumes a higher position than Christ and God, and is worshipped as the benevolent *Matha*. Mary as such is worshipped by the Hindus on her own merit without drawing comparisons to any of the Hindu Goddesses like Lakshmi, Saraswathi, Durga or Parvathi; she holds her own ground as the mother of God or as the mother of Christ. Among her devotees a distinction can be made, like the sick and suffering, the diseased, and those seeking success in education and employment : those whose basic needs are yet to be fulfilled. The rest, whose basic needs have already been fulfilled, come to seek mental peace and to pray for the unfortunate amidst them. In the former category, the emphasis is on seeking material benefits, while in the latter category the emphasis tends to incline towards seeking spiritual gain.

Vows and Offerings: Symbolism and Syncretism

Certain vows and offerings related to the study have been noted down; they notably contain a lot of syncretic elements in their observances and practises. Some of the practises bear remarkable resemblances to the practises prevailing in the temples of the Hindus. In the realm of offerings made to the shrine after the harvest, one does come across similarities in the Hindu and Christian forms of offerings.

Colour of the Attire as an Offering

Men and women who come seeking any favour visit the shrine wearing a saffron-coloured dress as part of their offerings; this involves the person in prayer and piety becomes the part of the person. He or she who undertakes a vow wears the dress as part of the offering and also as a token of humility and respect to the *Matha*.

Various colours of the dress represent the various aspects of the *Matha*, Mother Mary. For example, brown colour represents immaculate conception, white colour represents purity, and blue colour represents the colour of the *Matha*.

Different colours are also identified with different apparitions of Mother Mary. In Vailankanni, the immaculate conception of the Matha as seen by the Hindu boys was brown in colour, hence, one can come across a large number of men and women coming to the shrine clothed in brown. Light saffron and dark saffron colours represent the Indian tradition, particularly the Hindu tradition, identified with pilgrims undertaking a journey to the Holy Hindu shrines; and a reflection of the same can be seen in the pilgrims visiting the shrine of the *Matha*. No specific colour of the attire, however, represents the kind of vow or offering that is made.

The Cult of the Matha

There have been five main stages and types of shrines in the historical development of the popular cults of the Virgin Mary.

1. The Prototypical Palestinian and Roman shrines.
2. Post Islamic "reduplicative" European shrines.
3. Colonial shrines, which replaced the shrines destroyed during the reformation in Europe.
4. European shrines of the high and late middle ages.
5. "Apparitional" shrines which developed during the early Industrial Revolution and continued throughout the present century with a markedly chiliastic and apocalyptic character. (V. Turner, pp. 162).

Since 1960, Fatima in Portugal, and still earlier in 1600 A.D., Guadalupe in Mexico, and Beauring and Banneux in Belgium, have achieved recognition even outside the Catholic Church and attracted hundreds of thousands of pilgrims annually. Yet, only a small percentage of the numerous Marian shrines have become pilgrimage centres. And wherever this has happened, a vision has often been the precipitating factor : either a vision (or dream) in which the virgin asked that a shrine be erected to her on a given site or one in which she revealed, to some lowly person, a hidden image of herself that later became the centre of a new cultus. This pattern has been fairly constant over the centuries (V. Turner p.149). As such, Vailankanni is also one of the few places where the apparitions of Mother Mary were seen, and the resultant devotions to the *Matha* have over the years assumed a cultic phenomenon.

In popular usage, "devotion to Mary" is synonymous with the Cult of Mary. Technically, however, "Cult" with reference to Mary means the external recognition of her excellence and of the superior way she is joined to God; and "devotion" adds the notion of an interior readiness for cult. Hence, the words devotion and cult are used interchangeably.

A new religious practise, which can be ascribed as part of the popular devotion is the concept of taking on the *mala* in the name of the *Matha*, which has almost assumed the form of a cultic phenomenon in Vailankanni.

The pilgrims call it as "*Mathaku mala poduruthu*", i.e., "putting on *mala* in the name of the *Matha*". This phenomenon is of a recent origin; according to some of the informants, this practise was started in Vailankanni around 10 or 15 years ago. Initially, it was started by the people from Madurai travelled on foot (*padayatra*) to visit the shrine of the *Matha*, wearing saffron colour clothes and a rosary with the cross being the equivalent of the *mala*. Gradually, the practise spread to other districts like Pudukottai, Salem, Tirunelveli, and Kanyakumari. Now people from all over the state are part of the movement, and it has also spread to nearby states like Kerala, Karnataka and Andhra Pradesh. Both the informants and some members of the clergy whom I interviewed agreed that this is an influence of the Hindu pilgrims who undertake pilgrimage to Sabarimalai, a very popular Hindu shrine of Lord Ayyappa (son of Shiva and Parvathi), in Pathanamthitta District in Southern Kerala.

The process which the pilgrims undergo before embarking on a pilgrimage to the shrine is quite similar to that of the existing practises followed before undertaking a pilgrimage to Sabarimalai of the Hindu order : the indigenous practises that existed for centuries even before the arrival of Christianity into India, as many of the religious elements have been assimilated and reinterpreted in a syncretic manner.

The Process

The process of a pilgrim or devotee who has taken on the *mala*, i.e., the beads, is acceptance of the pilgrim to visit the shrine of Lord Ayyappa. The *mala* and the dress, which is usually black or saffron in colour is blessed and given by a Guru : usually a person who has made at least 18 visits to the shrine on foot. The devotee who takes, on the *mala* has to observe certain prescribed procedures for a stipulated period of 40 days. The devotee has to bathe in cold water twice daily once early in the morning before sunrise and again later at midnight; soon after he has to recite the *mala* which contains 108 beads, the devotee is supposed to take only one meal a day, usually a vegetarian meal cooked by himself, and not by women of certain age. There are restrictions on non-vegetarian food, liquor and smoking, which have to be strictly adhered to. The devotee is supposed to sleep on the floor only and perforce address everybody as "Swamy" and not by his/her name during the course of his penance. The code of procedure has to be maintained throughout the stipulated period of 40 days before the pilgrim or the devotee embarks on a final journey to the shrine. The final pilgrimage to the shrine is undertaken either individually or with a collective group of pilgrims and devotees. There is a taboo, which restricts girls above 12 years of age and women below 50 years of age from undertaking a pilgrimage to the shrine, as some aspects of purity and pollution are observed in the Hindu shrine.

The Reinterpretation and Reorientation of the Process in the Christian Context:

For pilgrimage to the Sabarimalai's Hindu shrine, the process and procedure that a pilgrim has to undergo has been clearly established by tradition. But pilgrimage to Vailankanni doesn't have any established tradition, besides there is no restriction for girls and women of any particular age visiting the shrine with or without the *mala*.

Moreover, pilgrimage to Sabarimalai is seasonal, i.e., November to January 14th of every year, which coincides with the winter solstice, whereas pilgrimage to Vailankanni on foot by putting on the *mala* and dress coincides with the Christian calendrical event of Lent.

Meaning of Lent: For the Roman Catholics it is a period of repentance for sins; it is a time during which preparation is made for one's sins, for e.g., foregoing food and activities, which one enjoys, in memory of Christ's suffering, thus resulting in starting a new life with the Risen Jesus; in other words to cultivate one's habit to lead a virtuous life.

The period of Lent falls 40 days before Good Friday, i.e., between February and March : the period during which Jesus fasted for 40 days and 40 nights before his crucifixion at Calvary in Jerusalem.

These 40 days before Good Friday had been conveniently chosen by some pilgrims from Madurai District of Tamil Nadu to conduct a *padayatra* to the shrine of the *Matha*. As mentioned earlier, some pilgrims said that this concept of taking on *mala* in the name of the *Matha* is a phenomenon which emerged around 10 or 15 years ago.

The concept of taking on *mala* in the name of the *Matha* is a personal choice, for one's personal and individual satisfaction. It doesn't have any divine, canonical, or textual sanction in the Catholic dogma. In Vailankanni it is a pure imitation of the concept of pilgrimage to the Hindu shrine of Sabarimalai. The pilgrims have adopted the concept through assimilation, reinterpretation and reorientation of the whole process in the Catholic context.

The Process in Vailankanni

If a pilgrim has undertaken a vow to visit the shrine of the *Matha* on foot, s/he has to undergo the following process: The dress is purchased along with the rosary; the rosary is here equivalent to the *mala*, i.e., a necklace of beads, which contains a cross (crucifix). S/he gets the dress and the rosary blessed by the Parish priest; here the Parish priest–who doesn't have any objection to bless the devotee or pilgrim who has undertaken a vow to visit the shrine of the *Matha* or replaces the traditional Guru of the Hindus. Invariably, the pilgrim undergoes the same process, which a Hindu pilgrim undergoes. The same restrictions on food, attire, speech, address, code of behaviour and mannerisms are followed by the pilgrim. Lent is also a period of fasting and prayer for Catholics; as such no non-vegetarian food is cooked or eaten. However, there is no restriction on the pilgrim to accept food prepared by a woman.

It is an act of purifying oneself before undertaking the pilgrimage to the shrine. The penance for 40 days that a pilgrim undergoes is, according to a Catholic, an act of redeeming oneself for the sacrifice of Jesus, who had died for the sins of mankind. The period of 40 days coincides with the Lent, which is called "*Tawaskala*" in Tamil. Pilgrims who wish to seek some favour undertake the journey coinciding with the *Tawaskala*, i.e., Lent, 40 days before Good Friday and Easter. Often such pilgrimages are undertaken as an act of seeking some favour and are also subsequently undertaken for the fulfillment of a vow, as an act of thanksgiving.

The clothes and the *mala* (rosary) indicate that the person is going to undertake a pilgrimage to Vailankanni; the dress is in itself a reminder and a marker of the journey. It is a process of keeping oneself away from certain vices and also an indication to others to keep a distance from the person, as he has undertaken a vow to dedicate himself to God through fasting and prayers or an act of self purification and self mortification before undertaking a journey on foot to the holy shrine. The *padayatra* is a redemption of that pledge to bear all difficulties on the way to the holy shrine; for the pilgrim it is something sacred and the process that he undergoes before the journey is in itself a ritual to that end.

Invariably both men and women wear clothes of varying colours depending upon their convenience and availability. Often such colours reflect the area and place where they come from. They undergo the same process of purification before undertaking the journey.

Majority of the pilgrims, both men and women wear the saffron clothes which they call "*Kavi*" *in* Tamil. Some of the pilgrims wear blue clothes along with a blue towel. The blue colour is a representation of Mother Mary. The essence of cultural pluralism is to ensure that every religious or social group is allowed its own cultural space in which it has the right to practise its own beliefs and traditions.

Conclusion

The pilgrimage process in Vailankanni reflects the Pan Indian character of the shrine also with its share of pilgrims from outside the country. The throng of pilgrims both Hindu and Christian to the shrine since the apparitions to the two Hindu boys has been retained in the popular consciousness of the people. Countless persons from different religions believe in the gentle presence of the Blessed Mother here and honour her. In the realm of informal worship and popular devotion, Roman Catholicism altogether assumes a different form by its adherents who are allowed to practise their own indigenous way of worship. It is the non-liturgical aspects in the form of various offerings that dominate the informal way of worship. The resultant devotion to the Mother over a number of years has paved the way towards a new religious practise among her devotees which can be ascribed as the best example of syncretism and cultural pluralism. The entire process of taking on the "*mala*" has Hindu connotations wherein many a Hindu trait has been borrowed and reinterpreted in the Christian context in a syncretic manner. The offering of hair to the *Matha* is unique in a Christian pilgrim center, and some of the cultural practises followed around the Kodimaram like prostration, circumambulation, tying threads with turmeric, etc., indicate that the cultural practises followed have Hindu orientation, though the deity being worshipped is Christian. In course of time such practises got established both between the Hindu and Christian pilgrims visiting the shrine. The visit of Muslims is unique in a Christian pilgrim center. The conduct of mass in various languages speaks highly of the cultural and linguistic diversity of the shrine. The accumulation of both the Hindu and Christian forms of worship in a singular congregation of devotees at the shrine represents the quintessence of the vast pluralistic cultural and religious diversity of India. The sacred complex of Vailankanni adds to the cultural dimension of an ancient civilisation, which is also experiencing the process of cultural homogenisation and globalisation.

References

Archbishop P. Arokiaswamy, 2003. *Why We Catholics Venerate Mary*, Bp. Gabriel Publications, Shrine Basilica, Vailankanni-611111.

B.R. Ambedkar, 1997 (reprint). *The Buddha and his Dhamma*, Diksha Bhoomi Publications, Nagpur.

Das, N.K., 2003 (ed.). *Culture, Religion and Philosophy, Critical Studies in Syncretism and Interfaith Harmony*, Rawat Publications, New Delhi.

E. Alan Morris, 1997. *Pilgrimage in the Hindu Tradition : A Case Study of West Bengal*, Oxford University Press, New Delhi.

Fr. Gabriel, 1997. "The Shrine History of Vailankanni, Shrine." Basilica of Our Lady of Health of Vailankanni.

L.P. Vidyarthi, 1962. *The Sacred Complex of Hindu in Gaya.*

Makan Jha, 1971. *The Sacred Complex of Janakpur in Nepal.*

Makan Jha, 1974. *The Sacred Complex of Ratanpur in MP.*

Helen, K. Bond, Seth, 2003. *A Companion to Religious Studies and Theology*, Edinburgh University Press Ltd.

Ignatius Irudayam, 1997. *Christianity and Tamil Culture*, Dr. S. Radhakrishnan Institute for Advanced Studies in Philosophy, University of Madras.

Rowena Robinson, 2003. *Christians of India*, Sage Publications India Pvt.

Ltd., New Delhi.

Vasudeva Rao, 2003. *Living Traditions in Contemporary Contexts : The Madhva Math of Udupi*. Orient Longman, New Delhi.

Victor Turner and Edith Turner, 1978. *Image and Pilgrimage in Christian Culture*, Columbia University Press, New York.

Mundadan. A.M., 1984. *History of Christianity in India, from the Beginning upto the Middle of 16th Century* A.D., Vol. 1, Theological Publications in India, Bangalore.

Oomen, T.K., 2002. "Pluralism, Equality and Identity", *Comparative Studies,* Oxford University Press, New Delhi.

PART–IV
Linguistic Pluralism

18

The North-East Scenario: A Linguistic View

R. Senkuttuvan

Language is an integral part of human behaviour. It is the primary means of interaction between people. Speakers use language to convey their thoughts, feelings, interactions, and desires to others. We learn about people through what they say and how they say it; we learn about ourselves through the ways that other people react to what we say; and we learn about our relationship with others through the give-and-take of communicative interactions. Language is enriched by its use, and the meanings transmitted are social as well as cultural. Although people within a given culture share many assumptions about the world, they are not a completely homogeneous group. People are differentiated on the basis of gender, age and status in all societies. In addition, distinctions of class and ethnicity are used to segment population in modern nations.

India is rightly called the epitome of the world–a statement which is true, both anthropologically and linguistically apart from other considerations. As far as languages are concerned, India is represented by almost all families of world languages–Indo-European, Mongolian, Dravidian, Austric, etc., and the North Eastern Region (NER) of India is considered as a treasure of languages.

The phenomenon of language in North-East India is fascinating and awesome in its variety and culture. For a linguist, there is no difference between a language and a dialect. Each dialect can express anything needed for the society and so it is as good as any other dialect. This difference is marked when we study it from the socio-linguistic viewpoint. One of the dialects gains importance owing to some reason and then it becomes a language and it is accepted as a norm for other dialect groups.

Sapir and Whorf tried to find out the exact link between language and culture. Hockett explored the possibility of finding the exact link between the Chinese language and the Chinese culture, but he ended in a blind alley (Hoijer, 1954). Everybody will have to agree that a language is meaningful in the cultural context only because that particular language has grown within that particular culture, and serves the purpose of the bearers of that culture only. The language must have terms for all material objects which exist in that particular culture. The language must also include concepts for all the non-material ideas with which the culture normally deals. Some linguistic peculiarities cannot be explained as impressions of the culture on it.

Cultural pluralism is fundamental to the belief that all citizens are equal. Multiculturalism in India ensures that all citizens maintain their identities, take pride in their ancestry and have a sense of belonging. Acceptance gives each Indian citizen a feeling of security and self-confidence, making them more open to diverse cultures.

India has embraced diversity or cultural pluralism in both policy and practise. The Indian Constitution – the source of many state policies – can be called a basic multicultural document, in the sense that it provides for political and institutional measures for the recognition and accommodations of the country's diversity.

Cultural diversity is viewed as one of India's most important attributes, both socially and economically. Multiculturalism bespeaks of the existence of many different groups of people in one society. For example, people of different races, political or religious beliefs – the beliefs that it is possible and good for different groups and people to live together peacefully in a community, and co-exist in dynamic relation to one another enjoying more or less equal rights and opportunities. When unity and diversity are integrated in this way, unity does not remain abstract passive and diversity does not lead to fragmentation and isolation.

It is important to cultivate a common sense of belongingness among the diverse communities and to help them identify each other in the wider society. North-East India is the most linguistically and culturally diverse region in our country. It truly supports India's identity of "unity in diversity". All the eight states in this region, namely Assam, Arunachal Pradesh, Meghalaya, Manipur, Nagaland, Mizoram, Tripura and Sikkim have their own culture and traditions. These states are predominantly tribal lands inhabited by numerous tribal communities that are called rainbow states, and their languages belong mainly to Indo-Aryan, Sino-Tibetan and Austro-Asiatic linguistic families. Each of these tribal communities has a unique culture, which is totally distinct from the others. The main aspects of culture such as custom, tradition, language and life-style demarcate one community from the other.

Language in North-East India is a melting pot of various languages; each tribe is presumed to have its own language, and each language is presumed to be spoken by just one tribe. A map of the tribes is expected to look no different from a map of the languages. Tribes and languages are even called by the same name. For example, the Angamis speak Angami, the Garos speak Garo, the Mizos speak Miso, and so on; in fact, there are about a hundred or so languages that are spoken in the North-East.

Language is probably the most easily identifiable and accurate instrument of articulating the rich runs and wisdom of an ethnic group. It is the chief vehicle to connect oneself with others as well as with the whole community, and with other cultural groups. According to Dand Crystal, language is the primary outward sign of a group's identity. Language becomes an indicator of a community ethos. We realise that without language it would be impossible to adequately articulate the richness of one's cultural and ethnic identity.

Language Problem in NER

The language problem in the North-East is no doubt baffling and complex. But given the will and determination, all problems however baffling and complex these may be, these can be solved to the satisfaction and benefit of all. Each tribe speaks a different language which is not understood even by its immediate neighbouring tribe. For instance, the people of Arunachal Pradesh speak over 50 languages. In Nagaland one tribe does not follow the language of another tribe. The AIR broadcasts programmes in at least 15 tribal languages for Nagaland.

The population of the NER is multilingual in composition and character. In this context, to venture to offer a ready-made and acceptable solution to all, off the sleeve will certainly seem over ambitious, if not ridiculous. The solution needs careful study of the situation and the needs and aspirations of the people inhabiting the region from time immemorial. Therefore, the matter may best be left with the people depending solely on their collective wisdom to find out the best possible solution to the otherwise vexed and complex problem in the region. But thanks to the collective wisdom of the people, they could find out at least one workable solution and carry out the normal activities of trade and commerce, administration, education and their day-to-day activities as effectively as possible under such a situation. In the process, the society slowly and steadily with increased realisation and also under the compulsion of living together for mutual benefit and progress, gradually emerged as a multilingual society. For example, Arunachal and Nagaland developed new languages, now termed as Nagamese and Arunachalese – a kind of Assamese which are understood by the different people there. This newly developed Assamese language is a kind of *lingua franca* for the people of the said region. It also illustrates a point of linguistic importance that prescriptive grammar cannot keep a language in an iron jacket all the time – it changes, it grows, it expands, and serves the people by doing away with the communication gap. But a point here needs to be stressed that Nagaland and Arunachal have evolved a workable solution of this type, even though Hindi is also used in a restricted domain. In this process, the society also tends to become multilingual. It is now seen that a man in this region uses at least three languages in his day-to-day activities. The way of life and the nature of work of a person normally decide the number of languages one will have to use to carry out his normal functions in life.

Therefore, we find a person; say in Shillong (i.e., Meghalaya State) who uses Malayalam at home, Khasi outside home, English and Hindi in office, Hindi and Bengali in the market, and so on. This pattern may be more or less similar in other parts of the region with slight changes in one or two languages depending on the area of operation of the person concerned.

In Assam, the situation is a little different. Assamese is the state language. However, in the districts of Cachar and Silchar, Bengali is the official language at the district level. Assamese and Bodo are the major indigenous and official languages while Bengali holds official status in the three districts of Barak Valley. Linguistically, modern Assamese traces its roots to the version developed by the American Missionaries based on the local form used near Sibsagar District.

Bodo is an ancient language in Assam. All the major rivers in the NER are named using Bodo-Kachari words (e.g., Dihing, Dibru, Dihong, etc), revealing that it was once the most important language. Bodo is presently spoken largely in lower Assam (Bodo Territorial Council area). After years of reflect, now Bodo is gaining the limelight and its literature is developing. Other languages of Tibeto-Burman origin and related to Bodo-Kachari are Mishing, Karbi, Dimaca, Rabha, Tiwa, etc. Rajbongshi, also known as Kamatapuri or Goalpariya, is also widely spoken by the people in Western Assam. Nepali is also spoken in almost all parts of the state and the NER.

However, the problem of language is nothing new to the region. It had also existed before but thanks to the collective wisdom of the people, they could find out a workable solution and carry out their normal activities of trade and commerce, administration, education and their day-to-day activities as effectively as possible under such situation. In this context, the society slowly and steadily grew, with increased realisation and also under the compulsion of living together for mutual benefit and progress. This was also observed in the Munda area of Malkangiri in Orissa state (*Desiya Bhasa*).

Now in Arunachal Pradesh, a new trend is emerging in the language pattern. At the school level, the medium of instruction is Hindi, because of the imposing government policy. Now attempts are made to codify the new variety of Assamese prevalent in that part of the region. This is one instance to show how a language grows out of necessity and functions effectively and satisfactorily to meet the local needs and aspirations of the people.

However, it needs mention here that while Nagaland and Arunachal have evolved a workable solution of this type, other areas like Mizoram, Meghalaya, Manipur and Tripura are yet to evolve a common and acceptable indigenous system of communication. These areas are generally dependent on English. A kind of Hindi is also used in a restricted domain. But it cannot be said that the people are not communicating amongst themselves. They do so, and in this process, the society also tends to become multilingual.

Focus on Lyngngam

The State of Meghalaya was described as the "Scotland of the East" by the first British colonial who gained entry into this enchanted land of lush green mountains and meandering rivers. This place was first referred to as Meghalaya by S.P. Chatterjee, and the name was officially adopted when it attained statehood in 1971. Meghalaya has five administrative districts namely, West Garo Hills, East Garo Hills, West Khasi Hills and Jaintia Hills. The climate of the Garo Hills is comparatively warmer than that of the Khasi Hills, with fairly high summer temperatures and moderate winter temperatures.

Ethno-History of Lyngngam

Ethno-linguistic information includes family ancestry and socio-cultural traits of Lyngngam, who inhabit the area between the West Khasi Hills and the South-Garo Hills districts in Meghalaya; the ethnic identity of these people is a matter of much debate.

The Khasis and Garos practise matriliny but while the former speak a language of the Mon-Khmer family, the latter speak one of the Tibeto-Burman family. According to Gurdon (1974), Grierson (1928), Radtrome (1977), Bareh H. (1967), etc., the Lyngngam were considered as one of the five Khasi sub-tribes or dialectal groups (J.B. Bhattacharjee, 1978). Sangma (1981) stated that there are about 12 sub-tribes or dialectical groups of Garos, but their Endo-Ethnic name is Langam.

Genetic Admixture

The intermixture between two populations of separate gene pools, through marriage, is important in bringing about changes in the genetic make-up of a hybrid group. It takes place generally due to migration. Thus, the terms migration and gene-flow are synonymously used in population genetics, although genes may flow into a population from migration of individuals (especially males) from outside. However, such a casual gene-flow is considered to be less important in changing the genetic composition of a population. A genetic study (Langstieh, B.T. and B.M. Reddy, 1999) has indicated that the Lyngngam are not related to either the Khasis or the Garos especially in respect of the ABO blood group system. One of the possible explanations for such deviation of the Lyngngam population from the neighbouring population may be due to a different recombination of gene-types as a result of intermixture.

Genomics of Lyngngam Language

The languages of the Mon-Khmer family fall into five groups. The first group includes a number of closely-related forms of speech used by the inhabitants of the hill country of the lower and middle Me-Kong.

The second includes the Mon or Talaing spoken in Pegu, by the Anamese of Anam, and a number of minor dialects (including Stieng and Behnar) spoken in the latter country. The third group consists of the various dialects of the Khmer spoken in Cambodia. The fourth or Palanng-wa group includes the dialect spoken in the North-East of Mandalay, the language of the war, and a number of other dialects spoken in the hilly country around the upper middle course of the Chindwin and the Me-Kong (Grierson, G.A., 1928). Amongst them may be mentioned Kha-nuk Orkhun le-met and Riang. The fifth group consists of the various dialects of the Khasi language.

The Mon-Khmer vocabularies and the Munda languages of Central India, Noncowry language of the Nicobars and the dialects of the early inhabitants of Malaccal are so remarkable and of such frequent occurrence, that a connection between all these tongues cannot be doubted, and must be considered as finally established by the labours of professor Kahn.

The Man-Khmer Lyngngam have mono-syllables : every word consists of a single syllable, while Khasi, is an apparent dissyllable : it is actually a compound word. On the other hand, the Munda, Noncowry and Malacca languages contain many undoubted poly-syllables. This is a very important point of difference between the languages, as it is an important factor for the classification of languages.

This ancient substratum may have been the parent of the present Munda languages, or it may have been the parent of the present Mon-Khmer languages. It cannot have been the parent of both, and it is possible that it was the parent of neither.

Logari writing in the early 50s is believed to belong to the Mon-Khmer family of which it was the parent, and that the speakers were a mixture of two distinct races, i.e., that of Eastern Tibetans, or Western Chinese, who came across the Himalayas and mingled with the Australo-Iravidioms of India proper, who are now looked upon as the aborigines of India. These are the languages of the so-called Organ Utan, or men of the woods, Asked Senang, Organ Bemia and others.

Logan J.R. published a series of papers on the Ethnology of the Indo-Pacific islands, which appeared in the *Journal of the Indian Archipelago*, most of them were studied with advantage, though much has been superseded by later inquiries.

Brief Social Structure of Meghalaya

Meghalaya is predominantly inhabited by three tribes, the Garo, the Khasi and the Jaintia. There is no definitive historical account of the origin of the people of the region, since it is occupied by tribal groups, who until recently lived in physical isolation and had no script of their own. However, there is some reference to them in the *Buranjis* of the Ahoms.

The pre-historic evidence found in Meghalaya has contributed significantly towards establishing the fact that Paleolithic man lived here. Till 1960, there was an abundance of Neolithies that surfaced in the Garo Hills, but recently a daily paper news wrote about the gigantic man who appeared to have lived in the Lyngngam area. Pebbles, core and flake tools are evidence to this, though no human fossils have been found so far.

In Meghalaya, social divisions exist in the form of 21 communities of various lineage or clans which regulate marriage and indicate status. Most of them claim to follow the norms of community endogamy, but clan exogamy is observed by 20 communities, and inter-community marriage is reported in 19 communities. The common form of acquiring a mate is by negotiation, mutual consent, courtship or elopement. Besides, five communities practise polygamy which is either sororal or non-sororal.

All the segments of the three major tribes, the Garo, the Khasi and the Jaintia, have been identified and described at length. These tribes share a matrilineal tradition under which descent goes through the female line and the child belongs to the clan of the mother. But it is important to mention that matriliny among the Garos does not imply that females dominate the males. Infact, it is only a mode of transmission of property from one generation to another. On the other hand, the Khasis and Jaintias have a matrilineal system in a more meaningful way where women enjoy a better social status and position than the Garo women.

In the recent years, tribal matriliny has been under stress, mainly as a result of growing male dominance. There is a demand for the suspensions in such cases where gender is counterpoised to ethnicity.

Today, most of the Lyngngam have embraced Christianity and any reference to the religious beliefs of the Lyngngam, therefore, is only to the ancestral religions. The Lyngngam have a very vague notion of sin. Only that which hurts another is considered as sin, though practises like head hunting are not considered a sin. The idea that breaking the law is sinful is foreign to them. Sexual relations outside marriage are also not considered as sinful.

Apart from the sacrifice offered on the birth of a child, various other sacrifices are offered to the spirits; for example to the spirit or god of the forest, the god of illness, the god of cultivation, etc. They believe that there is life after death and that the spirits of the dead continue. There are no *Lyngdoh* or priests among the Lyngngam. The elders occasionally perform sacrifices. The Lyngngam, have a sacred mountain called Wakpangaram which is about 100 km from Sonapahar. Sacrifices were offered there in the past. It was also believed to be the abode of the souls of the departed Lyngngam, and symbolises a kind of heaven for them.

The Lyngngam were a head hunting people till about 1850; and the Rashir Clan of the Lyngngam seem to have continued the practise until recently. There are indications that some of them were also cannibalistic. Infact, the Khasi called the Lyngngam "*bam briew*" meaning man-eaters. Head hunting among the Rashir Clan seems to have been part of a ritual. Usually, they celebrate a second funeral, especially for the grandmother and the mother, which includes burying their bones; and on such occasions, the men of the clan cut off the head of a victim and take it for burial. If that was not possible, at least the blood of the victim was brought and buried with the bones.

The Lyngngam burial was an exclusive function. In earlier times, if any stranger who had nothing to do with the ceremonies was found wandering in the vicinity of the village, where a burial was taking place, he was killed and buried along with the dead. The Lyngngam believed that the spirits sent such strangers to them.

Head hunting for burial was considered to be one of their rights. The spirit of the hunted person was believed to belong to the devil, and if more heads were offered to him, he would increase the clan's prosperity. The Rashirs also had their own way of deciding the number of heads that are demanded by the devil or the evil spirits. Sometimes, the dying man asked for the head of a particular person. At other times, the corpse or the skeleton was supposed to stand up and tell how many heads it wanted. A relative of the dead man would go out to get them. Such practises are seldom reported now. In fact, there are very few cases of murder among the Lyngngam now.

In the words of Gurdon (1907-91) : "In the country of the Lyngngam, the crop belongs to the *Kur* or the family." The Lyngngam villages like those in the Khasi Syiemships, do not pay any rent to the *syiem*. If outsiders cultivate within the areas, set apart for different Lyngngam villages, all of them including women have to pay eight annas each to the villagers in whose circle they cultivate. There is usually a mutual understanding between the inhabitants of the Lyngngam villages that certain tracts of land belong to their respective villages. Sometimes, however, there are disputes between the different villages regarding the lands. Such disputes are settled by the Lyngngams' *Sirdars* of the villages or by the *Sirdars* together with two Lyngngams of the *Syienshing*. If the disputes cannot be settled by the officials to the satisfaction of the parties, they are taken to the *syiem* of Nongstoin, who tries the case with aid of the state *mantris* (machinery).

Today, most of the Lyngngam have embraced Christianity and belong to different Christian Churches. Any reference to the religious beliefs of the Lyngngams, therefore, is only to their ancestral religion. Like most of the tribal people of North-East India, the Lyngngam were animistic in their religious beliefs, practises and norms of worship, especially ancestral worship. They believed in the existence of spirits and their presence in forests, rivers, etc. The Lyngngam believe in a "primeval ancestress" for whose welfare a cow is sacrificed.

The Lyngngam were among the most backward and underdeveloped people in Meghalaya, some fifty years ago. They lived in inaccessible, rain-swept, malaria-infested jungles, deprived of educational opportunities and human contact with the wider world; and of people, ideas and medical care.

Their behavioural patterns were most primitive. Search for food and drink were their only known pursuits. Culturally, they still lived in a sort of "stone-age". They survived on roots and fruits from the forest and covered themselves with leaves. Broad pieces of tree bark were used as blankets. They slept near fire in mud huts, and personal hygiene was minimal. Hygienic practises like bathing were frowned upon, since it was believed that a bath would weaken the body.

Christianity has, however, remarkably changed the Lyngngam community. It has led them to devise new value systems and attitudes and consequently, to new patterns of behaviour, both personally and collectively.

Since Christianity came into the Lyngngam area, the level of literacy and education has been rising steadily. The average literacy among the Lyngngam may be estimated to be about 10% or more. Some are already reaching the high school level, but college education among the Lyngngams is still in the priority stage. However, there are a few who are attending college and university in Shilling and Nongstoin. Today, there are about 90 Church-run primary schools in the Lyngngam area, through which they are practising and adopting cultural pluralism as well as linguistic syncretism.

References

Ahmed, T.J.S., Sengupta and A.K. Ghosh.1997. "A Genetic Study on the Lyngngam of Meghalaya", *J. Hum. Ecol.* 8 : 473.

Bareh, H. 1967. *The History and Culture of the Khasi People*, Guwahati: Spectrum Publications.

Bhattacharjee, J.B. 1978. *The Garos and the English*, New Delhi. Radiant Publishers.

Grierson, G.A. 1928. *The Mon-Khmer Family in languages of North-Eastern India : A Survey*, Vol. 1, pp. 1-57, New Delhi, Gyan Publishing House (Reprint 1987).

Langstieh, B.T. and B.M. Reddy. 1999. "The Origin and Ethnic Position of Lyngngam among the Tribes of Meghalaya : An Exploratory Study". *J. Indian Anthrop. Soc.* 34 : 265-275.

Mathur, P.R. 1979. *The Khasi of Meghalaya*, Hyderabad. ICSSR.

Nagaraja, K.S. (unpublished MS). *A Lexico Statistic Study of Khasi and Lyngngam.*

Nagaraja, K.S. 1995. *The Status of Lyngngam Mon-Khmer Studies*, 26, pp. 37-50.

Nongsiang, E.D. 1995. "Various Forms of Festivals and Ceremonies of the Lyngngams", in K.R. Marak and R. Wankhar Shillong (eds.), *Festivals and Ceremonies in Meghalaya*. Department of Arts and Culture, Government of Meghalaya, pp. 120-123.

Rodborne, T. 1977. *U Khasi*, Shillong: Mrs. Rodborne.

Sangma, M.S. 1981. *History and Culture of the Garos*, New Delhi. Cosmo Publishing.

Singh, K.S. (ed.). 2002. *People of India*, Meghalaya. Volume XXXII.

Thapa, R. and A.K. Ghosh. 1998. "Demographics of the Lyngngam of S. Sengupta, Meghalaya India", *J. Hum, Eco* 9. pp. 629-631.

19

Cultural Pluralism: The Indian Scenario: In the Context of North-East Region

Harka Bahadur Chhetri Atreya

Introduction

The term "culture", if we try to magnify to its real sense, goes back to the stage of human beings when they were only limited to living on agriculture and taming animals. What they did for their livelihood, was known as culture and nothing more than that.

The movement of people, due to their increasing numbers and for seeking food, shelter and safer places, perhaps, compelled them to be competitive for their respective needs and identities. And hence, today, people are competitive in the defense of their language, culture, literature or religion that they feel as their important elements of identity.

Thus, culture as we mean today, is an identification of a speech community, i.e., their traditional customs, rites and rituals, faiths and beliefs, behaviour and manners and also the dances, dresses, artistic style, etc. In short, it is the identity of a particular lingual community, whatever may be the religion. Culture, in its true sense of today, is a full-fledged life-style with the preservation of language and literature as their distinguished identifications from others. Thus, it is said that loss of culture is the loss of identity.

Indian Scenario

A great nation, more like a continent, i.e., *Bharatvarsha*, or India, as named by the foreigners, was a vast country in its geographical boundary since the history extracts. *Dharma* was the backbone of the society, and the identity which ruled them properly. The Vedic literature, *Sindhu-Sabhyata*, and later the "*ahimsa parama dharma*" of Lord Goutama Buddha, 2500 years ago, were some of the simplest elements of the Indian Cultural identification. From Srilanka to Afghanistan and from Dwaraka to Burmadesh, India was a single entity, though there were many languages – colloquial or written, dialects, and literature.

The fifty traditional kings of the present state of Tripura as mentioned in the Rajtarangini of Kashmira, and the description of the Mahabharata war where a number of *Danava* soldiers took part from Pragjyotishpura, i.e., the North-East of present India, clearly prove the multiple cultural identity as single, though there were occasional warfare or war-games among the small kings and states which continued till the British invasion. In sum, it can be said that there existed competitions, wars and invasions, but not like of the present day cultural competitions.

As our concern is Cultural Pluralism in the National Scenario, the participant wants to represent his own area : the Greater Assam, from what he has read in his early days of school education.

Assam and the North-East Region

Before 1972, the present North-East Region (NER) was known as Assam or in our memory, as Greater Assam. The British captured Assam in 1826 through the Yandabu Treaty signed in Burma and till 1838, the tribal kingdoms of the different present states, were all annexed and united into one as Assam.

The Cultural Assam

Pragjyotishpura, as mentioned in the Mahabharata era, was later known as Kamrupa till the Ahoms of Burma attacked in A.D. 1228 under Su-ka-fa, the Burmese King that is, the first Ahom King. No doubt, there was Hindu religious and cultural influence from the middle India, and there was the Kairataja religion of the then Kirata people who are now known as the Bodo-Kachari or the Bodo people. The immigrant's history of these Bodo people dates back to 3000 years B.C., according to historians like Dr. S.K. Chatterjee, R.M. Nath or Dr. Banikanta Kakati. Thus, the culture of Assam is a composite culture of the Assamese lingual people, Bodo speech community and other Indian Austrics, Aryan and the Dravidian communities.

Mutual Influences of Culture

The reformation movements during the 14th and 15th century to the 16th century in the European countries might have influenced India also, in the form of the Bhakti Movement in India. The same trend at a time reached Pragjyotishpura or in the modern Assam while the prophet Sri Sri Sangkar Deva came to middle and north India and met Kabirdasa and Guru Nanak. Thus, there was no cultural terminology in use, and religion played a dominant role in all aspects of social life. So, the socio-religious reformation took roots in Assam in the form of the Bhakti Movement with Sangkar Deva during A.D. 1449-1548 : a saint and preacher, poet and playwright, philosopher and reformer, artist and composer, "all rolled into one", (to quote Dr. V.S. Agrawal, the eminent Indologist) : as its foundation head.

The Kairataja, a tribal religious-cultural people were slowly converted to the Vaishnavite cult founded by Sangkar Deva in the far east of India. The converted people like the Moran and Matak, Barahi, Chutiya, Lalung, the Coches, Saraniya, etc., were all the Monoplian Kachari people sub-divided into many sub-communities, who maintained their own traditional tribal identities in reserve, but identified themselves with the mainstream in the composite Assamese culture. Many of them might have forgotten their dialect also as they adopted the Assamese language and literature as their own. So, like other riverine civilisations of the world, the old cultural civilisation of Pragjyotishpura or Kamrupa on the banks of the great Brahmaputra was reformed, restructured and galvanised into one as the Assamese culture, since the later part of the 15th century. In fact, the present Assamese culture is an invaded culture of the Ahoms on the Kairataja religious culture, reformed and moulded by the Vaishnavite philosophy of Sangkar Deva through the "one God, one principle", on Lord Krishna. It is a kind of Krishna cult throughout the present small Assam under *Ek Sharana Bhagawati Dharma.*

According to the historians, prior to the Ahoms or the Mongolian footprints on this riverine or alluvial soil, the Austrics had already left their footprints and crossed over to the Andaman and Nicobar Islands. Whoever was left behind, were known as Monkhemr or the Khasis who continued their culture of *jhum* cultivation on the hills and the betel-nut plantations till today.

The Present Scenario

The present Assamese culture, based first on the Austrics for their agriculture and betel-nut plantations, was definitely inspired and influenced by the Bodo culture that flourished 3000 years ago, with respect to designing clothes, dresses, dances and arts, etc. The influence of the Vedic culture after the presence of Narada, a disciple of Lord Vishnu, did much : he named the province as Pragjyotishpura, which means advanced in the astrology as in the east. Thus, a social milieu took place in Pragjyotishpura of the east, and carried a long tradition of mutual influence of the cultural heritage through Kamrupa to the present Assam among the Austrics, Aryans and the Mongoloids.

The Mongolian and other Cultures

The Bodos or the Boros are a race of the Mongoloid people described as the inhabitants of a country lying to the north of the Himalayas and in the Western belt of China. This country is known as Bod, meaning a homeland of a particular racial community. "In pre-historic period, Tibet or Tribistan, was perhaps divided into five parts : Har-bod, La-bod, Kosh-bod, Ti-bod and Tse-bod. People descended from Kosh or Kosh-bod, at a time known as Kosh-hari or Kochari who lived in the Kosh-bod area. Kosh + Hari = dynasty, fragmented to Kochari in the modern period."

In the Bodo Language "*Bod*" means land or country, and hence, the Bod province of West China is directly related to the Bodo people as their aboriginal homeland. The movement of people as a universal habit for food, shelter and security, might be the cause of the migration of Bodos through the banks of the River Brahmaputra in the North-East and from the Tista River bank in the Tibet-Sikkim ways to north Bengal valley. Their history in the Pragjyotishpura or Kamrupa, i.e., in the present Assam, dates back to 2500 to 4000 years ago. This is mentioned by Dr. S.K. Chatterjee in his history, and R.M. Nath in his book "The Background of the Assamese Culture".

Dr. Chatterjee further says "The whole of Assam (barring the eastern parts inhabited by the Nagas and the south-eastern parts inhabited by the Kukichins), and North-East Bengal was the country of the great Bodo people". (Kirata-Janakriti, p. 46).

Earlier to the Bodos, the Austrics including Monkhemr or the Khasis had already left their footprints in the Brahmaputra Valley; all historians agree on this argument. Thus, many linguists, historians, social thinkers and anthropologists come to the same conclusion that dwellers in the NER, whether they are called ethnic, aboriginal or indigenous are all immigrants. The fact is that all of them were immigrants who came here either earlier or later in the time frame.

Thus, the present Assamese culture which was converted from the Ahom culture after A.D. 1228, with the Ahom annexation into Kamrupa from Burma, was again reconverted to Assamese culture through the great saint of vaishnavism Sri Sri Sangkar Deva after A.D. 1449. In fact, the present composite culture of Assam is a new product of the assimilation of the Burmese, Aryan and Mongolian cultures. It is a social affinity that produced the Assamese culture, though the tribals continue to have their own distinguished culture.

Thus, nine different sub-branches, with their stem as the Bodos, follow their religions Kairataja or the Kirata religion more of less in their traditional religious institutions through the two philosophical dogmas.

The *Satras* and *Namghars* are the main religious institutions of the Sangkari religious culture in Assam. Such *Namghars* are more than thousand in number and so are the *bathowthansali* and the Brahma temples of the Bodos which are more or less equal to the number of Churches of the Bodos. *Kherai* is the prayer dance and song, *Bagroumba* is the welcome dance to the heavenly god and *Baisagumwchanai* is the new year's welcome dance of the Bodo culture. Apart from this, in the Assamese culture, the Bihu festival is celebrated in the month of April, September and January every year. The Bihu is celebrated by all the Mongoloid sub-communities in Assam including the Nepalese and Maroaries. Though the Biharis or the Hindi speaking people, the Bengalis, and the Punjabis, who live there, follow their own traditional cultures, they also celebrate the Bihu festivals.

The Bihu festival relates with the Baisakhi in Bengal, Bihar and Kerala, Chandramana Ugadi in Karnataka, Baisakh in Nepal, ChaitraBisu in Tamil Nadu, Pongal in the southern states and so also of the Punjabis and Kashmiris, Gujaratis and the Marathis. The *Satras* and *Namghars*, infact, have remained limited in the Assamese speech communities until today. That the Sangkari culture should have spread to other communities and outside the said state, is also a demand of time sequence.

The said Mongoloid sub-communities, i.e., the tribes, with their separate but identical language, culture, dresses and dances, warfare weapons, art and manner, and behaviour, or in appearance too, represent their similarities. A dominant Austric dynasty in Assam with the Dravidian lingual people represents mainly 60 lakhs of the population and more than 6 lakhs of them have dominated more than 850 tea gardens in Assam under the company management. The Santals outside the tea gardens follow Singbonga (Sun God principle) while others in the garden including the Oraon (Dravida), Khariya, Bhuyan, Kurmali, Munda, etc., have a mixed culture of rites and rituals. Those who are converted to Christianity in the garden area go to the Church every Sunday, but the women continue to wear *Sindur* (head spot).

The Austrics follow their natural culture because they have no temples like the Hindus, but the Dassera and Dipawali are commonly celebrated by all the communities of Assam. The Austrics also celebrate Baha, Sahray, Karampuja, Golwari, Tusupuja, Jhumur dance and so on.

Historical Background

The Dharma Raja Yudhisthira of Mahabharata after the great war of Kurukshetra and the *Rajasuya Yajna* for his supremacy, left free the horse declaring it as uncaptured. The horse was caught by Babru Vahana in Manipur, as mentioned in the *Dharmashastra*. So were the past relations of small provinces with the greater *Bharatakhande-Jambudwipe*. Historians and Anthropologists who comment on the quotations in the Ramayana and Mahabharata say that this region was fully dominated by some tribal kings named *Danavas* and *Ashuras* or *Mlecchas*, and before them, there were footprints of the Negrito and the Austrics whose cultural traits remain with the Hmar and the Khasis in the present Meghalaya State.

According to Twipra Chronicle Rajmala, there were 184 kings, who ruled the Twipra Kingdom for five thousand years. The Rajmala and the Chronicles of Kashmira and Rajtarangini compiled by Kalhana, are the only two written chronicles in India. They have narrations about relations between the Aryans and the Twipra Kingdom during the Mahabharata period, when the Twipra Kings joined the Kurukshetra war. After the war was over, Triluchan, the great King of Twipra was invited by Maharaja Yudhisthir to visit Indraprastha on the occasion of the *Rajasuya Yajna*. On this occasion, Maharaja Yudhisthir presented a throne to the Twipra King as a symbol of friendship.

All the eastern regional minor provinces were under small Tribal kings earlier to A.D. 1228, i.e., the attack of the Ahoms on Kamrupa. More or less, the provinces were united in cultural milieu. The East India Company annexed Assam in 1826 under the Yandaboo Treaty in Burma. It later annexed Jayantiya Hills in 1835, Upper Assam in 1838, Sadiya and Lakhimpur including the NEFA areas in 1842, Nagaland in 1864, Garo Hills in 1873, and Luchai Pahar in 1882-1898. All these minor states were districts of Assam, i.e., the Greater Assam, at one time. The British had demarcated the border of Nagaland District in 1925 and ultimately, it was separated as a state.

When the capital of Assam was brought from Shillong to Guwahati, it paved the way for hill districts to demand to be identified as full-fledged states. This led to the creation of Meghalaya, Manipur, Mizoram,

Tripura and Arunachal Pradesh as full-fledged states in this region.

Sikkim was ruled by Chhogyal for a long time, before it was annexed by India in 1975, and was declared as a state under the Union of India with local administration. All these states have some peculiarities of people with their settlements in the geographical isolations or land-locked situations, with many languages, rites and rituals, cultures and customs in a long tradition. Being at a long distance from the National Capital, they are unwantedly far, for the last 60 years, from the constitutional as well as developmental steps taken by the Government of India.

Richness of the North-East

A foreign researcher, Dr. Robbins Burling, Professor Emeritus of Anthropology and Linguistics at the University of Michigan, after his long study tour in the NER, said on June, 2009 at a gathering of the students and teachers in the Guwahati University premises that except for New Guinea, parts of Africa and Amazon, such diversity does not exist today. Further he said, "For me the most fascinating discovery has been the huge wealth of languages that North-East India possesses, which could be well over a hundred". Referring to his familiarity with Nagamese, he hoped that scholars and researchers from different parts of the world would carry out similar field studies in the North-East, an experience that was of great benefit to him personally as well as academically. He suggested that some clever people and local Universities should seize the opportunity for this appreciable and living heritage, and encourage the people to provide learning through their local languages.

In fact, this scholar while moving from place to place during a research (project) in 2003-04 and 2006-07, on the socio-culture of the Adivasis and the Bodos in Assam, found different language-speaking people every 100 miles, in the locality of the upper and middle Assam. This is very common in the whole NER, which inspires the scholars and researchers towards deep thought. This is rare in all other parts of India.

Thus, the socio-economic set-up and cultural varieties based on languages, is very common in the states of NER.

The North-East Scenario

Apart from the main cultural groups, i.e., the Assamese, Bodos, and the Austrics, the six states in the region : seven including Sikkim : follow their local traditional cultures separately. In Arunachal Pradesh, there are tribes like Abor, Aka Angami, Khamti, Singphow, Apatani, Pakheals, Khamyangs, Deoris, Mishings, Turunqs, Dafla, Tihak and Tangsas, etc. Some of them have been converted to Buddhism while others follow their own tribal culture without any religion, as we know it today. Likewise, people in Nagaland represent their individual culture through Nagamese language. They are Ao, Angami, Sema, Lotha, Thaadou, etc. The Meitei, i.e., Manipuri language represents the state but there are other dialects representing Luwang, Khuman, Angom, Moirang, Khaba-nganba, Chenbai, and Mangong, etc. There are about 33 lingual groups in Manipur.

Mizoram, the Christian state second to Kerala in literacy, is dominated by the Zomi people followed by other communities like Kuki, Naga, Manipuris, etc. Tripura is a small state with a long tribal traditional culture. The Kok-Boroks are the main dominating tribal group under the Sino-Tibetan language family, while the Debbarma, Jamatia, Kolgi, and Miring tribes also have a presence; but Hindu culture and Bengali language have dominated the state till now which can be compared to Jharkhand, a tribal state having Urdu as the state's representing language. The Khasi Hills, now known as Meghalaya, represent the Khasis, Monkhem (Austrics) and the Garo (Mongoloid with other sub-communities). The Sikkim State in the Indian Union after 1975, represents Nepali language speaking people like Rai, Limbu, Gurung, Tamang, Lepcha, Bhote, Sherpa, Magar, Sunuwar, Danumar, Tharu, Hamal, Dhimal, Damai, Kami, Sarki, Gaine, Chhetri and Brahmin. The other states are eastern regional states that use Hindi as the inter-state *linguafranca* in their common communications and in business transactions.

Conclusion

The influence of the missionaries after 1840 was only through religious preaching for conversion into the Christianity. Nagaland and Luchai Hills, i.e., the present Mizoram were mostly influenced by this religious culture; some Bodo and Adhivasi people in the plains were influenced too. Presently, the people converted to Christianity go to the Churches, while the others to their Mongoloid and the Austric cultural and religious traditional places to worship Shivrai and the Singbonga as their Supreme Being.

The whole Mongoloid population under Sino-Tibetan Language family group, at present is divided into two religions cultures, i.e., the followers of the Shivrai and the followers of Christianity. The followers of Shivrai, inspired by the Shivrai temple mountain that existed in the North Mongolia province, in fact, follow the five elements as the Hindus do : the five organs of perception, i.e., *Khaoswm* to control five actions, etc., have deep relation with the five elements of the Hindu Philosophy. The *Siwbwrai* roars with the five spiritual sounds *ong-hring-khling-fwt-che* creating the universe with the sun and others stars and planets.

Thus, pluralism in cultural India can never be denied but preserved, uplifted and saved sincerely.

The Dalits have been counted in a percentage-wise basis in the number one class cities like Delhi, Mumbai, Chennai, etc. But it is a shame to the country that, while the nation is going to become one of the super power countries of the world, the poor people, dalits and the tribals are speedily pushed back to the unwanted classes. Does it signify that the nation is developed? And are the people proud of their super power?

So, for the sake of the down-trodden people for their development, considering the national level, a direct method of plan and project in the long term is to be followed by the central and the state governments in understanding and uncompromising ways.

References

P.N. Dutta. 1985. *Glimpses into the History of Assam*, Guwahati. Bani Prakashan. pp. 113-15.

Kameswor Brahma 2002. *The Bodo: Mouth Piece*. Kokrajhar. Bodo Sahitya Sabha.

Sydney Endle. 1911. *The Kach Baptist Mission*. Tezpur. Paris.

M. Neog. 1987. *Asomiya Sahityar Ruprekha*, Ghy. Chandra Prakashan Tihu. pp. 216-34.

B.L. Brahmachaudhury. 1993. *The Bodo: At a Glance*, Bongaigoon. Tribal Cultural Institute. pp. 42-45.

H.B. Chhetri. 2007. *The Bodos: A Socio-Cultural Study of Assam*. Kolkata. Ministry of Culture.

H.B. Chhetri. 2007. *The Adivasi Culture of Assam*, Kolkata. Ministry of Culture.

PART–V
Cultural Pluralism and Ethnic Groups

20

Emerging Patterns of Cultural Pluralism Among the Burmese Settlers in Great Andaman: An Anthropological Perspective

D.V. Prasad and *S.A. Azeez Saheb*

Introduction

Burmese settlers were brought to Andaman Islands as convicts during the British reign. After Independence, they were let free along with other convicts and allowed to return to their native place. However, a few remained in Andamans due to their conjugal relations with the local settlers, migrants, and Anglo-Indians. Those who expressed their willingness to settle in Andamans were allotted land for plantation and residential purposes. Later they were allowed to bring their spouses and children from mainland Burma. Some Burmese immigrated voluntarily to work as labourers in the forest; and as elephant-care-takers, forest guards, etc. Descendents of these first and second generations constitutes the present Burmese population in the Bay islands.

The Burmese who got married to "Locals"[1] possess passports issued by the administration on the condition of renewal on a yearly basis. Whereas their descendants were entitled for Indian citizenship based on their matrilineal or patrilineal parenthood. In due course of time, they were categorised as pre-1942 settlers. Under this positive discrimination, the Burmese can avail government benefits at par with other settlers who came to Andamans prior to 1942 as freedom fighters. Those who already cleared the forests for horticultural activities after settlement were also given title deeds, i.e., land protection licenses. The remaining Burmese settled in government jobs, as labourers in saw mills, timber works, as carpenters, and in other private jobs.

Due to contact with the non-Burmese, they have accepted certain new cultural traits in place of their own. Slowly they got absorbed along with the changes that took place in due time and were identified with the non-Burmese who mingled with them for the past few decades through matrimonial relations. In spite of this, they still claim their own identity through their religion and language in the isles. During Burmese festive occasions they come together at the Buddhist Monasteries situated in Port Blair, Wandoor (Memio), and Mayabunder and express their solidarity through celebration of Buddha Poornima, Deewali and Holi. However, there is little impact on the host cultures with which they interact.

In this context an attempt has been made to understand the continuity of structural features of social organisation and existence of other cultural practises that have been absorbed in the life-style of the Burmese. Prior to understanding the plural situation, it is pertinent to understand the socio-cultural, economic, political and religious aspects of their own society.

Historical Transect

During pre and post British periods, Burmese largely inhabited different parts of Andamans. They encroached forest land and cleared it for their livelihood and settlement. The Burmese are experts in construction of wooden houses and some of the existing wooden living structures in remote areas of Port Blair are testimony to this fact. Apart from their individual settlements, they collectively cleared some plots of forest and constructed a monastery on their own. This place was demarcated and named as the Andaman Buddhist Mission, and is locally known as "*Phonghy Khyongi*". The Burmese visit this place during festive occasions.

During 1967-68 the Burmese were allowed to return to their native land and vice-versa (i.e., some of the Indian nationals were allowed to return to this place as per the diplomatic agreement between India and Burma). During that period all the ethnic Burmese left except those who married the "local" settlers and decided to stay back. This move greatly affected their community living and the maintenance of the monastery became more problematic because the original *Phonghy* (priests) also left in 1967 along with their community elders. The remaining Burmese were in a dilemma, regarding the continuation of the Mission in absence of a priest. Hence, they brought this matter to the notice of Bodh Gaya requesting for the maintenance of Buddhist monastery in Andaman. The proposal was readily accepted and a trained *Phonghy* was sent to look after the monastery. Though the *Phonghy* hailed from Assam, he was a Nepali. Hence, the present Nepalese population also identify with this Buddhist monastery.

Thereafter, phenomenal changes occurred in the maintenance of the monastery's property. Encroachment of monastery land by the local settlers for commercial as well as settlement purpose took place with the connivance of the new incumbent. According to the original settlers, this was a source of income for the maintenance of monastery premises. But the act of intrusion was resisted by the non-Burmese Buddhists and they brought it to the notice of the administration. As a result, the monastery was sealed off temporarily with a view to bring this property under the direct control of Indian Government. However, the *Phonghy* with the help of then Secretary of Buddhist Mission, Burmese women and other followers, filed a case in Circuit Bench of Calcutta High Court against the administration. Meanwhile, they changed the earlier name of the temple from 'Andaman Buddhist Mission' to 'Burmese Buddhist Mission' and formed a committee overnight. Actually this committee had no earlier role in the maintenance of monastery lands and activities, as everything was under the direct control of then *Phonghy*. When the Burmese Buddhist Mission won the case against the administration, its Secretary was murdered by unidentified persons. This enmity between the non-Burmese Buddhists and the *Phonghy* badly hit the monastery's activities. Due to this many believers stayed away from the maintenance of monastery and curtailed their relations with the *Phonghy*.

Soon after this, the committee assumed authority over the present Buddhist Mission area and undertook its maintenance with the income from the shops established in the area. The authorisation obtained from the managing committee by the shopkeepers paved the way for settlement of different communities. Earlier there were three *Dharmasalas* (choultries) to provide shelter for the destitute. However, at present no *Dharmasala* is found in this area except the settlement of the Burmese and other communities. This is attributed to having a non-Burmese *Phonghy*, instead of their own. The corrupt practises of the new *Phonghy* forcibly converted the monastery into a commercial and residential area by leaving only the Buddhist shrine. Soon after his demise, the new *Phonghy,* who also hailed from Nepal, filled this vacancy. At present, the income generated from the rented houses of the existing shrine premises are utilised for its maintenance, celebration of festivals, etc.

The concept of plurality is evident in the formation of the new managing committee, which consists of President (Nepali), Vice-President (Bengali), Secretary (Tamil), Joint Secretary (Bengali), Treasurer (Nepali), and seven executive members. Among them, four members represent the Burmese community while the rest are from diverse communities. Though the secretary looks after the regular activities of the shrine, the final authority is vested in the hands of the *Phonghy*. However, the role of the *Phonghy* has come down slowly, and is now limited to the maintenance of shrine. The rest of the powers are now in the hands of the Executive Committee. As such it assumed a syncretic character in composition, activities and followers.

Profile of the Burmese

The Burmese were divided into different groups on the basis of territorial distribution. They are mainly Burmese, Davey, Kachen, Sen, San, Muwai, Yakahami, Kaya, and Karen (Singh, 1994). In the Andamans only the Burmese and Karen groups have settled, while the majority of the Buddhist preachers (*Phonghy)* hail from the Yakahami group; however, persons from any other group may become a *Phonghy* through the practise of strict celibacy.

They speak Burmese for intra-community communication. But the present generation is not acquainted with the script, except for the old women. Now they acquaint with Devanagari script and use Hindi in their daily communication. Apart from Hindi, they also speak their spouse's language like Bengali, Tamil, Telugu and Oriya.

Earlier they lived in joint families. But now the nuclear type of family is prevalent among them, followed by a few cases of extended and joint family set-up. Soon after marriage, the bride comes to live in the bridegroom's house for a permanent settlement. Joking relationships are observed among the close relatives of the kin group even in the changed scenario. This is observed mainly between women and their elder sister's husband; a man and his mother's sister's unmarried daughter; and between grandparents and grandchildren; it is in the form of verbal teasing, but no vulgar words are used. No avoidance is observed between daughter-in-laws and the father-in-laws, or a man and his elder brother's wife.

The Andaman Burmese were generally endogamous in nature; but due to the non-availability of mates from among their own group, they now choose spouses from diverse cultural backgrounds. Monogamy is the ideal practise among them, but in case of death and divorce, remarriage is permitted, based on their personal choice. Practise of concubinage in the case of broken marital relations is less common. There is no communal restriction in this regard, as earlier these cases needed acceptance from community associations. Succession is reckoned still on the basis of patrilineal rule : the eldest male member acts as a head of the family.

Traditionally they consume the Burma rice (which is in black colour and tastes sweet after boiling), *khousoo* (noodles), *nappi* (dish made from prawns), along with fish, pork, venison meat, mutton and chicken. The preparation of indigenous *nappi* in typical Burmese style projects their identity. For this, huge quantities of prawn (very small in size) are collected and smashed in a big container. Then they squeeze the flesh to drain out the water. Spices and salt are added and the paste is stored in earthen pots. This they use often as a ready mix. This method of preparation was also adopted by other settlers who had regular interaction with them.

Asivoye is a council of elders among the Burmese for their social control. Apart from dispute resolution, the council assists in maintaining the solidarity of the group. Though *Asivoye* had significant contribution in their political life, advice/opinion of the *Phonghy* is mandatory.

Basically, the Burmese are experts in wood related works, i.e., logging, supply of wood to saw mills, carpentry works, building of wooden houses, and so on. Due to their expertise in forestry-related works, the Forest Department engaged the Burmese for wage labour in the forest. Now, due to restrictions on forestry works, they have undertaken government service, horticulture, wage labour, and private contract works. Those who reside in the remote villages engage in multifarious activities ranging from cattle rearing, poultry, vegetable and fruit crops, and raising gardens along with betel nuts and coconut. Cultivation of traditional variety of Burmese rice by some of them can also be noticed in interior islands.

As religious faith strengthens the bonds of relations in the group, the Burmese express their solidarity through their attachment to Buddhism. *Phonghy Khyongi* (monastery) is one of the oldest religious shrines in Port Blair. Though they worship other religious gods and goddesses, they preserve their ethnic identity through celebration of Buddha Poornima, Holi and Deewali in a syncretic manner. This is evident from the display of Gautam Buddha's idol along with other religious idols at the worshipping site inside their houses. For the above-mentioned celebrations, all the Burmese come together at the monastery just one day before the event. Preparations for the occasion including decoration, cleaning of shrine precincts, and food preparation are done collectively under the guidance of the *Phonghy*. Those who convert to Christianity and other religious faiths also visit and participate in the monastery during ceremonial occasions. They believe in supernatural forces and visit *tantriks* (sorcerers) and their *Phonghy* to ward off evil spirits, which cause illness to their family members.

The Burmese often consult the *Phonghy* for treatment of illness. Based on the gravity of the illness, he offers herbal medicines to the victims. Even while laying the foundation for the construction of a new house, opening a new house or shop, harvesting of new crop and likewise occasions, the presence of the *Phonghy* is essential. As such, the *Phonghy* holds a respectable position in their society. This is evident from the offering of the first share to him from the special dishes prepared during ceremonial occasions. But after contact with other communities, the role and status of the *Phonghy* has come down and he is now treated at par with the other Burmese.

Life Cycle Rituals

Birth

Pre and post-natal care is most important in the native Burmese society. During pregnancy women continue their usual life without any restrictions. It is only during the peak months that she is relieved from household chores. No avoidance is observed with regard sexual intercourse during pregnancy period. It is purely a personal choice. The expectant mothers are prescribed a special diet during their confinement. Vegetables like *kumda* (pumpkin), *began* (brinjal), *karella* (bitter guard) and *kheera* (cucumber) are restricted. After childbirth, the mother is not allowed to eat chilli, venison meat, pork, cold items, and some aquatic foods like *gobra machi* (saw fish), and *magur* (crocodile), as they feel that these will affect the baby. To recover the strength, nutritious food is given to the delivered mother. *Tousia* (soup) made with fish, meat, and vegetables and *nappi* is given for the continuous nourishment of the mother.

Soon after the delivery, the mother and the newborn child are rested in a separate room, which is screened off, and no man is allowed including her husband. On the seventh day, they observe a ritual to get rid of birth-related pollution. *Winsewde* is an elder woman who is an expert in handling delivery cases and plays a crucial role in providing the necessary services to the parturient women. She uses soaked mud brick for massaging the delivered mother to relieve her from labour pains. Later vermilion water vapor is given to reduce her drowsiness. Then *Hinja* and *Tousia* prepared from fish and chicken are also given for instant energy. The *Winsewde* is rewarded in cash and kind for her midwife services.

Pollution of the new birth lasts for seven days, after which the mother is given a ceremonial bath. With regard to tonsure of the child, days may vary from one week to two months. On the auspicious day, an elder male person gives name to the newborn child. This is followed by a grand feast to the relatives. The mother is not allowed her daily chores until the completion of this ritual.

Education

Though family is the primary unit for socialisation of the Burmese children, most of the formal and informal education of the child takes place in the monastery. Here they teach the Burmese dialect, customs, traditions, values and social etiquette. Thus, each and every Burmese child is taught at the monastery under strict discipline. This resembles a kind of residential type of education. All the children come early in the morning and engage in prayer. Soon after this, they divide into three to four groups and leave for the collection of food for their *Phonghy* and other members of the monastery. After return to the monastery, they mix the food which was collected from various households. The food is first served to the *Phonghy* and the remaining food is distributed to the poor in the monastery. Maintenance of temple precincts and garden is also done by its students. Punishments for wrong-doings are severe.

In their worldview, childhood perceptibly merges into adolescence by the observance of initiation ceremony (*Phonghy banana*), which is compulsory for both boys (*khoienji*) and girls (*mithelan*) after attaining a preferable age between 10 to 14 years. Children of this age group are brought to the monastery and taught the Buddhist principles and mantras for a period of 15 days. During this time, they are not allowed to go to their respective houses; they sleep in the monastery itself. All the requirements of the children are looked after by the *Phonghy*. After this, the process of the initiation ceremony begins. First the children are decorated like princes (*raja*) and taken in a procession throughout the area along with a bandwagon. Next, they are brought into the monastery or sea coast, where they remove their attire and hair. Then they dress as the *Phonghy* (old dress) in the midst of chantings by the *Phonghy*. They are supposed to spend three days in the same dress. Later this ceremonial dress is sent to their respective houses. Those who wish to become a *Phonghy* (religious monk) should attain 20 years of age and have to adhere to strict celibacy. He should go through vigorous training with regard to spiritualism, commensality rules, and other principles of life. This training may range from two to five years depending on the person's capacity to learn. Then four chief *Phonghys* in the marked precincts of the monastery conduct the initiation process. However, after the departure of the Burmese and the introduction of formal education at schools, this system has lost significance in the present context.

Puberty and Marriage

Information regarding puberty of a girl is not disclosed to the family members except the elder women. No ceremony and taboo is observed at the end of her seclusion. The selection of marriage partner was purely the parent's choice in the recent past. During the negotiations, the boy's parents would send a message about their visit to the girl's residence. Then the groom's family members along with their close relatives and community elders would proceed to the house of the girl. It was customary for the groom's party to carry new clothes, and a ceremonial ring for the becoming bride. Bride price was common earlier. After their mutual consent, the eldest person in the group would fix a date for the marriage according to the Burmese calendar. There was no significant role for the Phonghy during the marriage ceremony. Due to his celibacy, he is bound to avoid marriage ceremonies. However, the first feast food is offered to him at the *Phonghy's* residence, and the newly married couple takes blessings from him in return.

The eldest person (who is well versed with Burmese text) performs the ceremonial rites during marriage. He joins the hands of the groom and the bride and asks them to utter the marriage oath, towards a long lasting relationship forever. The next day the *Phonghy* is invited to the bridegroom's house for the performance of worship. He chants *sutras* from the Buddhist text and teaches *Dharma* to the newly married couple. While doing this, he asks the groom to tie a thread to the bride's forearm. This symbolises the wedlock of the couple who are to live together during the travails of their life.

Death

In case of death among the Burmese, the dead body is kept outside the house on the floor. Pieces of white pumpkin are spread over the body to prevent the stinking smell and damage of the corpse. Sometimes the body is preserved for up to seven days for a last glance of the person to his/her farthest relatives. They keep a small piece of small metal or currency coin inside the mouth of the dead person. They believe that this piece of metal is useful in overcoming the crisis of the departed soul, and helps to reach the destiny. If the dead person is unmarried, parted plantain is kept beside the coffin symbolising his/her partner. They believe that a person cannot die without marriage after rebirth. The Phonghy visits the house and prays for the soul of the dead. In some cases he also visits the burial ground for prayer.

Before they lift the coffin for procession, they break a pot of water believing that this breaks all kinds of attachments with the expired. Anybody from the procession can carry the funeral bier. The dead body is kept in a wooden box and is carried to the burial place in a procession. All the members irrespective of age and sex participate in the procession. Some of the close relatives (in groups of odd numbers three or five) go to the burial ground and prepare a pit for the cremation. They wait till the arrival of the procession, and when the procession comes near the site, throw stones towards the procession symbolising the prevention of further deaths in the family concerned. After completion of the burial procedure, all the participants hit the mound several times for calling the soul to the last food. Those who prepare the burial pit take some earth from that mound and carry it back to the house. Due to pollution of the deceased person's house, their consanguine kin prepare food for those who return from burial. They keep aside some food so that the persons who bring earth from the burial can offer food for the dead. All these procedures are completed before the sunset.

The next day, the *Phonghy* conducts worship at the deceased's residence to ward off the evil spirits. He ties a sacred thread to the four corners of the house to prevent the entry of the dead soul into the house. After one year, they observe a mourning ritual and invite their close kith and kin. They also invite the *Phonghy* to the house and conduct a *pooja* on the dead person's name. On the mourning day, they also visit the burial ground and light candles on the mound. They offer a feast to the gathered relatives. Further, they observe ancestral worship during all ceremonial occasions including annual and life cycle rituals, crop harvest, house warming ceremonies, etc.; they do not consume food without offering to their ancestors first.

Celebration of Festivals

Apart from the above-mentioned life cycle rituals, the Burmese also celebrate festivals as per their traditional calendar. They are mainly *Tankem* (Holi), *Pavarana* (Deewali), and Buddha Poornima. At present they manage to obtain the special calendar from the Burmese people who are residing in mainland Burma.

Tankem *(Holi)*

This is a major festival observed during March-April to mark the arrival of the Burmese New Year, and is celebrated for three days continuously. On the outset of the day, they gather at their monastery and clean the surroundings. All the Burmese irrespective of age and sex take part in the cleaning works. On the first day, they play *Holi* with scented water; they do not use colours. They never tease aged people; rather they spill little drops on their foreheads as a mark of respect. However, pouring scented water and teasing is permissible only among joking relatives. On the second day, they attend worship at the monastery in front of Lord Buddha and accomplish the remaining works with collective effort. On the third day, they celebrate New Year. For this, a *sharbat* (sweet lemon water) is prepared in huge containers and distributed among their neighbours. However, they now-a-days play *Holi* with colours, following the Hinduistic tradition; later they distribute *sharbat* as a mark of their own festival.

Pavarana *(Deewali)*

This is celebrated during September-October, on a *poornima* (full moon) day. It is different from the Hinduistic tradition in observance of ritual process, as well as date and time. They observe June to August as one *poornima* and during this period the *Phonghy* avoids going outside the monastery. This is the season of agriculture and hence they don't want to disturb the agricultural activities. After the arrival of the new crop, they celebrate Deewali. They light candles in their houses and visit the monastery to worship, along with *prasadam* (offering of eateries), which consists of several articles of ritual significance including currency notes and coins. However, in the Andamans, this is being replaced by the great Hindu tradition.

Buddha Poornima

The Burmese celebrate Buddha Poornima to mark the occasion of the birth anniversary of Lord Gautam Buddha in the month of May. One day before the occasion, the *Phonghy* visits the nearest Buddhist temple for hoisting their traditional flag. The flag consists of five colours in both vertical and horizontal dimensions representing the five *Dharmas* of Buddhism, i.e., not to lie, not to steal, not to luxury, non-violence, and giving alms. On the auspicious day, the *Phonghy* proceeds to places where there are Buddhist settlements, and conducts prayers at their respective centers. He lights the candles and incense sticks in front of the idol and near the flagpole. While chanting mantras, he unfurls the flag amidst the gathering. Soon after this the devotees light candles and incense sticks in front of Lord Buddha's idol. Then the *Phonghy* teaches the principles of *Dharma* to the followers by sitting on the floor in front of the idol. When the preaching is over, the august gathering drops coins in a tumbler filled with water, which is kept in a plate. Then the eldest person from the gathering slowly empties the water from glass in the midst of chantings by the *Phonghy*. The money is deposited in a charity box and used for the monastery's development. It is believed that just as the water flows from higher to lower places and meets at one place, all their ancestors will meet together in one place. The coins, which they offer in the tumbler, are to forfeit the sins that are committed by their ancestors. Later, traditional food is served to all the attendants.

The entire process is also repeated the next day. After formal worship, the *Phonghy* narrates the life story and message of Gautam Buddha. Later he shows videos of the sermons of the Buddhist chief. Soon after this, food is arranged to the present gathering. During this ritual, giving alms to the orphanage is encouraged by the *Phonghy*.

Existence of Pluralism

Due to their marital alliances with people of diverse cultural backgrounds, the present Burmese observe the traditions of their spouses during life cycle and other ritual occasions. This is also attributed to the weakening of the Buddhist Mission's influence, scattered households, and modern education.

Earlier all the Burmese lived together in Burmese communes (*Asivoye*) at several places. Their social life was well organised and controlled by their community association headed by the elders. Soon after the departure of their fellowmen, these communes disappeared in due course of time and the remaining population mingled with people of other religions with whom they had conjugal relations. No trace of their community association is found at present; in fact, they now follow customs and traditions of their spouse's cultures, and have adapted to the modern forms of social control, which is based on statutory law. The role of the *Phonghy* and other elders have lost their significance in strengthening inter and intra personal relations in the present context. This is due to lesser numerical strength and identification with other community members.

Besides the Buddhist shrine, the temples of Non-Burmese like Bengali, Tamil and Nepali, and other communities are also visited by the Burmese settlers, where they offer worship along with their spouses. Their traditional customs and traditions have been weakened; and each and every aspect of their social life has been dominated by their latter tradition. The practise of other's customs is now being observed in naming, marriage ceremony, and death and funeral rites. As a result, Burmese identity is slowly vanishing from the minds of the forthcoming generations. The typical Burmese physical feature is the only parameter at present to identify these analogous people.

In some cases it is observed that syncretic practises are still maintained with the mutual consent of both husband and wife while visiting shrines during the ceremonial occasions, and in performing birth, naming, puberty, marriage and death rituals, as well as annual festivals of the host communities, along with their traditions. Due to lack of proper knowledge of Buddhist principles, the host people and their children are not undergoing any initiation ceremony at present unlike in the past.

The customary practises in the performance of life cycle and annual rituals are not strictly adhered to now. During festive occasions, the Burmese visit the monastery and later on a party is arranged by inviting their close friends and some of their relatives. Traditional marriages are replaced by court and registrar marriages to get Indian citizenship for their children.

Mutual exchanges of cultural traits took place in the initial period, but now their practises are being completely replaced by their respective host traditions. The dominance of patriarchy indirectly contributed to the absorption of host cultural practises. Moreover, the process of westernisation and modernisation is also contributing to the perpetuation of pluralism among the present generation.

Further, conjugal relations with local settlers have brought about tremendous changes in the traditional life of the Burmese people in the islands. Due to non-availability of spouses among their groups, inter-religious marriages were preferred to community endogamy. As such, Port Blair is termed as mini-India by the local settlers since inter-caste and inter-religious marriages are common. The Burmese have almost lost relationship with their relatives in the mainland and are now living as settlers. The criteria for marriage are not social, but based on the economic position of the family concerned. Marriages based on mutual love and consent are also prevalent among them. As such rule of exogamy and endogamy is not strictly practised due to mixed social composition in the Isles.

Even after the marriage, some of them continue to maintain their identity in the form of consuming traditional foods like *chowmin*, *nappi*, and coloured Burmese rice; and the dress pattern of women. But these are observed only on special occasions, and it is no longer being preserved in the present context. As they engage in diverse occupations, the traditional preparation of *nappi* is very miniscule. This art of preparation has been learned by the local settlers, i.e., the Ranchi community who also buy it from them occasionally. No Burmese are interested to wear their traditional dress (i.e., blouse and wrap around) even during festive occasions; only the old women continue to do so. They feel shy to wear their traditional dresses; instead, they show preference towards the modern dresses, sarees, *chudidars*, and so on. Feeling of ethnic identity is coming down among the present generation due to the influence of media, communications, and the very nature of socialisation.

Their association with non-Burmese has also resulted in the change of their traditional names. As the typical Burmese names were difficult to pronounce, they voluntarily assigned themselves new names that the non-Burmese are familiar with (for e.g., Newsain changed her name to "Usha Devi"; and Mamotin changed hers to "Beena" for the convenience of her husband). Majority of Burmese women are known with dual names: one is their own Burmese name and the other is a non-Burmese name for easy recognition; and likewise for the Burmese men. This is attributed to their alien cultural impact. In the process, they forgot the original script of their original dialect, except for the old women in these islands. Their children are not acquainted with the Burmese language.

Earlier they avoided face-to-face contact with the older people as a sign of respectable fear towards them. When they faced their elders on the way they bent their body and head and passed them from the side. Participation in meetings and decision-making process was restricted to the community elders. Such types of practises have now disappeared and the communal or elder people have no control on the present generation. Chronic alcoholism, chewing tobacco and pre-marital sexual relations are now rampant among the younger generation due to lack discipline and proper control.

Due to the absence of their traditional social organisation, the attitude of the children towards their value system is not in vogue as it was prevalent earlier. They were adapted to an alien cultural system through the influence of their surrounding environment. The parents, due to their preoccupations in modern living, spend lesser time in the company of their children, and free themselves from their responsibility by sending them to schools and tuitions. Most spend their leisure time watching television. As a result, a wide generation gap between the aged and the younger generation has developed. However, the families residing in interior islands still maintain their cultural attributes along with the other cultures.

Acknowledgement: The author is grateful to the Director, Anthropological Survey of India, Kolkata, for the facilities, support and encouragement during my stay at the Andaman and Nicobar Regional Centre, Port Blair, and in developing the work in this form. Further, I would like to acknowledge my humble gratitude to the settlers of Phonghy Khyongi and Memio, and the in-charge of the Andaman Buddhist Mission in Port Blair for allowing me to conduct field investigation in the respected areas. It is very difficult to mention names of the assistants who rendered assistance in Port Blair Town, but my sincere thanks goes to everyone. The views expressed in this paper are those of the author alone.

Note

1. The term "Local" refers to the settlers of Andaman Islands who are given positive discrimination by the Andaman and Nicobar Administration, Port Blair.

References

Coomer, P.C. 1994. *The Burmese People of India: Andaman and Nicobar Islands* (ed.) K.S. Singh. Vol. XII. Calcutta. Anthropological Survey of India.

Das, S.T. 1982. *The Andaman and Nicobar Islands: A Study of Habitat, Economy, and Society*. New Delhi. Sagar Publishers.

Directorate of Economics and Statistics, A and N Administration, Port Blair 2005-06.

Hunter, D.E. and Whitten, P. 1976. *Encyclopedia of Anthropology*. New York. Harper and Row Publishers.

Kochar, V.K. 1965. "Social Panorama of the Andaman and Nicobar Islands and Prospects of Anthropological Research." *The Andaman and Nicobar Information*. Port Blair. No.11, pp. 5-16.

Oomman, T.K. 2003. *Pluralism, Equality and Identity: Comparative Studies. New Delhi*. Oxford University Press.

Pandit, T.N. 1976. "The Ethnic Situation in the Bay Islands." *Yojana*. No. 20(13).

Sharon Bohn Gmelch. 1986. "Groups that don't want in: Gypsies and other Artisans, Traders, and Entertain Minorities." *Annual Review of Anthropology*. No. 15, pp. 307-30.

Singh N.I. 1978. *The Andaman Story*. New Delhi. Vikas Publishing House.

21

Society and Culture Among the Kallu Pandarams of Kerala

P.R.G. Mathur

Introduction

Of the communities known locally as "Pandaram", I have already conducted field work and prepared reports on the Jangam Pandaram and the Poo Pandaram. The Jangam Pandarams speak Telugu, subsist on ritual begging and farm labour. The Poo Pandarams speak Tamil, were traditionally garland-makers to the Pattar (Tamil Brahmin) temple, ritual mendicants and have been recently engaging themselves as farm labour. The third community known as "Pandaram" is the Kallu Pandaram or Kall-Andi. They are distinguished from the other two communities by their occupation; they are highly skilled and engage in polishing *navaratnam* gem stones. They speak Telugu in the family and among themselves; however, they cannot write the script. They use Malayalam for all other purposes and most of them are fluent in Tamil also. They say that originally they were Jangams, but because of their occupational pattern, they differentiated from that community.

There was a dispute over the rights of management of the Ardhanareeswara Temple at Tiruchengode (Tamil Nadu) between the Jangam Pandarams and the Kallu Pandarams. The case was contested in court, and the final verdict, it is understood, was that the management should be vested in both the communities, and that the temple festival should be conducted alternately by each community. The two communities were distinguished on the basis of their occupation.

In Kerala, Kallu Pandarams are distributed in Kalvakulam of Koppam (revenue) Village, Palghat Municipality and Nalleppally, Chittur Taluk, Palghat District. They have a tradition of migration from Pokkanad in

Andhra Pradesh; they say they migrated because of famine and unemployment. They first settled in Kangayam, Tiruchengode, and other places in Tamil Nadu, while some came to Kerala. Many settled in the Coimbatore area, where they are still found in large numbers. The Kallu Pandaramsin Kerala maintain marital and other relations with those in Tamil Nadu, especially near Coimbatore. Now-a-days more than half of the original settlers in Kerala have returned to Kangayam, Coimbatore, Mysore, and other places in search of employment.

Demographic Structure

The Table below shows the distribution of Kallu Pandarams in the Palghat District, and to the extent I could trace, of those who have recently out-migrated from Kerala.

Taluk	*Revenue Village*	*Hamlet*	*No. of Families*	*Estimated Popul-ation*
Palghat	Koppam	Kalvakulam	60*	345
	Pudusseri	Kunnathurmedu	3	18
Chittur	Nallepally	Kallandi Thara	40*	230
Outside Kerala	Mysore		15	80
	Mandya		6	35
	Bangalore		15	95
	Trichengode		50	260
	Erode		12	72
	Tirupur		20	85
	Pollachi		8	45
	Ooty		5	30
	Coimbatore		65	345
	Kangayam		60	325
	Madras		5	30
	Bombay		3	15
Total			**367**	**2,010**

* These families constituted our informants. The out-migration was estimated on the basis of their reports

A household survey of the 100 families marked with an asterisk (*) in the table above was conducted. Out of the total population of 332, there were 168 (50.6%) males and 164 (49.4%) females; it was found that 264 (79.5%) were literate, and among them 82.74% were males and 125 (76.23%) were females. Every household reported that at least one or more members had out-migrated to Tamil Nadu or Karnataka, over the last 25 years, in search of employment. They continue to be in contact, and maintain their ritual relationships with the original settlements, by visiting it and worshipping the Mariyamman and Vinayagan temples of the settlements, during the annual festival.

Our field study was conducted in the Kaluvakulam settlement of Koppam in Palghat Municipality, and in Nallepally of Chittur Taluk. A house-to-house survey was conducted, covering various socio-economic aspects, including life cycle rituals and religious beliefs. The main method adopted includes genealogical tables prepared in order to trace the marital status, endogamy and relation with out-migrated families.

Settlement Pattern

The Kallu Pandarams in Nallepally inhabit lands assigned to them about two hundred years ago by the Chondath Nair chieftain family. According to them, 300 families had originally settled there; but today, only 40 could be traced, and of them, 15 members have recently out-migrated. Some of them sold out their properties before going away. They are settled on both sides of a Panchayat Road, in a roughly linear pattern. Though the houses are close together, they are not row-houses, sharing partition walls, as in Tamil Nadu. All of them are tiled and of substantial construction. The front veranda is large and enclosed, to form the work area, where they polish the stones. None of them engage in cultivation, even in their own homesteads or backyards. The settlement is called "Andi Thara"; if more specification is required, it is identified as "Kallandi Thara".

In Kozhinjampara Village, a few Kallandi families purchased agricultural lands for cultivation; but after a couple of years, they gave up the effort and went to Coimbatore. This area, however, is still known as "Kallandi Challa", even though there are no Kallandi families living there now. The settlement maintains a temple dedicated to Vinayagan, and another to Mariyamman.

The temple of Vinayagan is a tiled structure. Just outside the main temple, there is a raised platform in front accommodating the Nandi bull; a little further away to the left is a stone snake head. Just opposite to the temple, there is a dilapidated *Saraswathi Mandapam*, a hall, and about 100 yards away, on a raised platform, there is a *Muni Appan*, a human figure in stone.

The Mariyamman Temple is about 300 meters away. It is also a tiled structure; just outside to the left, there are three stone snake heads and a *Muni Appan* a little farther away. There is an open ground in front of it. There are two wells, one for the community, and the other, owned by a comparatively affluent Kallu Pandaram. They have always had access to public tanks and bathing places, used also by the Nairs.

The Kalvakulam settlement in Koppam, Palghat Municipality, is named after the tank there, and the Kallu Pandaram houses are located around the tank. They are separate, but close to one another; a few are terraced, most are tiled and one or two have thatched roofs. When a joint family gets partitioned, a corresponding partition is built through the house. The municipal road goes round the settlement. The municipality has provided water taps and lighting in their houses.

Caste Hindu families live in close proximity with the Kallandi Tharas. In Nallepally, the Ankarath and Chondath Nair chieftain families also live close to the Thara. In recent years, in Kalvakulam, other communities have been living on rent in the Thara, in the more substantial houses.

Social Structure

The Kallu Pandarams claim superiority among the three Pandaram communities. While the Jangams had tacitly accepted this, the Kallu Pandarams challenge it. Although the Poo Pandarams were originally supplying flower garlands to Brahmin temples, they "demeaned" themselves by adopting mendicancy. While Jangams accepted food and water from the other two, Poo Pandarams did not do so from either of the other two. Kallu Pandarams also do not take food and water from the other two. The Kallu Pandarams say that they have no connection whatever with the Poo Pandarams because the latter speak Tamil. They disclaim relationship with the Jangam, even though they speak Telugu, because of the latter's mendicancy. Our genealogies do not show any evidence of inter-marriage between Kallu Pandarams and either of the other two Pandarams, except one case, where the caste council ostracised the partners of an inter-caste marriage, and those who supported it. It was also reported to us that if a Kallu Pandaram, because of friendship, accepts an invitation from either of the other two, he will not accept cooked food from them; he will take only betel leaves, arecanuts, and fruits, which are not regarded as entailing pollution.

However, some of the younger members have started accepting coffee and snacks from Jangam Pandaram friends.

The Kallu Pandarams accept water and food from Nair families, but Nairs do not accept food or water from them. The Kallu Pandarams of Nallepally say that even though they usually do not perform *Andiyuuttu* or *Kaavadiedukkal*, because of their traditional obligation to the Chondath family, who had given them the land to settle in, they were invited to and had conducted these rituals for that family every year until the implementation of the Kerala Land Reforms Act. They link their tradition to the history of the Chondath family, according to which the original "Chondath Mannadiars" were in-migrant Telugu speakers; this family became extinct and the properties were escheated to the Cochin Government. Subsequently a Nair family, known in Walluvanad Taluk as the "Pudumana Panikkars", was gifted, for services rendered to the Cochin Rajah, with the properties and titles of the "Chondath Mannadiars". The Kallu Pandarams say that astrologers prescribed the conduct of the *Andiyuuttu* so that the lineage may not again become extinct; the Nair family settled the Kallandis in the place, and entrusted them with the conduct of the rites. Until the Chondath family was partitioned, there used to be an annual *Andiyuuttu* on *Thaipooyam* day, when the entire settlement, including women and children, would be fed in the *randamkettu* (the second courtyard). Even though the members of the Chondath family would take their meals only after the Kallu Pandarams were fed, the latter were not allowed to take their bath in the family tank – surprisingly, they were allowed to wash their hands in it after their feast!

In Nallepally, the Kallu Pandarams had roles to play in the annual festival of the village deity, Chunangi Bhagavathi, managed by the Chondath family. In the annual festival, the Tamil population of the village, and the Kallandi families, participated in the *Kummatti* rite, when they could touch the outer veranda of the Nair family's house. However, they were not allowed to enter the shrine of the Goddess. They could take bath in the tank attached to the temple, even though the Ezhavas and other "untouchable" communities were not allowed to do so. In the Siva temple of the Pattar settlement in Nallepally, they could approach the *nalambalam*, a privilege denied to the Ezhavas.

In Kalvakulam, the tank was not open to the untouchable castes, but Kallandis could use it; in fact, it belonged to them. The Pattars did not use the tank, and denied Kallandis access to tanks in their settlements, though the Nairs used the tank. Kallandi temples were not open to the Ezhavas and other untouchable castes.

Thus, the Kallandi appear to have been ranked just below the Nairs and above the Ezhavas; they had access to public facilities like roads, etc. The Pattars insist that they should stand three paces away, lest there should be approach pollution; but the Nairs observed only touch pollution against them. The Kallandis observed untouchability against the Ezhavas, and other castes, including the other two Pandaram communities. They were honorifically called "Pandaram" by members of other communities, and refer to themselves using the same term. Of late, some of them have started styling themselves as "Jangam" and "Veera Saiva Jangam". Our informant told us that they started doing so because some influential Jangam gentlemen have been instructing them to establish a larger identity with the Veera Saiva community.

Kinship and Marriage

Eleven sub-castes have been identified among the Kallu Pandarams; they are known as *kulams*: Chakrathu; Panniraam; Uddannam; Chivanga; Vaira; Pesala; Thevanna; Ramangiram; Thirumalla; Vathiri; and Panlangiri. (The word "*kulam*" is suffixed after each name). The names appear to be after the mythical founders of the respective clans. Three more clans are known in the Coimbatore area, viz., Vakkadudam; Anappa and Jadi. Marriage of two individuals belonging to the same clan amounts to incest. They are strictly endogamous within the community; breaking of this rule entails ostracism or excommunication. In the past, breaking of the commensality rules resulted in the same punishment.

Formerly, marriages were conducted before the girl attained puberty; however, this is not strictly observed now. Polygyny, especially sororal, is permitted. Maternal uncle-niece and bilateral cross-cousin marriages are preferred. Polyandry, levirate and divorce are not allowed. Widow remarriage is totally prohibited, but a widower may re-marry with the permission of the caste council; the deceased wife's younger sister is the preferred mate for a widower.

The Kallu Pandarams had, until recently, a powerful caste council in each settlement. It consisted of ten members acceptable to the community by consensus; it had a headman known as *muuppu*; this office tended to be hereditary. Without the permission of this council, life cycle rituals could not be conducted. The council also considered cases of violation of caste norms, and marriages and remarriages required the prior sanction of the council. There were no corresponding councils at the regional or at the global level for the community. Now-a-days, in the two settlements studied, viz., at Nallepally and at Koppam, there are "Vinayagan Temple Committees", constituted through election from the households, each of whom contributes Rs. 50 to Rs. 60 per year. These committees have chairmen, secretaries, treasurers, etc. Of late, they have been usurping some of the functions of the traditional councils. The presence of the *muuppu*, however, continues to be indispensable at the life cycle rituals.

The following case-histories illustrate the dynamics of these councils:

In Koppam, about 20 years ago, one Sivamany, now working as an overseer in the Kerala State Electricity Board, married a Poo Pandaram girl from Tamil Nadu. The caste council withheld its permission, but he was supported by seven families belonging to his clan. All of them were ostracised; they continued to be treated thus for three years. They were comparatively affluent. In the meantime, the husband of the sister of one Krishnaswamy, an uncle of Sivamany's, died. Only the seven ostracised families attended the burial, then, Sadasivan, the head of one of the ostracised families, approached the traditional caste elders for a compromise. Our informant, Nanjappan (70), mediated and a settlement was made, whereby the ostracised persons had to pay Rs. 525 as fine to the council, and Rs. 150 to the temple committee; after the payment they were re-admitted.

The sister of one Sundarajan, working as a peon in the District Court of Palghat, was employed as a clerk in the British Physical Laboratories (BPL) Ltd., in Palghat. She was married in 1993 to a Jangam Pandaram, who was a police constable. Neither the traditional council nor the temple committee took serious notice of this marriage. This shows the tendency towards greater laxity in such matters. In Nalleppally, the community is still orthodox in caste matters. However, there have been no instances of violation of caste norms reported from this area. The genealogical tables also do not reveal any marriage outside the community, though partners have been selected from eligible families settled in Kangayam, Coimbatore, Mysore, etc.

Conceptually, the micro-caste unit functions as an effective interacting group, or a "kindred of recognition which comprises a population within which marriages can take place without enquiries as to the credentials of membership" (Mayer, 1965). It contains enough people, segmented into exogamous clans, to satisfy the search for partners. Among the Kallu Pandarams, marriage is usually restricted to members of the micro-caste; but because of the out-migration, improved means of communication, regional economic development, and constant interchange of residence, the matches can be found from members of the community living in other localities. Thus, the concept of the micro-caste was geographically extended over a region, without being detrimental to the endogamous character of the community.

The Kallu Pandarams are patrilineal and patrilocal. Marriage severs a woman's membership from her natal clan, as she joins her husband's clan. Joint family was the norm, with the Pater of the family being the undisputed head. The tendency is now for the families to break up into nuclear units; interestingly, the richer the family, the longer it remains joint. The girls married into a joint family keep off from their father-in-law and brothers-in-law. The mother-in-law avoids her son-in-law. After the death of her husband, the widow continues to be in the household, if there are children; if childless, she returns to her natal home. As widow-remarriage is prohibited, her position in society and life in general are unhappy.

Material Culture and Economic Activity

The dress of the Kallu Pandarams is different from that of the other two Pandaram communities. The men wear the "four-cubit *veshti*" by simply wrapping it around the waist. On ritual occasions, they are required to wear the "eight-cubit *veshti*", with the ends tucked up between the legs; this style is also becoming obsolete. They wear shirts when they go out. Women wear a long piece of cloth, *podavai*, covering the body and the breasts; now-a-days they wear under-clothes and blouses. The younger women are taking to sari. Widows wear white blouses and coloured saris. Married men and women wear *minchi*, a toe ring on the big toe of the right foot; married women also wear the *Tali*. Most of the men and the widows put *vibhuti* (sacred ash) on their foreheads after bath.

The Kallu Pandarams are non-vegetarian but avoid pork and beef. Tea is their favourite beverage. They do not take alcoholic drinks, unlike the other Pandarams, the Nairs, and the Ezhavas of the locality. The men use tobacco in all forms, but women only chew it along with betel leaves and nuts. Men and women observe fast every Monday, in honour of Lord Siva.

Technology of Gem-making and Economic Organisations

The Kallu Pandaram community is distinguished because of its unique skill in gem cutting and polishing. They say that the skill has been passed down from generations. Each household owns the tools of the trade.

There are five grinding and polishing machines. They consist of a wooden frame, *pattara*, on which are two wooden uprights (*kaalu*). Between these uprights, a rotary beam or drum (*danta*) is fixed, to which can be attached a variety of grinding discs called *chaana*. A strong thread tied to a wooden bow is wound round the drum, so that it can be rotated by moving the bow to and fro.

To make the grinding disc for the *Kara chaana*, emery powder of various grades is melted to an equal quality by weight of *kolarakku* (lac). The molten material is pressed between two iron moulds and allowed to cool and solidify. This disc is used to make the rough cuts and size the *dalam*, i.e., the gem-stone or glass jewel. The raw *dalam* is cut to a convenient size with the help of the *vairauusi*, a diamond tipped chisel. It is then attached with molten lac to a finely cut wooden strip, about 15 cm long, which can be conveniently held between the thumb and the fingers of one hand, pressed against the *chaana*. While this is done, water is plentifully used to lubricate and cool the gem stone so that it does not crack due to the heat generated by the friction.

The next stage is the *Vandi chaana*. It is lighter, being made of finer grades of emery powder. The *dalam*, after the first cutting and polishing, is transferred to another stick. For further polishing, the *Nysaana* (corruption for "nicer *chaana*?"), still finer emery powder is used. This is specially used for gold, and moonstones. The fourth, the *Mara chaana*, is critical. It is made of enamel powder instead of emery. It is used only for polishing. The final polishing is made on *Palaka chaana*; it is made of *murukku* or mango wood by the local carpenter. The sacred ash or *bhasmam* from the Palani Subrahmanya Temple, supplied by one Chittanathan Co., is smeared on the wooden disc. Great care is taken when using this to avoid scouring of the material being polished.

The stock in trade consists of "nine gems" (*navaratnam*); they are (all costs per carat of approx. 250 mg) : *Pushyaragam*, imported from Burma, costing Rs. 500; *Maanikkam*, obtained from outside Kerala @ Rs. 5000; *Muthu*, from Tuticorin, @ Rs. 1000; *Vaidooryam*, from merchants in Trivandrum @ Rs. 1000; *Pavizham*, from Tuticorin @ Rs. 50; *Gomethakam*, from Trivandrum @ Rs. 50; *Pacha*, from Burma and Sri Lanka @ Rs. 4500; *Vairam*, imported from Belgium @ Rs. 3500; and *Niilam*, from Burma, @ Rs. 1500.

In addition, the Kallu Pandarams also cut and polish *paalakka*, *naagapatam* and *manga* (green coloured Belgian glasses), which have great demand in Kerala; *karuppukallu*, black glass bangles, is popular in Andhra Pradesh. The material is supplied by the goldsmiths and jewelers. The cheaper items like Belgian glass and Black glass bangles are stocked by the Kallu Pandarams. Now they supply polished gems throughout India; and Kerala, Coimbatore and Bangalore are among their best markets.

Trade in gemstones enabled the community to find favour with the feudal chieftains of the past, including the Nambuthiris and ruling families; the Pattars respected them for their esoteric knowledge of gemstones. Now-a-days, the increasingly affluent class of jewelers and merchants seek them to cut and polish the gem stones for their "fashion jewelry creations". These factors have raised the social status of the Kallu Pandarams.

Income

For cutting and polishing 100 Belgian glass stones (*paalakka*, *naagapatam*, *manga*), a Pandaram has to work for two days, from 8 am to 6 pm, sitting hunched up over the *chaana*, and taking utmost care to see that the precious raw material is not damaged. He gets Rs. 200 for the 100 finished pieces; his cost includes the purchase cost of the *dalam* (= Rs. 25); and wear and tear of the equipment estimated at Rs. 15. Therefore, the margin is Rs. 160. If he employs another worker, the wages payable would be (@ Rs. 30 per day for two days) Rs. 60. His profit is therefore Rs. 100 which he earns in two days.

In the case of the *navaratnam*, the stones are usually supplied by the clients, in these days, the jewelers. The Pandaram charges double the normal wages, viz., Rs. 60 per day. We do not know how much the jewelers make out of the sale of the cut and polished stones. We understand that the trade has greatly declined. Only two families in Nalleppally and three in Koppam are being entrusted with *navaratnams*. The demand for Belgian glass items is fairly steady.

We studied the case of Nanjappan of Koppam. He received orders for cutting and polishing 300 glass stones : *naagapatam*, *paalakka* and *manga*, in various fashions. He had to supply these within two weeks. The order was from a goldsmith of Kongad. He can cut and polish at most 1500 stones per month. He has to invest Rs. 375(@ Rs. 25 per 100 pieces) on the raw material. His own wages at the going rate of Rs. 30 per day for 30 days is Rs. 900; wear and tear of the emery coating alone works out to Rs. 450; thus, the total cost = Rs. 1725. He realised a sale price of Rs. 3000; so the margin was Rs. 1275, which does not cover the replacement charge of the capital equipment, including the woodwork. In other words, his monthly income, including imputed wages is Rs. 1275 + 900 = Rs. 2,175. Usually he buys a stock of 1000 raw *dalam* at a time, costing Rs. 250, depending upon availability and colour combinations. No allowance has been made for the interest charges on this amount.

In spite of our best efforts, our informants would not disclose their trade secrets with regard to the *navaratnam* stones. We got the impression that the supplies come through various channels, the agents of which are sworn to secrecy. Our informants told us that they get double the normal rate of wages for polishing these costly stones. Some Pandarams, e.g., Raju of Koppam, are also commissioned agents for these stones; he goes to Madras and other places for the trade and supplies the stones to his caste men. One Kandaswamy of Nallepally has a virtual monopoly in the trade of black glass pieces, from Andhra Pradesh.

An interesting development has been that unemployed literate young men belonging to Nair, Ezhava, Christian, Muslim and Mannan communities are recruited by the Pandarams, trained in the skills of cutting and polishing, and engaged on daily wages, varying from Rs. 15 to Rs. 30 per day, depending on the experience. One Gopalakrishna Pandaram has employed four Ezhavas; this is locally termed *kallupani.* Raju, the commission agent, has employed more than 12 workers, including four of his own sons, who have failed in the SSLC. Nanjappan employs, besides his two sons, a Nair, a Mannan, a Christian and a Muslim.

An Ezhava has established a gem-stone cutting and polishing unit in Koppam, where he employs four Kallu Pandarams, including the son of an Assistant Sub-Inspector of Police; the boy has a Diploma in Civil Engineering from the Industrial Training Centre. Another Kallu Pandaram, PDC-passed, and son of a peon in Government Service, has started *kallupani* in his own house.

However, the tendency is for the industry to shift from Kerala. Several reasons are adduced by our informants. The first is that there is increasing demand for polished precious stones outside Kerala, whereas here, the main demand is only for the comparatively cheaper glass pieces. The demand in Kerala is also varying and not steady throughout the year; the work is therefore in fits and starts, and the Pandaram experience a lot of uncertainty and corresponding losses, in the matter of inventory purchases and locking up of capital. Some people, e.g., Nanjappan, obtained loans from the banks, but found the rules and procedures inflexible, the uncertainties of the business made the banks apprehensive.

Migration and Occupational Mobility

Out-migration began about 25 years ago. Six families from Nallepally migrated to Mysore. One of them, the late Mara Pandaram, leaves behind two sons, Krishnappa and Purushottaman. Both of them married from Coimbatore. They specialised in making silver ornaments. They have settled down in Mysore, but visit Nallepally to participate in the temple festivals. Krishnappa's son, Maran, has passed the SSLC and is employed in the Telephones Department in Mysore. He also married from Coimbatore. Purushottaman's son, Nanjappan, is engaged in *kallupani* in Mysore; he has also married from Mysore.

The late Narayana Pandaram sold his property in Nallepally and migrated to Mysore 20 years ago. He worked there polishing gemstones. His sons married girls of the same community that had already settled at Mysore; they now work as tailors. The late Marappa Pandaram migrated to Mysore about 15 years ago and engaged in *kallupani*. His wife is still alive in Mysore; his son Nanjappan is a tailor. Mara Pandaram has been working as a tailor in Mysore for more than two decades. His eldest son, Saktivelu, a matriculate, is employed in the Forest Department in Mysore; his youngest son, Velayudhan is still in *kallupani* at Mandya. Both of them sought their wives from Coimbatore. Veera Basavan has been working as a tailor in Mysore for the last two decades. He married from Koppam; has three sons and a daughter. The sons have obtained their brides from Coimbatore, Nallepally and Koppam. One of them, Subrahamaniam, is an engineer employed in the Karnataka PWD. Another son continues to be a gem-stone worker, and the third is a tailor.

Migrants to Coimbatore have been attracted by greater opportunities there. Basavayya Pandaram started a jewelry shop there about 20 years ago; he had married from Palghat. He has three sons employed as goldsmiths; the third also has a grocery shop. The grandson of the late Subrahmania Pandaram, who had migrated to Coimbatore 25 years ago, is now employed in a nationalised bank. His brother runs a "gold-covering of ornaments" business. We noticed that several KalluPandarams have taken up goldsmith works and business related to that metal, after settling in Coimbatore.

The KalluPandarams are included in the OBC list of Tamil Nadu for all purposes. This may be another reason for the out-migration; for example, ten families that migrated from Nallepally to Kangayam have now multiplied into 30 families; they are employed as goldsmiths, tailors and workmen in automobile workshops. They have not given up their traditional occupations. They get the benefits of free education and some are employed in service.

Resource Endowments

In Nallepally, five Kallu Pandaram families own lands ranging from 75 to 250 cents each. They purchased these lands, and now cultivate them, engaging Ezhava and Harijan workers; they do not work in the fields themselves. In Koppam, the maximum holding owned by a Kallu Pandaram is 250 cents, which the owner obtained by purchase. Out of the 100 households surveyed in detail in Koppam and Nallepally, 46 owned between one and 10 cents of homestead plots, three owned between 11 and 25 cents; one between 26 and 50 cents; and none owned more than 50 cents. While two had more than two acres of agricultural lands; two between one and two acres; three between 51 cents and one acre; one had only 50 cents. This is one of the most landless communities in Kerala.

Employment in the tertiary sector is reflected in the following table, prepared after surveying 100 households:

Category	*Number Employed*
Government servant	5
Process server	2
Assistant Sub-Inspector of Police	1
Lineman in KSEB	1
Sub-Engineer, KSEB	1
Secretary, Co-operative Society	1
Employed in private companies	3
LIC Officer	1
Electrician	3
Tailor	9
Nurse	1
Automobile workshop workers	8
Painter	1
Bus driver	2
Auto driver	1

contd. . .

Category	*Number Employed*
Artist	1
Workshop owners	2
Stationery shop owner	1
Selling balloons	2
Upholstery and mattress manufacture and sale	2
Gem-stone commission agent	2
Contractor	1
AMIE qualified Civil Engineer in private employment	1
Lottery agent	1
Retired Government servant	3
Retired private company employee	1
Retired pensioner	1
Family pensioner	1
Old age pensioner	1

Disabled pensioner

It is observed that employment of women in the tertiary sector is very meager. Only one is in Government service (non-gazetted). The highest position attained by a member of this community in Kerala is that of the Assistant Sub-Inspector of Police. Five women are employed as maid servants. It is remarkable that unlike the other two Pandaram communities, agricultural and manual labour has attracted very few members of this community: only seven, of whom there are women, have sought employment as manual labourers.

All of these Kallu Pandarams own residential plots and houses. Most have capital in the form of the tools of their trade. The fact that they have no resource other than their specialised skill is one of the factors that explains their readiness to migrate. If business is dull then they have to go to places where the opportunities are greater. Occupational mobility is also identified with out-migration; perhaps the community feels less constrained by the traditions of their homes in Kerala.

Educational Status

Out of the 100 families comprising 332 individuals, the following table shows the educational attainments.

Standard	*Total*	*Male*	*Female*
Illiterate	68	29	39
Standard 1 to 4	49	25	24
5 to 7	66	32	34
8 to 10	93	49	44
SSLC Passed	36	18	18
PDC Passed	4	3	1
Graduate	3	3	0
SSLC + Typewriting	5	3 2	
SSLC + ITC	5	5	0
PDC + Nursing	1	0	1
Graduate Nursing	1	0	1
AMIE	1	1	0

It is observed that most of the dropouts are either after the 7th standard, or after SSLC, which is only roughly one-third of those who attempt it from this community pass. The illiteracy percentage is 20%. The proportion of those who have passed the SSLC is 10.84%; graduates including one in Nursing is 1.80%; and the lone engineering graduate forms 0.30% of the sample.

Our informants said that their children preferred to take up the family trade, to which they are apprenticed even as school children. This makes them neglect the grit required to pass the SSLC. Education costs them the fees, as they are not entitled to any concessions. Outside the state, where concessions are available, they have persevered in their studies. Even in Kangayam in Tamil Nadu, there are a number of SSLC passed persons. In Mysore, one of them is a Graduate Engineer, and another is a Forester.

Sacred Beliefs

Unlike the other two Pandaram communities, the Kallu Pandarams worship Vinayagan as the main deity. Mariyamman and Muniappan are the subsidiary deities. Each clan has an *adimadaivam*, viz., a deity to whom they are supposed to be bound. The Kallu Pandarams of Koppam are bound to serve the Thonkukulatthil Bhagavathy, the family deity of the Nairs. In Nallepally, they are similarly bound to the Chunangi Bhagavathi, the village deity.

Every morning, before they start work, each Kallu Pandaram worships Vinayagan. Annually, they perform the Mariyamman Pongal in April-May. The Kallu Pandarams conduct the fire walking ceremony at Koppam; this has been discontinued at Nallepally. Pongal is celebrated on a Wednesday instead of Friday. At Nallepally, the Pongal is first offered to a "*Vanadevata*" located some kilometers away, before it is offered to Mariyamman. The flowers used for decoration of the pots are red lotuses and marigold, instead of jasmine, as among the other two communities. Goats and fowls are sacrificed to propitiate Muniappan, who is believed to be the protector of the locality. The festivals of Vinayagan Chathurthi and Navaratri are celebrated.

Ritual Significance of *Navaratna* Gem Stones

Our informant, Nangappa Pandaram (60) told us that *navaratnams* are used in rings to ward off the evil effects of malefic planets under each *dasa*, or position of the stars, and also to bring good fortune. They believe that the *dasaasandhi*, the badly accepted meeting of two life-periods, may entail even death, unless protected by the influence of the gemstones. The following *navaratnams* are used to nullify the evil effects of the various *dasas*:

Name of Dasa	*Navaratnam to be used*
Sani (Saturn)	*Niilam* (Turquoise)
Vyazham (Jupiter)	*Pushyaragam* (Topaz, Yellow Sapphire)
Surya (Sun)	*Manikkam* (Ruby)
Chandra (Moon)	*Muthu* (Pearl)
Rahu (Dragon's Head)	*Vaiduryam* (Cryso Beryl Cat's eye)
Chova (Mars)	*Pavizham* (Coral)
Kethu (Dragon's Tail)	*Gomethakam* (Garnet)
Budha (Mercury)	*Pacha* (Emerald)
Sukra (Venus)	*Vairam* (Diamond)

It is interesting to note that the belief in this system is widely held, even among the educated Muslims. The Pattars believe in this absolutely; and the demand is very high from Tamil Nadu.

Life Cycle Rituals among Kallu Pandarams

Birth

The pregnant women among the Kallu Pandarams are prohibited from doing heavy household work. It is customary to send her in the seventh or ninth month to the natal home after the *Siimantam* is conducted at the husband's house. Her matrilineal kinfolk bring cooked rice, tamarind juice and other eatables; she is presented with new clothes; each relative puts a glass bangle on her wrists. She is then taken to her mother's home. In the ninth month, the husband's people send a variety of eatables to her.

When the labour pains become acute, the expectant mother is secluded in a dark room with elderly experienced midwives belonging to the community. The midwife buries the placenta in a corner of the house compound. Now-a-days, the delivery is in a hospital. The mother is bathed in warm water and her clothes are changed. The baby is washed in warm water and wrapped in warm clothes, after which it is put to the breast. When the stem of the umbilical cord heals and drops off, it is put in an amulet and tied around the waist of the child.

The Kallu Pandarams observe birth pollution for 15 days. The *Mattu* is supplied by the local *Mannathi*, and worn on the first, third, seventh and fifteenth day after delivery. The *Mannathi* is paid in kind and cash. During the pollution period, the mother is given pepper soup and neem oil. Now, the tendency is to reduce the pollution period to ten days. An iron knife is always kept under the bed, to ward off evil spirits. On the fifteenth day, the mother lights a wick lamp at the place where the umbilical cord was buried; she performs a special puja there.

On the sixteenth day, a black thread is tied around the baby's waist, and a black bangle is put on its wrist. Friends and relatives are treated to a feast on that day. The first feeding of cereal food is in the tenth month; ear lobes of babies of both sexes are pierced on the same day. This is absolutely essential in the case of girl babies, because if later she should die without the lobes having been bored, her body can be buried only after the ears of the corpse are bored.

The first tonsure is done only after the baby attains the first year of life. Parents might have vowed to take the baby to Palani for this ceremony. If it takes place at home, a Tamil-speaking barber (*Ambattan*) does it and is paid in cash and kind. The baby is named by its parents on completion of the third year; usually the grand-parents' names are chosen.

Puberty:

At menarche a Kallu Pandaram girl is secluded in a separate room for 15 days, and prohibited from seeing the menfolk. The maternal uncle brings a set of new clothes on the first day itself. She wears the *Mattu* on the third, seventh and fifteenth days. On the fifteenth day, she takes a purificatory bath and is taken to the house of the headman (*muuppu*); she is then taken in a procession, with *Nadaswaram* music, to the Vinayagan and Mariyamman temples. At home, there is a feast, after *punyaham* is sprinkled by the *muuppu* and the house is whitewashed. Maternal uncles, relatives and friends present new clothes, ornaments, coconuts, etc.; cash presents ranging from Rs. 50 to Rs. 100 (*banduma*) are also made. The present trend is to reduce the number of days of pollution to ten.

Marriage:

The only recognised mode of a finding a mate among the Kallu Pandarams is by negotiation. In the past, pre-puberty marriages were in vogue, and either the mother's brother (maternal uncle), or a bilateral cross cousin was the preferred husband for a girl. Even now, this is observed. The bride-price is fixed; it used to be Rs. 25 and was reduced to Rs. 11 and further to Rs. 6.25 later; in addition, saris, cosmetics, coconuts, fruits etc., have also to be presented to the bride.

Polygyny was permitted as a special case, especially if a man wanted to marry sisters (soraral polygamy). It was normal for a man to marry the younger sister of his deceased wife. Polygamy was unknown; so was levirate. Divorce was not permitted. Widow remarriage was also prohibited. At marriage, a girl ceased to be a member of her natal (father's) clan, and was integrated into the clan of the husband. They were strictly patrilineal and patrilocal. Ties are maintained with families who have out-migrated to Tamil Nadu and Karnataka, especially for marriage alliances.

If a suitable consanguineous kinswoman is not available, the boy's parents look around for a suitable girl through match-makers, who may be relatives or friends. Family reputation is the most important consideration. Enquiries are made among the families who had out-migrated from the locality. The girl's parents, on the other hand, give weightage to the prosperity and earning capacity of the proposed groom's family. Horoscope matching is essential. Betrothal (*nischitataambuulam*) is conducted; the parents of the prospective bride and the groom meet in the girl's house, with the respective *muuppus* in attendance. The groom's parents present betel leaves, arecanut, plantain fruits and a sari to the girl; now-a-days, gold rings and ornaments are also included. The *muuppu* of the girl's settlement asks aloud whether any one has any objection to the proposal; silence is taken as consent to it; the groom's parents pay the bride price, and a sum of Rs. 15 as contribution to the Vinayagan temple committee of the girl's settlement.

The months of *Chingam* (August-September), *Thulam* (October-November), *Vrischigam* (November-December), *Makaram* (December-January) and *Meenam* (March-April) are considered auspicious for marriage; *Kanni* (September-October) and *Karkitakam* (July-August) are especially inauspicious. The parents of the groom and the bride are expected to invite relatives and friends jointly, and present betel leaves and arecanuts along with the invitation.

On the night before the wedding, a *muhurtakal* : a branch of a *paala* (*Alstoniascchcholaris*) tree, is erected; it is wetted with cow's is milk. The bride's party (typically about 50 strong) comes to the groom's house to invite him formally (*mappilaazhithal*); a feast is served. After a *linga puja* performed by the *muuppu* of the groom's settlement, the groom and his party accompany the bride's party in a procession to her house. They are received by her parents; the groom's mother puts bangles on the bride's wrist in the *Pandal* itself. The *muuppu* and five "gurus" (elders) of the bride's settlement perform a *linga puja* keeping five *kalasam* (pots filled with water), offering fruits and *panchamrtam*. The *muuppu* then ties the *lingam* on the right forearm of the bride and groom. The *lingam* is taken off after the wedding ceremonies, and carefully preserved by hanging over a picture of Lord Siva or Subramania; the *lingam* will be required for important rites when the person ultimately dies. This is preliminary to the marriage; all are accommodated by the bride's father.

On the following day, it was a custom in the past to seat the couple on a wooden plank and bathe them jointly; this has now been given up. Turmeric is applied on their face; the pair wear gilt head gear (*pattam*);, the bride's maternal uncle's wife puts the *minchi* (toe ring) around the big toe of her right foot; the groom's father's sister does likewise for the groom. A piece of turmeric covered in a betel leaf and tied with a thread soaked in turmeric round the wrist of the pair; this is *kankanamkettal*. The bride is then brought to the marriage booth, and seated at the right of the *muhurtakal*. The groom's father's sisters as well as the bride carry a *nandavilakku*, viz., a wick lamp placed in an earthen container around the *kal*. The *muuppu* of the bride's settlement hands the *Tali* over to the groom; he ties it around her neck. They exchange garlands. They also exchange betel leaves, rice and arecanuts; all the relatives and friends throw rice grains and *tulasi* leaves as blessings. The couple exchanges sweetened milk and plantain fruits (*madhuramkodukkal*). The *kankanam* is then removed; the feast follows.

In the past, there used to be a number of joking and merry-making customs like the couple searching jointly for gold and silver rings in a pot of water; the one who gets the gold is believed to be the dominant partner in the forthcoming married life. Though not completely given up, the custom is getting obsolete.

Death:

When the death of a Kallu Pandaram draws nigh, the *Panchakshara* and *Yamakantham* (in Tamil) are read aloud. The sons, daughters and relatives gather around; holy water is dripped into the mouth through *tulasi* leaves. When life is extinct, loud wailing, especially by the women, is set up. The *muuppu* takes charge of the ensuing proceedings. Information is sent to all concerned; the *Praya* (Scheduled Caste) are engaged to dig a pit in a corner of a grave-yard; both in Nallepally Panchayat, and the Palghat Municipality graveyards, a separate corner is reserved for Kallu Pandaram burials.

Gingelly oil is dropped into the mouth of the corpse, and it is bathed by the caste-men; it is then kept in a sitting position on a chair. The mouth and ears are closed with a new cloth; the caste-men and relatives pay their last respects. The *lingam* which the deceased had worn at the time of marriage, and carefully preserved, is now again tied round his/her neck, after a *linga puja*; a little rice is cooked with turmeric and served to the deceased; it is later carried along with the body to the graveyard.

The eldest son is the chief mourner. The body is bathed a second time, with water brought by him; and is kept in a sitting position on the floor; another *linga puja* is conducted; the *muuppu* appoints four *nandigal* (pall-bearers) to carry the body in a *theru* (decorated car made of green bamboo and leaves); the pall-bearers must be married persons. If the deceased had been a married man, a new white cloth is placed by the chief mourner; if the deceased had been a married woman, a new coloured sari is used; her ear lobes, if not pierced, are now pierced; her ornaments, and *minchi* are removed, and the *Tali* is removed and tied to the right wrist of the husband if surviving.

The *nandigal* now proceed to put the body in the *theru*; a *neivilakkupandam*, is performed; all the grandchildren go around the body with wick lamps soaked in ghee. At the burial ground, the *muuppu* touches, with his right toe, the forehead of the deceased; this signifies the blessings of the entire community on the soul of the deceased. If the deceased happens to be an unmarried woman, the body is interred head onwards. In other cases, the body is first interred up to the neck; another *linga puja* (*paada puja*) is performed; the face is smeared with *bhasmam*; they say that it should look like a *lingam*. Then the pit is filled up. The chief mourner takes a pot of water which he carries thrice round the grave and breaks it at the head. The chief mourner washes the feet of the *nandigal*. The pot of turmeric rice is dumped there.

The mourners return after a bath. There will be no cooking in the house of the deceased on the day of the death; food is supplied by the neighbours. On the third day, the *nandigal* return to the graveyard; vegetable dishes and food items relished by the deceased while alive are cooked and taken to the grave yard, where they are served to, and eaten by the *nandigal*, after portions are symbolically served to the departed soul, in reality to the crows.

For death, the purificatory ceremony among the Kallu Pandarams used to be on the fifteenth day; now they prefer to do it on the tenth. The *muuppu* officiates at the last rites. Cooked rice is served to the crows. The next day, an image of the deceased is prepared out of earth; the chief mourner takes a dip in a tank or river and throws the image into the flowing water. They visit a nearby Pattar temple dedicated to Siva. The chief mourner throws a bit of butter against the temple door; the Pattar priest opens it; the mourner enters and fastens the mouth of the Nandi (stone image representing Siva's Bull) with a cloth in which green gram is tied; the priest conducts a puja offering *pachamaavu* (rice dough), plantain fruits, coconuts, etc. The mourner prays aloud that the soul of the departed may go to Kailasam, the abode of Siva. At the anniversary of the death a *sraadha* is performed.

The major changes in the recent past have been the reduction in the period of pollution at birth, and other life cycle rituals from fifteen days to ten. Marriage ceremonies are now conducted in a day, instead of three, abandoning some of the rituals. Bride price continues to be paid but has been reduced from Rs. 25 to Rs. 6.25.

General Observations

Social Status

The Kallu Pandarams have not been generally considered as socially backward. They had access to public places, temples and shrines, belonging to the upper castes. They did not depend mainly on agricultural labour or manual labour. Instead, they were highly skilled artisans, and recognised as such. They were not identified under the traditional system with crafts or occupations; they were not considered to be lowly, impure or undignified, or stigmatised. Instead, their traditional occupation gave them prestige and access to the royal lineages, and Brahmins. They were not considered as polluting or unapproachable. They were not subjected to discriminatory treatment, like denial of access to public places. The participation of women and children in the economic activity of the community was negligible. Even now, very few women in this community are engaged in manual work, including as maid servants.

They have no representation in any elected body, including at the Panchayat level. The atmosphere is not congenial for total development, as it is dominated by the craft. They lack the motivation, but have the ability; they migrate to places where their skills find more profitable utilisation. They live in rural, semi-urban and municipal areas. Their settlements are close to those of the caste Hindus.

Educational Status

Only 10.84% of our sample has passed the SSLC. This is much less than the state and district averages. The number and proportion of graduates in the community is negligible, and far below the likely district and state averages. There are two engineers, one of whom is working in Mysore, and one Graduate Nurse in this community, again, very negligible percentages. There are no Judiciary Officers, Chartered Accountants, Doctors, etc. Dropouts among the students occur after SSLC, while dropouts among the age group of 7-15 are not very high. They do not show apathy or indifference to education, but perceive that it is irrelevant to their way of life and their traditional skilled artisanal occupation. They were not denied access to formal education; but they were considered educationally backward.

Economy

They were identified with a traditional craft, viz., a very highly skilled one of cutting and polishing gemstones including the *vairam* (= diamonds) and *navaratnams*. They lacked a resource base in landed property; they owned the tools of their trade and the stock in trade only. They do not own any educational institution. They own their cottage industry establishments of gem cutting and employ others, including those belonging to other communities. The family income is highly variable; it depends on the orders received for gem-cutting, and the type of gems processed. One case we examined in detail shows that the monthly income would be lower than that of a "permanent" agricultural worker under the Kerala Agricultural Labour Act, 1975, in the district.

Test of Adequacy of Representation

Neither in numbers nor in the quality of representation in Government service, does the community come anywhere near what may be considered "adequate". The highest Government appointment achieved by a member of this community in Kerala is that of an Assistant Sub-Inspector of Police; there is a "Sub-Engineer" in the Electricity Board, and an officer in the LIC. A Graduate in Nursing is employed in a suitable capacity. In Karnataka, a Kallu Pandaram has become a Forester; and his brother is an Engineer in the Karnataka PWD.

An Analysis of the Life Stories:

(a) Endogamy and the "Extended Micro-caste": The Kallu Pandarams are even now very particular to adhere to endogamy. They seek partners from their own community. Nallepally seems to have been the premier or original settlement in Kerala. When the population of the community at Nallepally and Koppam became too closely inter-married, they sought brides from the same community, in settlements outside Kerala. The first preference was naturally to the nearest, viz., at Coimbatore; then to Kangayam, followed by Mysore.

(b) The community combines location mobility with a willingness to try occupational mobility also. Goldsmith was their first preference; then they adopted various other occupations like tailoring, employment in workshops and establishments, and trade. The greater choice of occupations outside Kerala tended to move Kallu Pandarams to other areas. Marriage encouraged the trend.

(c) They, however, continued to prefer coming back whenever things improved vastly, as in the case of "Mysore Nanjappan", or when life brought unpleasantness, as in the case of his daughter, Veni, whose story points out how, in a community which prohibits divorce, a woman with her child still dares to desert her husband, because of the comparative affluence of her father.

(d) The life stories also show the community's perception of the irrelevance of school education. Veerammal was proud of her son's achievement in becoming an Assistant Sub-Inspector of Police, even though he had not passed the SSLC; her grandson, who was "highly educated", however has to depend on the traditional occupation. This is reflected in the notable paucity of Kallu Pandarams who have passed the SSLC.

(e) The "Extended Micro-caste" is new in anthropological literature. Mayer (1965), the famous proponent of the theory of the "Micro-caste", contemplated small communities limited both in numbers as well as in geographical spread. The distinguishing mark was that everyone knew everyone else, and marriage could be decided without detailed enquiry about membership. Among the Kallu Pandarams, we see this trait. Even though geographically spread out in three states, they still know all the families by reputation. Thus, we have here a community, which is a "Micro-caste", even though spatially widely spread over a "meso" region.

References

Mathur, P.R.G. 1969. "Caste Council among The Namputiri Brahmins of Kerala", *Eastern Anthropologist*, Vol. XXII, No. 2.

Mathur, P.R.G. 2007. "Sanskritisation of Non-Brahman Communities in Kerala in Misra", P.K. *et al. (eds.)* M.N. Srinivas. *The Man and His Work*, Jaipur. Rawat Publication.

Misra, P.K., 2007. Rereading M.N. Srinivas as an Ethnographer in Misra, P.K. *et al.* (eds.) M.N. Srinivas. *The Man and His Work*, Jaipur. Rawat Publication.

Srinivas, M.N. 1951. "The Social Structure of a Mysore Village", *Economic Weekly*, 30 October.

Srinivas, M.N. 1952. *Religion and Society among The Coorgs of South India*. Oxford. Clarendon Press.

Srinivas, M.N. 1955. *India's Villages*. Bombay. Asia Publishing House, 1960.

Srinivas, M.N. 1966. *Social Change in Modern India*. Berkeley. University of California Press.

Srinivas, M.N. 1976. *The Remembered Village*. Delhi. Oxford University Press.

22

Bishnupur : A Site of Cultural Pluralism

Samira Dasgupta

India is a country that encourages multiple cultures with a tune of harmonious co-existence. Multiculturalists accept and respect cultural diversity, stress its inevitability, and hold that diverse cultural groups are all equal members of society. Bishnupur—the Kingdom of Malla Dynasty is an ideal universe to study the role of various cultural expressionist groups or ethnic groups in mobilising the tourism industry along with its heritage contribution. It is true that countries are becoming culturally diverse, in part as a result of globalisation, technological changes and migration. Bishnupur is a place where all practises of different cultural groups have a peaceful co-existence, in an exemplar environment of cultural pluralism in India.

Wanderlust is a basic nature of humans. Tourism with multi-dimensional activities has evolved as one of the largest and gainful industries, which can be definitely called an engine for economic development. Tourism as a phenomenon means the movement of people within their own country or across its national border. According to Wahab (1975), Tourism primarily consists of three elements: man, who is the creator of the act of tourism; space, and time.

Tourism industry has emerged as one of the biggest revenue earners for our country. On the one hand, it generates employment opportunities, and on the other, it initiates infrastructural development – as a facility, which is the base, the stimuli for diversification of the economy and for the development of other industries at the local level.

Under this backdrop, the vast and varied cultural universe, as well as the great cultural heritage of India, with its splendour of beauty, both natural as well as architectural monuments, fetch a good number of tourists even from abroad. When such a tourist spot is identified, it also becomes the abode of artists and artisan groups, and their products obviously have a market that ultimately influences the tourism industry.

The main aim of this paper is to study Bishnupur of Bankura District in the light of tourism. Bishnupur is a site that has emerged as one of the potential areas of tourism development through its importance as a historical-cum-heritage site (due to the existence of Malla Kingdom in this area). The artisan groups' products found here are additional attractions for the tourists. Often the myths, legends, etc., are depicted and disseminated through these products, which carry extra weight with the tourists both at home and abroad.

Bishnupur Sub-division

Bishnupur Sub-division is in the eastern side of the district. It is situated between 22°54' and 23°25' North latitudes and between 87°15' and 87°46' East longitudes, extending over 700 sq miles. It is bounded by the River Damodar on the north, Hooghly and Midnapur districts on the south, Burdwan on the east and by the Bankura Sub-division on the west. Bishnupur is situated in a position that was used as a corridor for Hindu pilgrimage from north to south India and from Mathura and Vrindaban to Puri in Orissa (west to east India). Bishnupur is popularly known as Mallabhum. The name Mallabhum is derived from the name of the Malla Dynasty which ruled over the place from the eighth century AD till the 18th century AD. Bishnupur is home to some tribal communities such as the Santal, Munda, Kora, Kheria and Bhumije. In addition to the tribal communities, there are caste groups such as the Bauri, Gope, Bagdi, Khaira, Mete, Layek, Keot, Jele, Dhibar, Sadgop, Tili, Teli, Mahishya, Kaibarta, Sankhabanik, Kanshari, Tambuli, Tantubai, Barui, Kamar, Kumar, Sonar, Mal, Malakar, Dhopa, Dom, Sutar, Kshatriya, Brahman, Vaidya and the Kayastha, who live in Bishnupur, along with some Muslims and Christians.

Cultural Profile of Bishnupur

Agriculture is the mainstay of the economic life of the people in Bishnupur. The other occupations include silk weaving especially the Baluchari sari and tussar silk, pottery, lac industry, conch shell works, brass and *bel* metal work, lanterns, *Dashavatar Tash*, and other miscellaneous types of works. All these occupations are found in the Bishnupur Sub-division and its adjoining places.

The Malla kings, who ruled over Bishnupur, were believers in the Shakti cult. Adi Malla, the first Malla King, established Goddess Dandeswari Devi Mrinmoyee as their tutelary deity. It is said that there were some Malla kings who were devotees of Lord Siva and ultimately of Gauriya Vaishnavism during the reign of Bir Hambir (1565-1620).

In Bishnupur, among the local deities and local festivals, Dharmaraj, Manasha, Sitala, Bhadu, Tusu, Gajan, Ravan Kanta are very important.

Ethno-Historical Background of Mallabhum Bishnupur:

There are different opinions about the origin of the Malla kings. According to legend, Adi Malla, the founder of the Malla Dynasty, was originally a Kshatriya brought up by a Bagdi woman and later by a Brahman. He was presented some zamindaris by the King of Pradyumnapur, and ultimately became the king. In another opinion, Raghunath was a ghatwar of a ghat or path at Laugram. Ghatwars were infact the guards of the ghats/paths in the jungle. It is said that for their services, they enjoyed those lands as tax-free property. Adi Malla was originally a Bagdi. Satisfied with his faithfulness, the king presented him some tax-free zamindaris and gradually, through his efficiency, he became the king of the place. The Malla territory was established in the Rarhanchal of lower Bengal in the early years of the Muslim rule and just after the Sen Dynasty. Later, Bishnupur was a Samanta *(tax-free) Kingdom of the Mughals.*

There were at least 60 Malla kings who ruled from seventh to eighteenth century AD. During the reign of Bir Hambir (1565-1620), the Malla kingdom had experienced a new religious environment of Gauriya Vaishnavism through the Vaishnava Pandit Srinivas Acharya who not only influenced the Malla kings, but successfully placed the Gauriya Vaishnavism deep into the hearts of the people of Bishnupur, the then Mallabhum. Several temples of Vaishnava cult were built by the Malla kings with different names, architectural identities and with the deities in different positions, styles and shapes. Some of these are Madanmohan Shyam Rai, Jor Bangles, Radha Madhab, Radha Gobinda, Malleshwar, Kalachand, etc., which are important tourist attractions. Several reservoirs, forts, stone gates, chariots, etc., were also constructed. Gumghar Palace, Dal Madal Canon, Lalgarh Fort (now a botanical park), etc., are other tourist attractions in Bishnupur. All these were constructed during the Malla rule.

Almost all the temples are under the supervision of the Archaeological Survey of India, and only in three temples, among these, rituals are performed. There is a huge structure of pyramidal shape called the Rash Mancha constructed during the reign of Bir Hambir, which is an excellent contribution of the Malla reign. Almost all the temples are important from the archaeological point of view, with various carvings and decorative works on terracotta structures depicting the stories of Ramayana, Mahabharata and the Puranas. The temples are the conglomerations of north, west, and east Indian styles. The structure of the temples can be classified into three types, based on the design and/or number of towers: duel type, ratna type, and chala type.

The duel type temples have a single tower : some temples have a *sikhara* type of tower. Among the temples of ratna type, some have *ekratna* or single tower, while some have *panchratna* or five towers. The chala type of temple is built with Bengal's chala or hut styled tower. It may have two slopes (*do-chala*), four slopes (*char-chala*), or eight slopes (*at- chala*). Bishnupur is also famous for its different types of art and craft items, folk songs, and dances. Together with its music of Bishnupur *Gharana*, all these enriched Bishnupur as a tourist place. In the year 2000, the place was declared as a World Heritage Site. During the study, all the important tourist spots and the Ethno-Historical background of the Malla Dynasty are taken into account as these are historically important Heritage Sites.

Arts and Crafts

Bishnupur is known for its various types of arts and crafts. Among all the crafts, weaving of Baluchari sari, pottery and terracotta works, *sankhasshilpa* or conch-shell industry, followed by *Dashavatar Tash*, lanterns, etc., are other important items, which also glorified the name of Bishnupur. In the present study, all these craft items are included.

Baluchari Sari

The Baluchari and Swarnachari saris are very famous items among the cottage industries of the Indian tradition, and they have glorified the name of Bishnupur through their excellent designs and workmanship. However, this was originally not a product of Bishnupur. Baluchari textiles were originally developed in a village named Baluchar, situated in the banks of River Bhagirathi in the district of Murshidabad. The Baluchari weaving dates back to the 7th century AD, and since then it has undergone several changes in designs and motifs. Later on, it developed and flourished under the royal patronage of Nawab Murshid Quli Khan. The sari was then known as Badsa sari.

In the year 1950-51, Kamala Devi Chattopadhyay, the chairperson of All India Handicraft Board, wanted to revive the Baluchari work. She discussed this with Subho Thakur, the then Director of the Regional Design Centre, Kolkata, who with the help of Akshay Kumar Das, a retired designer at the Regional Centre, and the original inhabitants of Bankura District, decided to revive the industry in Bishnupur. The weaving community of Bishnupur locally known as Tanti or Tantubai also weaves tussar silk, but Bishnupur is now famous for its Baluchari sari weaving. In case of Baluchari sari, two types of silk threads silk : thread from Bangalore and Silk thread from Malda are used.

The Baluchari sari is particularly known for its designs. Generally figure designs are found with demonstrations of mythical stories from the Hindu Epics, Ramayana and Mahabharata, such as Bhishma's *Sarasajja*, conversation between Lord Krishna and Arjuna in the battle ground, *Swayambarsabha* of Sita, Ram's Marich *badh* (killing), Ravan's-Sita-*haran*, *Pancha Pandav* along with Draupadi, etc., together with some animal and floral designs. Figures are weaved generally all over the sari, but the designs on the *anchal* or *pallu* and border are always heavy in comparison to the body of the sari. The cost of the sari varies according to the designs and the quality of the thread and ranges from Rs.1200 to more than Rs.10000.

The Swarnachari sari, the other variety of sari, is more similar to the Baluchari sari in their colour texture and designs. The same variety of silk threads is used; the only exception is that for Swarnachari sari they use *jari* to prepare the design. While in the Baluchari textile, *jari* is occasionally used only in the warp threads of the border of the textile, in the Swarnachari textile, *jari* is compulsorily used along with warp and weft threads. The colour of the *jari* may be golden, silver, or copper.

The Baluchari and Swarnachari saris, especially the Baluchari sari, have a great demand in the markets of India. It is said that such saris are worn by the Hindu women both in India and abroad. The Muslims do not wear it, because the sari is designed with animal or human figures. Wearing of such figure designs is taboo in their *Shariyat*; moreover, they do not wear such saris because mythical stories from Hindu epics are illustrated in the designs. The Muslims have no restrictions, however, with the textile with floral design. In early times in Murshidabad, Baluchari saris with floral design were used. Sometimes human figures were also weaved in the body, *pallu* and border of the textile. But all those were related to the daily life of the royal families and worn by the women of the royal families of Murshidabad. These saris are generally not weaved for regular use but for rituals and ceremonial occasions (Chattopadhyay, 1985).

The Baluchari and Swarnachari saris are weaved by the Tantubai community in Bishnupur; they are Hindu and believe that they were born as per the wishes of Lord Siva. According to them their forefathers were brought to this place by the Malla kings to weave tussar silk clothes and *gamchha* (locally weaved towels), saris, bed sheets, etc.

Conch Shell (*Shankha*) Products

The *Sankhakars* or the *Sankharis* opine that the demand for *Sankhas* or conch shell bangles is not so high among the tourists. On the contrary, they prefer to purchase various conch-shell items such as hairclips, broaches, incense stands, candle stands, pen stands, etc. As per the demand of the tourists, they make various types of items on wood, glass, fibre, velvet, and even of terracotta, along with the conch-shell items. Among all these items, terracotta and velvet ornaments are popular among the tourists. Interestingly, very few of these items are prepared by some of them; most of them are brought from Kolkata.

Sometimes, instead of breaking a conch-shell into pieces, they extract the fleshy portion inside it by controlled hammering on the lip portion, then make beautiful engravings, on the whole conch-shell depicting stories from Ramayana, Mahabharata, *Dashavatar Tash*, Durga's *Dasha Mahavidya*, *Krishna Lila*, etc. These are very costly, and Indian tourists can hardly afford to purchase them. Generally the foreigners purchase these. The *Sankharis* say that due to less availability of the raw material and its high cost, now-a-days some of them have shifted to other raw materials such as coconut shell, gourd shell, wood apple shell, snail, etc. Engravings on those shells are also appreciated, and a National Award was given to one of the craftsmen for such type of work. They also prepare flower vases, incense stands, candle stands, spoons, salt pots, coasters, plates, etc., with these materials. Generally, tourism has less influence in the market for these products. They are usually supplied to different parts of India and abroad. According to the *Sankhakars*, though the tourists purchase the items, their economy cannot depend on the tourism industry. However, they are still in favour of tourism, as the Indian tourists who visit their place and appreciate their work publicise their products. The tourists who come from abroad are the main customers for their engraved conch-shells, which are costly. Various Non-Governmental Organisations also take initiatives for selling their items where again tourism has its influence.

Pottery and Terracotta Works:

Pottery and terracotta works are other important craft-works. The village of Panchmura is well known for its pottery and terracotta works. It is said that traditionally, these potters prepared vessels, small terracotta horses, elephants, bulls, etc., and all the votive offerings to the deities. They prepared these items by hand and called them *hatpakanoghora* (pinched horse), *hat pakanohati (*pinched elephant), etc., in addition, articles such as small pots and incense stands. Gradually, with the introduction of the wheel, they began to prepare various types of items. Among those a special variety of horse is famous not only in India but also abroad.

The other items are *Manasa Chali Bonga Hati*, *Pradip* or lamp, incense stand, *Ghat* or sacred vessel, household utensils, etc. Now-a-days, they also make various types of show-pieces such as dolls, wall plates, and other some small items such as ashtrays, pen stands, etc. According to them, the tourists prefer small items, as they are easy to carry. The foreigners have a craze to collect the votive items such as *hath-pakanoghora* and *bongahati*.

During the field investigation in Panchmura, it was observed that a potter's family was busy preparing invitation cards using terracotta plates as per the order of a tourist who had visited very recently. According to them, tourism in Bishnupur is definitely appreciable. It helps improve the infrastructure of the place; besides, it has also opened new job avenues. But at the same time, they informed that they are less connected with the tourists. In general, the tourists have no idea about their village. The tourists come and purchase their items from the local shops where they supply their products. Due to this reason, the shop owners enjoy the lion's share of the profit. They wish to have regular contact with the tourists so that they can sell their items directly to the tourists and exchange their ideas with them, so that new ideas can evolve in their craft items.

Lanterns

Lantern is one of the famous handicraft items of Bishnupur. It is made by the Kalu community and prepared mostly from scrap materials of corrugated sheets of iron ware. A few artisans also use brass instead of corrugated sheets. The specialty of the lantern is that it requires less fuel – that is, kerosene oil. It is handy, easy to carry, and costs less in comparison with other varieties of lanterns. Hence, poor village people can afford to buy such lanterns. It does not go off in wind and storms. It is very popular in rural Bengal, and is a compulsory item for the farmers who guard the fields during the night. In general, very few tourists are aware of this industry; hence, the tourism industry has no impact on this craft.

Bel Mala

The *Bel-mala* (garland made of wood apple shield) is another cottage industry in Bishnupur, which is solely prepared by the Muslim women, and used as a ritual item by the Hindus. To the Vaishnav, a *tulsi mala* (garland of basil wood) is a very important ritual item. But basil wood is not sufficiently available as per requirement. So to meet the demand, *bel* or wood apple is also used. However, the bel *mala* has no importance for the sake of tourism industry, nor the tourism industry has any gain from this handicraft.

Dashavatar Tash

Bishnupur is a repository of different types of cultural items. *Dashavatar Tash* (cards) of this place is other very attractive item. It is said that it has come to the land of Bishnupur during the Malla era initially, as a game for the recreation of Malla kings in their leisure time. A touch of Gauriyo Vaishnavism was present in each and every nook and corner of Mallabhum. Lord Vishnu's religion was the heart, pulse, body, and the soul of Bishnupur, and Madanmohan was the tutelary deity of the Malla kings whom they believed guided the Malla kings to run the kingdom. In this atmosphere, the Malla kings could not forget their own Madanmohan even in the games. Before playing the game, it was mandatory that they should get some purification either by taking a bath or by wearing clean clothes and washing the hands and feet with water.

Dashavatar Tash is a set of cards with ten different incarnations of Lord Vishnu. They are *Matsya* (fish), *Kurma* (tortoise), *Baraha* (boar), *Nrishingha* (father of Prahlad : Lord Krishna's disciple), *Baman* (a dwarf man), *Balaram* (Lord Krishna's elder brother), *Parashuram*, *Dasharathi Ram* (Lord Krishna born as the King of Ayodhya), and *Jagannath* (Lord Krishna) in the place of *Buddha,* and *Kalki*. This game was started in the durbar or royal court of Bishnupur about 400 years ago during the reign of Bir Hambir (1556-1620).

It is reported that Kartick Fauzdar first prepared the *Dasavatar Tash* at Bishnupur upon the order of King Bir Hambir. In fact, the Fauzdars were originally the *Sutradhar* or *Sutar* by caste whose traditional occupation was carpentry. They originally were the inhabitants of Laugram of Jaipur Police Station. The Malla kings brought them as soldiers. But Bir Hambir selected Kartick Sutradhar from that group and gave him the responsibility to prepare *Dasavatar Tash.*

Satisfied with the skill, style of composition, design and painting of the *Tash*, the king honoured him with the title 'Fauzdar' and presented him 250 *bighas* of cultivable land. Infact, the land was presented to him particularly for making a pot of Devi Durga as per the directions of the king. Gradually, making the *Dashavatar Tash* became one of the very important occupations for Kartick and his family. At present there are four Fauzdar families of his descendance and till date they continue to prepare the *Dashavatar Tash* and other *Pata-Chitras.*

At present, very few persons can play the game. Presently *Dashavatar Tash* is less important as a game but gets a very important position as a set of art piece in the world of the artists and the people with an artistic mind. Presently, several researches are going on regarding the *Dashavatar Tash.* The very interesting part of it is its drawing. The sketches have no accurate or proportionate measurement but have a different look. Again, the colouring is very bright and very attractive, and as a whole *Dashavatar Tash* is appreciated as a cultural item of this place.

Dokra Art

The Dokra art of Bikna Village in Bankura District is a very important craft. Though it is not an item of Bishnupur, it still has an impact on the tourism industry in Bishnupur. The tourists who come to visit Bishnupur are always attracted to the Dokra items kept for sale in the local market.

Bishnupur Gharana

In Bishnupur, like other art and crafts, music also holds a very important position. The songs and music are classified in three categories: (i) Folk songs, (ii) *Kirtans* and (iii) Classical music: Folk songs are the outcome of spontaneous emotion of the local folk. *Kirtans,* on the other hand, are primarily the devotional songs which have emotional as well as spiritual themes, especially on Radha and Krishna. The classical songs can be described as an impact of Gauriya Vaishnavism during the 16th century on the life of the people of Bishnupur. Radha Krishna were present everywhere, in each and every aspect; and every moment of life.

With the introduction of Gauriya Vaishnavism in Mallabhum through Srinivas Acharya, a new school of music, the Bishnupur Gharana was evolved by *Ustad* Bahadur Khan during the reign of Raghunath Singh II. *Ustad* Bahadur Khan was one of the descendents of Tan Sen. Bishnupur Gharana style of music is very popular especially among classical music-lovers in India.

Gharana is a term only used to identify style in classical music. The word *Gharana* is derived from the word *ghar* which means a home. So *Gharana* denotes a *ghar* or a home that is a school or family of a group of musicians with a specific style and certain characters, which differentiate it from the other *Gharana.*

All the craftsmen and the artists have a positive attitude towards tourism industry in Bishnupur and the tourists. They say that if the tourists are connected with them then their own crafts will definitely get boosting, which ultimately will bring economic development to Bishnupur. Opinions on tourism in Bishnupur was taken from different persons associated with the tourism industry, including Government officials, NGOs, and other local people. All have a positive attitude towards tourism. According to them, as an effect of tourism, the place is developing. The temples are getting special care, attention, and also protection. Several job avenues are emerging in connection with the tourism industry. Some infrastructural development is there, though not sufficient.

Lastly, the tourists were interviewed. It was found that the tourists in general visit the place to see the temples, their architecture, and other places of historical importance in this heritage site. Incidentally, it was found that most of the tourists are educated up to not less than graduation level, and with a monthly income of not less than Rs. 5000. They have given suggestions for the development of tourism in this place.

The Heritage Site

Bishnupur sub-division of Bankura District is a place completely filled with varieties. It is rich with culture and heritage, fairs and festivals.

Sometimes the place is referred to or mentioned through the stories of the Malla Dynasty: stories of bravery, heroism, and brilliant and glorious acts, and achievements of the Malla kings and the Malla Dynasty. Again and again in the stories Raghunath Singha and his beloved Lalbai's eventful happenings come into discussion. There are events of bravery, found in the stories of the rescue of Jagat Singh, the son of Man Singh, from attack during the time of *Samrat* Akbar. There are stories, which tell how Bir Hambir came in touch with the Vaishnava Guru, Srinivas Acharya and after that how he became over-flooded with the outburst of emotions of Vaishnavism. The whole Mallabhum was submerged in that emotion. In every nook and corner of Mallabhum – its sky, its air, and even in its each and every particle of dust – there is the humming of a name, the name of Madanmohan. Sometimes he is called Madanmohan, sometimes Kalachand, sometimes he is called together with his love Radha as Radhey Shyam or Shyam Rai or Radha Lal Jiu. In these names, several temples were built by the Malla kings. The excellent architecture, sculptures and designs signify the efficiency and artistic minds of the Malla kings. Bishnupur became the temple town and was known as a second Vrindavan. The temples, roads and reservoirs were all named after Lord Krishna, Lord Vishnu, or their own bosom friend, Madanmohan. In connection with Madanmohan they have several stories. Today also after a long period, some of these mythical stories are popularly narrated to the tourists. All these stories, architecture, sculptures, arts and crafts, etc., bring a special attraction to the tourists of Bishnupur.

In Bishnupur, the Malla kings established several temples of Radha-Krishna. All of them are very attractive with the varieties of architectural designs, spell-bound terracotta figurines demonstrating sometimes a war, or the king's luxurious life-style, and sometimes about the then society, its norms and customs, etc., along with the very beautiful artistic floral and geometric designs which are, till date, among the best architectural monuments of India. Among the temples, some important temples are Shyam Rai temple, Radha-Shyam Jiu temple, Jor Bangla, Madanmohan temple, Kalachand temple, Radha Lal Jiu temple, Jor Mandir, etc., which are very important for their beautiful architecture and terracotta designs on the walls. Among the glorious deeds of the Malla kings, Rash Mancha, a different type of structure with unusual architectural style charms one's mind. It is a place, where during Rash festival, all the deities from different temples are brought and worshipped. There is a Shiva temple in Bishnupur, which is also declared to be of national importance under the ancient monuments and archaeological sites. The king's palace (though at present is in a ruined condition), Gumghar, the reservoirs (locally known as *bandh*), the Dal-Madal *Kaman* (cannon), Lalgarh (the eco-park), *Patharer Darja* (the stone gate), etc., are all very attractive. It is said that all these are the attractive spots, taken by the Archaeological Survey of India and declared to be of National importance.

Observation and Conclusion

Bishnupur is a treasure land of arts and crafts. It has its excellent weaving of Baluchari *sari*, its terracotta works, *Dashavatar Tash*, *sankha* industry, etc. Its excellent music of Bishnupur Gharana brings a heavenly atmosphere, which gives joy, peace and satisfaction to the life of the people, and has a very important position in the cultural life of Bishnupur. All these along with the temples and the other spots together establish Bishnupur as a very important tourist place for the tourists, throughout the world.

Lastly, the researcher has noticed that tourism as an exogenous component and a stimulating agent have caused occupational opportunities, and makes a few suggestions to improve the impact of tourism in Bishnupur:

- Due to promotion of tourism, this heritage site is getting protection and proper conservation.
- Proper advertisement of the tourist spot is primarily needed with guide maps, hoardings and assistance booths in the railway station.
- Smart, knowledgeable guides should be there.
- The craft items are also attractions for the tourists. But direct contact of tourists with the craftsmen is needed for the interest of the tourism industry.
- Some musical programmes should be arranged for tourists, which will be an additional attraction for the tourists.
- Though some infra-structural development is there, they are not enough for a site declared as a World Heritage Site.

To conclude, Bishnupur, as a tourist spot, has tremendous potential. Proper coordination between several departments is urgently needed to improve all spheres connected with tourism industry at this place. It is also evident how different ethnic groups with their cultural potentialities promote tourism industry in the environment of a multicultural society.

References

Samira Dasgupta, Rabiranjan Biswas, and Gautam K. Mallik 2009. *Heritage Tourism: An Anthropological Journey to Bishnupur*, New Delhi: Mittal Publications.

Wahab, S. 1975. *Tourism Management*, Jaipur. Rawat Publications.

Wahab, S. 1987. "Sustainable Tourism in the Developing World" in Salah Wahab and John, J. Pigram, (ed.) *Tourism Development and Growth : The Challenge of Sustainability*, London. Routledge.

23

Indian Pluralism: Changes and Concern

K. Bhamini Raghavaiah, C.E. Subramanya **and**
K. Rajasekhara Reddy

Introduction

Every civilisation evolves certain unique features of its own, which in their entirety and inter-relatedness, constitute its dominant configuration and differentiate it from other civilisations. Indian civilisation is distinguished from other civilisations of the world in respect of its continuity, heterogeneity, accommodating ethos, and composite character. The migrant groups and communities brought their respective traditions and behaviour patterns from their native lands. In the course of time, however, they lost contact with their places of origin and underwent an extensive process of indigenisation. The process of adaptation and interaction among the various groups brought about, on the one hand, India's characteristic diversity and, on the other, a composite cultural tradition.

The process of acculturation, which was set into motion as far back as the third millennium BC, continued unabated during the successive periods of Indian history and led to the intermingling of a variety of cultural traits and features. From early times, tribal folk cults and ritual practises were incorporated and assimilated into the corpus of Brahmanism. Totemic deities such as fish, tortoise and boar were made into incarnations of Vishnu. The incorporation and assimilation of regional features into the mainstream of the Vedic culture is attested by linguistic and philological evidence as well. From very early times, Vedic society was internally differentiated and pluralistic, rather than monolithic and homogenous. It was an amalgam or synthesis of Aryan and non-Aryan, including tribal elements. In other words, since its very inception, Hinduism appears to be a "mosaic of distinct cults, sects and ideas".

The process of acculturation and integration has been extensively at work at the regional level. Though each group or community has a distinctive identity and ethos of its own, it does not exist in a social vacuum. Rather, it forms part of an extended and dynamic network. Often, interaction, exchange and integration characterise inter-community relations. The sharing of space, regional ethos and cultural traits cuts across religions and sectarian differences and binds the local people together. What is characteristic of any civilisation is not its being but its becoming. By virtue of its characteristic pluralism and its continuously evolving synthesis, India represents a nation in the making, a nation which is continuously unfolding its civilisational potentialities. This view is reflected in a statement of Jawaharlal Nehru to the effect that "Indianness is a matter of feeling, a dream, a vision and an emotion."

India clearly has access to important gateways of globalisation, such as, well-established channels of media and commerce; it also has its own unique, a large NRI community, large and potentially important gateway of globalisation. Today, issues related to culture are often dealt with in relation to cultural diversity, a concept that has only recently replaced the notion of cultural exception. The shift from one term to another is not merely semantic. It reflects the emergence of a broadened concept of cultural stakes in the context of globalisation. These stakes are no longer strictly reduced to the need to maintain an international balance in the production and exchange of cultural goods; they rather convey a growing concern to defend identities (national, geographic, religious, historical, etc.) in a globalised world where culture naturally has its place. This high degree of concentration stems from the growing cultural industrialisation that entails its own limits. By its very nature, the production of a cultural good is grounded in an original artistic and cultural contribution. Systematically streamlining this production could gradually erase all originality and risk taking in the creative process, leading *ipso facto* to a trivialisation of cultural products that could lead to loss of public interest. Cultural industries do more than just meet functional needs.

Since ancient times, Indian civilisation has had a pluralistic and composite character. The pluralistic and composite ethos of Indian civilisation, which began germinating during the Vedic period, was supplemented by the rise of Buddhism and Jainism, and was further reinforced during the early medieval period which witnessed the early flowering of the Bhakti Movement. The distribution of material traits, at the regional level indicates a certain complementarity that is marked by both local differentiation and inter-penetration. Often, a cluster or complex of material traits, at the regional level, unites different sections and communities.

Cultural development is the process of self-sufficiency which, at a macro level, is fulfilled by the community itself and, at a micro level, by the individuals and groups. On this same basis, it is directly the result of endogenous cultural creativities against prevalent methods of the transfer of science and technology. But development by itself is a historical change, i.e., the communities move and transit from one historical stage to another. In fact, preparing the community for development is a historical necessity, depending on time and place.

The pattern of development of policy-making in each country is peculiar to that country, but the laws of development are general and comprehensive. Therefore, the transfer of technology can be effective in the progress and development of, orient communities only when they are in harmony with the social and cultural conditions of such communities. Protection of cultural identity and reinforcing it are of vital importance. Similarly, technology constitutes the reality of time. Our goal must be to protect our cultural identity by using the gifts of technology rather than sacrifice the former for the sake of the latter or ignore the benefits of technology.

Development induces continual interaction between tradition and modernity, generating creative tension between the two sets. Even though modernity is the ascendant idea system, it can neither replace nor erase tradition completely. Modernisation only compels tradition to reformulate its ideas and to redefine its functions in the light of modernity. Thus, what is implicit in tradition is made explicit; more systematic what is random. In other words, tradition makes a structural adjustment : a total transformation, during the process of modernisation.

The only tentative generalisation we can make at the present state of our knowledge is this: Modernisation is a relatively universal process but mediated by specific cultures. The system has made us look down on our own culture, on our own indigenous solutions and institutions and influenced us to mistrust all knowledge and information that originates from those we persist in calling the poor as backward and primitive.

Another major dilemma is the lack of space for individual growth. In this great desire to help the so-called poor and in the name of development we have encroached on individual space, violated privacy, forced people to think in a certain way and penalised those who have rejected government assistance for a good reason.

Conclusion

The fact, that the different cultural areas overlap makes it particularly difficult to identify goals and principles for action. Today, it raises the question not only of the effectiveness of national policies and measures in the field, but also that of the definition of the tools making it possible to weigh and measure flows of cultural exchanges and diversity. Hence, the importance of establishing forums for debate and discussion sites to draw up such principles.

This should be the main thrust of the public debates focusing on diversity – promoting practical solutions that make it possible to reconcile the needs of the economic dimension of cultural exchanges with the needs of their identity-related dimension.

References

Baidyanath Saraswathi. 1996. *Interface of Cultural Identity*. New Delhi. Motilal Banarasidass Publishers Pvt. Ltd.

Christoph Eberhard and Nidhi Gupta. 2005. "Legal Pluralism in India : An Introduction." *Indian Socio-Legal Journal* XXXI, pp. 1-10.

Madan. L. Goel. 2007. *Pluralism, Dissent and Democracy in India*. i.varta.com.

Muuray J. Leaf. 1998. *Pragmatism and Development*. USA. Greenwood Publishing Group.

Raymond Bradley William. 1996. *Christian Pluralism in United States: The Indian Immigrant Experience*, Cambridge. Cambridge University Press.

Surendranath Dasgupta. 1949. *History of Indian Philosophy*. Vol. IV. Cambridge. England University Press.

List of Contributors

Amitabha Sarkar, Anthropological Survey of India, 27, Jawahar Lal Nehru Road, Kolkata – 700 016.

B. Francis Kulirani, Anthropological Survey of India, Southern Regional Centre, Manav Bhavan', Bogadi, Mysore – 570 006

B. Krishna Reddy, Department of Folklore & Tribal Studies, Dravidian University, Kuppam–517 425.

B.R. Ghosh and **S. S .Ghosh,** 1720, Near Hampi Circle, Hebbal 2nd Stage, Mysore.

B.R. Vijayendra, Anthropological Survey of India, Southern Regional Centre, Manav Bhavan', Bogadi, Mysore – 570 006.

Bhamini Raghavaiah K., Department of Anthropology, University of Mysore Manas Gangotri Mysore.

C. Raghu, Anthropological Survey of India, Southern Regional Centre, Manav Bhavan', Bogadi, Mysore – 570 006.

D.V. Prasad, Assistant Anthropologist, Anthropological Survey of India, Southern Regional Centre, Manav Bhavan', Bogadi, Mysore – 570 006.

Elizabeth Zachariah, Vadakedarampil, Maramon-post, Kerala.

H.K. Bhat, Department of Anthropology, University of Mysore, Manas Gangotri, Mysore.

Harka Bahadur Chhetri Atreya, Central Institute of Indian Languages, Mysore.

Imtiaz Ahamad, B-361, Vasanth Kunj Enclave, New Delhi, 110007 .

K.G. Gurumurthy, C/o, S.A.A.Saheb, 1747, Hebbal 2nd Stage, Mysore-570017.

M. Sasi Kumar, Anthropological Survey of India, Southern Regional Centre, Manav Bhavan', Bogadi, Mysore – 570 006.

N. Subba Reddy, A-7, Annad Sheel Enclave, Nandinagar, Banjara Hills, Hyderabad.

Nilanjan Khatua, Anthropological Survey of India, Southern Regional Centre, Manav Bhavan', Bogadi, Mysore – 570 006.

PRG Mathur, Ananthakrishna Iyer International Centre, For Anthropological Studies, (AICAS), Palakkad, Kerala- 678571.

Pragati,V., Department of Anthropology , Pudhucherry Institute of Linguistics and Culture, Pudhucherry -605008.

R. Rajendra Prasad, Anthropological Survey of India, Southern Regional Centre, Manav Bhavan', Bogadi, Mysore – 570 006.

R. Senkuttvan, Anthropological Survey of India, Southern Regional Centre, Manav Bhavan', Bogadi, Mysore – 570 006.

S.A.A. Saheb, Anthropological Survey of India, Southern Regional Centre, 'Manav Bhavan', Bogadi, Mysore – 570 006.

Samira Dasgupta, Anthropological Survey of India, 27, Jawahar Lal Nehru Road, Kolkata-700016.

V. Jayarajan, Chairman, Falkland, International Centre for Folklore and Culture, Trikaripur (Kerala).

Index

C

D